Critical Essays on
CLIFFORD ODETS

CRITICAL ESSAYS
ON
AMERICAN LITERATURE

James Nagel, General Editor
Northeastern University

Critical Essays on

CLIFFORD ODETS

edited by

GABRIEL MILLER

G. K. Hall & Co.
BOSTON, MASSACHUSETTS

Published 1991.
10 9 8 7 6 5 4 3 2 1

Library of Congress Cataloging-in-Publication Data

Critical essays on Clifford Odets / edited by Gabriel Miller.
     p.   cm.—(Critical essays on American literature)
  Includes bibliographical references and index.
  ISBN 0-8161-7300-1 (alk. paper)
  1. Odets, Clifford, 1906–1963—Criticism and interpretation.
I. Miller, Gabriel, 1948–   . II. Series.
PS3529.D46Z65 1991
812'.52—dc20   91-6424

Printed and bound in the United States of America

For my brothers
Richard and Moshe

Contents

♦

General Editor's Note

◆

This series seeks to anthologize the most important criticism on a wide variety of topics and writers in American literature. Our readers will find in various volumes not only a generous selection of reprinted articles and reviews but also original essays, bibliographies, manuscript sections, and other materials brought to public attention for the first time. This volume, *Critical Essays on Clifford Odets,* is the most comprehensive collection of essays ever published on one of the most important modern writers in the United States. It contains both a sizable gathering of early reviews and a broad selection of more modern scholarship. Among the authors of reprinted articles and reviews are Joseph Wood Krutch, Brooks Atkinson, John McCarten, Edith J. R. Isaacs, R. Baird Shuman, and Gerald Weales. In addition to a substantial introduction by Gabriel Miller, there are also three original essays commissioned specifically for publication in this volume: new studies by George L. Groman, Norma Jenkes, and Frank R. Cunningham. We are confident that this book will make a permanent and significant contribution to the study of American literature.

JAMES NAGEL

Northeastern University

Publisher's Note

◆

Producing a volume that contains both newly commissioned and reprinted material presents the publisher with the challenge of balancing the desire to achieve stylistic consistency with the need to preserve the integrity of works first published elsewhere. In the Critical Essays series, essays commissioned especially for a particular volume are edited to be consistent with G. K. Hall's house style; reprinted essays appear in the style in which they were first published, with only typographical errors corrected. Consequently, shifts in style from one essay to another are the result of our efforts to be faithful to each text as it was originally published.

Introduction

◆

GABRIEL MILLER

When Clifford Odets died of stomach cancer on 15 August 1963, the obituaries all played essentially the same tune, which, with a few notable exceptions, still echoes today: he was eulogized either as a "promising" playwright whose talent had gone unfulfilled or as an emblem of the thirties whose significance was greater than his talent. In his *Writers on the Left,* Daniel Aaron refers to him as the " 'Golden Boy' of the Left theater,"[1] applying the convenient label most often used to pigeonhole Odets's career and to dismiss it with an implication of failed potential. Essentially Odets is considered a relic of another time, whose work sheds light on the way we lived then but little else—a writer once full of sound and fury, but one whose career was, in the end, of no lasting consequence.

On the surface, the final years of Odets's life seemed to confirm this unflattering judgment: having produced no plays after completing *The Flowering Peach* in 1954, and his last credited works were two undistinguished films, *The Story on Page One* (1960), which he also directed, and an Elvis Presley vehicle, *Wild in the Country* (1961). Not only had he spent too much time in Hollywood, neglecting his theatrical career, but he had also "named names" before the notorious House Un-American Activities Committee (HUAC) in 1952. Shortly after his death, NBC premiered *The Richard Boone Show,* which was to feature a group of actors performing a different original teleplay each week; Odets had been intended to supervise the scripts, and to write four of them himself. The program, however, was a failure, and the two completed Odets scripts did not redeem his reputation.

Unfortunately, these last barren years of Odets's life have tended to eclipse and nullify his considerable accomplishment. Neither his commercial appetite nor his political apostasy was ever really forgiven by the intellectual establishment, and the messy circumstances of his life have thus clouded the critical perception of his art.

Ultimately Odets was the victim of his own celebrity. He was the object of constant media attention: his every remark was recorded and quoted in the columns: his marriage and divorce from two-time Academy Award–winning actress Luise Rainer was accorded considerable coverage in the newspapers, complete with pictures. In 1935, when Odets was king of Broadway (by the year's end, he had four plays running), George Ross wrote:

They spoke last year of the emergence of a flaming playwright, of the Theater's White Hope, of the new O'Neill, and they were speaking this year, in the same circles and in whispers and in less reverent tones, of Clifford Odets . . . [he] had been seen with Tallulah Bankhead, had been noticed talking to Beatrice Lillie, . . . had been observed at Fire Island week-ending with Fannie Brice, the Gershwins, Gene Fowlers and the like. . . . "Will Odets," it often was asked at numerous soirees, "keep his head after all that acclaim or will he go in for social climbing, Hollywood and cocktails at five?"[2]

The lure of such fame has, of course, compromised many American writers: its flattering distractions are subtly shadowed by the popular assumption that celebrity itself corrupts, and critics are on the lookout for signs of it in the writer's works. Odets himself was keenly aware of this double-edged blessing, as he indicated in 1961: "You don't want to change, you want to hold on . . . but you're just kind of swept off your feet, with wire services and interviews and people telephoning you; the parties you're invited to, the people who just take you up."[3] In his 1940 journal he wrote, "The so-called practical and realistic world has impinged itself upon my consciousness. The nature of the beast comes clearer to me each week, and one must actively take arms against it or be corrupted into a twisted cynical rascal of a diplomat. What a shock to march up a hill, banner in hand, and suddenly look down on that Hollywood in the valley! The first impact can stun you for life!"[4] Odets would reflect more extensively on the stresses of the celebrity syndrome in *Golden Boy* (1937) and *The Big Knife* (1949).

His enormous successes in the thirties were, in fact, to haunt him throughout the forties and fifties, because critics inevitably approached his later plays with reference to the earlier ones. As early as 1941 Odets seemed to have attained the status of a historical character, and so appraisal of his new work as an evolving effort eluded many critics, a number of whom preferred bashing his reputation instead. As John Gassner wrote in his review of *The Country Girl* in 1950, "It is not fair to make esteem for the work of a writer's ardent youth a lien on his entire life."[5] In the same spirit of defensive eulogy Elinor Hughes wrote, shortly after Odets's death, "It is a strange reflection upon the career of Clifford Odets, . . . that he was still being regarded at the time of his death as a promising playwright."

A careful and detached examination of his plays and the manuscripts now available show that Odets was, in fact, a serious, self-conscious writer obsessed with formal experimentation and dramatic expression. Consistently passionate about his art and the role of the artist, he sought to give voice to his love for man and the human spirit while also warning of the dangerous tensions inherent in man himself, in the American experience, and in the increasingly threatening global situation. His career represents no clichéd model of great talent ruined by success, for however short he may have fallen of the glittering promise of his youth, the record of his achievement remains substantial: he wrote some of the very greatest of American plays—*Awake and Sing!*, *Paradise Lost*, *Golden Boy*, and *The Country Girl*—and in the process tackled such profound and compelling themes as man's search for wholeness and fulfillment, the chasm between the spiritual ideal and the lure of the flesh, the family as trap and as haven, the wasteland landscape of the modern world, and the peculiar nature of American society. Only O'Neill wrote theatrical dialogue as effective as Odets's; only O'Neill and perhaps Williams succeeded in shaping the American experience into tragic form as powerfully as Odets did. As a poet of the theater, he has no peer. His body of work should rank near O'Neill's, and with those of Williams and Miller, in the forefront of American drama.

Since his death, however, Odets's work has received scant attention from academic critics. Despite six book-length studies and half a biography, his reputation remains, at best, in limbo. The university presses and most academic journals have ignored him. Such neglect is hardly unique to Odets, of course, for American drama as a whole commands little regard in the academy. With the exceptions of O'Neill, whose monumental stature dominates the field, no American playwright is deemed worthy of sustained scholarly attention: while Miller, Williams, and Albee are accorded some notice in the journals, they have yet to be the subjects of university press books. Even the editors of anthologies of American literature disdain to reprint more than a few standard plays; indeed, not until its 1985 revision did the *Norton Anthology of American Literature* include any plays at all.

In the case of Odets, this climate of neglect threatens to enshroud a brilliant if fitful career in a kind of historical obscurity, preserving his name for the record while ignoring or smoothly patronizing the work that first brought it to prominence. Of the eleven plays Odets completed and saw produced during his lifetime, only his first six are generally available today, collected in *Six Plays of Clifford Odets*, which was originally published by Random House in 1939 and which Grove Press has kept available since 1979. His five later plays are out of print, although *The Big Knife*, *The Country Girl*, and *The Flowering Peach* can be read in acting editions published by Dramatists Play Service. *Night Music* and *Clash by Night* are not to be found except in the original hardcover editions published by Random House, discoverable only in libraries and used book stores.

Odets's plays are, inexplicably, rarely anthologized. *Waiting for Lefty* is occasionally included as a representative thirties work, but even this selection seems dictated in part by the play's convenient brevity and relative notoriety. Harold Clurman includes *Awake and Sing!* in his anthology *Famous American Plays of the 1930's*.[6] Harvey Swados, in his anthology *The American Writer and the Great Depression*,[7] includes nothing by Odets, despite the fact that he was arguably that decade's most famous writer; indeed, in that anthology, which runs over five hundred pages, the sole representation of the theater is three scenes from Marc Blitzstein's *The Cradle Will Rock*.

Among the other primary materials collected in anthologies is Odet's monologue "I Can't Sleep," first performed by Morris Carnovsky in 1935, which can be found in *The Anxious Years,* edited by Louis Filler,[8] and in Margaret Brenman-Gibson's biography *Clifford Odets, American Playwright: The Years from 1906–1940.*[9] Odets's screenplay of *None but the Lonely Heart,* which he adapted from the novel by Richard Llewellyn, is in *Best Film Plays of 1945.*[10] The musical version of *Golden Boy,* which opened after Odets's death, was published in 1965,[11] and a paperback version appeared a year later[12]; even though Odets's name appears as coauthor, the work is primarily that of Williams Gibson, who provides a valuable introduction. Odet's adaptation of Konstantin Simonov's *The Russians,* retitled *The Russian People,* appears in *Seven Soviet Plays,* edited by Henry Wadsworth Longfellow Dana.[13]

The most important Odets work to appear since his death is *The Time Is Ripe: The 1940 Journal of Clifford Odets,* published in 1988 with an introduction by Gibson. In addition to the biographical information contained in it, the journal's primary value lies in the insight it provides into Odets's character and his attitude toward art and writing. It clearly establishes that the root and heart of Odets's writing was emotional, spiritual, and confessional. The overt romanticism manifested there should put to rest the critical cliché that Odets was simply a didactic political writer. Another important collection is Eric Bentley's *Thirty Years of Treason,*[14] which contains Odets's HUAC testimony of April 1952.

Some of the most insightful commentary on Odets's work can be found in Brooks Atkinson's reviews of the plays for the *New York Times.* Atkinson reviewed all of Odets's plays, from *Waiting for Lefty* (11 February 1935) to *The Flowering Peach* (29 December 1954). He also contributed a sensitive eulogistic reminiscence (3 September 1963) in which he attempted to refute the negative tenor of the obituaries that labeled Odets a failure. Atkinson's reviews are judicious and sober: unlike many of his contemporaries, he did not judge Odets's work on the basis of stereotypical preconceptions; he was able to see each play as part of an evolving career. Like others, he regularly commented on Odets's extraordinary gift for dialogue and his ability to create exceptional individual scenes, but Atkinson was also careful to elucidate theme, invariably following up his reviews with more extended essays on the plays in the Sunday paper. He was one of the few critics to discern Odets's change of direction in his last three plays and to evaluate them as more than commercial fluff. In addition to the plays cited above, Atkinson also reviewed *Waiting for Lefty* and *Till the Day I Die* (27 March 1935), *Awake and Sing!* (20 February 1935 and 10 March 1935), *Paradise Lost* (10 December 1935 and 29 December 1935), *Golden Boy* (5 November 1937 and 21 November 1937), *Rocket to the Moon* (25 November 1938 and 4 December 1938), *Night Music* (23 February 1940 and 3 March 1940), *Clash by Night* (29 December 1941 and 11 January 1942), *The Big Knife* (25 February 1949 and 6 March 1949), and *The Country Girl* (11 November 1950 and 19 November 1950).

Two other judicious newspaper critics were John Mason Brown, whose reviews of Odets's early work are generally excellent, particularly his discussion of the Chekhovian flavor of *Awake and Sing!* and his nearly unique appreciation of the strengths of *Paradise Lost*. Brown's reviews first appeared in the *New York Evening Post*, which eventually became the *New York Post*. He later reviewed Odets's plays for the *New York World-Telegram* and for the *Saturday Review*. The other discerning reviewer was Richard Watts, Jr., who wrote for the *New York Herald Tribune* in the late thirties and covered Odets's last three plays for the *New York Post*. Most notable are his reviews of *Rocket to the Moon, Clash by Night,* and *The Country Girl*.

Odets's best critic, however, was his colleague, friend, and cofounder of the Group Theatre, Harold Clurman, who also directed the original productions of *Awake and Sing!, Paradise Lost, Golden Boy, Rocket to the Moon,* and *Night Music*. His historical memoir of the Group Theatre, *The Fervent Years*,[15] remains the best account of the Group and also an excellent source of biographical information on Odets. Clurman discusses the productions of Odets's first seven plays, all staged by the Group, and also provides information on an early Odets fragment, *910 Eden Street,* and on Odets's unproduced labor play *The Silent Partner*. Most important, Clurman's account shows how the Group's ideals shaped Odets's playwriting, particularly inspiring the building of his plays around an ensemble, and how the political and social currents of the thirties influenced his thinking. Clurman characterizes the contradictory impulses that inform Odets's work: his fervent romanticism, his susceptibility to moments of extreme despair, his love and hopes for mankind, and his sad presentiments that those hopes would remain unfulfilled.

Clurman also wrote introductions for the published versions of *Awake and Sing!, Paradise Lost,* and *Golden Boy,* all of which were included in the 1939 edition of *Six Plays of Clifford Odets*,[16] and he provided an evaluation of Odets's entire career as an introduction to the Grove Press reprint in 1979. Clurman's reviews of *The Big Knife, The Country Girl,* and *The Flowering Peach* are collected in his *Lies Like Truth*, a compilation of his theater reviews and essays.[17] Like Brooks Atkinson, Clurman wrote an obituary essay in the *New York Times*,[18] in which he analyzed Odets's true accomplishment as a playwright; it remains one of the most moving and insightful essays on Odets's career. Recently another friend and colleague, Elia Kazan, who appeared as Agate in the Broadway production of *Waiting for Lefty*, as Fuseli in *Golden Boy,* and as Steve Takis in *Night Music,* writes eloquently of Odets in his autobiography *A Life*.[19]

Other interesting accounts published during Odets's early career are the *Time* cover story on Odets, occasioned by the opening of *Rocket to the Moon*[20]; Edith Isaacs's early evaluation of Odets's strengths and weaknesses as a play-

wright, "Clifford Odets: First Chapters"[21]; John McCarten's rather unflattering *New Yorker* profile, "Revolution's Number One Boy"[22]; and Brooks Atkinson's essay on Odets and the Group (occasioned by the 1939 revival of *Awake
and Sing!*), "Group Theatre Plus Clifford Odets."[23]

The first book-length study on Odets appeared during his lifetime:
R. Baird Shuman's *Clifford Odets* (1962), a volume in Twayne's United States
Authors series.[24] In the preface to her biography of Odets, Margaret
Brenman-Gibson relates that the playwright mailed her a copy of that book
in July 1963; referring to it as a biography, she wrote, in a letter to Odets,
"You must admit it is quite a feat to deal with a guy like you and somehow
turn it into a bland exercise."[25] Brenman-Gibson was a bit harsh: Shuman's
volume was intended to be not a biography, (although it contains a biographical chapter) but an introduction to Odets's work as a playwright. The book is
uneven, but Shuman does provide sensitive readings of *Awake and Sing!*,
focusing correctly on the interplay of the family members and the fraud
inherent in their dreams of success, and of *Paradise Lost,* pointing out the
interplay between realism and symbolism. Unfortunately, he replays too
many of the clichés of Odets criticism in his constant emphasis on proletarian
realism and social politics, even applying this approach to *The Country Girl,*
which was Odets's first play devoid of significant reference to the external
world.

Edward Murray's *Clifford Odets: The Thirties and After* appeared in
1968.[26] Murray devotes detailed chapters to eight of Odets's plays, concentrating on structure and theme. He thinks little of *Paradise Lost, Waiting for
Lefty,* and *Till the Day I Die,* and so excludes these works from consideration
in his book. Murray provides a useful corrective to Shuman's proletarian /
political approach, highlighting instead the personal aspect of Odets's writing and the darker side of his work. Murray's introductory chapters to the
two parts of his book ("Odets and the Thirties" and "After the Thirties") are
more interesting than his chapters on the plays, in which he fails to examine
carefully the thematic issues he raises, particularly Odets's efforts to fuse the
personal and the social, and the apparent contradiction between Odets's need
to believe in the "perfectibility of man"[27] and the often violent, pessimistic
thrust of the plays. Murray is best on Odets's last three plays, and he is the
first critic to evaluate seriously and sympathetically the much-maligned *The
Big Knife.*

The third book on Odets, published in 1969, was Michael Mendelsohn's *Clifford Odets: Humane Dramatist.*[28] Mendelsohn had previously published an excellent two-part interview with Odets, "Odets at Center Stage"
(1963),[29] and his book clearly benefits from the personal association. His
discussions of the plays, unfortunately, are brief and superficial, and his
division of the work into "The Early Plays: Written in Anger," "The Middle
Plays: In Moderation," and "The Post-War Plays: In Maturity" is perfunctory
and problematic. *Clash by Night,* for example, can hardly be classified as

moderate, while whatever "anger" might be discerned in *Awake and Sing!* is surely not comparable to that which pervades *The Big Knife*. Mendelsohn does, however, provide the first analysis of Odets's film and television work; he also deals briefly with *The Silent Partner*.

The best of the early books is Gerald Weales's *Clifford Odets: Playwright*,[30] which was reprinted in 1985 by Methuen as *Odets: The Playwright*. Brenman-Gibson's appellation of biography more appropriately applies to Weales's book than to Shuman's, for it is the first attempt to provide a detailed accounting of Odets's life. Weales, a lively writer, covers his material with style, verve, and intelligence. Although he does not want to distinguish Odets the playwright from Odets the celebrity, he nevertheless recognizes his subject as an artist who left some remarkable plays and an important body of work: "With Atkinson if not for his reasons, I am ready to discard the failed dramatist cliché. Odets left a body of work—flawed and imperfect as it is—that from *Waiting for Lefty* to *The Flowering Peach* shows him as one of our most talented playwrights."[31] This is certainly an accurate assessment and one that Weales undoubtedly believes, but his book does not substantiate it. Emphasizing the life at the expense of the art, Weales fails to examine many of the plays with the extended scrutiny they deserve. He begins by labeling *Awake and Sing!* Odets's best play—which, in light of his own biographical / chronological method, might lead one to conclude the Odets never went beyond the work of his youth.

Still, there is much of value in this book, and it remains a balanced and provocative study. Weales deals not only with Odets's eleven produced plays but also with all of his film and television work, as well as the unproduced *The Silent Partner* and *The Cuban Play*. More recently Weales published "Clifford's Children: or It's a Wise Playwright Who Knows His Own Father,"[32] in which he discusses Odets's influence on Williams, Miller, Carson McCullers, Lorraine Hansberry, and David Mamet.

The first study to depart from the chronological play-by-play approach was Harold Cantor's 1978 *Clifford Odets: Playwright-Poet*.[33] First isolating what he considers Odets's central themes—"The Family Trap," "The Sell-out," and "The Crisis of Love"—Cantor proceeds to discuss central symbols and structural devices such as his "imagination of disaster" and fertility images. He concludes with an analysis of Odets's dialogue. A major advantage of Cantor's study is that in concentrating on themes and techniques, he succeeds in removing Odets for once from the social context and so is able to address the works without recourse to questions of contemporary reference. Odets's concern with timeless themes and his reliance on recurring symbols are thereby demonstrated clearly for the first time in lengthy analysis. If Cantor, like Murray, tends to quote too much, and if his commentary tends to read rather like a list of references, this study nonetheless makes an important contribution in tracing out "the figure in the carpet" of Odets's dramatic artistry. The book also provides an excellent bibliography of secondary materials.

The single most important book on Odets is Margaret Brenman-Gibson's mammoth biography *Clifford Odets, American Playwright: The Years from 1906–1940.* This work chronicles Odets's life through the premiere and failure of *Night Music,* when he was thirty-four years old; a promised second volume has not yet appeared. One of the book's strengths, which is also its primary weakness, lies in the sheer accumulation of detail; the 748 densely printed pages contain frequent references to the copious explanatory notes at the back. Brenman-Gibson apparently cites every scrap and scribble from Odets's hand in reconstructing his story, leaving one to wish at times for a more selective rendering of the material. Surely no more detailed account of Odets's life will appear: Brenman-Gibson received the full cooperation of Odets's children, who provided her all of their father's papers, said to have filled an entire moving van.

Brenman-Gibson's aim was to adopt Odets's comment, "I will reveal America to itself by revealing myself to myself," and to apply it literally by constructing not only a psychoanalytic biography of Odets but also a social and cultural history of the America that produced him. She takes for a model her mentor Erik Erikson, who advocated psychohistory, as exemplified in his *Young Man Luther: A Study on Psychoanalysis and History.*[34] While Brenman-Gibson is a perceptive social critic, usefully illuminating the connections between Odets's career difficulties and the problematic qualities of American culture, she treats his life more as a fascinating case history than as the formative experience of a major artist. The mountain of personal material is presented and examined in clinical depth, while too many of the plays are probed for what they reveal psychologically about Odets rather than for their intrinsic worth as works of art. Brenman-Gibson's analysis of *Rocket to the Moon,* which she considers Odets's best play, is, however, definitive.

The most recent book on Odets is my own, entitled *Clifford Odets,*[35] in which I attempt to describe Odets's central themes and images and to portray his tireless experimentation with form as the necessary vehicle for these recurring concerns. Recognizing a distinct Chekhovian flavor in Odets's early plays, I demonstrate that he succeeded in transforming Chekhov's style and grafting it onto the American scene in *Awake and Sing!* and *Paradise Lost.* His attempt to fuse popular film culture and the philosophy of Nietzsche to create the tragic form in *Golden Boy* and his variations on the tragic formula in *The Big Knife,* his experiments with the romance genre in *Rocket to the Moon* and *Night Music,* and his use of melodrama in *The Country Girl* and *Clash by Night* are also explored. My book is the first to consider all of Odets's published work in detail, as well as his film and television work. Also analyzed are the early fragments *910 Eden Street* and *Victory,* and the extant scripts of *The Silent Partner* and *The Cuban Play.*

A number of extended essays that are included in books of wider scope deserve mention. The most important is Frank Cunningham's "Clifford Odets," in *American Writers: A Collection of Literary Biographies.*[36] Cunningham argues that Odets should be ranked with Williams and Miller and O'Neill in his concern with great themes, while providing some rather eccentric evaluations of Odets's work, ranking *Clash by Night* and *Night Music* among his greatest plays. Gerald Rabkin's study of politics in the American theater of the thirties, *Drama and Commitment,*[37] presents the best essay on Odets as a political writer. A fine, comprehensive study of the American theater and the Depression is Malcolm Goldstein's *The Political Stage,*[38] which offers two chapters on the Group Theatre, in which are discussed the seven Odets plays produced by that ensemble. Two useful overviews of Odets's careers as a playwright and as a screenwriter can be found in *The Dictionary of Literary Biography* volumes on American Dramatists by Beth Fleischman[39] and on American Screenwriters by James Goodwin.[40]

Three other essays on Odets appear in books that deal with more specific themes. Robert J. Griffin's "On the Love Songs of Clifford Odets," in *The Thirties: Fiction, Poetry, Drama,* regards Odets as an imaginative spokesman "of the romance of the 30's because his personal sentiments and aspirations mirrored the decade's captivating ideals."[41] In "Clifford Odets and the Jewish Context," in *From Hester Street to Hollywood: The Jewish American Stage and Screen,* R. Baird Shuman deals with Odets as a Jewish writer.[42] George Groman discusses Odets's appearance before the HUAC in "Waiting for Odets: A Playwright Takes the Stand," in *Politics and the Muse.*[43] Winifred L. Dusenbury, in her *The Theme of Loneliness in Modern American Drama,* provides sensitive readings of *Night Music* and *Rocket to the Moon.*[44]

Finally, the most important resource for the study of the career of Odets is The Billy Rose Theatre Collection of The New York Public Library at Lincoln Center. Over the years Odets's son, Walt Whitman Odets, has been donating material incrementally to this collection, which includes multiple drafts of most of Odets's plays, as well as such unpublished work as *The Silent Partner, The Cuban Play, 910 Eden Street, Victory,* and *At the Waterline* (a radio play). These manuscripts demonstrate Odets's struggles with form during the evolution of his plays. The collection also includes diaries, appointment books, photographs, clippings that Odets kept for use in his work, paintings by Odets, and drafts of his essays. Not all of the material in the collection has been catalogued.

Notes

1. Daniel Aaron, *Writers on the Left* (New York: Harcourt, Brace and World, 1961), 319.

2. George Ross, "So This Is Broadway," *World-Telegram,* (20 September 1935), 16.

3. Arthur Wagner, "How a Playwright Triumphs," *Harper's Magazine,* (September 1966), 70.

4. Clifford Odets, *The Time Is Ripe: The 1940 Journal of Clifford Odets* (New York: Grove Press, 1988), 70.

5. John Gassner, *Theater at the Crossroads* (New York: Holt, Rinehart and Winston, 1960), 129.

6. Harold Clurman, ed., *Famous American Plays of the 1930's* (New York: Dell, 1968), 19–93.

7. Harvey Swados, ed., *The American Writer and the Great Depression* (New York: Bobbs-Merrill, 1966).

8. Louis Filler, ed., *The Anxious Years* (New York: Capricorn, 1964), 214–17.

9. Margaret Brenman-Gibson, *Clifford Odets, American Playwright: The Years from 1906–1940* (New York: Atheneum, 1981), 354–56.

10. John Gassner and Dudley Nichols, eds. *Best Film Plays, 1945* (New York: Crown, 1946), 261–330. Reprinted by Garland Publishing Co. (New York, 1977), which uses the same pagination.

11. Clifford Odets and William Gibson, *Golden Boy* (New York: Atheneum, 1965).

12. Clifford Odets and William Gibson, *Golden Boy* (New York: Bantam, 1966).

13. Henry Wadsworth Longfellow Dana, ed., *Seven Soviet Plays* (New York: Macmillan, 1946), 389–454.

14. Eric Bentley, *Thirty Years of Treason* (New York: Viking Press, 1971), 498–531.

15. Harold Clurman, *The Fervent Years* (New York: Knopf, 1945).

16. Clifford Odets, *Six Plays of Clifford Odets* (New York: Modern Library, 1939).

17. Harold Clurman, *Lies Like Truth* (New York: Macmillan, 1958).

18. Harold Clurman, "Clifford Odets," *New York Times,* 25 August 1963, sec. 2, p. 1.

19. Elia Kazan, *A Life* (New York: Knopf, 1988).

20. "White Hope," *Time,* 5 December 1938, 44–47.

21. Edith Isaacs, "Clifford Odets, First Chapters," *Theatre Arts* (April 1939):257–64.

22. John McCarten, "Revolution's Number One Boy," *The New Yorker,* 22 January 1938), 21–27.

23. Brooks Atkinson, "Group Theatre Plus Clifford Odets," *New York Times,* 26 March 1939, sec. 11, p. 1.

24. R. Baird Shuman, *Clifford Odets* (New York: Twayne, 1962).

25. Brenman-Gibson, xii.

26. Edward Murray, *Clifford Odets: The Thirties and After* (New York: Ungar, 1968).

27. Murray, 13.

28. Michael J. Mendelsohn, *Clifford Odets: Humane Dramatist* (Deland, Fla.: Everett/Edwards, 1969).

29. Michael J. Mendelsohn, "Odets at Center Stage," *Theatre Arts* (May and June, 1963): 16–19, 74–76 and 28–30, 78–80.

30. Gerald Weales, *Clifford Odets: Playwright* (New York: Pegasus, 1971).

31. Weales, 186.

32. Gerald Weales, "Clifford's Children: or It's a Wise Playwright Who Knows His Own Father," *Studies in American Drama 1945–Present* 2 (1987): 3–18.

33. Harold Cantor, *Clifford Odets: Playwright-Poet* (Metuchen, N.J.: Scarecrow Press, 1978). Cantor also analyzes Odets's use of Yiddish dialect in "Odets' Yinglish: The Psychology of Dialect as Dialogue," *Studies in American Jewish Literature,* 2 (1982): 61–68.

34. Erik H. Erikson, *Young Man Luther: A Study on Psychoanalysis and History* (New York: W. W. Norton, 1958).

35. Gabriel Miller, *Clifford Odets* (New York: Continuum, 1989).

36. Frank Cunningham, "Clifford Odets," in *American Writers: A Collection of Literary Biographies,* suppl. 2, pt. 2. (New York: Scribners, 1981), 529–54.

37. Gerald Rabkin, *Drama and Commitment: Politics in the American Theatre of the Thirties* (Bloomington: Indiana University Press, 1964), 169–212.

38. Malcolm Goldstein, *The Political Stage: American Drama and the Theater of the Great Depression* (New York: Oxford University Press, 1974). Of special interest are chapters 4 and 10.

39. Beth Fleischman, "Clifford Odets," in *Dictionary of Literary Biography, vol. 7, Twentieth Century American Dramatists, pt. 2,* ed. John MacNicholas (Detroit, Mich.: Gale Research, 1981), 126–39.

40. James Goodwin, "Clifford Odets," in *Dictionary of Literary Biography, volume 26, American Screenwriters,* eds. Robert Morsberger, Stephen O. Lesser, and Randall Clark (Detroit, Mich.: Gale Research, 1984), 235–39.

41. Robert J. Griffin, "On the Love Songs of Clifford Odets," in *The Thirties: Fiction, Poetry, Drama,* ed. Warren French (Deland, Fla.: Everett/Edwards, 1967), 193–200.

42. R. Baird Shuman, "Clifford Odets and the Jewish Context," in *From Hester Street to Hollywood: The Jewish American Stage and Screen,* ed. Sarah Blacher Cohen (Bloomington: Indiana University Press, 1983), 85–105. See also Shuman's "Clifford Odets: A Playwright and His Jewish Background," *South Atlantic Quarterly* 71 (1972): 225–33.

43. George L. Groman, "Waiting for Odets: A Playwright Takes the Stand," in *Politics and the Muse: Studies in the Politics of Recent American Literature,* ed. Adam Sorkin (Bowling Green, Ohio: Bowling Green State University Popular Press, 1989), 64–78.

44. Winifred L. Dusenbury, *The Theme of Loneliness in Modern American Drama* (Gainesville: University of Florida Press, 1960).

REVIEWS

◆

[*Waiting for Lefty* and *Till the Day I Die*] (1935)

Joseph Wood Krutch

A new production by the Group Theater supplies the answer to a question I asked in this column three weeks ago. Mr. Clifford Odets, the talented author of "Awake and Sing," has come out for the revolution and thrown in his artistic lot with those who use the theater for direct propaganda. The earlier play, it seems, was written some three years ago before his convictions had crystallized, and it owes to that fact a certain contemplative and brooding quality. The new ones—there are two on a double bill at the Longacre—waste no time on what the author now doubtless regards as side issues, and they hammer away with an unrelenting insistency upon a single theme: Workers of the World Unite!

"Waiting for Lefty," a brief sketch suggested by the recent strike of taxi drivers, is incomparably the better of the two, and whatever else one may say of it, there is no denying its effectiveness as a tour de force. It begins *in media res* on the platform at a strikers' meeting, and "plants" interrupting from the audience create the illusion that the meeting is actually taking place at the very moment of representation. Brief flashbacks reveal crucial moments in the lives of the drivers, but the scene really remains in the hall itself, and the piece ends when the strike is voted. The pace is swift, the characterization is for the most part crisp. and the points are made, one after another, with bold simplicity. What Mr. Odets is trying to do could hardly be done more economically or more effectively.

Cold analysis, to be sure, clearly reveals the fact that such simplicity must be paid for at a certain price. The villains are mere caricatures and even the very human heroes occasionally freeze into stained-glass attitudes, as, for example, a certain lady secretary in one of the flashbacks does when she suddenly stops in her tracks to pay a glowing tribute to "The Communist Manifesto" and to urge its perusal upon all and sundry. No one, however, expects subtleties from a soap-box, and the interesting fact is that Mr. Odets has invented a form which turns out to be a very effective dramatic equivalent of soap-box oratory.

From *Nation*, 10 April 1935. Copyright 1935, The Nation Co., Inc. Reprinted by permission.

Innumerable other "proletarian" dramatists have tried to do the same thing with far less success. Some of them have got bogged in futuristic symbolism which could not conceivably do more than bewilder "the worker"; others have stuck close to the usual form of the drama without realizing that this form was developed for other uses and that their attempt to employ it for directly hortatory purposes can only end in what appears to be more than exceedingly crude dramaturgy. Mr. Odets, on the other hand, has made a clean sweep of the conventional form along with the conventional intentions. He boldly accepts as his scene the very platform he intends to use, and from it permits his characters to deliver speeches which are far more convincing there than they would be if elaborately worked into a conventional dramatic story. Like many of his fellows he has evidently decided that art is a weapon, but unlike many who proclaim the doctrine, he has the full courage of his conviction. To others he leaves the somewhat nervous determination to prove that direct exhortation can somehow be made compatible with "art" and that "revolutionary" plays can be two things at once. The result of his downrightness is to succeed where most of the others have failed. He does not ask to be judged by any standards except those which one would apply to the agitator, but by those standards his success is very nearly complete.

"Waiting for Lefty" is played upon what is practically a bare stage. It could be acted in any union hall by amateur actors, and the fact accords well with the intention of a play which would be wholly in place as part of the campaign laid out by any strike committee. Indeed, it is somewhat out of place anywhere else for the simple reason that its appeal to action is too direct not to seem almost absurd when addressed to an audience most of whose members are not, after all, actually faced with the problem which is put up to them in so completely concrete a form. The play might, on the other hand, actually turn the tide at a strikers' meeting, and that is more than can be said of most plays whose avowed intention is to promote the class war.

As for the other piece, "Till the Day I Die," there is much less to be said in its favor. The hero is a young German whose loyalty to the Communist Party survives the tortures applied by fiendish storm troopers, but a note on the program suggests the reason why the play lacks the air of reality. It was "suggested by a letter from Germany printed in the *New Masses*," and obviously the author had too little to go on. However much "Waiting for Lefty" may owe to a Marxian formula, both the characters and the situation come within the range of the author's experience and there is a basis of concrete reality. "Till the Day I Die" is founded upon nothing except the printed word, and the characters are mere men of wax. In so far as we believe it at all, we do so only because we have been told that such things do happen. There is little in the play itself to carry conviction, and neither its hero nor its villains seem very much more real than those of the simplest and most old-fashioned melodramas. The acting in the two pieces is as different as they are them-selves. Mr. Odets's Germans strike attitudes and declaim. His strikers are so real—perhaps so actual would be better—that when the play is over one expects to find their cabs outside.

[*Awake and Sing!*]
(1935)

BROOKS ATKINSON

After experimenting with scripts from several different hands, the Group Theatre has found its most congenial playwright under its own roof. Clifford Odets, whose "Awake and Sing!" was acted at the Belasco last evening. He has been for some time one of the Group actors, and he is the author of "Waiting for Lefty," the dynamic play in one act which has been done several times at special performances this Winter. Now he is writing in three acts a vigorous and closely matted drama of Jewish life in the Bronx, and nine members of the Group Theatre play it with stunning power. Having considerable power in his own right, Mr. Odets has written a drama that is full of substance and vitality; he is not afraid to tackle a big job. But it is necessary to add that he does not quite finish what he has started in this elaborately constructed piece. Although he is very much awake, he does not sing with the ease and clarity of a man who has mastered his score.

The home-life of his Bronx family is volcanic. His characters are drawn in several directions. Having brought up her family by force of her own character, Bessie Berger is a tyrant whose one ambition is to preserve her home. Under her roof she harbors a husband who is an amiable bungler and an aging father who is a student of revolution and a lover of the great arts. Her daugher is an unhappy and rebellious girl who creates the first crisis in the play by confessing that she is pregnant by a boy whose identity she will not reveal. Her son is a scatter-minded lad whose impulses are thwarted by his mother. For good measure, there is also a bitter neighborhood racketeer who is in love with the daughter and rebels against all his own impulses. These are the main characters. They are all excitable, restless and at loose ends; and they are generally flying at one another's throats.

Although Mr. Odets has a story to tell, his method is to infuse it with the development of his characters; the story cannot be dissociated for a moment from its people. In other words, he means to be a dramatist rather than a playwright. In this instance the defect of the method is the lack of clarity and simplicity in his writing. Although his dialogue has uncommon strength, his drama in the first two acts is wanting in the ordinary fluidity of a play. For two acts it is turbulent—packed with noisy, lunging humanity. In the last act Mr. Odets comes to at least two conclusions, and the daughter and son who have been dwelling in the dust awake and sing the melody of free people. When he succeeds in loosening the play from the bonds of his tense craftsmanship, Mr. Odets has the fervor and the skill in direct assertion that are the admirable qualities of "Waiting for Lefty." He may not be a master yet, but he has the ability to be one.

The Group Theatre actors play as if they felt at home inside Mr. Odets's Bronx saga. As the lonely, dreamy old man Morris Carnovsky plays with endearing gentleness; he is an actor of artistic eminence. Jules Garfield plays the part of the boy with a splendid sense of character development. As the daughter Phoebe Brand gives her most attractive performance. Stella Adler as the overbearing mother, Luther Adler as the half-malignant cigar-store lounger. J. E. Bromberg as a braggart garment vendor, Art Smith as the footless father and Sanford Meisner as a bloodless son-in-law give clearly imagined performances. Although Harold Clurman's direction seems to this reviewer to be overwrought and shrill, no one can complain that it is lacking in conviction.

So the Group Theatre batters its way on. To this student of the arts "Awake and Sing," in spite of its frenzy, is inexplicably deficient in plain, theatre emotion. There is something unyielding at the core of the play. Charge that comment off to the higher criticism. The pleasant news is that the Group Theatre has found a genuine writer among its own members and knows how to set his play to rattling on the boards.

[*Paradise Lost*]
(1935)

John Mason Brown

Although taken as a whole "Paradise Lost" is not a play that adds to Clifford Odets's stature as a dramatist, neither is it one that subtracts from it. In spite of the fact that it is overstuffed and confused—yes, and that it is often feeble just when it stands most in need of strength—its three overwhelmingly glum acts include excellent scenes, scenes that are richly and poignantly written and that flame volcanically into life in Mr. Odets's best manner.

The truth is that it is a poor play, even though one is constantly made aware of the fact that a dramatist of exceptional powers has written it. Mr. Odets has uncanny ears for dialogue. He is a master of conflicts which erupt suddenly into climaxes of terrific force. He is equally sensitive to the smaller values by means of which character is realized. And he sees deeply into human agony and frustration. But it soon becomes regrettably clear in "Paradise Lost" that it is not his own eyes upon which he has depended to study the world in this American version of "The Cherry Orchard," but Chekov's microscope.

Chekov and Mr. Odets

The trouble with his borrowing Chekov's microscope is that Mr. Odets is not always able to keep the instrument in focus. He knows the externals of the Chekovian method. And he makes such flagrant use of them that they become annoying. But he does not seem to realize at all times what it was that lay at the heart of that method.

Chekov never wrote just to be writing. He loved to make copious use of the seemingly irrelevant, of small talk which apparently led nowhere, and of idiosyncrasies which were ventilated in speeches that appeared to be going off on tangents. But Chekov was too much of an artist not to make every detail count. Cutting one of his plays for production would be a thankless task.

From *New York Evening Post*, 10 December 1935. Reprinted with permission from *New York Evening Post*. © New York Post Co., Inc.

He could dispense with plot because he could put character and flavor in its place. The mood his people created was his plot. His irrelevancies were relevant. His inaction was his action; his apparent formlessness, his shrewdly achieved design. Every part of the jigsaw puzzles of his dramas was needed. These were the paradoxes of his amazing techniques.

In telling in "Paradise Lost" of the unhappiness suffered by two American middle class families during these years of economic crisis, Mr. Odets has made much more deliberate use of the Chekovian method than he did in "Awake and Sing!" There one felt it in spite of Mr. Clurman's denials in his preface to the published play. Here one can not escape it.

Mr. Odets has filled his play with men and women who admit their Chekovian parentage in most of their speeches. These people—particularly the eccentrics who must sing odd songs or dance or play in the familiar manner of Chekovian eccentrics—do not always do honor to Chekov. Often they employ his indirections to such a willful extent that, without meaning to, they become laughable parodies of his method. But often, too, as they prattle on between the bigger and the better scenes about canaries, stamps, fathers, wars, peace, misery, the economic system, the days before the war, or death, they cease to be laughable or exasperating because of some sudden and perceptive turn in Mr. Odets's dialogue, when he has his own say in his own arresting way.

Dream Men and Real Ones

Mr. Odets has one of his characters say, "The way I see it, there's two kinds of men—the real ones and the dream. We're just the dream." What "Paradise Lost" implies is that the middle class people who have accepted defeat under the present system are "dream men." They become "real" in the play, not as disasters descend upon them, but by seeing the light—the Communist light, we presume—and by dreaming of better days ahead in a woefully didactic curtain-time speech that Mr. Carnovsky is forced to deliver.

The two families with whom Mr. Odets's play is concerned are the Gordons, who live downstairs, and the crazy Katzes, who live upstairs. Mr. Gordon (Morris Carnovsky) has for years been Mr. Katz's (Luther Adler's) partner in business, but eventually discovers that Katz has stolen all of the firm's money. Gordon is a liberal and a man of honor, who raises the wages of his workers and gets into financial difficulties for so doing. Katz is an unscrupulous sweat-shop tyrant, half-mad and tortured by the fact that his slavish wife has presented him with no children. We see him only occasionally and for no good reason never learn what finally happens to him. But we are made fully aware of his misery.

Gordon also has his worries. His wife (Stella Adler) is an amiable woman who is stronger and more practical than he is. His daughter (Blanche

Gladstone) is a neurotic pianist who is condemned to sex-starvation when she decides she cannot afford to marry the impoverished violinist who loves her. One of the Gordon's sons (Sanford Meisner), who likes to dress up in a tuxedo because it makes him "feel good," is slowly dying of sleeping sickness. Another (Walter Coy) is a former Olympic champion who, without having a job, marries the silly daughter of an old stamp collector (Roman Bohnen) who lives with the Gordons, and then seeks a gangster's death when he learns his wife has been unfaithful to him with his best friend (Elia Kazan). Gordon's home crumbles and they are evicted a year after Mr. Katz's failure. At this point Mr. Gordon sees the light and delivers his skillless little spiel.

AN EXCELLENT PRODUCTION

It is not the absence of plot, in the long-abandoned sense of the word, that one misses in "Paradise Lost." It is the presence of many, too many plays that have been crowded into one. The result is a drama which seems as disjointed as a card catalogue.

One wishes Mr. Odets had shown a surer control of his material. One wishes that he had thought it out (not only intellectually but dramatically) as Chekov would have done, so that every character and detail possessed some final relation to the whole. One wishes that its good writing had been put to a better use and that its abuses of the Chekovian method had been blue-penciled in the second draft. Then it would not be the occasionally brilliant, often interesting, but generally unsatisfying proof of Mr. Odets's exceptional talent that it is.

The production which "Paradise Lost" has been given is in the Group Theatre's very best manner. It is studded with performances by Luther and Stella Adler, Morris Carnovsky, Sanford Meisner, Roman Bohnen, Elia Kazan, Bob Lewis, William Challee and George Pembroke which are as rich in implication and in depth as are the best passages in Mr. Odets's writing. The acting is of a kind which more than justifies the Group's ideals. Due to Mr. Clurman's ever-sensitive direction, it has been coordinated into an ensemble which boasts high and uncommon virtues.

Mr. Odets may have failed Chekov in "Paradise Lost," and failed him badly, but he has not failed the actors in Group. He has tried too much, done some of it badly, and piled more miseries on top of one another than can remain believable or be taken seriously. Nevertheless, there are several scenes and innumerable touches in this disappointing new play of his which justify any one's strong belief in Mr. Odets as the most promising of America's younger dramatists. They are the scenes which he alone could have written.

[*Golden Boy*]
(1937)

BURNS MANTLE

They may be saying this morning that Clifford Odets, who came back to the theatre last night with a new drama called "The Golden Boy"—they may be saying that Clifford's Hollywood contaminations are apparent because his newest play is typical picture stuff, save for an unhappy ending.

But they will have some trouble proving their point. Practically any story of achievement stalked by menacing failure is picture stuff, and "The Golden Boy" reveals the best of the Odets genius for recreating a believable realism in both story and characters. His touch in these particulars is as sure, and his feeling for their development is as true in the new play as they were when he wrote "Awake and Sing" or even "Waiting for Lefty."

INTERESTING STORY

"The Golden Boy" is a carefully sustained study of an Italian boy whose artistic and creative urges were at war with the common American ambition to acquire wealth and publicity.

He went into the box fighter's business because he discovered that he was a born fighter and because he was at the moment tired of fiddling. He may also have been suffering from some slight glandular maladjustment.

He stayed in the box fighting business because he fell in love with his manager's gal, and found that she, too, was a wandering and misunderstood soul.

He won his way to a championship, even after the girl's loyalty held her to the other man. Then he won her back and, realizing that they had made a failure of their lives, took her for a death ride in his Duesenberg.

No, there is no noticeable loss of power in Odets' writing, and nothing lost in the keenness of his observation, or the rough but effective fluency of his style. He is still interested in the problems of the culturally submerged and hopefully ambitious.

From *New York Daily News*, 5 November 1937. © 1937 New York News, Inc. Reprinted with permission.

He knows the people about whom he writes, their problems and their reactions. His play will interest any one who acknowledges a similar interest. Most of us could live quite contentedly a great number of years if we never happened to meet any of these folk, but, meeting them, the story they tell, with Odets as interpreter, is holding.

Luther Adler, an actor of splendid technique and a long list of fine characterizations, has a great chance as the Golden Boy of this legend. None of the younger players could have done better than he.

Frances Farmer, come over from the movies to play the girl, is also nicely cast and splendidly equal to the job. She neatly caught the mystified reactions of a hardboiled daughter of the darkened ways.

The gentle Roman Bohnen has some little difficulty being as tough as a prizefight manager should be, but Morris Carnovsky is nicely in character as the mystified and hurt Italian father.

There are, as is usual in a Group Theatre production, a half dozen bits expertly played and completely realized, including those by Jules Garfield, Robert Lewis, Elia Kazan and Lee Cobb.

The settings are by Mordecai Gorelik and the direction by Harold Clurman, competent workers in the theater.

[Rocket to the Moon]
(1938)

RICHARD WATTS, JR.

Mr. Odets continues to be the most exciting and the most exasperating of the younger American dramatists. Once more he is revealed as a writer of really brilliant first acts, of fine and moving dialogue, of true and breathing characters, of brooding power and of plays that end by being curiously disappointing. This latest of his studies in the lives of the depressed classes has an opening act that is not only the finest thing that Mr. Odets has ever written but is as eloquent and stirring as anything in the recent theater. He is contemplating the emotional life of a dentist in his early middle years and since the dentist doesn't seem to have much business he and those about him have plenty of time for discussing their thoughts and emotions. And what talk it is, incisive, dramatic, realistic, lyric and capable of bringing characters and their ideas into glowing life! Then, halfway through the second act, both talk and plot seem to get out of hand and the play begins to languish.

It should be emphasized that "Rocket to the Moon" is a play decidedly worth seeing. Even when Mr. Odets is growing vague and uncertain in the manipulation of his story and the maneuvering of his people, occasional scenes and speeches and minor characters emerge eloquently and with flashes of sharp clarity. In the last act, for example, he casually tosses in the character of an unsuccessful salesman, a role seemingly of little importance to the narrative, and somehow the scene takes on a wonderful quality of friendliness and compassion. It is not such interruptions that interfere with the drama, since it is the souls of the brooding, lonely, unhappy people, not their adventures in love and dentistry, which are of importance. Mr. Odets can get humor and heartbreak and a wry sort of pity in his contemplation of people, but he cannot always manage them in their plot activities or make his cosmic observations seem important as thinking.

The central character of "Rocket to the Moon" is the quiet, modest and sensitive dentist, bedeviled by a brusque, efficient and somewhat nagging wife and a sardonic, witty, faintly satanic father-in-law, and falling into hopeless, baffled love with his flutter-brained and romantic-minded little

From *New York Herald-Tribune*, 25 November 1938.

secretary. It is obvious that all of them might have been familiar, routine figures in a familiar, routine triangle. Mr. Odets, however, makes them real and bewildered and helpless in a civilization that they do not understand and in which they cannot fit, and somehow these little people and their problems become exciting and important. In truth it is in part because the people are so believable that it grows so exasperating when the playwright manages their fate and their drama amid the longwinded confusion that interrupts the second and third acts.

The acting and the direction seem to me exceptionally fine. The most showy role of the play is that of the satanic father-in-law and it is richly and colorfully played by Luther Adler in one of his most effective performances. There is an uncommonly fine portrayal of the role of the little secretary by Miss Eleanor Lynn, who handles the part splendidly, even when the character goes in for an embarrassing touch of "Candida" in the last act. There are good performances, too, by Miss Ruth Nelson as the wife, Art Smith as a beaten dentist who turns blood-donor, Leif Erickson as a breezy doctor, Sanford Meisner as a dance director from Hollywood and William Challee as the traveling salesman. The most difficult role of all, however, is that of the dentist, who might easily seem half man and half mouse, if Morris Carnovsky, that brilliant actor, did not make him such a touching and dignified human being. "Rocket to the Moon" is a baffling combination of brilliance and confusion.

[*Night Music*]
(1940)

RICHARD LOCKRIDGE

Boy meets girl in the theater this season and together they meet New York. They meet with a difference in Clifford Odets's "Night Music," which opened at the Broadhurst last evening, and a philosophic detective chaperones them through the maze. They and those they meet have that odd, intense individuality which people have in the Odets world, where old men mumble their life stories eagerly on park benches and angry husbands reveal their domestic tribulations furiously in hotel lobbies.

But they are boy and girl all the same, and telling of them has mellowed Mr. Odets. "Night Music" is easygoing beyond any of his plays, and it is focused on individuals rather than on theme. It straggles a little here and there and is, I think, minor Odets; it is also crankily alive and full of pungent dialogue and often very funny. Now and then, too, it is more simply moving than Odets's plays often are and the characters, for all their idiosyncrasies, are rather easier to know. A lot of them, however, are mighty odd people, and the hero is one of the oddest.

He is a hungry, angry young Greek-American, whose predicaments are as singular as his temperament. He is taking a couple of monkeys to Hollywood at the start, and one of them makes a grab at the necklace of a pretty girl. In the turmoil young Steve Takis loses his airplane ticket and his wallet, mislays his monkeys and meets the girl. And when, released, he pursues her angrily, he gets knocked down by a stage hand, inherits a fox fur of doubtful lineage and fails bitterly in love.

The girl is an actress in flight from Philadelphia, respectability and a collar-ad suitor. Chance gathers her and the boy up together, and the elderly detective saunters after them to play providence. They sleep a night on a park bench and wrangle with Philadelphians in a Greek lunchroom and always the insecurity of their lives is a shadow accompanying them. The boy is a sensitive, furious youth, full of bluster and innocence and "hung up by the ears." He voices his desperation and anger at the World's Fair and admits love in a musty hotel room. But it is not until he finally loses his job while

From *New York Sun,* 23 February 1940.

waiting for a plane at the airport that the girl and the detective teach him to turn back to the city and fight, arm and arm with friends.

The vigor of the play grows out of the boy's character, and the characters of those he meets. He meets those strange, arresting people of the Odets world—sailors and unhappy husbands, suitcase thieves and hurrying fur salesmen and men who talk to themselves. He meets drabs with cats and men walking dogs and drunken men and insane vegetarians, because the people who interest Mr. Odets most are the peculiar ones. Now and then they interest him a little too much, and he lingers over minor idiosyncrasies while his play stalls. But by and large, Mr. Odets's strange people are as interesting as he thinks they are—and probably even more strange than he thinks them.

But "Night Music" does not go much beyond its characters. It is a minor play because it is not shaped to any vital purpose. In its very different, intensely subjective fashion, it is reporting as its cousin, Elmer Rice's "Two on an Island" is reporting. Except for its optimistic insistence that youth will be better off if it is not downhearted, "Night Music" has little to say about the world which its author views with such nonconforming eyes. It is a familiar play about unfamiliar people.

Like most plays produced by the Group Theater, it is acted with interest and variety, and like almost all designed by Mordecai Gorelik it is visually picturesque. Elia Kazan plays the leading role with sharp vigor and great perception. Morris Carnovsky, who seems never to miss, acts the part of the detective with vast comprehension. Miss Jane Wyatt plays the girl with simplicity and tenderness. A dozen of the Group familiars—Sanford Meisner, Roman Bohnen, Philip Loeb, Art Smith and the rest—dart in and out of the many scenes in brilliantly characteristic flashes.

[*Clash by Night*]
(1942)

JOSEPH WOOD KRUTCH

With almost perfect unanimity the critics turned thumbs down on Clifford Odets's new play "Clash by Night" (Belasco Theater). The tone of the reviews was, indeed, one which seems reserved almost exclusively for dealing with works by new authors previously greeted with wild enthusiasm, and it is difficult not to feel that the reviewers, in the process of cooling off, frequently do somewhat less than justice to those they are afraid of having praised too much. Nearly every fault found in "Clash by Night" is, to be sure, really there. Certain scenes, for example, are unquestionably over-long and the catastrophe, like that in most of the author's other plays, seems weak or at least less imaginative than the opening passages lead one to hope. But Mr. Odets, being a good writer, cannot be adequately described as the sum of his defects, and to me it seems positively monstrous to treat him as though he could. Whatever its faults, the new play has originality and power, and I am willing to wager that its severest critics will remember it long after they have forgotten other pieces successfully launched on the wave of their enthusiasm.

In subject matter and tone "Clash by Night" belongs in the category with "Rocket to the Moon." The setting is equally drab, the persons equally unbeautiful, and the story deliberately banal in much the same way. But like "Rocket to the Moon" all this is both more interesting and less painful than it seems to have any right to be because Odets has qualities very few of his contemporaries possess in anything like an equal degree. He had them from the very beginning, and they were responsible for the impression which "Awake and Sing" was able to produce, but they have become clearer and clearer as he has abandoned the preaching of a doctrine and left the plays to stand or fall by their imaginative force.

The first of these qualities is one of the most mysterious and most nearly unanalyzable in the whole repertory of artistic magic—namely, the power of making things seem real. This has, of course, no necessary connection with what is called realism, and it is, on the other hand, identical with what ought to be the primary meaning of the word "imagination," or the power of creating imitations of reality which seem like reality itself. One recognizes it when one finds oneself accepting personages and actions directly and on their own terms rather than as typical characters or situations, when they remind one of nothing except themselves and not of either fiction or, even, experience. The quality is not incompatible, as in this case, with the fact that both the characters and the situations can be crudely described as banal or, as in the case of Shakespeare, with the fact that they can equally well be described as directly in an established convention. They are merely so completely realized that their existence is independent of either the actuality or the convention with which it is possible intellectually to connect them.

This power Mr. Odets has to a degree unequaled by any of his American contemporaries except Erskine Caldwell and Eugene O'Neill. In addition he has the power of communicating a special sort of compassion peculiarly his own. The preacher takes us down into the lower depths to arouse our indignation, the sentimentalist in order that we may discover there impossible virtues, and the decadent merely that we may wallow with him in congenial mud. Mr. Odets has been occasionally a preacher, but never a sentimentalist or a decadent, and at his best he is none of these. His people are certainly not beautiful people, and in "Clash by Night" there is not a single character "sympathetic" in the ordinary sense of the word. Yet there is not one with whom one does not sympathize, not one who is not pitiable, not one whom the spectator does not understand.

In his earlier plays Mr. Odets had a villain, "the social system." His best characters are still persons to whom lack of money is recurrently the dominant fact in life, but he has grown less and less interested in demonstrating this fact as a fact, more and more interested in picturing from the inside the tragedy of men and women who are victims of passion no less than of economics. Many of them have, like Odets himself, the gift of compassion, but suffering and frustration generate an egotism which overrides even compassion, and the result is a kind of tragedy which his plays define more and more clearly—the tragedy of those who hurt others not in blindness or malice but only because they are themselves in agony.

None of this could mean much if Mr. Odets did not have the power of imagining his people with extraordinary solidity. But since that power has been given him, he is already one of the most impressive dramatists of our generation, and about "Clash by Night" I should like to make a prediction. If it is not too precipitately removed from the boards it will find a rewarding audience.

[*The Big Knife*]
(1949)

WILLIAM HAWKINS

In "The Big Knife," Clifford Odets has written a play that gathers momentum in its windup and ends with the emotional impact of a mule's kick square in the face.

His theme is the worship of Mammon, and his choice of background is Hollywood, which gives him two big advantages. In the first place the motion pictures' familiarly make the most exaggerated fiscal returns for success of any industry extant. Beyond that, there is no other setting where such a theme could be so violently and rawly personal, because nowhere else is individual reputation so vulnerable an asset.

This is the story of Charlie Castle, a top-ranking picture star, disgusted with ordinary work he is doing, irritable, casual about his wife, and yet captured by acclaim and wealth.

When faced with the fact, he really loves his wife deeply, but things have come to a point where she wants to abandon their marriage, unless he makes an effort to recapture his integrity as an actor and a man.

THREATS ARE MIGHTY

He would refuse to sign a new 14-year contract, but unfortunately a scandalous incident of his hit-and-run driving has been covered up by his studio, and the threats are mighty.

A pathetic little tart who was in his car when the accident took place is threatening to talk. It is when an executive of the studio suggests that she be ruthlessly removed from the scene that Charlie sees he is hopelessly embroiled in an immoral morass. The threatened disaster of the play's beginning becomes real and far reaching.

There will be endless arguments about the special nature of a Hollywood story, and it will be easy to quip that a man with a $13,000,000 contract ought to get along.

From *New York World-Telegram*, 25 February 1949.

More important is the fact that the author has relayed a valid criticism in terms that make it terrifically effective on the stage. The play starts casually, even slowly, as it creates an atmosphere of nervous dissatisfaction in the middle of physical luxury. After it gets rolling there are still scenes played at retarded tempo, but they are so real in their tension that they are sometimes indecently exposing.

JOHN GARFIELD IN LEAD

In the end one wonders just how far the exposure of the sordid truth can effect the absolute and amoral monarchs of the subject business. They seem beyond paying off in human terms, but the smaller ones for whom there is hope offer the promise of emotional resolution.

John Garfield's is, of course, the major role, and he seems to have stuffed its frustrations inside himself until they burst out of their own accord. It is a tense part of a man who recognized the brutality of threats against him and others around him, knows the emptiness of his own tempting glory, and realizes that happiness is now beyond his capabilities.

Nancy Kelly is admirable as the wife, whose love for the actor prevents her decisions from sticking until it is too late. Her assignment is one of continual harassment, which she modulates effectively, and she closes the play with a devastating moment of despair.

There is a highly polished portrayal of the studio head by J. Edward Bromberg. In normal terms it is not an entirely believable character, but picture people can and do confirm that its facets are understated. Mr. Bromberg plays it with monstrous quiet.

Paul McGrath is doing one of his best jobs in years as the sycophantic assistant, and Reinhold Schunzel makes an utterly convincing figure of the star's manager.

As the touching little trollop, dancing fearfully to her doom, Joan McCracken performs a pathically revealing scene, and Theodore Newton is a sturdy, sensible Horatio as a writer.

[*The Country Girl*]
(1950)

RICHARD WATTS, JR.

Out of the material of the most familiar of backstage plots, Clifford Odets has provided a tense and absorbing play, which offers cheering proof that the one-time master of the so-called "propaganda" drama can write with all his old skill and sensitivity when he gives up his contemplation of social problems and goes in for a straightforward story of love and the theatre. It is called "The Country Girl," and it was acted brilliantly at the Lyceum Friday night by a fine cast headed by Paul Kelly, Uta Hagen and Steven Hill. Among its other virtues it gives Miss Hagen an opportunity for her most skillful performance.

The narrative is, indeed, so artfully and freshly managed in the writing and playing that it probably will not be until you are out of the playhouse that you will pause to remember how frequently the plot has been used by dramatists in the course of stage history. Under the talented Odets touch it doesn't seem to matter much, but what he has given us is the customary story of the alcoholic actor, whose weakness for drink has ruined his career, and who is helped in his comeback fight by the heroic loyalty of his faithful wife. It requires no small skill to make the familiar tale so dramatically arresting.

TRIANGLE

Mr. Odets has, however, managed this minor miracle, not by any tricks of story-telling, but by observing his characters with such intelligent compassion and writing of them with all the feeling for hapless humanity which made his social plays so exciting a feature of American playgoing in the thirties. In his hands, "The Country Girl" becomes a sort of triangle play of the theatre, in which the loyal wife and an earnest young stage director battle for the soul of the weak and selfish but once-great actor. It is no small triumph that the three of them somehow seem people worth bothering about.

From *New York Post*, 12 November 1950. Reprinted with permission from *New York Post*. © New York Post Co., Inc.

Odets is, I think, particularly skillful in letting his characters develop as you see more and more of them. In a way, the story is seen through the eye of the director, who, from his youth, has worshipped the famous actor. At first, his admiration makes the husband's weakness seem a cruel result of the wife's neurotic selfishness, and the wife is apparently the poor fellow's evil genius. It is only slowly that it becomes evident that it is the husband who is guilty of pathological cruelty, through his inability to be honest about himself, while the wife is the victim of her gallant fidelity. By that time, you also come to see why the director was so mistaken in his judgment.

THE ACTOR'S WIFE

Although the wife is the sympathetic figure of the story, in the usual fashion of such backstage stories, Mr. Odets never makes the error of being sloppily sentimental about her. She is not simply the long-suffering martyr of so many plays and movies. She has strength, courage and pride, and with all her loyalty, there is a limit beyond which she will not surrender her personal identity to the husband who imposes on her. And, while the author has no illusion about the selfish weakness of the actor and the blindness of the director, he makes both of them worth a measure of sympathy. The backstage atmosphere is, of course, excellent, although the playwright of the story struck me as perhaps a trifle too meek.

Never before, it seems to me, has Miss Hagen played with anything near the moving excellence she reveals as the wife. It is one of the notable performances of the season. Mr. Kelly is always a splendid actor, and he plays the husband with complete honesty and none of the familiar cliches of such a role. Mr. Hill's performance as the director indicates that he is a man who is going to be heard of in the theatre. The author has also directed with skill, and Boris Aronson's sets are, of course, just what they should be. "The Country Girl" brings back Clifford Odets as a force in American playwriting.

[*The Flowering Peach*]
(1954)

BROOKS ATKINSON

Mr. Odets' new play is a beautiful one. His finest, in fact. "The Flowering Peach" he calls it. It opened at the Belasco last evening with a tender, lovely, humorous performance.

Imagine the fable of Noah's voyage told in terms of a temperamental though closely united Jewish family and there you have the plan of "The Flowering Peach." Years ago Mr. Odets came into the theatre with another play about a Jewish family. In "Awake and Sing" the members of the family were temperamental and united, too.

The tone of "The Flowering Peach" shows how far Mr. Odets has traveled since the cocksure days of "Awake and Sing." The brassy, ricocheting dialogue has matured into humorous, modest talk about great subjects that neither Mr. Odets nor the rest of us are likely to solve. For the new play is the story of mankind living out its destiny under the benevolent eye of God.

There were giants on the earth in those days of the Deluge. In spirit Noah was the greatest. It is Mr. Odets' mood not to put him on a pedestal but to characterize him as the worried head of a family of ordinary individuals—a peevish though loving hero who feels himself close to God. As Noah, Menasha Skulnik, previously celebrated as a low comedian, gives a memorable performance in terms of comedy, temper, pettiness and devotion. Call it a masterpiece of character acting and you cannot be far from the truth.

No doubt, the first half of "The Flowering Peach" is the more endearing. The second half is a little repetitious and garrulous. But no matter, really, for the story of how Noah persuades his skeptical family that God has given all of them a mission, how they bicker, yet do the job obediently, how God helps them solve the most prodigious problems, how they scamper into the ark when the rains fall—all this, told with sympathetic humor in the form of a folk fable, ought to be enough to delight and move any theatregoer.

In the second act the voyage concludes triumphantly with the grounding of the ark, the flowering of the peach and the departure of the family in

From *New York Times*, 29 December 1954. Copyright © 1954 by The New York Times Co. Reprinted by permission.

their several ways to replenish and fructify the earth. It is a triumphant conclusion, but after a long series of quarrels and sorrows that symbolize the eternal questing of God's children.

Mr. Odets is every inch a theatre writer. That is probably the reason why this fantasy always seems real and human and respectful of the unseen Lord of the skies. As his own director and in association with other theatre artists, he has staged an idiomatic performance. Mordecai Gorelik has designed a whole series of settings in fable style; and Abe Feder, the lighting expert, has arranged sunshine, storms, nights and days and the final rainbow in a deeply emotional vein. Alan Hovhaness has composed an evocative musical score that serves the pulsing moods of the play admirably.

All honor to Mr. Skulnik for his touching, humble, virtuoso performance. But Berta Gersten also contributes a notable performance. As Noah's wife, she plays with sardonic sharpness of speech, but with fortitude, patience and forgiveness as the matriarch of the race. She has stature and homely eloquence.

The other parts are well defined individuals. Martin Ritt is a tower of strength as Shem. Nor is there anything slovenly in the other characterizations. Mario Alcaldo as a stubborn though capable Japheth, Leon Janney as a trivial-minded Ham, Osna Palmer as an industrious Leah, Janice Rule as a placid Rachel with a stone lying in her heart, Barbara Baxley as a coquettish Goldie who learns to respect some unworldly people—these are perceptive performances that grow in richness and understanding as the story tests the characters.

If you listen closely you can probably discover a message of hope for the sullen world of today. But Mr. Odets is not setting himself up as an oracle. He does not pretend to have the magic formula. Contemplating the long history of the race in terms of some disarming people, he is facing the world with respect and humility. "The Flowering Peach" is his testament to the endurance and native wisdom of mankind.

EARLY EVALUATIONS

◆

Revolution's Number One Boy
(1938)

JOHN McCARTEN

Clifford Odets is thoroughly dissatisfied with the contemporary theatre. The poor scripts, the awkward direction, and what he calls the "lack of creativity" depress him, and he cannot stomach the rank commercialism of the actors. Therefore he rarely goes to any plays except his own. And although he takes a proper pride in being generally accepted as the most promising young playwright in the country, he is by no means certain that the drama is his best medium of expression. He is inclined to think that he should have been a composer all along. His interest in music dates back to his early childhood, when he used to listen to his father playing the pianola. Later on the family got a phonograph, and Odets can still remember how moved he was when he first heard the Sextet from "Lucia" on a Victor Red Seal. As a boy, Odets' favorite instrument was the harmonica. He was given piano lessons for a while, but he refused to practice. It wasn't until he was twenty-five that he began to regret his childish indolence. That was when he started to write a novel about a boy who was well on the way to becoming a great pianist until he lost his left hand in an accident. Odets has since destroyed the novel, but the theme recurs in "Golden Boy," his most recent play, which concerns itself with a brilliant young violinist who breaks his hand on an opponent's head while battling for the lightweight championship.

Odets' penthouse at 1 University Place is seldom empty of music. When his electric phonograph isn't playing record after record of Mozart, Tchaikovsky, and Beethoven, Odets is usually either singing or improvising chords on his Hammond organ. He sometimes interrupts a conversation with an aria. His singing voice is a rather uneasy baritone, but there is utter confidence in the sweeping gestures with which he dramatizes his delivery while coursing a melody.

Odets gesticulates constantly. His hands, which are extremely long and graceful, are never still. He likes to talk standing up because it gives him a chance to stride up and down, tossing his head, swelling his chest, and

Originally published in *New Yorker* (22 January 1938). Reprinted by permission; © 1938, 1966 The New Yorker Magazine Inc.

39

throwing his arms around. He often indulges in the second-balcony stare, the head back, the brows raised, the eyes opened wide behind heavy tortoiseshell glasses. He goes about his conversational histrionics with a great deal of intensity for besides being a frustrated composer, he is a frustrated actor. Most of his acting career was spent playing stock in New York and Philadelphia, and doing bits for the Theatre Guild and Group Theatre. As an actor he was seldom more than adequate. "I was too tense," he is apt to explain. "I couldn't relax." Because of his bushy hair and prominent features, he was a highly unlikely juvenile. Usually he was cast in small character rôles, and he experienced one of his acutest disappointments the day his picture was displayed outside a theatre in Chester, Pennsylvania, with his face so shrouded in the whiskers required for his part that he could barely recognize himself. He has never been completely reconciled to the fact that he was not a great actor. The directors, he feels, were grievously unaware of his potentialities. His first rebuff as an actor was administered by the great Mamoulian when he was directing "R.U.R." for the Theatre Guild. Odets had been hired to do a walk-on, but in the course of the rehearsals Earle Larimore suggested that he be given a couple of lines. Mamoulian instantly bridled. "He is no good," he declared flatly. Odets has hated Mamoulian ever since. When Odets was in Hollywood last year, Mamoulian sent word that he would like to do a picture with him. "You tell that————that he is the only director I loathe and won't work with," said Odets. The message was delivered verbatim to Mamoulian. He wasn't offended, though. He still insisted that he and Odets could do a wonderful picture.

Whatever his frustrations as an actor and a composer, Odets has been conspicuously successful as a playwright. Since his "Awake and Sing!" was presented in 1935, he has been compared to O'Neill, O'Casey, and Chekhov. At thirty-one, he has aroused more earnest and ecstatic discussion among the critics than any other dramatist who has appeared in the last decade. The prevailing critical opinion of Odets is summed up neatly in the following excerpt from some extended comments by Richard Watts, Jr.: "It is pretty clear by now that Mr. Odets's talent for dramatic writing is the most exciting to appear in the American theatre since the flaming emergence of Eugene O'Neill as an author of one-act plays about the sea. Mr. Odets has fire and freshness and vast vitality. He has a shrewd sense of dramatic situation; his dialogue has power and pungency, and his characters, even those sketched briefly in cartoon form, invariably have the stuff of life in them."

Despite such high praise, however, Odets doesn't find Mr. Watts and his fellow-critics very helpful. "In 'Awake and Sing!,' " he points out, "they said I didn't have any plot. Then in 'Paradise Lost' they said I had too much plot. Now they say that it's too bad to submerge the characters of 'Golden Boy' in a plot." Apart from the plot question, Odets thinks that the critics were all wrong in their unanimous disapproval of "Paradise Lost," which he regards as his best and deepest play. He has an idea that they were influenced against it because he tried to explain it to them before it opened. Odets' explanation of the play, which was mailed to all the critics, emphasized the fact that the people of "Awake and Sing!" and "Paradise Lost" had a Chekhovian quality. The debate as to whether or not the benighted characters of "Paradise Lost" were Chekhovian lasted through a good part of the 1936 season, with Heywood Broun, Archibald MacLeish, and Theodore Dreiser, among others, upholding the affirmative. The play was a flop.

The real heroes and villains of Odets' plays are always invisible and always the same. No matter who the characters happen to be, they are incessantly badgered by the Capitalist System, and at the third-act curtain it is pretty apparent that only the Revolution can get them out of their unhappy predicament. Odets has never wavered in his grim faith in the efficacy of revolution. But since he surrendered to the gold of Hollywood during the run of "Paradise Lost," some of the more emphatic revolutionists of the Communist Party have joined skeptical members of the bourgeoisie in accusing him of having sold out. Odets resents the accusation. Even though he likes to carry five-hundred-dollar bills around in his pocket and lives in a penthouse, he is unfailingly interested in the plight of the masses. His most celebrated exploit on behalf of the world proletariat was to lead a commission of fifteen liberals to Cuba during the summer of 1935 to investigate conditions under the Mendieta-Batista dictatorship. The commission didn't get very far. The members were arrested as soon as they arrived in Havana and deported the following day. Probably the most lamentable result of the investigation was the detention of a couple of New York school teachers, who were arrested in the general confusion although not members of the commission at all. Luckily, they were not deported with the others, and were able to continue to Mexico, where they had intended to go in the first place. On his return to New York, Odets, in the name of the commission, announced that Jefferson Caffery, then American Ambassador to Cuba, had a heart of sugar and that Vice-Consul Edgar of Havana was a fish. He also announced that another delegation would be sent to Cuba, but it hasn't been as yet. Since then his support of the proletariat has been mostly moral. Odets says that he is not and has never been a member of the Communist Party. He admits, however, that he is highly sympathetic with its aims. It helps, he points out, to keep the masses socially hopeful. Odets' concern for the masses was excited originally by Victor Hugo's "Les Misérables," which he read while he was living in the Bronx. That was nearly twenty years ago, long before he learned the dialectics of the class struggle.

Odets has a way of referring to himself in the third person. The habit manifests itself most persistently when he talks about his childhood in the Bronx. He is apt to get rather emotional, too, when the reminiscent mood is on him. "This boy," he said recently, "was a very ordinary middle-class boy, unconsciously ambitious, but with a kind of purity and unselfishness. He did

typical things, for everything about him was typical, typical, so typical."
Odets is continually astonished that there was nothing in his early years save
a certain facility for writing English compositions to indicate that he would
someday be a famous playwright. His steadfast ambition as a child was not to
write plays but to act in them. He determined to become an actor after
playing the Prince in "Cinderella" while he was in the first grade at P.S. 52.
He gave the part everything he had and, as he recalls it, was terrific. His
parents, though, didn't take his acting very seriously. They expected him to
outgrow it. He was their only son and oldest child, and they were hopeful
that he would enter a respectable profession.

The Bronx that Odets depicted in "Awake and Sing!" was one of the
gloomiest places in the world, but the Bronx he actually lived in was quite
pleasant, full of trees and open fields, and his family got along fine there.
Odets' parents came to the Bronx in 1908, when he was two years old. Up to
that time they had been living in Philadelphia. Odets' father is a native of
Philadelphia and for a number of years worked as a printer there for the
Curtis Publishing Company; his mother, who died in 1935, came from
Rumania. They moved from Philadelphia to the Bronx because Odets' father
thought that he could establish himself more securely in New York City than
he could anywhere else. Jewish, like the Bergers in "Awake and Sing!," the
Odets family lived near the corner of Beck Street and Longwood Avenue,
which was then a rather elegant section. Their apartment was in one of the
three elevator buildings that the Bronx had to offer. They had a Maxwell
when the possession of a car was a certain sign of affluence, and as he went
onward and upward, Odets' father was able to send his wife on a couple of
year-long visits to California for her health, accompanied by their two daughters. Both Odets' sisters are younger than he is. Florence, who is twenty-one,
is studying dramatics, with Clifford's help, at the school of Madame Tamara
Daykarhanova in Manhattan. Genevieve, who is twenty-eight, is married to
a haberdasher named Howard Levy and lives in Philadelphia.

Odets *père* started out in the Bronx as a feeder in a small print shop.
From feeder he progressed to pressman, which paid quite well, and it wasn't
long before he had money enough to start a printing shop of his own. Since a
good many of his customers were direct-mail advertisers who wanted him to
arrange their copy and layouts, he hired a copy man and set himself up as a
direct-mail advertising agent. By 1927, when he decided to take a job as
vice-president and general sales manager of a boiler company in Philadelphia,
he was functioning as a merchandising counsellor and was the owner of an
agency that brought about $200,000 when he sold it. He retired a couple of
years ago.

Clifford Odets rebelled against formal education when he finished his
second year at Morris High School. Since Odets the elder was anxious to have
his son learn the advertising business, he tried to train him to become a
copywriter in his agency. But Clifford just sat around writing poetry, and

finally his father, who thought anything would be better than that, told him to go ahead and be an actor. Odets started out with a little group of ardent amateurs known as the Drawing Room Players, who put on one-act plays at the Heckscher Theatre. Then he joined Harry Kemp's Poets' Theatre, which was a coöperative venture. The Poets' Theatre had its headquarters in the basement of a church at Fourth Street and Avenue A, where the poetic drama was glorified in all its variations, from Percy Bysshe Shelley to Harry Kemp. Odets liked the Poets' Theatre fine, even though his share of the coöperative's profits ran to less than twenty dollars in a year. Unfortunately, just when everybody had agreed that he was to be Don Juan in "The Don Juan Legend," the Poets' Theatre went broke. By this time, however, Odets had a group of his own, made up of former members of the Drawing Room Players. He had no theatre, so he offered his group to various radio stations, and on and off from 1925 to 1927 they performed as a sustaining program. In the same period, Odets functioned independently as the Roving Reciter, relying heavily on the works of Robert W. Service and Rudyard Kipling for his material. He didn't confine his roving reciting to the radio. He was often among the ringers sent out by the vaudeville chains to insure the success of their amateur nights. He received only a dollar a performance for appearing as an amateur, but his rendition of "The Shooting of Dan McGrew" usually took one of the prizes, which brought him from three to seven dollars more. On the strength of his reputation as the Roving Reciter, Odets occasionally got a few weeks' work with one of the stock companies around New York. He made his most extended tour with a troupe that was sustaining itself on "Abie's Little Rose," a play whose theme had a lot in common with the Anne Nichols masterwork. As Abie, Odets played all through the coal fields of Pennsylvania. He made his last appearance in a town called Hawley. There the tour ended abruptly when the manager was thrown in jail as a dope fiend. To get out of Hawley, Odets had to wire his father for money. Then he headed for Oak Lane, the Philadelphia suburb to which his family had moved after his father gave up his agency.

When Odets returned to his birthplace he was twenty-one, and his parents were beginning to wonder whether he'd ever be able to support himself. "Their son," says Odets, "was not industrious. He had temperament. He was moody. In a word, he was artistic."

Among the works of the artist as a young man were a couple of short plays he wrote for the radio. One of them, entitled "Dawn," opened with a man dying (of natural causes) at sunrise and wound up with his being nursed back to health by a woman from his past. "Dawn" was never put on the air because Odets thought it needed a little revision. But "At the Waterline," his other radio play, was produced by three stations, two in New York and one in Philadelphia. In "At the Waterline," Odets himself appeared as the hero, Garfield Grimes, a blue-blooded stoker on a grain ship who discovers the woman he is trying to forget on top of a boiler just as the ship is going down. Amid the welter of coincidences in "At the Waterline," the high point of the dialogue is reached when Garfield Grimes suggests that it may be possible to escape from the sinking ship through the ash-ejector. It is then that Billy Buzz, Grimes' fellow-stoker, observes, with magnificent understatement, "He is a deep one." Odets made his farewell appearance on the radio when "At the Waterline" was performed over WIP in Philadelphia. For the next two years he was fairly regularly employed by Mae Desmond's Stock Company, which played West Philadelphia, Chester, and Camden, New Jersey. Mac Desmond's repertory was infinitely varied. It included practically everything, from "Way Down East" to "White Cargo." Odets' most memorable rôle was that of the overwrought lieutenant in "What Price Glory?" His interpretation of the part was so graphic that it stirred even Mae Desmond herself. "I want you to know," she told Odets, "that I think you have talent." She was a reticent woman, and that was the only comment she made on his acting during the two years he was with her company. In the spring of 1929, Odets left Philadelphia to appear on Broadway in a play called "Conflict," in which he understudied Spencer Tracy, who had the lead. Shortly afterward, Odets got a job with the Theatre Guild.

"There is no better way to measure your life," says Odets, "than to say 'I loved that girl then and she meant this or that to me.' " But it is a girl with whom he was not in love who stands out in his memories of Philadelphia. She was a girl he met and impressed while he was one of Philadelphia's little group of liberated thinkers. Odets remembers her with satisfaction because she was the author of this encouraging tribute: "Every girl should have one Cliff Odets in her life." The first girl to whom Odets became attached, however, didn't recognize him as a desideratum. She spurned his love for that of a chauffeur. This happened at Fishers Island, a few miles off New London, during the summer of 1925. Odets wanted to spend this summer, as he did several others, working as a dramatic counsellor at various camps for boys. But there weren't any openings at the camps, and he took a job running a laundry mangle at a hotel. It was his first and last attempt at manual labor. He recalls it with a distaste as keen as the pleasure with which he recalls his romance. The girl by whom Odets measures this phase of his career was a school teacher from Springfield, Massachusetts, who was waiting on tables at the hotel where Odets was employed. "It was," says Odets, "one of those horrible, exquisite, addolescent affairs, with something of the Sorrows of Young Werther about it." The Sorrows set in when the girl, to whom he had been sending poems daily, advised Odets that the man she was going to marry had just arrived at the hotel, driving his boss's limousine. Odets thereupon determined that someday, when he was a famous man, he would go to Springfield and make a speech from the observation platform of his train. Then if the girl jumped out of the crowd to speak to him, he intended to tell her coldly that she had had her chance. He attributes a profound significance to the fact that although "Midnight," in which he had the juvenile lead, in 1930, was short-lived it lasted long enough for him to appear in Springfield in his only starring rôle. "She might have been in the audience," he points out. "Ironical."

While Odets was with the Theatre Guild, he lived in a cheap hotel on Sixtieth Street, where he was able to get credit during streaks of unemployment. The hotel was full of characters whose morality was as low as their funds often were. Odets had a room on the ground floor, and when he wasn't working he used to lie in bed all day listening to the chatter of the people outside his door. He brooded a great deal about the meaning of life, but his conclusions were always vague and unsatisfactory. Among his acquaintances at the hotel was an unemployed specialty dancer with whom he occasionally had a few drinks. She interested him became she seemed to be trying to escape from something. Odets was sympathetic with her, and eventually she confided her troubles to him. She had, it developed, been so terribly humiliated while performing at a Miami night club that she had lost faith in her ability as a dancer. Her anxiety had been caused by a drunk who had sportively dropped an olive on her navel as she back-somersaulted near his table. When Odets heard this, the conviction grew upon him that he was living in a strange, tragi-comic world. In fact, he says, it made him feel like a Dostoevski character. The feeling hung over him for the next few years. It culminated in 1932, when he was understudying Luther Adler in John Howard Lawson's "Success Story." By then he was so steeped in melancholy that he wanted to make himself as unattractive as possible in order to keep life at arm's length. This impelled him to shave off his hair, grow a beard, and adopt turtleneck sweaters as a distinguishing feature of his attire. Even though the Dostoevski mood has left him, Odets is still addicted to sweaters. He likes them because they are casual and convenient, and in keeping with the general air of informality that he diligently maintains in his dress. His sweaters cost from twenty to thirty dollars.

Odets was one of the original members of the Group Theatre. He was in "Roar China!," a production of the Guild Studio, the Theatre Guild's subsidiary from which the Group eventually evolved, and he sat in on the fervid meetings at which, during the winter of 1930, the future of the Group was plotted. While the Group was in the process of being organized, Odets, in the solitude of a furnished room on West Eighty-second Street, wrestled with his soul. He says he was trying to find out what was the matter with him. With eremitic zeal he would remain in his room for two and three days at a stretch, sustaining himself chiefly on canned herring with tomato sauce and shredded-wheat biscuits. When he took the room, Odets had intended to write, but he got too involved in studying himself to accomplish much on the creative side. Apart from some voluminous letters, his literary activity was restricted to making entries in his diary. The carbons of the letters are preserved in a correspondence file that Odets still maintains today. It contains duplicates of practically all the letters he has ever written. The carbons have been an invaluable aid to him in analyzing his development, and he makes a point of reading them over every now and then. But however helpful at present, the letters didn't do much good in 1930, and Odets was a gloomy fellow when he headed for Brookfield Center, Connecticut, the following summer to rehearse his bit in "The House of Connelly," the Group's first production.

In his first two seasons with the Group, Odets wasn't particularly outstanding, and he was oppressed by the belief that nobody thought very much of his acting. He started to write a play called "9–10 Eden Street," which was about the intelligentsia of Philadelphia, but he put it aside before he finished it. Then, while the Group was holding summer rehearsals at Dover Furnace in Dutchess County, he worked on a play about Beethoven. His dissatisfaction with the Beethoven play is revealed pretty succinctly by his diary. "Now I see again in myself flight always flight," says the diary. "Here I am writing the Beethoven play, which when it is finished may not even be about Beethoven. Why not write something about the Greenberg family, something I know better, something that is closer to me?" Once he had made up his mind to write about the Greenberg family, Odets felt a lot more cheerful. A few days later he observed in his diary, "I look at the baby that was me and rejoice." Odets started to write his new play in a cold-water flat on West Fifty-seventh Street, where he lived with some other Group members following the disastrous failure of Dawn Powell's "Big Night" in 1933. He finished it in Warrensburg, New York, while rehearsing in "Men in White," which the Group put on in 1933. When Odets submitted his play to the directors of the Group, none of them thought much of it. Harold Clurman admitted that it might have some merit, but doubted that it was actable. It wasn't until 1935 that they were willing to produce it. In the meantime the play had been held a year by one Frank Merlin, whose contribution to the 1934 season was a turkey called "False Dreams, Farewell." Odets' play was first called "I Got the Blues," but finally appeared as "Awake and Sing!" The Greenbergs of the diary wound up as a family called the Bergers.

"Awake and Sing!" emerged on Broadway when the great migration to the Left that marked the later years of the depression was at its peak. Since the play clearly suggested that things were going to be a whole lot better after the Revolution, the Leftists acclaimed Odets as a revolutionary oracle. Meanwhile the critics, who were more or less agreed that the revolutionary note was dragged in, saluted Odets as an infinitely promising playwright. In the midst of it all, the Group brought out "Waiting for Lefty," the one-act play with which Odets had won a *New Theatre–New Masses* play contest a couple of months before, together with "Till the Day I Die," an anti-Nazi companion piece. "Till the Day I Die" provoked little comment, but "Waiting for Lefty," which had had several New Theatre benefit performances at the Civic Repertory before the Group brought it uptown to the Longacre, added to Odets' reputation both as a playwright and as a prophet of the Left. It was a sympathetic description of the causes behind a taxi-drivers' strike. "Waiting for Lefty" was presented all over the country by little-theatre groups to which the New Theatre League, the radical group sponsoring the *New Theatre Magazine,* had released copies of the script, and was awarded the Yale Drama Prize for 1935. On various dubious pretexts, it was suppressed more often than any other play in the history of the American theatre. With three plays on Broadway and "Paradise Lost" already announced, Odets began to hear from Hollywood. Although the offers for his services ran as high as $4,000 a week, he refused to have anything to do with the movies until "Paradise Lost" proved unsuccessful. Then, to get money enough to save the show, Odets took a job in Hollywood. By that time the best offer was $2,500 a week. He sent $4,000 back to the Group before "Paradise Lost" finally failed. He hasn't put any money into the Group itself since. He and his wife, however, have a twenty-five-per-cent interest in "Golden Boy" which they acquired for $5,000.

In Hollywood, where the class struggle is a burning if academic issue, Odets was the hero of the studio Leftists. His advice on the methods the screen writers could use to contribute to the cause was listened to with eager interest. When he spoke at the Masonic Temple at a benefit for the *New Theatre Magazine,* the place was packed. Cocktail parties in his honor were events of moment. He was even threatened by a Fascist at the Brown Derby—the ultimate tribute. When, in January, 1937, he married Luise Rainer, who was then being shown in "The Great Ziegfeld," the publicity was awesome. Odets worked on three scripts while he was in Hollywood. For Paramount he wrote "The General Died at Dawn" and "Gettysburg," and for Walter Wanger "The River Is Blue." Of these, only "The General Died at Dawn" has been produced. Shooting on "Gettysburg" will start in the spring. "The River Is Blue," which has a French background, is being rewritten, Odets' version having been ideologically at odds with the Wanger preconception.

Odets sometimes talks like one of the more lyrical characters in his own plays. It is not at all unusual for him to break into something like "How sweet and nice to get up in the mornings to see the glitter of the day—like when you were a kid." He doesn't get up in the morning, though. He gets up around noon. While he has his coffee, he likes to listen to a record full of brasses. The brasses, he says, affect him like a cold shower. Odets is more sensitive to music now than ever. He thinks the sensitivity may be explained in part by the fact that his sense of smell is no longer acute. Before his nose went back on him, he could go into an empty room and tell who had been there simply by sniffing. Since he has a theory that nature never dulls one faculty without making another keener, he is convinced that his hearing improved as soon as his sense of smell declined. He is almost as proud of his hearing as he is of his looks. He admits frankly that he knows he is attractive. He is fairly tall and husky, and in profile vaguely resembles a pickerel. In his abstracted moments, he could easily be mistaken for one of the more earnest students of N.Y.U.

Odets returned from Hollywood last July, and aside from one brief visit back to the Coast has remained here ever since. When he is in New York, he doesn't get around town much. Concerts are his chief diversion. He prefers serious discussions to the hoopla of the night clubs. He drinks heavily about four or five times a year, and in his cups he tends to be truculent. During the first flush of his success, he spent a few weekends on Fire Island in the earthy company of Fannie Brice, Billy Rose, and Lou Holtz. He also stayed a while as a guest at Henry Varnum Poor's place in New City, where, in the mystical shadow of High Tor, he worked on "Paradise Lost." While he was staying at Poor's, he occasionally spent weekends with Charles MacArthur and his wife, Helen Hayes, whose place in Nyack is nearby. His friendship with the people of New City was never more than casual, and he doesn't see much of them any more. The same is true of his friendship with Ruth Gordon, Beatrice Lillie, and Tallulah Bankhead, whom he went around with for a while. Now his most frequent companions are actors in the Group. He is sure nobody really understands him, and that makes him feel lonely.

When he completed "Awake and Sing!" he decided that in comparison with the other playwrights in the country he was highly talented. He has seen no reason to alter that point of view.

Along with his penthouse at 1 University Place, Odets maintains a one-room apartment on another floor which serves as an office for his secretary. He himself works at a big modernistic desk in his living room, which also contains his Hammond organ and his phonograph. As inspirational aids, he has a mask of Lenin on one wall and a mask of Beethoven on another. On top of his bookcase, which runs the whole length of the room, there are a number of bright and pensive photographs of Luise Rainer. Miss Rainer, who has spent two eight-week vacations from Hollywood at his penthouse, does not like the place. She thinks it's too small and says that the furniture is too masculine. But Odets intends to keep the apartment until his wife comes to live in New York permanently, in 1942, when her contract with M-G-M runs out. He's going to write a play for her so that she'll have something to do after she leaves Hollywood. The Odetses are surcharged with temperament, and their home life is rarely placid. Their outbursts, however, are brief, and as artists they both regard their domestic turmoil as a healthy outlet. One of the traits they have in common is a love of ordinary people. They would both like to stand on the Library steps at Forty-first and Fifth Avenue and watch them go by. When they tried it, though, everybody stared at them, and they returned to their penthouse feeling sad and upset. In her sad moments as well as her glad moments, Mrs. Odets likes to sit on a window ledge and look up at the sky. Odets whistles, hums, or sings when he is happy, broods in fierce silence when he is mixed up emotionally.

He is never without his notebook. When he is working on a play, he jots down ideas whenever they come to him, no matter where he happens to be. When he overhears people talking, he makes a note of the striking characteristics of their speech. Later on, his secretary types out the notes and files them away. Odets also clips everything in the papers that might be of dramatic interest and cuts out any pictures that might be of help to him in visualizing his characters. He has sufficient material on hand, he says, to keep him busy for the next ten years. He'd like to sit at his desk until he completes all the plays he has in mind. Unfortunately, the $65,000 he made in Hollywood last year was cut into pretty deeply by the California state income tax, the federal tax, and his agent's commission. That's why he's going back to work in Hollywood again. He worries a lot about money. "When you get a little," he says, "there are all kinds of people out to gyp you." He has a hard time finding a restaurant in the Village where he can get a good meal at a reasonable price. He eats only one meal a day because he finds that a faint hunger stimulates his mind.

In whatever he does, Odets is anxious to convey to the masses a message of hope for the future. To reach the broadest possible audience, he would prefer to write for the movies. The trouble is that the studios censor his scripts so severely that it is only on the stage that he can relate his message without distortion. For that reason he hopes that the Federal Theatre will give his next play simultaneous productions throughout the country. The new play, which he intends to have ready for production any day now, will be called "The Silent Partner" and will reveal some further evils of the capitalist system. "It will," says Odets, "be the best labor play ever produced in this country or in any other country."

Clifford Odets: First Chapters
(1939)

Edith J. R. Isaacs

It is only four years since *Awake and Sing* was produced by the Group Theatre and Clifford Odets won the favor of the majority of New York critics over night. The production at the Belasco was not the first that had been heard either of the playwright or of his play. Odets had been a "Rover Reciter," an actor in radio and in stock before he understudied Spencer Tracy in Vincent Lawrence's *Conflict.* He had gone on tour for the Theatre Guild, and had played small parts in Guild productions in New York. It was there that he met Harold Clurman, a play-reader for the Guild, heard through him the idea for a group theatre, shared in its early discussion meetings and became a charter member of the Group acting company. By that time Odets was beginning to accent an early taste for playwriting, and when the Group went to the country for the summer to try out new plays and to work out acting problems, he gave them the script of *Awake and Sing* to experiment with. The Group was interested in the play, but not enough to risk a production which required more money and a stronger and surer ensemble than they had at that time. Somebody gave the play to another producer, Frank Merlin, who promptly took an option on the script.

That was the point at which people began to hear of Mr. Odets. Nobody who knew Mr. Merlin and saw him that summer escaped his praise of the bright new star in the playwriting firmament. But it needed more than enthusiasm to back a production of *Awake and Sing.* It needed a cast of competent character actors, well rehearsed. No company of players picked up casually in the Broadway manner could make those unhappy individuals look and act like a family—each with a double set of nerves, none with a grain of common sense (no Odets character has every had that modest virtue), all with large chips on their shoulders, moving blindly through an upset world, all suffering from different personal disharmonies, but all basically alike, and all bewildered. The play did not attract Broadway's "angels"; so the option, once renewed, was finally dropped.

A little later, when Odets was acting with the Group company in Boston, he heard of a New Theatre League one-act play contest, for which the

Originally published in *Theatre Arts Monthly* (April 1939).

time was nearly up. He is said to have locked himself in a hotel room for three days, and to have come out with *Waiting for Lefty,* which won the prize and was soon exciting audiences to action at the New Theatre League Sunday nights. Before long everyone was talking of this compelling little play about a union meeting during a taxi strike, with its cut-backs showing the hardships and injustices in the lives of the men who bore the brunt of the strike's burdens; showing, too, the evils that beset the union, pointing the way out. Audiences at labor centres, at left-wing political rallies, at the theatre where the Theatre Union held sway, were all equally stimulated by the vigor of the play's attack, the novelty of its method, by the effective and theatrical speech, and by the excellent acting of some of the Group players, including Russell Collins and Elia Kazan.

The Group decided quickly that it was worth taking a Broadway chance on Odets while the enthusiasm was still hot; that not only *Waiting for Lefty* but *Awake and Sing* must have an uptown production. Since the former was too short for a full evening, *Till the Day I Die* was written as a companion piece, and within thirty-five days Odets had three plays running on Broadway and was arousing more discussion in theatrical circles than any man since Eugene O'Neill. *Awake and Sing* ran for 137 performances. *Till the Day I Die,* although it showed distinct progress in every way over the earlier play, was too far to the left in ideology, and in spots too brutal, to meet public favor, and lasted only 96 performances. *Waiting for Lefty* still goes on, not on Broadway, but in almost every corner of the land where an active young theatre group is playing, and in many places abroad. It has carried Odets' name around the world.

Waiting for Lefty is special pleading, with a sure-fire sentimental approach. By its method it neither takes nor gives time for thought; it is an excellent acting exercise; the dialogue is deft and vigorous; and it keeps an audience wide awake by inventions that would be called tricks if they were less successful. Few authors have opened the door to fame so easily.

Paradise Lost, which was well along in writing before *Waiting for Lefty* was begun, appeared in the theatre a year later. But what Odets had learned from watching his other plays in production was not transferred to *Paradise Lost,* and the muddy play met with little favor. The next year and a half belonged to Hollywood and the movies, from which Odets returned with *Golden Boy,* which most critics consider his finest play and many people consider his own saga. *Golden Boy* was produced November 4, 1937, with the Group acting company at its best and Luther Adler better than his best. It carried the Group and Odets both far forward, even as far as to a success in London. This year there is *Rocket to the Moon,* a banal triangle whose originality goes no farther than a water-cooler in a dentist's office, a play which has most of the faults of the earlier plays, including a pretentious earnestness, and the great virtue of the earlier plays—good parts for the actors. Reading *Rocket to the Moon* is not rewarding.

So much for the record. It is easy to see that a young man who has blazed such a trail within four years must be taken seriously in considering the hopeful horizons of the American theatre.

Odets has, indeed, from the very first, been taken seriously by his associates, his critics and his audience; almost, one might say, as seriously as he takes himself. In spite of much phrasing about "the mass as hero" and "social *vs.* personal viewpoint," he is the most subjective of playwrights. When you read his plays, as when you see them, you have the distinct impression that two-thirds of the time it is Odets talking. This makes it difficult to face his work as objectively as criticism should regard it, which is, in itself, a criticism of the work. But the plays have stood the test of the theatre—both in performance and in audience response. And if we aim to know our threatre, we should know how they do it. It may be well, therefore, to measure the faults in Odets' writing and thinking, and go ahead from there to find the things that give his plays importance.

What is most wrong with Odets is undoubtedly the fact that his imagination is bounded by his experience and that he is not the broad and profound social philosopher he thinks he is. He feels deeply about the things which are most obviously wrong with the world today—war, injustice, tyranny, economic instability, poverty. He believes, as millions of people do, that the way out of all this is as straight, if not as simple, as Marx has made it. He intends his plays to do active service for the cause of more humane living. But his social background is almost invariably false and falsifies his conclusions.

In *Awake and Sing* and *Paradise Lost,* Odets believes he is writing about middle class people and their decay. Harold Clurman says this explicitly in his introduction to the latter play: "To make this clear we must state what is meant when we speak of middle-class 'decay'. The two most striking facets of the middle-class situation today are: first, the economic insecurity that deprives it of its former prestige as the bulwark of civilization, and inspires it with a fear of becoming reduced to a social class to which it has always considered itself superior; second, an awareness has grown upon the middle class that most of the ideas by which it has lived no longer correspond to the reality around it." But Odets' people are definitely not this lost "bulwark of civilization." They have never shared the sense of stability in their place and social position, the inborn feeling of security in relation to labor and the land, the unity with their friends and neighbors expressed in their social clubs and business affiliations, the general unimaginative faith in government, the church, the press, the majority, the banks and the law, and the certain righteous sense of personal, communal and national duty and obligation which are the marks of the middle class. There are plenty of middle-class people, of course, who do not fit completely into any such simple picture. There is at least one member of almost every middle-class family that does not; and that is true of all social generalizations. But

Mr. Odets' people in *Awake and Sing* and *Paradise Lost* have none of the qualities associated with the middle class. Although they may have had more money at one time, as the Gordons in *Paradise Lost* had, may have had a horse and carriage, may have owned their home for a while and with an over-sized mortgage, may have paid their bills, may even have sent their sons to war, you know from their speech, their associates, and from the tone of their minds that personal, mental, financial, social security they have never had. They have always been lonely, unhappy and without roots. They seem to have no heritage, no traditions, no pleasant ties, and having lost the thing they had and treasured most, namely money, they are more unhappy than ever, afraid and ashamed to live without it. It is their permanent spiritual lack, sharpened by an immediate economic crisis, which has made them morbid, frustrated, decadent. It is in themselves that they are underlings, not in their stars.

There are a hundred plays waiting to be written about the decay of the middle class, but none of Mr. Odets' plays is among them.

Another fault that must be charged against Odets is that his characters, except in *Golden Boy* and *Till the Day I Die,* end as they begin, in spite of violent changes in the circumstances surrounding them. There is, to be sure, almost always one character who sees the new light and expresses it at the end of the play in a tag line or a grandiose speech; but even that man's light always carries its shadow before. The other characters are what they are, and what happens in the play makes little difference. Odets seems to think that when he is accused of this he is being accused of not constructing a "well-made" play in the fashion of Pinero. But the effect of action on character is something quite different. Every good play must have a good plot or it cannot move forward, for the plot is only the plan of a play's progress. When an author wishes, as he has happily the right to do, to substitute something better than a 'well-made' situation-plot, he must be careful to have a character-plot. If he does not, his play will turn into a preachment or die on his hands—as *Paradise Lost* died. When Mr. Odets wrote the paragraphs that follow here, he was either rationalizing his own limitations or talking plain tosh:

> Plots are primer stuff, easily learned. Since the whole truth must be told, the most difficult problem is to avoid gratifying situations and stories. These people of our bourgeois American life must be treated with more dignity and heart than the banality of clicking plot! . . .
>
> Excuse us if we insist upon life brought to the stage instead of the stage brought to life. Excuse us if we do not accept the dictum that any deviation from Ibsen and the Pinero form is a deadly sin. . . . But please allow us to continue to respect the men and women all around us and make the theatre serve an earnest examination of their lives and backgrounds. In interesting new theatrical forms, with poetic conceptions. With character understanding. With fresh dialogue. With love.

Each of Odets' faults has almost its counterpart in creative quality. Against his extreme subjectiveness can be placed his wise desire to express the natures and the problems of the people that he knows. Against his errors of cause and effect, his intention to give his plays a social background and to make them purposeful enough to carry the burden of their content. Against the fact that he himself does most of the talking in his plays, there is the fact that the talk is exceptionally alive and theatrical, speech for an actor's tongue. Against the fact that the majority of his characters are clichés, the recognition that in almost every play there is at least one that is a real creation, sometimes only a subordinate character, sometimes a leading figure, but recurrently one that has three dimensions and a soul.

In *Awake and Sing* it is Moe Axelrod, who stands out from that family of decaying Bronx neurotics like a well-wrought piece of sculpture, and yet for whose verity Odets gave himself a difficult assignment even in his first stage direction: "Moe Axelrod lost a leg in the war. He seldom forgets that fact. He has killed two men in extra-martial activity. He is mordant, bitter. Life has taught him a disbelief in everything. . . . He has been everywhere and seen everything. All he wants is Hennie. He is very proud. He scorns the inability of others to make their way in life, but he likes people for whatever good qualities they possess. . . ."

In *Paradise Lost* it is Gus Michaels, with only half a mind; in *Rocket to the Moon* the pretty, stupid, romantic little girl, the dentist's unsatisfied office assistant hunting the earth and the heavens for someone with love and the grace to use it. In *Till the Day I Die* and in *Golden Boy* it is the central character (which gives these plays their inner strength) and, in the latter play, several also among the minor figures that are something more than clearly defined types—Tom Moody the fight manager, Eddie Fuseli the gangster, Tokio the trainer. Wherever these figures appear, they leave no doubt that when Odets creates a new character instead of a new mouthpiece, his play gains a more vivid life and moves forward on its own impulse.

Till the Day I Die has had far less recognition among students of Odets' work than it deserves—less than it must have if the potential powers of the playwright are to be appraised. The reason for this neglect is simple enough. *Till the Day I Die* is a story of young Communists in Germany just after the beginning of the Hitler regime, and their brave and tragic struggle for the cause in which they believed. When the subject of a play is anathema to a critic or an audience, it is easier to let the play slip by unnoticed than to study it for what it reveals about the dramatist. Moreover, even for those who are willing to look a Communist play fairly in the face, there is an added repulsion in the brutality of certain scenes in *Till the Day I Die,* notably the one where a Nazi agent hammers the hand of the young violinist. That scene was a mistake, the error of a man who had not learned to trust his audience to understand more than the facts they see, or who perhaps had not learned to

trust himself to make them understand. But Odets makes up for that mistake
by another scene which is close to what the Greeks did with the messengers
who described the battles or the murders that were the crux of the story but
which, by Greek temperance, were kept from the actual stage. This is the
scene where Ernst Tausig, the ardent Communist youth who has started out
boldly and bravely, comes back beaten, mutilated, dazed, with "sulphur
running in his veins," to explain to his brother and to the girl he loves what
the Nazis have done to him, the record of a young soul's fall from its high
places to destruction. It is all done in a page or two. The words Odets has
written for Ernst Tausig have not quite the beauty and strength he achieved
in parts of *Golden Boy.* But with all its imperfections the scene is good enough
not to be passed by in a record of what Odets has done, as an indication of
what he can do.

Golden Boy shows all of his capacities farther developed. He has a good
story to tell, and he tells it. His characters respond to the events around
them. His thesis is a real one, heightened for dramatic use. His chief failure
lies in the end he has chosen for his play.

Golden Boy is a young Italo-American who could be a good violinist if
his hands were not more hungry for gold than for the touch of strings, if Joe
Bonaparte were not himself more determined to have power than to have
music. He becomes a successful prize fighter, kills his adversary in a fight,
drives away from the scene at breakneck speed in a high-powered car and is
himself killed.

In writing the many-scened play Odets keeps his story going fast and
the tension high. The reserve that he lacked in the earlier plays comes
through triumphantly in a short scene like the one between Eddie Fuseli, the
gangster-patron of Golden Boy, and Lorna, his boss' sweetheart. The two are
in Joe's dressing-room listening to the end of the big fight; Fuseli knows that
Lorna is in love with Golden Boy and is afraid that Lorna has upset him, that
he is about to be beaten. Lorna herself is stiff with fear. But this is all that
Odets needs to say to indicate so much:

EDDIE: (*Listening intently*) He's like a bum tonight . . . and a bum done it! You!
(*The roar grows fuller.*) I can't watch him get slaughtered. . . .
LORNA: I couldn't watch it myself. . . . (*The bell clangs loudly several times. The
roar of the crowd hangs high in the air.*) What's happening now?
EDDIE: Someone's getting murdered . . .
LORNA: It's me. . . .

Harold Clurman's introduction tells what Odets was trying to accomplish in
this play:

What the golden boy of this allegory . . . wants is to free his ego from the
scorn that attaches to "nobodies" in a soeicty in which every activity is viewed

in the light of a competition. He wants success not simply for the soft life—automobiles, etc.—which he talks about, but because the acclaim that goes with it promises him acceptance by the world, peace with it, safety from becoming the victim that it makes of the poor, the alien. . . .

Yet with this deeply and subtly subjective material, Odets has attempted to write his most objective play—a play that would stand on its own feet, so to speak, as a good show, a fast-moving story, a popular money-making piece. He has tried to bridge the gap between his own inner problems and the need he feels, like his hero . . . to make "fame and fortune." . . .

And *Golden Boy* did bring Odets the success and, no doubt, some of the fortune he needed for his contentment. More was to be hoped for from him after this than *Rocket to the Moon*. But it is well to remember that it is only four years, almost to the day, since *Awake and Sing* was produced. And Odets' path is obviously not straightforward, but full of ups and downs that are the fruit of difficulties which his own nature and experience create for him.

In an English journal, some time ago, there was a "letter to the editor" which said extremely well something that seems to express Odets' accomplishment exactly, although it had nothing at all to do with Odets. It was in answer to the familiar complaint that the actor, or perhaps the director or designer, was trying to usurp the playwright's dominance in the theatre. But it did not begin its apologia, as we usually do, by trying to show how useful these other artists are in aiding the dramatist to do his job. It went quite the other way around, the only right way. It said that when a man writes a play, "what actually happens is that a new literary plot and dialogue is added to the art of the theatre, which can and does exist quite independently of words, and whose foundations were laid long before verbal language ever existed. If the dramatist himself has a sense of the theatre, and not all dramatists or so-called dramatists have, his literary offering may be 'translated' into a convincing theatrical production in which the eye plays as great a part as the ear, if not a greater one."

Is not this exactly the talent that has made all of us, even those who are not satisfied with Odets' plays, listen to him—the sense that he is—by his nature—a man who sees people and ideas first as they move across a stage, and tries to write words that will make their passage through the scene sound right as well as look right?

If you add the fact that Odets has the rare gift of theatrical rhythms, and a vocal sense that seldom betrays him, are you not establishing the picture of a real man of the theatre?—the kind of man who—if he can forget himself a little more, parade his theories a little less, give himself as generously to his people and his stories as he does in *Golden Boy* and *Till the Day I Die*—can offer the playhouse not only the strength and the immediacy but the lyric beauty that it needs and that it repays so well.

INTERVIEWS

◆

Odets at Center Stage
(1963)

MICHAEL J. MENDELSOHN

INTERVIEWER: I have a number of general questions and some specific ones; do you have any preference as to where we begin?

ODETS: No, any way you choose to go is all right with me.

INT: Well, let's begin with the idea that the playwright belongs to the theatre, rather than to the library.

ODETS: Well, essentially there are two kinds of playwrights. Both can be excelling, but it would be necessary to make a distinction between the playwright who was essentially a theatre man and not a man of literature—not a man of the library, that is. If I talk about past and very great playwrights, it's obvious from the very style and form and cut and shape and pattern of their work that men like Molière and Shakespeare were men of the theatre, not men of the library. And you see it on every page of their plays. They write with their feet solidly planted on the platform, and they write with a very knowing and frequently cunning theatrical knowledge, in the sense of what the audience is getting—they don't follow literary canon so much as they follow theatre canon.

INT: At the same time, a piece of dramatic literature, when it is completed and bound between covers, can stand the test of good literature—if it *is* good literature.

ODETS: Well, you have to admit that the two men I just mentioned, Molière and Shakespeare, wrote very great literature.

INT: Let's go back to the 1930s. Do you feel the social protest plays accomplished something in themselves, or were they simply a dramatic manifestation in American society that would have taken place anyhow?

ODETS: The plays undoubtedly came out of ascending values, out of positive values, out of the search of millions of American citizens for some way out of

Originally published in *Theatre Arts* (May and June 1963). Reprinted by permission of Michael J. Mendelsohn.

a horrifying dilemma—a dilemma which, by the way, I don't think is over. And the writer, or the playwright like myself, simply had to be alive and aware and partaking of this extraordinary ferment around him. The playwright then, as he always is, became the articulate voice of the aspiration of millions of people. If, for instance, you saw the opening night of *Waiting for Lefty,* you saw theatre in its truest essence. By which I mean that suddenly the proscenium arch of the threatre vanished and the audience and the actors were at one with each other.

INT: You say that the proscenium disappeared, and I feel that this was something that you were trying to achieve in *Waiting for Lefty*—

ODETS: Not consciously.

INT: Not consciously? Well, I'm speaking of the theatrical concept of naturalism versus the Thornton Wilder type of presentational play. Consciously in your plays, it seems to me you are staying within the proscenium, in all of your plays except *Waiting for Lefty*. Did you have that in mind?

ODETS: Well, sometimes there are formal ways in which one breaks down the proscenium arch and makes the audience a more active participant in what is going on on the stage. Formal ways consist, sometimes, in a new style for the writer, or sometimes in the physical construction of the theatre. We talk of "theatre in the round." These are all attempts to unify the acting material and the audience. They are, however, in my opinion, artificial ways. The real way to make the proscenium arch disappear, the thrilling and human way, what I should say is the *experienced* way, is to have your actors speak from your platform materials and values which are profoundly and *communally* shared with the audience.

INT: And, if this happens, it doesn't matter whether they address the audience directly, as in *Waiting for Lefty,* or talk to each other, as in *Awake and Sing?*

ODETS: It doesn't matter at all. When you have a community of values in the theatre (which is, of course, what we *don't* have), the proscenium arch disappears. The audience is not watching a play, and the actors are not playing to an audience which is seated passively somewhere in that dark pit which is the auditorium. Theatre in its profoundest sense—*all* literature in its profoundest sense—has come in periods when the plight or problem expressed by the actors was completely at one with the plight and problems and values or even moralities of the audience. This is why the literature of Homer and the Greek drama and the Bible, or, in music, works of composers like Bach have such size. It's because the artist, the composer, the writer, is not someone apart and inimical to his audience, not a man in *opposition* to the values he is expressing, but one who completely shares organically the very values of the audience for whom he is writing.

INT: In other words, the specific type of "presentation" or "representation" doesn't make any difference at all?

ODETS: Well, it does nowadays, when theatre consists, for the most part, of trifles, of weak slaps and gestures at something that you don't like. Or, for the most part, an acceptance of things around you. You take all of the light comedies. What are they about? How amusing adultery is. By the way, they constitute propaganda plays for adultery, whether we realize it or not. They have no positive values; they play upon the patterns of prejudice and the likes and dislikes of the audience. They do not lead the audience. They do not lift the audience.

INT: Are you familiar with *Waiting for Godot?*

ODETS: Yes.

INT: This is a pretty good statement of a negative. I thought of that when you said "no positive values."

ODETS: All you can say of a play like that—and, by the way, a small gem I should call it—all you can do is sit there sort of stunned and lament that the world is in a hell of a shape. You can be moved in a certain way. From that play I don't think you can be moved to try to lift yourself out of what it's saying into some higher living view of things. Unless, of course, you believe cutting your throat is a value!

INT: Do you accept the label "optimist" that has very often been pinned on you?

ODETS: "Optimist"? I would say that I have a *belief* in man and his possibilities as the measure of things, but I would not say that I was an optimistic writer. I would say that I have shown as much of the seamy side of life as any other playwright of the twentieth century, if not more.

INT: It seems that many of your plays, even with the depiction of the seamy side of life, end on a hopeful note.

ODETS: Sometimes the hopeful note is real, as, for instance, I believe it is in a play like *Rocket to the Moon,* and sometimes my critics are correct when they say that the optimistic note has been tacked on.

INT: *Awake and Sing?*

ODETS: No, not so much *Awake and Sing,* because I believe in the possibilities expressed in the last scene. I do believe that young people can go through an experience and have their eyes opened, and determine from it to live in a different way. I do believe that older and more crushed human beings can pass on some lifting values to the younger generation. I do believe that, as the daughter in that family does, she can make a break with the groundling lies of her life, and try to find happiness by walking off with a man who is not her husband. I believed it then, and I believe it now. I think I believed it more *simply* then. I did not express roundly or fully the picture, but I don't think that ending is a lie.

INT: What particular plays did you have in mind when you said that the optimistic ending was "tacked on"?

ODETS: Well, there is a certain kind of subtle theatrical use that doesn't really ask too much. For instance, what did *Waiting for Lefty* ask? It asked really that you go out on strike and fight for better conditions. Well, the people did do that. Along came the C.I.O. But it is not enough to go out on strike and ask for better wages; it is much better to go out on strike and say, "Now we have made a *beginning*." Frequently, the simplicity of some of my endings comes from the fact that I did not say at the same time. "This is a beginning; this will give you the right to begin in a clean and simple way." But these things are not ends in themselves. A strike and a better wage is not an end in itself. It will give you the chance to begin. It will give you the chance, in a democracy, to find your place, to assume your place and be responsible for your growth and continued welfare and happiness in that place.

INT: Why do you sometimes like to direct? Is there a particular reason?

ODETS: Yes, there are several reasons. First of all, I think that, frankly, I can direct my plays almost as well as anyone I know. Therefore, why not do it myself? I am very capable with actors; I was an actor myself for about 14 years before I became a playwright. The stage, the acting platform, is my home. I am not a library writer. A library writer should not direct his plays, but should find a competent director who will say more or less what he wants to say.

INT: As Archibald MacLeish did?

ODETS: Yes, or as Maxwell Anderson did. Maxwell Anderson was my idea (and I mean no denigration), my idea of a library writer, although he had a great deal of theatre wisdom, let me say. So, since I can handle the materials of a play of my own, why talk it over with a director? Why not do it myself? Secondly, in a play like *The Country Girl,* which is relatively, in the body of my work, a superficial play, I knew just exactly how that play should become successful. I wanted to do a successful production. And in that case I trusted no one else, because it seems to me that that play walks on a tightrope and that if it is not done almost with a certain speed and tension, it would plunge right down into the abyss. It took us a year to cast the play. The final casting didn't satisfy me, but there it was. With all of these considerations, I trusted only myself to get the result I wanted to get, and I did get it. Another director, by the way, might have brought added dimension to some of the scenes. He might see things that I didn't see. That's always a danger when you direct your own play. On the other hand, in the case of *The Country Girl,* I was looking for a certain kind of—to say it vulgarly—a swift, tense strongly-paced production. And I simply didn't trust it to anyone else's hands.

INT: Then, just as with the novelist, who has no one getting in the way, except perhaps an editor, you feel that the fewer people who get in the way of what comes out of your pen, the closer to the pure work it's going to end up?

ODETS: Yes, there is such an aspect to directing one of my plays. But an even more important aspect is simply the stimulation. It stimulates me as a writer to keep my feet and my hands on the stage. It's not that I'm interested in giving or showing the definitive meaning of a play. That side doesn't bother me too much. The stimulation is very important. It keeps you *alive* with the script, until the opening night. I used to find that I lost all interest in the script when someone else was directing, even a director I trusted and a director I admired and liked—let's say, Harold Clurman at his best. The whole thing went dead on me, so that when I had to rewrite, it was almost like I was approaching a strange new subject. But when I, myself, am directing the play, although aliveness comes in a different sphere, that of directing, which is quite different from writing, nevertheless it keeps me alive as a *writer.* So that I can leave the stage when I am directing and go to my hotel room out of town, as I did in *The Country Girl,* and three or four nights before the New York opening, in Boston, rewrite the last 15 pages, which made the play successful. But if I hadn't been directing that play, I would have been dead on it, and I wouldn't have written those last 15 pages as well.

INT: Your comment about the desire to have *The Country Girl* be a commercial success suggests to me something else. Can you say that your early plays were written to push forward a certain point of view, and that your later plays were written for more artistic considerations, or for more financial considerations? Is there any way to separate these things?

ODETS: I can separate them. The result may not always be what I think it is, but I have only two times—I don't know, I think I've written 14 or 15 or 16 plays, 12 or 13 of which have been produced—only two times did I sit down with the goal of writing a play that would be successful on Broadway and have a long run. The other times, I simply sat down to express a "state of being." Sometimes an ache, sometimes an agony, sometimes an excitement, the excitement which comes out of some kind of conversion, emotional lift, a sudden *seeing* where before one felt blind, and a sudden strength, whereas before one felt weak and muscle bound. It was always to express an inner state of being. I think that any creative writer sits down to express that. Sometimes it's a sense, a very vague sense of hurt, a vague mood, a vague sense of unhappiness, of, let me say, sometimes of disconnection. I don't think that any creative person in any craft or any medium can be creative unless he does sit down with that sense of expressing an inner state of being.

On the other hand I can see a certain shaped play dealing with certain materials, and I would like it to get across in a very successful way. So I will kind of put blinders on and not express the entire spread of what I feel about this material, but just make it theatrically viable, theatrically entertaining, and try to get across something that people will like, that will excite them. The first time I did that was once to keep the Group Theatre together in a play called *Golden Boy.* That was the other play, with *The Country Girl,* that I sat down deliberately to write a success. And, in both cases, let me say, "mission accomplished." As a matter of fact, I always held *Golden Boy* a little in contempt for that reason, knowing how the seed had been fertilized. And it was maybe three years later that I saw the play had more quality than I gave it credit for. I don't, however, think I would change my mind about *The Country Girl.* It's a good show; it's a theatre piece. It does have about it a certain kind of psychological urgency, because if you are creative, things do creep in despite the conscious impulse. For instance, there crept into that play a central problem of my own life. And this did give a certain urgency and heat to much that went on in the script. I didn't *mean* for that problem to come out; I cannily and unconsciously disguised it. But that is unconsciously what came out in the writing of that play.

INT: You wouldn't go so far as to attribute to *Golden Boy* the sort of allegorical analysis that George Jean Nathan gave to it—of this being your entire career, and—

ODETS: I will tell you frankly that since the days of my youth were past—from those days on I have had no interest in what George Jean Nathan has written about me or has written about any other playwright dead or alive, or anything about the theatre. I think he was a first-class phony. I will always think so, and I don't miss him and never would miss him.

INT: You've had 11 plays produced, aside from the translation in 1942—

ODETS: Is it 11 plays?

INT: So far as I've been able to keep track.

ODETS: You've got me; I haven't counted them.

INT: Eleven plus *The Russian People*—

ODETS: Oh, let's not count that! They wouldn't let me do any work on it. It was forbidden to change a word. But Mrs. Litvinov, the Ambassador's wife, Ivy Litvinov—a very literate and charming woman—at the last moment got me permission to rewrite and change some of the scenes, but I said, "Mrs. Litvinov, it's too late." (We were opening in New York after, I think, two weeks in Washington, D.C.) "We're opening in New York City in three or four days, and I can't rewrite anything now." I did, here and there, enrich the texture, but no changes were permitted. This was a Soviet governmental order, you know.

INT: Well, we won't worry about that one, but I was going to ask you—

ODETS: Well, it's such a bad play; I shouldn't like to be responsible for it. I have the credit for adapting it.

INT: Incidentally, how does one adapt a play from Russian? Do you get a literal—

ODETS: Yes, you get a literal translation, and then you go to work on it. It's like you buy a chair made of raw wood, and you say now how shall I finish this chair? How shall I upholster it? The essential frame is there; you've bought the frame.

INT: Well, I've counted 11 produced plays, anyhow, and—do you feel they move in a definite direction, from something to something, or is each one an individual expression of what you feel at the moment?

ODETS: I don't think that I've written two plays alike. This makes trouble for me, because the materials of the play or its shape always seem to baffle not the audiences, but the critics. They seem to expect one thing. I don't do that consciously, but I write out of what interests me, and perhaps I'm still naive.

For instance, in my next group of plays, of which I have five laid out or written in part, I wanted to write the most serious play first. It's called *An Old-Fashioned Man,* and probably that title will stay. But then I think, if I write that play, and open it in New York—it's a big play, and necessarily will be densely textured—it will lay me open to all sorts of charges of immodesty, of lopsidedness. It's the kind of play you simply cannot get on one viewing. So I think, well, why not come in quietly with a much more modest play? And then when that one has its brief moment I would go to one a little heavier, from their point of view a little more immodest, because it will be attempting more and will be saying more.

INT: Let me ask you about your early reading. Is Charlie Castle's list in the first part of *The Big Knife* your list, too?

ODETS: What is that list? Could you tell me?

INT: Victor Hugo, Ibsen, Upton Sinclair.

ODETS: No—well, I came to Ibsen at about the age of fourteen by being profoundly moved by seeing the actress Nazimova in a silent movie production of *A Doll's House.* I also saw her do—believe it or not—a silent movie production of Oscar Wilde's *Salome.* And when this happened, when the picture excited me that way beyond myself, or beyond my knowledge of why or what, I would go to the library and get the plays out and read them. I don't think I'd read, by the time I was twenty, more than maybe four Ibsen plays. Now when you come to Victor Hugo, you come to a different matter. He is my literary and spiritual grandfather. I *love* Victor Hugo. Between the ages of, I guess, thirteen and eighteen or nineteen I must have read almost every novel that Victor Hugo wrote, but was particularly moved, beyond my awareness or comprehension, by his novel *Les Misérables,* which I read through perhaps twice or three times, and read selected parts of many times later.

INT: How much of the Bible? It shows up in some of your plays; that's why I ask.

ODETS: I like to read the Bible. I would like to read it more. I believe much of what's in it. I want to write one more play—at least one more play that I know about—on a Biblical theme (that is after *The Flowering Peach,* which is about Noah and the Ark). I do want to write somewhere out of the two Books of Samuel, particularly the second Book, I want to write about the life of Man, through taking the materials of Saul and David. I want to show in David, who is pursued by a psychotic Saul, a young poet. And I want to show how the young poet becomes a very successful man—indeed, the most successful in his realm, because he becomes the King. And I want to show the life of Man from the time he is a poet until he dies an old man, unhappy, but somehow still a poet gnawing at his soul. I want to turn the various facets of his nature around so that you see what happens to men of big success and how they meet the conflicting situations of their lives. I don't know what tone it will be in; it certainly won't be in the street language.

INT: What about the Greek dramatists? Did you read them?

ODETS: I must tell you that again and again I have begun. When a good translation comes out I am inclined to buy it, and then make a kind of desultory, half-hearted move toward reading carefully and evaluating what I'm reading. But I could not say that I'm really acquainted with Greek drama.

INT: As to influences on you as a playwright, more from O'Neill or Ibsen or Shaw or—

ODETS: I am not influenced by O'Neill at all. I admired O'Neill. I am influenced by O'Neill—I take that back—in terms of aspiration, in terms of becoming a big American playwright, in terms of being some kind of distinguished human being that people respect, in terms of shaking the audience. I approached O'Neill very early, in his early plays, the sea plays, in the whole sense of the Provincetown Playhouse. And he was part of the inspiration of what I call my Greenwich Village days. At the time I got to Greenwich Village, around 1925, most of the so-called great ones had gone. Floyd Dell had moved; George Cram Cook was dead. Harry Kemp, they used to call him "The Tramp Poet," was still living down there. In fact, I was his leading man in something called The Poet's Theatre for two seasons. And O'Neill was part of this wonderful, glamorous world that a youth enters at the age of seventeen or eighteen. He was gone, but it was as if his fragrance, or the awesome sense of this man still lingered around the dirty alleys and streets— Macdougal Street, Macdougal Street meant the Provincetown Playhouse and Eugene O'Neill. In that sense I was influenced by Eugene O'Neill, but not directly by his work. I don't think that anywhere in my plays any influence of that kind shows.

I was influenced by a playwright named John Howard Lawson, particularly the only play of his I knew well, *Success Story*. I was influenced a little by Chekhov. Not by Ibsen, because you see my forms are not Ibsen's. But my chief influence as a playwright was the Group Theatre acting company, and being a member of that company, formed and trained and shaped and used by Lee Strasberg.

Interviewer: I wonder if we could talk about Hollywood for a little bit.

ODETS: Sure, We'll talk about anything you want as long as your tape holds out.

INT: It seems that your attitude toward Hollywood has shifted at the present time over statements that you made ten or fifteen years ago. Do you feel now that films provide you with enough latitude, or would you prefer to write for the stage, all other things being equal?

ODETS: Well, Hollywood allows an intelligent writer, a gifted writer, far more latitude than it did before. Hollywood has become decentralized. The big studios have broken down. There is much independent picture-making. There are many advantages, or many advantageous possibilities, in terms of making pictures and approaching how you will make them today, that simply were not true fifteen or twenty years ago. However, you do not sit down in Hollywood if you are a writer, even if you are a director, to express a state of being. You sit down to put together a "construct." You put together and make an extremely viable big machine that will use not only the technical resources of a Hollywood film, but will use the resources of several stars and will gobble up in the doing of the work five or six million dollars. I know that I, myself, could never sit down to express some small, lyric disquietude, something that was personally disturbing me. The returns that must come in are against that. The work is not private enough in Hollywood. The only one who can—given the trust of the people who are backing him—the only one in whose hands there is a possibility of something creative is the director. A director with a few clues, a few opening lines, a few sniffs of how scenes close, can make a creative work. You see it happening in

Italian films all the time—in the work of Fellini, in the work of so many of the other European men. They start with modest budgets, and they, so to speak, *dream* together a picture, which is what? The expression of how they see the life of a prostitute, how they see the life of somebody who needs a bicycle and doesn't have one. They *do* express that state of being; they *are* creative. That is practically impossible in Hollywood. No one approaches work that way. I have tried it; I have not been successful. I wrote and directed one picture about fifteen years ago that did catch something of what I am talking about, a picture called *None But the Lonely Heart.* I thought the last picture I wrote and directed, *The Story on Page One,* I thought that there I could do it too. But I got lost in a technical welter.

INT: Aren't there even more people who get in between the creative author and the final product that goes into the film can in Hollywood than there are in New York?

ODETS: Oh, yes, Yes, indeed, It's fantastic. It's unbelievable, making a picture and directing one. You become the "big white father" of people who worry about buttons on a suit, or how do you see her hair, or what dresses should she wear, or is the volume of sound full enough? The moment you enter the studio gate, you are besieged by people who come at you with all of this nonsense—all of which has its rightful place. And that essential thing which is the soul of something creative and really gifted, *that* all goes, unless you are more, let me say frankly, more competent than I am. I mean, for instance, "Gadg" Kazan has frequently shut out all of this nonsense and produced on the screen very sensitive, very living tissue—I'm inclined to think, perhaps better than what he has done on the stage. But Gadg has a hell of a lot more competence than I have.

INT: In that realm.

ODETS: Yes, in that realm.

INT: Aside from *None But the Lonely Heart,* how many films would you want to have your name associated with along with you best plays?

ODETS: Well, let them stand for what they are. They are technically very adept. I have learned a great deal from making and shaping these scripts. I don't know; I suppose that by now I've written—written or rewritten secretly for some friends of mine—fifteen or eighteen, close to twenty films. One need not be ashamed of them. I have not expressed anywhere any loss of standards. I haven't dehumanized people in them. I have even written a little picture that ended up being called *Deadline at Dawn.* I'm not ashamed of that. It's a little mystery thriller. I see it; it has its living moments. It's not merely that the dialogue is good. Or a picture that I rewrote called *Sweet Smell of Success.* It's professional work; I'm a professional writer. And I am never ashamed of the professional competence which is in these scripts. I have never downgraded human beings or a certain kind of morality. I'm not ashamed of any of them . . .

INT: Did you—I don't imagine in your early plays, at least, you wrote with any particular actor or actress in mind—but did you have John Garfield in mind when you started in on *The Big Knife?*

ODETS: There, I think in that play I did have John Garfield in mind. It's one of the few times where I did have a certain actor in mind. With the Group Theatre plays I usually had a vague sense of who would play the part, but only a vague sense. And I deliberately kept it general, and you can see, the Group Theatre acting technique crept right into the plays. I have often been accused of aping Chekhov, which is in no sense a *mean* thing. But the real truth is that with the Group Theatre ensemble acting company, I wrote not one or two leading parts with a lot of supporting players, but the early plays were written with equal-size parts for equal-size actors. So that a play like *Awake and Sing,* let us say, has seven leading parts in it. And that form was dictated by the composition of the Group Theatre acting company.

INT: I have a few rather specific questions that came up in my reading of your plays. In the Random House Modern Library version of *Waiting for Lefty,* in the *Six Plays,* there is a scene omitted, the scene with the young actor, which is printed in certain other editions that I've seen—

ODETS: Ah yes, that's simple. It seemed to me too untypical. What happened was that since we were actors working in the theatre and I wrote this play directly for our actors to act, to perform, it seemed to me that I would write in the difficulty of getting a job as an actor. Well, later, with a little backward glance, it seemed to me so untypical to include an unemployed actor and a casting agent, that I simply dropped it for that reason.

INT: Was it used in the Group Theatre production, that is, as opposed to the off-Broadway production?

ODETS: I know that when we opened the play and played it around for benefit Sunday nights, that we had the actor's scene in it, but I am not sure, when we brought it to the Longacre Theatre, that the scene was still in. Perhaps. I'm not sure.

INT: The scene is printed in an anthology of British and American plays and it's discussed by Joseph Wood Krutch and a couple of other critics who talk about the play. But it didn't turn up in the Modern Library, and I was just curious about that.

ODETS: That's what happened.

INT: I'm interested in *The Silent Partner* as it fits into the development of your playwriting during the Thirties.

ODETS: Well, this is a play which went into rehearsal and then was pulled at the suggestion of the Group Theatre directors that it would be a failure, that its theme was passé. It is a labor theme, it evoked those days in labor conflict when, in a major strike, there always would be two or three or four strikers killed. And by the time the play was to be produced, that atmosphere had passed and there had been legislation—F.D.R. legislation—and the nascent C.I.O. organization. However, in the development of my work it was very necessary, and I should have insisted that that play be produced. It's the kind of writing that I have not done since, and I don't think I'm capable of now. It was a heightened realism and reached a very tense height, a very tense fullness and richness. It existed as a very real play, naturalistic, and yet was on a symbolic level. And if I had continued writing from there on, after its production, in the same way, something extraordinary might have come out. The production was absolutely necessary for me. But I was not mature enough to insist upon it and almost not *nasty* enough to insist upon it, or not cold-hearted enough. I could easily be touched. They said, "This will make dilemmas and problems for the Group Theatre," and I kind of said, "Well, don't do it," and walked away quite hurt and let it go at that, little realizing how much the nonproduction of the play would harm me as a writer.

INT: And you'll still stand by the judgment that you expressed to the—to McCarten in *The New Yorker,* that it's the best labor play that was ever written in the United States?

ODETS: Yes, but that's not saying too much, because there haven't been too many good labor plays written in the United States. There have been very few of any quality written. There were the ones that Theatre Union did by Maltz and Sklar, and two or three other writers in that period, but this is really the best play about a strike ever written. And I told you I think myself, objectively, it's far superior to *The Weavers,* which is a classic.

INT: I gather you don't think much of Galsworthy's *Strife?*

ODETS: Oh, too genteel. That's strife that doesn't want to dirty its hands. It's wearing gloves. Edwardian gloves. I think Galsworthy had some unique talents, and, you know, we're apt to sweep away—you know, there's always, after a very popular writer dies, there's that period where for fifteen, twenty or twenty-five years he is consistently underrated. Oh, let's say in our time, perhaps you've seen that, you've seen a writer of considerable magnitude like Joseph Conrad, after he dies, being forgotten, neglected. Twenty years later people say, "Hey, this novel *Nostromo,* it's a great book." Or this one. I, myself, have never lost my love for Joseph Conrad. I, about every three years, will reread one or two, *The Nigger of the Narcissus* or *Typhoon,* or occasionally will run across one that I haven't read, and with great pleasure. But Galsworthy, too. I mean he's not of the rank of Conrad, but he has many virtues as a writer. . . .

We live in a time where you say something in one decade, and a decade later you're old-fashioned. They talk about me as *a* playright, or *the* playwright of the Thirties. I've set down some of my best plays outside of the Thirties, and I'll continue, I hope, to do more of my best plays in the Sixties! What are they going to call me in the Sixties, when I produce three or four or five plays which will obviously have quality? What are they going to still call me, a playwright of the Thirties?

INT: You probably got tired of reading of yourself as "the angry young man of the Thirties" or—

ODETS: It makes me very angry in the Fifties and Sixties!

INT: Is California still a place where "an honest apple tree won't grow"? That's from *The Big Knife.*

ODETS: Yes, I remember that line. At that time I had had California up to the neck and could never make peace with the place. Now I've learned to make peace with it. It seems to tolerate me, and I seem to tolerate it. And it has its virtues. Anyway, it all boils down, as I said in another play, to: "A place is never a place; a place is whom you're with." I'll let it go at that.

INT: These earlier attempts at playriting, or when you were feeling your way around in the early Thirties, with such things as *910 Eden Street*—these are all just workshop material that's buried away, or thrown away?

ODETS: They were very painful attempts to not only find my identity—not only to locate myself—but to write down the nature of neurotic illness, to try to come to some clear, objective sense of myself and my inability to handle and deal with life. They also had in them considerable ambition, which simply means a desire to be *a* playwright, to be a significant writer. They were very sad affairs, and I think they have no value whatsoever as plays or even scenes, although some day I will dig them out of the files and read what they're about.

I find it very difficult to read anything I've written in the past. Achieved or unachieved or successful. I find it very difficult to read an old play of mine. I should review my work some time. It's a necessary task, but I avoid it. I guess I'm avoiding just simply sitting in judgment on myself. Ibsen said that. Ibsen said that every time you wrote a play, you were pronouncing judgment on yourself. And there is a large truth in there.

INT: What do you think about Arthur Miller and the "tragedy of the common man"? Is Willy Loman [*Death of a Salesman*] related to Leo Gordon [*Paradise Lost*], for example?

ODETS: Well, Arthur has never approached or acknowledged the slightest influence from me to him. Nor have several other writers. And I was surprised, in some magazine, maybe *Atlantic* or *Harper's,* to find an article by him in which he mentioned the writers who had meant something to him, myself and Lillian Hellman. I'm surprised that he made even that acknowledgment. Our literary people—I don't mean this as accusation—nevertheless our literary people have very bad manners. They don't have the European grace, the European sense of one thing passing on from one decade to another, one generation to another, and acknowledging it, or approaching it with some sense of gratitude or some sense of wanting to tell. I, for instance, although I had not been influenced by him. I made several efforts to meet Eugene O'Neill. And I would have gone to him as a younger poet to an older poet. I did it with the Europeans here during the war, when there were so many of them here. I met Thomas Mann in that spirit; I met Franz Werfel in that spirit—

INT: Did you know Brecht?

ODETS: Oh, yes. I knew him well. I knew him over a period of five, six years. I didn't approach him that way, because I couldn't read too much of him in German. There were very few translations. We met rather as friends. We talked about general things rather than literature. His English was very poor. So that when I did meet Brecht, it was on a quite casual level. It had nothing to do with literature, although we did have one or two conferences about *Waiting for Lefty,* which he admired very much. He told me frankly he wanted to use the form; he wanted to take it over and make it into a kind of—either a tank full, or a truckload of Nazi soldiers on their way somewhere, using it as a unifying thing for individual scenes, just as in *Waiting for Lefty.* He was a strange man. I always saw him one way, as a medieval monk. He was surpassingly ugly. You didn't see his talent in his shrewd face, but, after all, I think when you do see talent in a writer—when a writer looks talented—he's nine times out of ten apt to be a phony. . . .

You asked me in a letter where characters come from. Well I can tell you. Every human being has his own gallery of characters which he himself is. The more gifted the human being, the larger his gallery of characters. What is that gallery of characters? It is a group of characteristics or relationships to certain key psychological types outside of yourself. If you are really creative, you can only write out of this gallery of characters. You're lucky if you have six or seven of them. If you're an ardent young man, it's easy to write an ardent young man. If you have in yourself really fatherly qualities, in your gallery there is a father who is fatherly or a mother who is motherly. If you are an opportunistic rascal, a sharp dealer, you can write that character. And the trouble with many writers is that they—in a begrudging, close, guarded way—hold onto a gallery, a personal gallery, by which, again, I mean psychological characteristics or trends in their own natures. They hold onto them and insist upon writing out of that gallery, although their lives have *changed* and they are now functioning out of a *different* gallery of characters. One needs patience. It needs courage to throw away that trademark that has become *you* and sit patiently and wait for new forms, new styles, new character to assert themselves or grow so strong and rich that they become the new gallery. And there's no patience in the United States for that. . . .

INT: Perhaps I'll ask you one more question. Where would Shakespeare be writing today if he were alive? Would he be writing for the New York stage, or would he be writing for the television industry, or the film industry?

ODETS: I don't think that can be answered. The times are so different. Can you, for instance, possibly conceive of a man today—this will answer your question in a cockeyed way; it will answer your question by asking *you* a question—can you conceive of a man writing some thirty-odd plays, at least ten or fifteen of them as durable as the Rocky Mountains, and once they have been written and produced, and he has made his shillings from them, turning his back on them, not having copies of them, not having them published or printed, and going back to some little town in Arkansas where he was born, and forgetting that he ever wrote the plays?

So that—and I just make this up in my imagination—an old man says, "Oh, you're Will Shakespeare. Ain't seen you around for a while, Will. Where you been?" (This is on Avon Street.) "Where you been, Will?" And Will says, "Oh, I've been to London town."

And the old man says, "Oh, been to London town? Well, watcha been doin' there?"

And he says, "Oh, scribblin.' "

Well, this is almost the attitude with which William Shakespeare went back to Avon. So you ask me your question, and I ask you this question. Can you conceive of such a thing happening today? So you see, the times were different, what it meant to be a writer was different then—

INT: Well, let me pose another very hypothetical question. Suppose there were no film industry today. Where would you be?

ODETS: Well, in some ways it would be much better for me, because I might have been more productive in the serious aspects of my work instead of the mere craft aspects.

INT: Perhaps, then, you could have made a living out of the theatre?

ODETS: Yes, I would have scrounged around this way and that way, gotten out from under this big tent and pitched smaller tents in many a wild and strange terrain. And good would have come out of it, more good than has come out of my present way of life.

INT: What I meant is, I suppose it's conceivable that not only you, but other serious writers—had there been no film industry—would have been able to earn a living that way.

ODETS: Same thing for TV. Of course, we're talking about America. You see, the European concept of a "decent poverty," in which framework you continue to grow and exist creatively, is unknown to America. We're so much here for success and its din and its awards and rewards, that we do not understand this concept of a decent poverty. An artist like Paul Klee, whom you see that I love, his pictures—this room is hung with his pictures—I doubt if this man ever made more than $75 a week in his whole life. That just took care of things. I call that a life of decent poverty. That concept is foreign to us, so that the moment someone has a little talent, as—for instance, in my playwriting class at the Actors Studio, I carefully handpicked some twenty-odd writers, five or six of whom I thought had a lot of talent. They couldn't wait to run to TV.

One student, without me remonstrating against the ideas, actually shouted at me, and said, "Well, your wife's got a baby sitter, don't you think *my* wife should have a baby sitter?" I said, "That is for you to decide. I think you should finish this play before you run to TV." Because he was approaching me like a poppa to make a decision, like he wanted moral sanctions from me. I said, "I won't give you these sanctions. Do what you want. But you should finish this play." It was the last I ever heard of that writer.

And everybody runs to TV. Generation after generation gets worse. Run to TV, run to the movies, make a small success, the movies snap you up, and then they're well on their way to being lost. Because talent—what's talent? In our country there's no profound training, such as, let's say the training of a German musician, a German composer. He starts with Bach. And no matter how he ends up—he may end up an Alban Berg or an Anton Webern or some of these fellows working with electronics now—nevertheless he's profoundly steeped in that culture, which is his musical culture from A, B down to Z. But in this country, where there's not that cultural heritage to pass on, if a fellow has a little talent, what happens? It's as evanescent as smoke. He's not well grounded in the past of drama, really. He doesn't write out of any cultural stream or continuity. So that the talent just disappears—like smoke. Before you know it, he has become a hack. He laments it, he has no respect for the work—or for himself.

How a Playwright Triumphs
(1966)

CLIFFORD ODETS

The following monologue—by one of the best American playwrights of the century—was originally a dialogue. It is drawn from an interview in Hollywood with Clifford Odets by Arthur Wagner of the Department of Theatre at Tulane University. The interview took place over a two-day period in September 1961, two years before Mr. Odets' death.

I had always wanted as a kid to be both an actor and a writer. For a while I thought I would be a novelist, but when I became a professional actor, my mind naturally began to take the form of the play as a means of saying something. I wasn't sure I had anything to say, because some of the other things I wrote were quite dismal. But being an actor. I began to think in terms of three acts, divisions of acts, and scenes within the acts, and whatever technique I have has been unconsciously absorbed—almost through my skin—with all the kinds of acting I have done.

Before *Awake and Sing!* I wrote a whole very bad novel and a few short stories, all of which I later tore up. The question is really not one of knowing how to write so much as knowing how to connect with yourself so that the writing is, so to speak, born affiliated with yourself. Anybody can teach the craft of playwriting, just as I can teach myself how to make a blueprint and construct a house, on paper. But what cannot be taught, and what I was fortunate in discovering, was simply being myself, with my own problems and my own relationships to life.

Without the Group Theatre I doubt that I would have become a playwright. I might have become some other kind of writer, but the Group Theatre and the so-called "method" forced you to face yourself and really function out of the kind of person you are, not as you thought the person had to function, or as another kind of person, but simply using your own materials. The whole "method" acting technique is based on that. Well, after attempting to write for eight or ten years, I finally started a short story that made me really understand what writing was about in the sense of personal affiliation to the material.

I was holed up in a cheap hotel, in a kind of fit of depression, and I wrote about a young kid violinist who didn't have his violin because the hotel owner had appropriated it for unpaid bills. He looked back and remembered his mother and his hard-working sister, and although I was not that kid and didn't have that kind of mother or sister, I did fill the skin and the outline with my own personal feeling, and for the first time I realized what creative writing was.

A playwright who writes about things that he is not connected with, or to, is not a creative writer. He may be a very skilled writer, and it may be on a very high level of craft, but he's not going to be what I call an artist, a poet. We nowadays use the term creative arts, or a creative person, very loosely. A movie writer thinks of himself as a creative person who writes films or TV shows. Well, in the sense that I'm using the word, he's just a craftsman, like a carpenter. He has so many hammers, so many nails, so much dimension to fill, and he can do it with enormous skill. But the creative writer always starts with a state of being. He doesn't start with something outside of himself. He starts with something inside himself, with a sense of unease, depression, or elation, and only gradually finds some kind of form for what I'm calling that "state of being." He doesn't just pick a form and a subject and a theme and say this will be a hell of a show.

The form, then, is always dictated by the material; there can be nothing ready-made about it. It will use certain dramatic laws because, after all, you have to relate this material to an audience, and a form is the quickest way to get your content to an audience. That's all form is. Form is viability.

"Most Talented"—But No Option

I was twenty-six years old when I started *Awake and Sing!*, my first play. I wrote the first two acts, and six months later, in the spring of 1933, I went home to my folks' house in Philadelphia and finished the last act there. That summer the Group Theatre went to a place called Green Mansions Camp [in the Adirondacks], where we sang for our supper by being the social staff. After he read *Awake and Sing!* Harold Clurman announced one night at a meeting of the entire company that the Group Theatre idea—that we would develop from our ranks not only our own actors, but our own directors and perhaps our own playwrights—was really working out in practice. "Lo and behold!" he said, "sitting right here in this room is the most talented new young playwright in the United States." And everybody, including me, turned around to see who was in the room, and then with a horrible rush of a blush I realized he was talking about me.

But the Group Theatre didn't want to do the play. Although Harold Clurman, who was kind of the ideological head, liked it, he didn't have the strength to push it through to production against the wishes of the other two directors, Lee Strasberg and Cheryl Crawford. Lee Strasberg particularly didn't like the play. He kept saying, "It's a mere genre study." Strasberg and I were always on the outs. Although he has many other qualities, I could take just so much of his, let me call it now, authoritarian or dictatorial manner, his absolutism. And I, who was one of the humbler members of the acting company—even though I had been there practically from the start—would flare out at him and we would be shouting at each other like a pair of maniacs across the bowed heads of the entire company of thirty or so other persons.

I kept pleading with Clurman to do my play, and he kept saying that it read so well he didn't know if it would act. I said it would act like a house on fire. And he said, "I don't know, I don't know," and I said, "Well, just take my word for it." I said it very fiercely. So he decided to try the middle act one night on the Green Mansions Camp audience—and it did just what I said. It played like a house on fire. I had felt sure it would, for I knew the theater very well by then. I'd been walking around on stages since I was a kid, putting on plays in high school, with amateurs, being a leading man and director of a company on the radio called "The Drawing Room Players." And when I saw that act up there on the stage I realized I had real writing talent, and right then I was not to be stopped or contained.

Well, now I thought surely that Group Theatre would do my play, but to my bitter disappointment they had not the slightest interest in it. Here was the Group Theatre with all its ideals, here was my own company with which I felt such a sense of brotherhood, and here was my play, which they could have just taken and done; I didn't want any money for it. Furthermore, it seemed to me better than the plays we were doing. The play we were rehearsing at this time [by Sidney Kingsley], called *Crisis,* seemed to all of us threadbare in texture. It turned out to be very successful—due chiefly to Lee Strasberg's extraordinary and beautiful production, and became very famous as *Men in White.* Well, I couldn't see why, if they could do *Men in White,* they couldn't do *Awake and Sing!*

However, just as *Men in White* was opening that fall on 46th Street at the Broadhurst Theater, a fellow I had acted with at the Theatre Guild, a nice man named Louis Simon, told me that he was now working with Frank Merlin in the Little Theatre right across the street. He said Merlin, who was looking for new American plays, had heard about *Awake and Sing!* and he suggested I give him a script for his boss. When I told him I didn't have any copies, he said, "Well, get some typed up and give me one and, who knows, next week you might have $500 advance royalties." I was very impressed with that possibility, so I had six scripts typed up for twelve bucks, which was one-third of my weekly salary of $35. And about five or six days later, I had a check for $500. I'd never seen so much money in my life. And since I had gone again before the Group Theatre and said, "Look, somebody wants to take an option on this play. You going to do it or not?" and they had practically thrown me out, it was with double satisfaction that I got my first option money.

Merlin was rhapsodic about *Awake and Sing!* He said, "This is the kind of play that America should be producing. It's the beginning of something new in the American theater." Then I thought, well, I'm going to get an immediate production here. But Merlin, poor man, made a fantastic blunder which changed his whole life. Now, Merlin had $50,000 to spend. A wealthy man had given his new wife $50,000 to play around with in the theater. She had walked in on Lee Strasberg and just said she wanted to hand this whole $50,000 over to the Group Theatre in exchange for a humble position as assistant stage manager, or whatever it was she wanted to learn. Well, Lee was such a kind of rabbinical student that he just turned and looked at her, kind of shrugged, and was silent. The woman felt very embarrassed and finally left and took the $50,000 to Frank Merlin at the Little Theatre.

Mr. Merlin, however, now made the sad mistake. He had another play, called *False Dreams Farewell,* which he said was an inadequate play, but a hell of a show. It had something to do with the sinking of the *Titanic* or the *Lusitania*—very expensive and elaborate. He put the play on first because he felt it was going to make money, and he didn't think my play would, and he lost about $40,000. If Mr. Merlin had done *Awake and Sing!* first—it was a small cast with one set and its operating cost would have run about $3,000 a week—it would have run for two or maybe three years. But he lost most of his money on this first venture.

This was now August or September of 1934, and the Group Theatre was determined, in the purity of its heart, that it would have to go away and do a new play when it might very well have continued the run of the very successful, and by this time Pulitzer Prize, *Men in White.* But purity prevailed and we went up to Ellenville, New York, to a big, rambling, broken-down hotel—don't forget, with its office and managerial staff the Group Theatre consisted of maybe thirty-six men and women and their children—and we had to find quite a large place to live in. We arrived practically when autumn was setting in at this old Saratoga-type wooden hotel, with all the bedding piled up, and we lived in an itchy and uncomfortable way there for about five or six weeks while we put into rehearsal a play by Melvin Levy, called *Gold Eagle Guy.* I had, perhaps unfairly, only scorn and contempt for the play because I thought *Awake and Sing!* was far superior as a piece of writing. Indeed, we all felt that *Gold Eagle Guy* was a stillborn script, and Luther Adler summed it up for us one morning at rehearsal when he said, kind of *sotto voce,* "Boys, I think we're working on a stiff." That morning we were almost improvising certain scenes, which we would later scale down to the playwright's words. Levy would get alarmed because the actors were not quite saying his words, and not using his punctuation. To this day there are playwrights who don't know their punctuation isn't very important in the recreation of the character they've written, or that, as we used to say in the Group Theatre, their script is only a series of stenographic notes.

The Words Gushed Out

In any case, I had been given my own room at this old hotel, which gave me a certain lift. It's surprising how very important a small satisfaction can be in the life of one who is moving away from what I can only call illness to some kind of health or strength. (You must remember the background to all of this was that before I was twenty-five I had tried to commit suicide three times; once I stopped it myself and twice my life was saved by perfect strangers.) Before this I had always been quartered with one or two and sometimes three other actors, but when they gave me my own room, with clean, white-washed walls, I began to feel they had some sense that I had some kind of distinction, and I was very happy.

I had by now started *Paradise Lost,* about a man, Leo, who was trying to be a good man in the world and meets raw, evil, and confused conditions where his goodness means nothing. Almost all of that play came out of my experiences as a boy in the Bronx. I saw people evicted, I saw block parties, I knew a girl who stayed at the piano all day, a boy who drowned, boys who went bad and got in trouble with the police. As a matter of fact, two of the boys I graduated with ended up in the electric chair and another boy became a labor racketeer. Not too much of that play was invented; it was felt, remembered, celebrated.

One night I had the idea for the scene in the play which I call the Fire Bug Scene. It just impelled itself to be written, and since I had no paper I wrote the whole scene as fast as I could on the white wall. The words just gushed out; my hand couldn't stop writing. Then later, I copied it down on the typewriter, but to this day the scene may still be on the wall of that old hotel.

The next day, well, I had that advance money from Merlin, and I had always wondered what real liquor tasted like. Prohibition was over, and all I had ever had was bathtub gin and very phony rye whiskey. I went into a liquor store and bought two cases of mixed liquor—two bottles of everything— Scotch, gin and rye, applejack, sherry, red port, and something called white port which I have not seen again to this day. And I and my particular chums in the Group Theatre, Elia Kazan, Art Smith, Bud Bohnen, and one or two others, went to town on all that stuff. I got to know what real liquor, real Scotch, tasted like. There was booze in those two cases that I have not tasted since. We went down to the village one night, got drunk, and got arrested. We had a helluvatime.

During this time, however, I was extremely discontented about my acting career. Many of us were fretful in those days, because we had higher hopes for ourselves than playing bits and walkons. I had been assigned to play two bits in *Gold Eagle Guy,* but I didn't have a part in *Success Story,* which we had done before and were now reviving out of town to keep us going while we were rehearsing *Gold Eagle Guy.*

John Howard Lawson's *Success Story*—a good play—had, by the way, a very decisive influence on me, by showing me the poetry that was inherent in the chaff of the street. I began to see that there was something quite elevated and poetic in the way the common people spoke. I understudied Luther Adler, who played the lead, and while I never got to play it, I came to understand that living quality in Lawson's play by studying the part and writing down how I thought I would approach it as an actor. Getting a part also meant that you would learn what the hell the technique was about. There wasn't time for too many technique classes, so there was more than an ego problem involved in our wanting good parts, for it was the only way we could really get the benefit of Strasberg's training.

The Strasberg-Clurman Team

Strasberg worked with a wide range, then, of techniques and things. There were times when you would do improvisation for a part—the sensation, for instance, for riding a train or boat. It would play only a small part in the play, but concentration was given to it. Or you would do exercises or improvisation for simply being cold, for re-creating winter on the stage. As a matter of fact, the Group Theatre built up a set of actors and actresses who were extraordinarily reliable in small parts as well as in leads. Say this woman is a nurse, and this actress would go away and she would be a nurse to the life. She thought about how a nurse waddled, and what kind of shoes she would wear, why she walks the way she does, and what her professional mannerisms are.

Anyway, one day I told Harold Clurman, who by then had become my particular friend among the three Group directors—he was a kind of older brother to me—I told him that since I had never got a part, I was leaving and was going to do something about playwriting. He pleaded with me to stay, promising he would see that I got a good acting part in the coming season, and indeed I think I was leading him on a bit because I wouldn't have known where to go. Where else could you go? All I really wanted was to have the Group Theatre do my plays. These early plays were made for the collective acting company technique. They're written for eight characters, with six or seven of the characters of equal importance. Well, this is purely from the Group Theatre ideal of a stage ensemble, and this so fetched me and so took me over that this was how I wrote. I don't think, still, that even today anyone could put together such a company with its very brilliant ensemble performance but Lee Strasberg. That was Lee Strasberg's baby and he was 100 per cent responsible for it. Later, with this perfected tool, this ensemble, anybody could direct them who had a common lingo, a common frame of reference. It was easy for Harold Clurman to direct *Awake and Sing!* or *Golden Boy* with this company that Lee Strasberg had put together—any actor could have directed it, by that time. And Lee Strasberg has never gotten enough credit for that.

Strasberg and Clurman were a unique team. The procedure was that the directors picked the plays—remember, though, that we didn't have our choice of dozens of plays. Strasberg and Clurman saw rather eye-to-eye about what was in a play. They wanted progressive materials, they wanted yea-saying rather than nay-saying materials. After the play was chosen Clurman would call the company together and would talk with extraordinary brilliance for anywhere from two to five hours, analyzing the meaning, talking from every point of view, covering the ground backwards and forwards. And if the actor's imagination was touched, somewhere, which was his intention, then the actor would catch something and begin to work in a certain way, with a certain image or vision of how the part should go, with here and there Clurman giving him a nudge. Strasberg would never say a word. He was the man who, in action, directing, would bring out the things which Clurman had abstracted. Strasberg understood the concrete elements which you give an actor. But the sense of the play, its characters, its meaning, what it stood for, Clurman is most brilliant at this thing.

How the Actors Took Over

Well, now we move up to Boston in the late fall of 1934 to open *Gold Eagle Guy,* and that's when I wrote *Waiting for Lefty.* I now had behind me the practically completed *Awake and Sing!* and about half of *Paradise Lost,* but somehow *Waiting for Lefty* just kind of slipped itself in there. Its form and its feeling are different from the other two plays, and I actually wrote it in three nights in the hotel room in Boston after returning home from the theater about midnight. It just seemed to gush out, and it took its form necessarily from what we then called the agit-prop form, which, of course, stands for agitational propaganda.

I really saw the play as a kind of collective venture something we would do for a Sunday night benefit in New York for the *New Theatre Magazine,* a Left magazine that was always in need of money. My demands were so modest that I tried to get two other actors in the Group Theatre who I thought had writing talent to assist me. One of them, Art Smith, came up with me one night to my hotel room and we talked around and around this thing, but he seemed rather listless about working with me, so I went ahead by myself.

As a matter of fact, the form of *Waiting for Lefty* is very rooted in American life, because what I semi-consciously had in mind was actually the form of the minstrel show. I had put on two or three minstrel shows in camp and had seen three or four other ones. It's a very American, indigenous form—you know, an interlocutor, end men, people doing their specialties, everyone sitting on the stage, and some of the actors sitting in the audience. There were a number of plays then, usually cheap and shoddy plays, that had actors in the audience. I had played in one called, I think, *The Spider,* in Camden, New Jersey, when I was in stock. I guess all these things conglomerated in my mind, but what's important for *Waiting for Lefty* is how it matched my conversion from a fellow who stood on the side and watched and then finally, with a rush, agreed—in this drastic social crisis in the early 'thirties—that the only way out seemed to be a kind of socialism, or the Communist party, or something. And the play represents that kind of ardor and that kind of conviction.

About ten days after the tryout in Boston we opened *Gold Eagle Guy* at the Morosco Theater in New York, and the play got very bad notices. In all New York theaters you automatically lose the theater when the play receipts fall below a certain figure, so we moved over to the Belasco. It happened that three or four or even five of my plays were done at that theater, which people thought was very glamorous, but I always thought it a rather crummy old joint, shabby, with uncomfortable seats. Anyway, to keep the play going the actors and the playwright took cuts in salary, but in a few weeks it closed and we were forced out into the cold winter. We had no new play to put into rehearsal and there was a sadness around the place.

In the meantime I'd gotten some of the actors together and had started to rehearse *Waiting for Lefty.* I gave Sandy Meisner, an actor friend of mine, some of the scenes to direct, and I directed the bulk of the play. Strasberg, who was quite resentful of it, told Harold Clurman, "Let 'em fall and break their necks." One of the main things about Strasberg was that he always hated to go out on a limb. He must save his face at all times. Almost Oriental. I suspect that the thing about Strasberg was that whenever the Group Theatre name was used or represented, it was as though his honor was at stake. He didn't like me, he didn't like what I had written, and he felt it would in some way be a reflection on him, on the entire Group Theatre. This man who could be so generous, sometimes could be so niggardly and begrudging. It was with great trepidation that I had proposed putting on this play at all, and when I asked him a few questions about handling a group, an ensemble, he'd answer me very curtly, and I thought to myself, "Oh, the hell with him. I'll just go ahead and do this myself."

And then, the night of the benefit, I had an enormous fight down at the old Civic Repertory Theatre on 14th Street to get my play put on last. They used to put on eight or nine vaudeville acts there for the Sunday night benefits and they wanted some dance group to close the show, but finally, because I threatened to pull it, they agreed to put *Waiting for Lefty* on last.

It was very lucky they did because there would have been no show after that. The audience stopped the show after each scene; they got up, they began to cheer and weep. There have been many great opening nights in the American theater but not where the opening and the performing of the play were a cultural fact. You saw a cultural unit functioning. From stage to theater and back and forth the identity was so complete, there was such an at-oneness with audience and actors, that the actors didn't know whether they were acting and the audience didn't know whether they were sitting and watching it, or had changed position. I was sitting in the audience with my friend, Elia Kazan, sitting next to me (I wouldn't have dared take on one of the good parts myself) and after the Luther Adler scene, the young doctor scene, the audience got up and shouted, "Bravo! Bravo!" I was thinking, "Shh, let the play continue," but I found myself up on my feet shouting, "Bravo, Luther! Bravo, Luther!" In fact, I was part of the audience. I forgot I wrote the play, I forgot I was in the play, and many of the actors forgot. The proscenium arch disappeared. That's the key phrase. Before and since, in the American theater people have tried to do that by theater-in-the-round, theater this way, that way, but here, psychologically and emotionally, the proscenium arch dissolved away. When that happens, not by technical innovation, but emotionally and humanly, then you will have great theater—theater at its most primitive and grandest.

Of course, the nature of the times had a good deal to do with this kind of reaction. I don't think a rousing play today could have this kind of effect because there are no positive, ascending values to which a play can attach itself. My own new plays will never arouse that kind of enthusiasm, but they will have searched out and will express what has been happening here in the last fifteen years. And this isn't going to be anything to dance and shout about, because what happened here in fifteen years is really frightening. One of the new plays, *An Old-fashioned Man,* will almost cover the American scene from the time of FDR's death to today. I think the play is of considerable import, but really the kind of import that makes you sit there and think, rather than the kind that makes you get up and burn with zeal.

However, we now had to face the closing of *Gold Eagle Guy.* There was an emergency meeting and we were told we would have to disband. It was at this time that the actors took over and upset the applecart. We took the theater out of the hands of the three directors, especially Strasberg's, who was still extraordinarily resistant to the idea of doing *Awake and Sing!* What happened was that the Theatre Guild wanted to do *Awake and Sing!* for their last production of the season. So I rather timidly asked at this meeting whether the Group Theatre was or was not going to do my play because I had another offer.

Strasberg got up and pointed his finger at me and said, "I have told you a dozen times. I do not like your play. Your play will not be done by the Group Theatre." And it was Stella Adler who got up and said, "Well, is it better to disband, and those people who can get jobs will and the rest are going to be cold and hungry, as they have been many times before? And what's the matter with this play? Why shouldn't we do it?" And one or two other actors chipped in and Strasberg began to fight with them. Clurman says that he just sat letting things develop, and they did. Strasberg said, "But the play doesn't have a third act." I said, "It has a third act. It's not as good as it can be, but I can rewrite that." And, lo and behold, in a wave of what I call the Group Theatre spirit, it was voted, without the directors' interfering, that the next play we would do would be *Awake and Sing!* And Lee Strasberg kind of withdrew as the active director, so to speak, and Harold Clurman directed it.

When I rewrote the third act of *Awake and Sing!* I built up the boy to a kind of affirmative voice in the end, more affirmative than he had been in the original. There were technical reasons for this change, but the change had occured in me, too—a growing sense of power and direction. If I was going up, everything had to go up with me. But as you see, it runs throughout the play. The boy is always resentful of who and what he is, of his position in the world. And he always wants to get married and he can't, because of, let me call it that economic factor in his mother, who is always very authoritarian, always making decisions for him. And the grandfather, as weak as he is, was always against the values by which his daughter and the household lives. He always sided with the boy. So tried and true, that play.

Awake and Sing! opened at the Belasco Theater in February 1935. The notices were legendary. In the meantime we had been playing benefit performances of *Waiting for Lefty* all around and it was getting more famous by the minute. Even the commercial managers, the Shubert office, had called me and asked to see a copy of it. In the general enthusiasm Strasberg jumped on the bandwagon and now suggested that we bring *Waiting for Lefty* uptown, and I said, yes, I would write another play to go with it, which later became *Till the Day I Die*. I had read in *The New Masses* what I thought was a letter that had been smuggled out of Europe, from a man to his brother in the [anti-Nazi] underground, and in a wave of enthusiasm I wrote, in three or four nights, a play based on that letter. That's how arrogant youth is, for it never occurred to me to clear it in any way with *The New Masses,* and it turned out that the letter was not a real letter at all, but a short story in letter form, and later I was approached and had to pay that man royalties. In any case, *Till the Day I Die* was paired with *Waiting for Lefty,* and the whole town wanted to see it. And the whole town wanted to see *Awake and Sing!* You know—"America has found a really important playwright"; "The Group Theatre has found its most congenial playwright within its own ranks. . . ."

For me, strangely enough, the success and fame was a source of acute discomfort. I didn't have the psychological strength to face this kind of onslaught. It had on me a strangely isolating effect, even more isolated and cut off from the very things I was trying to get to. Later on when I became really a successful playwright the Group Theatre acting members, my friends, started to treat me quite differently. However, that's ahead. All I wanted then in 1935 were some of the things that were mentioned in *Waiting for Lefty*—a room of my own, a girl of my own, a phonograph and some records. And I got 'em. Nothing more I wanted.

Then I ran into a nerve-racking period where I thought I was going to go to pieces, just out of emotional exhaustion. I understood in this period of my life how van Gogh felt. I understood the kind of insanity and frenzy of his painting. I almost couldn't stop writing. The hand kept going. It began to frighten me. With all this set in the matrix of an American success—nothing is more noisy and clamorous than that. There are enormous tensions and strains within it, because you don't want to change, you want to hold on. You want time to digest, but you're just kind of swept off your feet, with wire services and interviews and people telephoning you; the parties you're invited to, the people who just take you up. You want to savor these things, flavor them, but you'd like it on your own terms. You'd like the time to establish forms with which to deal with it, or else it will drive you cuckoo.

Some of it, though, was gentle and sweet, like my mother. This was in a way all she ever lived for, to see her son fulfilled. She hadn't been sick; she just lived another couple of months and died. My whole life changed in this period. Within three months I was not the same young man I used to be, but was trying to hold on to him.

In any case, I now began to finish up *Paradise Lost*. The play, with Harold Clurman directing it, was treated with dignity and importance, and the actors approached it in a very dedicated way. It opened on December 9, 1935. It's too jammed, too crowded, it spills out of its frame, but it is in many ways a beautiful play, velvety; the colors were very gloomy and rich. And no one who acted in it or saw it in that production will ever forget it. It got very bad notices from the working press, but from unexpected people like Clifton Fadiman it got quite extraordinary notices. But the play was by all means a practical failure, judging by the notices and the reception.

What Damaged the Plays

I was, by then, being offered all sorts of movie jobs. One man offered me $500 a week. He was then the head of Paramount; poor man, Budd Schulberg's father. I thought going to Hollywood was the most immoral thing I could do, and yet who wouldn't want to go to Hollywood? When I finally went it was with a sense of disgrace, almost. A man came from MGM and just to get rid of him I said I wanted $4,000 a week. He called the Coast and arranged to pay me $4,000 weekly. I didn't accept the offer, but the company was making their usual sacrifices trying to keep *Paradise Lost* going, and I thought finally I'd go to Hollywood and send back half my salary to the Group Theatre to keep the play going. So in the end I signed with Paramount for $2,500 a week and sent back half to the Group Theatre. That was really not enough to keep the show going, and it closed after another couple of weeks. I went out there and wrote a movie, *The General Died at Dawn,* which was full of good ideas, but in the end it was a set of clichés on which we made some good birthday decorations.

But I'm not really interested in talking about Hollywood. I am interested in investigating not so much why—I understand why—but how I tried to take some kind of real life I knew and tried to press it into an ideological mold. How, actually technically, I used to try many ways to make the materials of my plays say something that they really were not saying by tacking on a certain ideological posture. I think this did damage to the plays and the material, but I couldn't have done otherwise in that period. It's the one thing that really disturbs me about the early plays—that I would very easily, very fluently and naturally, give an expression of a certain kind of life, and then try to tell the audience what it meant.

I think very simply that the material was always richer than the ideational direction that I tried to superimpose upon it. It was just enough to give birth to the material and let it say what it had to say. And yet, still in all, the life which was expressed, was impelled by some ideological direction in which I was going. It's almost like not trusting the material to make a statement, but you have to add a comment that was not really indigenous to the material. Jack Lawson, for instance, was a distinguished playwright, but he ruined himself artistically by tailoring his materials to fit an ideological conception. The last play he wrote, *Marching Song,* was concepted along these lines, and it's dead as a nail. I think it's a crime to see what happened to this juicy, gifted playwright when he got an ideology. Fortunately, however, the Left movement didn't absorb too many good talents. When I started to write *Awake and Sing!* I didn't have a mission in life; I wasn't going to change society. When I came to rewriting it I was going to change the world—or help change it. I should have learned a lesson from Ibsen; that it's simply enough to present the question. "You in the audience think about it; maybe you have some answers."

Soon after I arrived in Hollywood I began working on a new play, *The Silent Partner,* which is a very sympathetic portrayal of a man from an old American family who is ousted from his plant when the new management takes over. His sons have kind of drifted off; one killed himself in Hollywood while drunk, by jumping into a pool which didn't have any water in it. I've never rewritten the last act, but five of the nine scenes in it are the best writing I've ever done. The Group Theatre was going to do the play but I didn't have it ready. I was kind of discontented with myself and with the way things were going. I had come out to Hollywood to do a movie and now I was getting mixed up with the woman who was going to be my first wife. Finally I rented a little house where I started to work on the play seriously but all the while I was beginning to resent being pushed into plays for the Group Theatre. A play, when I put it into rehearsal, would never be ready, but the Group Theatre needed it, for there was always the prospect of the actors going without work.

When the play was finally put into rehearsal I was not quite satisfied with it yet. I had to sacrifice some of what I call the poetic quality of the play, because the texture was very dense as originally written, and in attempting to make things more concrete the play suffered, but still it kept most of its virtue. By then, with the help of FDR's Adminstration, the strikers had won and had organized all over the country into the CIO, and the play was a little dated in the sense that these big strikes were now a year or two behind us. The play was also critical of the working class. Because the point was, you know, stop the foolishness. For God's sake, get serious or die. You're going to die for lack of seriousness.

After *The Silent Partner* was in rehearsal for three or four days Clurman said to me, "Look, we'll produce any play you write. But you know this will be a very heavy and expensive production. We budgeted it for $40,000." So I said, "Why are you telling me all this?" and he said, "Well, the play will fail. We'll be out all that money and the actors will be out of work. But if you want us to do the play we will."

So I said, "Well, when you put it that way you don't give me much choice. Pull the play, then; don't do it." And I was very hurt, but not intelligent or mature enough to say, "Stop the shit and do the play. It's necessary for me. And after all the sacrifices I've made, just do the play and lose $40,000. It's worth it to me." And I never even tried to publish the play.

The production of that play was necessary for me, because nobody in the U.S. was writing that way. To this day nobody can write that way, including me. Everything was extremely heightened. You didn't know whether it was real, or mystic. Were these real human beings? Where was this happening? It was the beginning of a new striking out for me. You see, later, when I wrote a play that was successful, like *Golden Boy*, the Group Theatre had a treasury at last. It was quite all right for them to lose money, most of the time out of my pocket, on experimental things—to give Bobbie Lewis or Gadget Kazan a chance to direct something, to do trash by Irwin Shaw. But while it was necessary and good to help Gadget or Bobbie Lewis to become a director, or to do a special matinee performance of an Irwin Shaw play, I was the first necessity. I never put my mitts up. I just walked away.

"Really Quite a Good Play"

And then the group Theatre again was breaking up. Again there were no scripts. First of all, there was some impossible ideal. There was a time when we turned down plays like Maxwell Anderson's *Winterset* as not good enough for us. We realized later that we made a grave blunder there, but nobody was resourceful enough to go out and look for plays; the larder was always bare. This is why my plays always went on before they were finished.

Anyway, it looked like the Group Theatre was through. Strasberg and Cheryl Crawford had left; everybody kind of voluntarily disbanded for six months, and Harold Clurman came out here to Hollywood. It was very difficult for him to take the Group Theatre breakup. So I said, "I'll tell you what, Harold, I have an idea. You get the company together on October first and I'll have a new play." I told him in about two sentences what the play was about. I just said there was an Italian boy whose father wanted him to be a violinist and he has true gifts for that, but he wants to be a prizefighter. I had married Luise Rainer by then, and my bride of maybe six or eight months said, "What is that about? It's nothing. It sounds crazy." Harold said, "Let him alone, Luise. He knows what he's doing." She couldn't understand it and was rather bewildered. But he understood that something could come out of that; he knew how I worked.

I went back to the apartment in New York with my one page of notes for the new play, and Clurman set two or three actors to watch me to see that I didn't run off. All that summer I worked on *Golden Boy,* and it was ready I think before October first. I really wrote that play to be a hit, to keep the Group Theatre together. And it was a hit, my first really big hit. It pleased me, which was foolish on my part. It pleased me because now I was being accepted as a Broadway playwright. Before that I was kind of a nutty artist who had some kind of wild gift, and now, only now, was I a man with a ten-million-dollar arm who could really direct the ball just where I wanted it to go.

I must say, I think now that the circumstances under which I had written the play are what make me not like it. I feel the same way about *The Country Girl.* It doesn't mean anything to me; it's just a theater piece. I felt that way about *Golden Boy* for years afterwards, because it seemed to me to be really immoral to write a play for money. But I did see it once out here. Charlie Chaplin had never seen it, so the two wives, Charlie, and I jumped into a car and went to see it at the Pasadena Playhouse, and on seeing the play quite objectively, I thought, "Gee, this is really quite a good play." There's something written into it—a quality of American folk legend—that I really had nothing to do with. It was a much better play than I thought it was. So after that I made my peace with that play.

We revived it for ANTA in 1952. John Garfield always wanted to play the part and Lee Cobb played the father. By then, there were such accepted clichés for playing the parts that Garfield and Lee Cobb fell right into the stereotypes. Every once in a while Cobb would slouch onto the stage, very successful, at ease. Nobody can be so at home on a stage as Cobb, you know. And I'd say, "What are you playing? Are you playing a successful actor, or this rather humble, but perceptive old Italian father?" It was hard to try to break the stereotypes in four weeks.

One play I did like is *Rocket to the Moon*. It was based on an idea which I had for a long time, although I didn't know the real theme of it until I wrote it. I knew the play was going to take place in a dentist's office and that there was going to be a little dental secretary there who was going to take him away from his wife. But I didn't know that the play would be, so to speak, about love in America, about the search for love, and all the things it turned out to be about.

Plenty of my ideas kind of germinated sometimes for two or three years. On the other hand, sometimes I get an idea and sit down and write from just one page of notes. I find that those things often come out best when I don't know what's going to happen, and in fact, most of the time I don't know what I know or what I think until I say it. Ask me what I think about the world, about the kind of morality in this country, oh, I can give you some intellectual talk about it, but it's not till I write a play that I know what I really think, that I know where I am in the whole mess and can really make a statement that I didn't know was in me to make. That's one of the reasons that keeps me writing plays.

How *The Country Girl* Came About (1952)

In the Words of the People Involved

ARMAND AULICINO

The Country Girl, *jointly produced by Dwight Deere Wiman, Clifford Odets and Lee Strasberg, opened in New York on November 10, 1950, and proved to be Clifford Odets' first hit on Broadway since his Group Theatre days.*

BROOKS ATKINSON *in the* New York Times, *next morning:* "Odets has never written with so profound a knowledge of people as he does in *The Country Girl*."

CLIFFORD ODETS *on how it began:* "Very simply, I have thousands of ideas in my files; twenty or thirty plays outlined at a time. The important thing is what impels me to work on any one of them. In the case of *The Country Girl* the idea wasn't worked out very much. I happened to see Charles Coburn in New York and he mentioned he wanted to do a play. I looked in my files and got this idea and soon began to write. I soon realized that Coburn was too old for the triangle of the two men and the girl. Practically speaking, however, if Coburn hadn't mentioned wanting to do a play, I might not have started *The Country Girl*.

"I wrote at least two or three versions of the play before showing it to anyone. No one saw it before the fourth draft. The differences in the versions were mainly rewriting of certain scenes pertaining to the dramatic structure. I didn't know until the second draft, for example, that Georgie wasn't a very destructive, bitchy woman. She really was in the first drafts. She had cancer too, and discovers in the middle of the play she hasn't much time left to live. I wrote that out, however—How God-like. You give someone cancer, then take it away. Maybe playwrights should cure cancer, instead of doctors. Put a sheet of paper into the typewriter, take it out and cancer is cured."

BROOKS ATKINSON'S *review said:* "At least for the time being, Mr. Odets has set the ailing cosmos to one side and written a plain, human story."

Originally published in *Theatre Arts* (May 1952).

ODETS: "I never wrote a play that didn't tell a story. The only thing is that I usually verbalized the implications. It may be that in *The Country Girl*. I didn't verbalize them—things like what makes a man like Frank Elgin a drunkard."

"When I start to write, I have a general idea of the play. It expands as I write. In *The Country Girl* my point of view was held in abeyance because I wanted to accomplish something particular. I wanted to take simple elements and make something sharp and theatrical out of them. I stated a fact, the story of these people, rather than speculated about the fact.

"Someone who writes or works creatively doesn't function on all fronts at once. I can always write a good theatre piece. I ought to be able to do that. I'm forty-five and I've spent twenty-seven of those years in the theatre. But it's not my interest to write just a theatrical piece. Every so often I want to correct certain technical problems that bother me: It's like writing myself a lesson. I write fluently, but to combine a certain linear drive of story with psychological drive is the real problem. I don't know anyone who can do it, who ever did it.

"Theatre must appeal to man's immediate perception. Writing plays isn't like doing oil paintings. You can't say if they don't get it now, then they'll get it forty years later; the play doesn't usually survive that long. I'm a popular writer and I don't want to write for the library."

LEE STRASBERG, *co-producer of* The Country Girl, says: "In the first draft he showed me Georgie was already a positive character and sympathetic. I had a feeling at the time that Odets was aware of the destructiveness in people. It's not a psychological play since he couldn't have changed the role of the wife the way he did if it were. Odets is like most intelligent people in the theatre today. They find that the ideas they cherish come over too personally so they seek to be impersonal or theatrical. I feel *The Country Girl* has the straightforwardness of his earlier plays such as *Waiting for Lefty,* the quality of taking the directness of life and using it. This is evidenced by the way he uses the theatre background in *The Country Girl.* The scenes don't have the propaganda of *Lefty,* but they do have the same directness in making their point. He tried to follow through with the theme of the story and not allow himself to tell the audience his own feelings."

BORIS ARONSON, *who designed the sets:* "If you're familiar with Odets' work, you know everything he writes is written personally. He was trying to get *inside* of the people because the story, like that of every great play or movie, when told in three sentences seems like nothing has happened. But when you *see* it, the *inside* has so much to it; so much humanity, and it's so deeply felt that the conventional story becomes something you identify yourself with."

Clifford Odets set The Country Girl *in a theatrical background.*

ODETS: "I might have set it that way because I missed the theatre."

LEE STRASBERG: "Odets first described the play to me as beginning in an empty theatre while rehearsals are going on."

BORIS ARONSON: "There is nothing more glamorous and more sad than backstage in the theatre. There is something about the very *nakedness* of a rehearsal which is dramatic because it it stripped of all the superficiality that's added later."

The entire subject of the theatrical background of the play reflects Mr. Odets' growth as a writer.

LEE STRASBERG: "This was his first show on his own. I felt it was an important thing for him to do. Anything that brought him closer to the theatre was good. As a director, he works from the character's point of view."

FORREST C. HARING, *company manager, on Odets' direction:* "His approach is different with each actor. He works nicely with them—takes them aside and talks quietly about what the people are like in his plays. He talks about the characters, rather than tries to demonstrate what the actors should do. He never reads lines for an experienced actor."

LEE STRASBERG: "Odets works logically. He explains what's supposed to be happening. He's very concerned about character behavior."

ODETS *on directing:* "The requirements of the play are such that each scene must be played as written—there isn't much room for interpretation by the director.

"To my mind there are three ways to direct a play. First, *critically.* That is, to analyze each scene and moment for the actors. Secondly, to direct it *synthetically,* to take the material of the play and create something new out of it by enlarging it. Thirdly, and the best way, is a combination of both. In the years I've spent in the theatre, I almost feel that it is better not to have the actors know too much of the philosophical overtones of a play. The affinity of the actor to the part is far more important. I'm against this business of philosophical nonsense where an actor with three lines wants to know what his motivation is to say 'Hello' to the lead during a minor moment."

BORIS ARONSON *on his settings for the production:* "My entire approach was based on the conception of Odets' trying to get *inside* his characters. The play is mostly about two people on stage. I felt there should be a feeling of great emptiness on the stage during the rehearsal scene as contrasted with the very limited, condensed and tiny place where they live, with everything cluttered up. I wanted to create the feeling you get with so many actors, that if they walked out, you'd feel they had never lived there at all. Then, there's the dressing room. I attempted to dramatize different things. The Boston one was very depressing: The beams overhead, the steam pipes showing and the walls broken down. That's because the play at that time is at its lowest point.

Frank is drunk, he is failing, etc. Finally, the most attractive setting, comparatively speaking, in color, proportion and design, was the last scene. This is where there's hope, where they succeed and can look forward to life confidently."

Within this setting, the play deals with the story of the three main characters: Of the alcoholic actor making a comeback, his wife who is losing hope of a life with him and the young director who has faith in the actor.

FORREST C. HARING: "As in the case of all playwrights, the characters are all different expressions of Odets. He was concerned with the problems of personal relationship and the adjustment necessary to solve them. Man cannot live alone."

LEE STRASBERG: "Odets has a romantic attitude of life. Not quite in the sense that 'Love conquers all,' but that in the feeling people have for each other there is a great deal of life force. He's concerned with the misunderstandings people have of each other and their cruelty. Not in the political or economic sense, but in a purely human sense."

In Odet's mind, Georgie was the leading character, but Boris Aronson leaned heavily toward Frank Elgin, the actor.

ARONSON: "That's because he's extremely important: Of course his wife's important too—but he's a combination: He has real glamor although he's a lot of trouble to his wife. That's why she stays with him. A real play is when two people are *both* right. No drama exists when one is a villain and the other pure gold. Georgie is very right and you understand her. And Frank, on the other hand, is an artist; he is sensitive and things go wrong and he takes to drink.

"The reason I lean toward Frank in terms of the environment of the play is because Georgie didn't have a chance to create a permanent home. So I couldn't dramatize it. She couldn't do it on the empty stage, in the little room—or in the Boston dressing room. That's why the only scene that was pleasant was the one in New York. I couldn't dramatize her world of living because she's fighting it all the time. She doesn't have the chance to do anything about where they are."

The last scene of The Country Girl *is the dressing room in New York during Frank's opening night in the play within the play.*

ODETS: "As it is now written, the action is resolved by Georgie sticking with Frank and Bernie going off alone. But the real interpretation of what will happen to these people is for the reader or the audience. The last scene was not in the play until four or five nights before the New York opening."

Odets knew he had a problem with the last scene but wanted to wait until the play went into rehearsal to take advantage of things he could visualize once the actors had assumed their roles.

ODETS: "The last scene is the best technical job I ever did. It could only be on opening night in New York. What woman would leave her husband then but a real positive horror of a gal. The audience wants to know about the wife and the director. Will she stay or will she leave him? Will Frank be a hit, will he hit the bottle again, etc. And all this is covered in only *nine* typed pages of script. I had more fun in rewriting the last scene than anything I've ever done. I was worried. I wanted to stay out another week, but it all worked out fine."

LEE STRASBERG: "I'm proud of his last scene, too. It was real 'reworking.' It was done by *working;* it didn't just happen. It was an actual problem that had to be dealt with, and he tackled it. This was an achievement for him!"

BROOKS ATKINSON: "Clifford Odets has really got down to work. *The Country Girl* is the best play he has written for years, perhaps the best play of his career."

ESSAYS

◆

Clifford Odets and the Creative Imagination

George L. Groman

Clifford Odets, for all of his adult life as a playwright and screenwriter, marveled at the gift of creativity, finding inspiration when that gift seemed within his grasp and enduring depression when it seemed beyond reach. His own experience operated as both a resource and an obstacle as he sought to resolve a number of personal crises—as a son whose father viewed his early acting and writing efforts with contempt, as a lover and husband whose stormy relationships ended in failure and bitterness, and as a creative artist whose need for privacy and discipline conflicted again and again with the temptations and demands of a public life and reputation. Yet whatever his own circumstances, Odets consistently sought fulfillment as a writer, viewing the creative act with reverence and continuing attention, and finding in the efforts of others inspiration as well as validation for his own creative identity.

Even as a boy, Odets was drawn to writers of powerful imagination whose heroes struggled with questions of identity and self-realization through social action or artistic effort. As a teenager Odets read Victor Hugo's *Les Misérables,* a book to which he would invariably return and comment on with great affection. Indeed, in his 1940 journal, he called Hugo "the rich love of my boyhood days" and went on to describe *Les Misérables* as "the most profound art experience I have ever had." The French author, as Odets noted, influenced him in ways that were to affect his later life as a writer and political activist: "Hugo . . . inspired me, made me aspire; I wanted to be a good and noble man, longed to do heroic deeds with my bare hands, thirsted to be kind to people, particularly the weak and humble and oppressed. From Hugo I had my first feeling of social consciousness. He did not make me a romantic, but he heightened in me that romanticism which I already had. I loved him and love him still, that mother [sic] of my literary heart."[1]

For a boy entering adolescence, Hugo's clear division of right and

This essay was written specifically for this volume and is published here for the first time by permission of the author.

wrong, his demarcation of heroes and villains, and the endless pursuits of the relentless Inspector Javert must have met the young Odets's need for suspense and adventure. More important, ultimately, was Hugo's gallery of characters who were capable of heroism *and* sacrifice—the saintly Bishop of Digne, whose every action is devoted to those in need; Fantine, who sells her hair and even her teeth, hoping to preserve the life of her daughter; the young radical and romantic Marius Pontmercy, who gives up an inheritance on political principle; and the hero of heroes, the solitary convict Jean Valjean, who benefits from the Bishop's generosity and repays him by pursuing a life of good works despite enormous personal sacrifice.

Odets was to continue his search for mentors of powerful and wide-ranging vision, and in the American writers Emerson and Whitman he found new inspiration and direction. As he wrote to Harold Clurman in 1932, it was the business-oriented Louis Odets, the writer's father, who first encouraged him to consider Emerson seriously. Margaret Brenman-Gibson quotes from this letter, in which Odets recalls his father leaving in his room "two volumes of a peculiar edition of Emerson 'made for business men.' In a gaily mocking account of this . . . [Odets] says, 'The devils quote and underline on every page glorious trumpet sounding maxims about success. They make Emerson the first Bruce Barton of his country. But I am reading with a clear brain and no interest in success.' Emerson is 'certainly the wisest American.' "[2]

Reflecting further on Emerson's importance to him, Odets wrote in his 1932 journal, "I am glad that Emerson lived before I did. He has made life a richer thing for many many [*sic*] of us. That is the function of all great men: that they reveal to us natural truths, ourselves and a realization of ourselves."[3] Writing again in the same journal, he reflected on Emerson in a way that seemed to echo Hugo: "Emerson says somewhere that heroes are bred only in times of danger. I would add great artists are too bred in such times. Now I see the world is drifting into such times. I am waiting to see what heroes and artists will spring from the people."[4]

Although Odets would come to share Emerson's belief that people are not fundamentally bad, he commented that few could or would rise to Emerson's call for "uncorrupted behavior."[5] That he continued to brood over this loss of Emerson's faith in his fellow humans is amply demonstrated in his plays and elsewhere. Even near the end of his life, in a telecast interview, he would remember "what Emerson called 'uncorrupted behavior' " as a quality "with which all children are born . . . when nothing outside of yourself influences you, when you are in command of yourself with honor, without dishonesty, without lie, when you grasp and deal, and are permitted to deal, with exactly what's in front of you, in terms of your best human instincts."[6]

To be sure, Odets could and did find many calls for "uncorrupted behavior" in Emerson's work and that of other writers, but what he seems to have valued most in Emerson was his belief in the range of human potentialities despite the limitations of time, place, accident, or fate. It was Emerson who had emphasized in "Circles" that "there are no fixtures in nature. The universe is fluid and volatile,"[7] and in "Fate" that nature, rather than being limited to destructiveness, "solicits the pure in heart to draw on all its omnipotence."[8] In "Circles" Emerson remarked that "the use of literature is to afford us a platform whence we may command a view of our present life, a purchase by which we may move it."[9] Such statements were meant to clear the way to new horizons and did so for Odets and countless others.

Like Hugo and Emerson, Walt Whitman assumed heroic proportions for Odets, who even kept a plaster cast of the poet in his room.[10] In 1940 he bought first editions of *November Boughs* and *Drum Taps,* as well as a collection of Whitman's letters to his mother.[11] In 1947, when Odets's only son was born, he named him Walt Whitman Odets.

If the large-scale models of Emerson and Whitman were encouraging, Odets nevertheless understood that American life might bring forth artists of quite different scope and temperament. In conversations with the composer Aaron Copland at Dover Furnace, the Group Theatre's summer retreat, Odets came to grips with this issue. He noted that "today the artists are not big, full, epic, and Aaron shows what I mean. They squeeze art out a thousandth of an inch at a time, and that is what their art, for the most part, lacks: bigness, vitality and health and swing and lust and charity. . . ." Odets concludes by asserting, "there I go to Whitman again. Of course that's what we need, men of Whitman's size."[12]

In another entry in the 1932 journal, Odets suggests that Whitman "roars in your ears all the time. When you swing your arms and the muscles flex, they are Whitman's muscles too."[13] Elsewhere Odets celebrates not only the strength that may come with well-being but also the sexuality and autoeroticism that made Whitman famous and, in the nineteenth century, generally disreputable: "I think with love o [sic] Whitman's lines, something like, 'Oh the amplitude of the earth, and the coarsness [sic] and sexuality of it and the great goodness and clarity of it.' And I myself feel that way with love for people and the earth and women and dark nights and being together and close to naked women, naked as I am naked."[14]

Eventually, Odets's excitement and passion would cool—a result of hard living, many personal and professional disappointments, and, simply, aging. However, it may be that Whitman's imagery linked to a sense of purpose remained embedded in the playwright's consciousness, as suggested by a passage written a year before his death: "The whole fabric of my creative life I have built a room in which every corner there is a cobweb. They have mostly been swept away and I must begin again, *spinning out of myself* [italics mine] the dust and 'shroudness' of that room with its belaced and silent corners."[15] The passage brings to mind Whitman's noiseless, patient spider involved in the act of creation, launching forth "filament, filament, filament, out of itself." Like the spider, the narrator's soul in the second verse of Whitman's poem (now personified) sends out "gossamer thread" to "catch somewhere," thereby hoping to end a pattern of isolation. If Odets, like the spider and soul of the poem, sought to reach out to others, he seemed also to be settling old scores here, undergoing a ritualistic purgation in a rather stifling atmosphere and, in doing so, readying himself for the task of creation, which Whitman's spider image so powerfully evokes.

Odets's search for heroic models extended to the musical world as well as to literature, and in the life and work of Beethoven he found a source of inspiration that was to last until his death. Odets listened to Beethoven's music frequently and intensively, wrote on Beethoven's importance as a creative artist and man of his time, and would sometimes self-consciously compare and contrast Beethoven's problems and solutions with his own. In his early attempts at fiction and drama, Odets used the maimed musician or composer as a central figure.[16] Indeed, in his unproduced play *Victory* he carefully modeled the hero, Louis Brant, on Beethoven himself. In later years in Hollywood, Odets also planned a screenplay on the composer's life, but the project was never completed.

Beethoven's early poverty, his difficult social relationships (often with women), and his dedication to his art (despite hearing problems and eventual deafness) greatly moved Odets. And in looking at W. J. Turner's biography of the composer, which Odets read while writing *Victory,* he would find one acquaintance of Beethoven remarking of him "that he loved his art more than any woman" and "that he could not love any woman who did not know how to value his art."[17] Later, as Beethoven's hearing problems increased in severity and further isolated him, the composer thought of suicide but desisted, "art alone" restraining his hand. At other times he wrote of seizing "fate by the throat" to reach his goals.[18] Clearly, for Odets, Beethoven was a truly courageous man and artist despite his personal difficulties.

Odets, in commenting on Beethoven's music, found the Eroica Symphony "an awesome and terrible piece of work" and his fourth piano concerto a composition in which the "characters of the orchestra never for a moment stop their exuberant conversation."[19] As for Beethoven's Seventh Symphony, he noted, one must "be virgin of heart and spirit to write it. Beethoven did not lose the innocence," though ordinary mortals give it up simply "to survive."[20] Odets's descriptions, quoted here, underscore the intensity of his feelings about Beethoven and sometimes suggest Emersonian parallels. They also indicate the kind of close thematic connections between music and literature the writer would make in his plays and films.[21]

As Odets struggled with form, so did the Old Master, but Beethoven triumphed again and again. As Odets put it, "every time he found a form for his content he simultaneously found that his content had progressed in depth and a new form was necessary—a very Tantalus of life! He, however, had the hardheadedness to see it through to the bitter end—he obviously died looking for a new form—and he died having pushed music to a level which before had never been attained nor has yet been equalled. Great unhappy man!"[22]

Finally, in Beethoven, Odets found a paradigm for the quintessential Romantic—a superman for all seasons—one who is "amazed, impressed, delighted, and enraged by the caprices of life." As Odets noted further, "It is the romantic who cries out that he is out of harmony with life—by which he means that life is not in harmony with his vision of it, the way he saw it as a youth with moral and idealistic hunger to mix his hands in it and live fully and deeply. The classic art is to accept life, the romantic to reject it as it is and attempt to make it over as he wants it to be."[23] The man and his method were for Odets a means of perception, a symbol of hope, and possibly a basis for social action and change.

When we turn to Odets's own work, however, we find a curious paradox. The heroic models have disappeared, and in their place the protagonists of his plays respond at a primal level to a brutal, self-serving world; either they are (or become) corrupt or they are overwhelmed by an environment over which they have little or no control. Indeed, the America that Odets lived in and responded to was far different from the private and idealized world about which he wrote with such intensity and even affection and that he later abandoned with such regret. In *Waiting for Lefty* (1935), Odets's first-produced and perhaps most well-known play, there is a rousing call for strike action by the rank and file of a taxi union after much indecision and argument. However, Lefty, the guiding spirit of the union, has already been murdered by unknown assailants, and even the ringing call to action at the end of the play suggests martyrdom as well as the benefits of solidarity. As Agate, one of the rallying strikers, puts it, "HELLO AMERICA! HELLO. WE'RE STORMBIRDS OF THE WORKING-CLASS. WORKERS OF THE WORLD. . . . OUR BONES AND BLOOD! And when *we die* they'll know what we did to make a new world! *Christ, cut us up to little pieces. We'll die* for what is right! put fruit trees *where our ashes are!*" [My italics.][24]

In *Awake and Sing!* (1935), Odets's Depression-era play centered on an American-Jewish family in the Bronx, the Marxist Grandfather Jacob is ineffectual even in his own family and ends his life by suicide. His grandson Ralph Berger, who surrenders the insurance money Jacob had left him at his mother's insistence, will in all likelihood have little influence in times to come. As a number of critics have suggested, his optimism strikes a false note as he faces the future without a clear sense of purpose, training, or money. Indeed, as more than one character comes to understand, despite arguments to the contrary, life *is* "printed on dollar bills." The well-to-do Uncle Morty, a dress manufacturer, will continue to have the respect of Ralph's mother Bessie, he will continue to oppose strike action vigorously and probably successfully, and he will lead a personal life without personal responsibilities, sleeping with showroom models and seeking other creature comforts. Moe Axelrod, the World War One veteran and ex-bootlegger, has by the end of the play convinced Bessie's daughter Hennie to abandon her much-abused husband and infant to seek a life of pleasure with him. To be sure, arguments for social or family responsibility may be found in this often moving play, but the resolution nevertheless seems to suggest a definition of success devoid of commitment or love.

In *Golden Boy* (1937), Joe Bonaparte,[25] a violinist turned boxer, does become a hero *for his time,* defined by physical strength and a willingness to incapacitate or destroy his opponents in the prize ring. Although he has read the encyclopedia from cover to cover (perhaps fulfilling Ralph Berger's quest for learning) and "practiced his fiddle for ten years," the *private* world he has created is no longer sufficient for him. It cannot offer him the sense of power or perhaps the ability to dominate others for which he yearns. Indeed, he is seduced by the monied world that surrounds the prize arena and by the temptations offered by the gangster Eddie Fuseli, who seeks to remold the Golden Boy and turn him into a fighting machine—careless of others, indifferent to love, and irrevocably cut off from family ties and memories of the past. As the reborn Joe aggressively puts it, "When a bullet sings through the air it has no past—only a future—like me." Joe returns to his dressing room after what is to be his last fight, and his trainer, Tokio, notices that one eye is badly battered, symbolic of Joe's impairment of vision on a number of levels. The triumphant fighter learns that he has killed his opponent in the ring, and he must confront the implications of the disaster. In rejecting a personal integrity, he has betrayed his moral and spiritual center, and at the end of the play he dies, an apparent suicide. His personal tragedy is an awareness of the vacuity his life has become. He is trapped in a world that he himself has made, rejecting his father's simple but encompassing Old-World Italian version of what his personal struggle must lead to: fulfillment of a dream predicated on the yells of a mob over ten rounds, the quick buck, and tabloid headlines forgotten at a glance.

Both *The Big Knife* (1948) and *The Country Girl* (1950) are plays that show the failure of art and artists destroyed by a world that demands too much, too fast, too soon. In *The Big Knife,* Charlie Castle has given up a promising career in the theater and a somewhat vague belief in political and social action[26] to become one of Hollywood's big stars. Like Joe Bonaparte or perhaps Odets himself, Charlie is plagued by the idea that he has betrayed his considerable talent in exchange for money and stardom. Early in the play, he argues that the theater is "a bleeding stump. Even stars have to wait years for a decent play." Now in the movie business, he cannot afford "acute attacks of integrity." In a succession of films, he reflects "the average in one way or another" or is at best "the warrior of the forlorn hope." As Hank Teagle, a family friend, puts it, "Half-idealism is the peritonitis of the soul. America is full of it."

Like Joe Bonaparte, Charlie understands only too well what he has become. He remarks that he has become an imitation of his old self, and young new actors now imitate—or parody—the imitation. However, it is Marion Castle, Charlie's estranged wife, who most emphatically reminds

Charlie of his self-betrayal, warning that he acts against his own nature. She says to him, "Your passion of the heart has become a passion of the appetite. Despite your best intentions, you're a horror."

Indeed, Charlie has taken a downward path. He is on the way to becoming an alcoholic, he has been unfaithful to his wife, and he has avoided prosecution for an accident that occurred during an evening of drunken driving by allowing a studio employee to confess in his place and serve a prison term.[27] Only when the studio management obliquely threatens to murder the woman companion turned blackmailer who was with him on the evening of the accident does Charlie assert himself by preventing a new crime. However, despite his one moment of decency, Charlie is lost. He has, over Marion's objections, signed a new contract with the studio moguls who have by turns enticed and threatened him. Too weak to face a loss of status, poverty, and the unstable life of the theater, perversely attracted by the life he has been leading, and yet filled with self-loathing, Charlie takes his own life. Marion, his wife, leaves with Hank Teagle, the writer who has been faithful to his principles and whom Charlie had called his Horatio. Indeed, it is Teagle who will tell Charlie's story to the world—the tale of a man who was certainly not a Hamlet in depth or breadth, one who could understand and even dream but who could not change himself or the world, which paradoxically offered him so much and so little.

In *The Country Girl,* a play better structured and developed than *The Big Knife,* Broadway director Bernie Dodd is ready to take a chance on a new play starring a has been, an older actor named Frank Elgin. Dodd is "in love with art" and tells Elgin's wife Georgie that although he could "make a fortune in films," he intends to continue in the theater, where important work can still be done. Elgin's brilliant performances in two mediocre plays, based on his intuitive understanding of character and situation, had long ago inspired Dodd and now lead him to believe that the old actor can excel again. However, there are real problems. Elgin is weak and self-indulgent, he is an alcoholic, he is a liar, he needs constant reassurance, and like Arthur Miller's Willy Loman, he needs desperately to be well liked. As the play develops, Bernie Dodd and Georgie struggle with each other and with Frank. Each of the three seeks personal fulfillment, but finally the play becomes the all-consuming and all-important issue. Frank Elgin does succeed (with the help of the two closest to him) in rising to his full stature as an actor. He vindicates Bernie's judgment and justifies (or necessitates) Georgie's remaining with him—after years of failure and disappointment.

In this play about theater life, Frank Elgin's transgressions are forgiven in the name of art and artistry. Bernie discovers that Frank has lied about his wife's past. He has told Bernie that Georgie was once Miss America (possibly to enhance his own prestige),[28] that she is an alcoholic, and that she is a depressive who has attempted suicide. Georgie learns that Frank has lied about her (his lies are partially based on a play in which he once appeared) and observes that he has begun to drink again. When the producer (Phil Cook), Bernie Dodd, and others in the company find out, there is turmoil, but there are no lasting repercussions. Because of Bernie's belief in Frank Elgin's talent, the actor is to continue in the play. Frank himself is simply following an old pattern. He has for much of his adult life drunk steadily, taken pills, and lied to relieve the pressures on him. When his and Georgie's only child dies, when he loses much of his money in producing a play, and when he begins to fail as an actor, the old remedies are close at hand. The conflict between the easy indulgence of the moment and the stern realities of working in a creative but uncertain world—with its quick rewards and even quicker condemnations—leads to the kind of disintegration Odets so often sought to depict. In this play, as in *The Big Knife,* intuitive understanding, talent, and artistry bring some forms of self-fulfillment and recognition, but are by themselves no protection against weakness or personal loss. In *The Big Knife,* Charlie Castle finds suicide the only way out. Frank Elgin is successful at the end of *The Country Girl,* but one suspects that his future success will depend on the continued availability of the long-suffering wife who mothers him, on directors and producers who excuse his frequent lapses, on unending applause, and on total self-involvement and self-delusion.

Odets, then, in his work revealed his fascination with the world of art and his belief that art may enhance our understanding of the human condition, though it cannot alter the environment or our responses to it. The romantic vision that Odets pursued so intensely in a personal way might seem ennobling or heroic, but in a world of shrunken values and failed personal lives, it offers only a sense, a resonance, of what might have been. Indeed, the romantic stance—as Odets portrayed it in the America of his time—was collateral to be called in, leaving only a shell without substance. Despite the excitements of the conflict, Odets's vision of the truth was profoundly pessimistic. That he portrayed it as he did often showed courage as well as artistry.

Notes

1. Clifford Odets, *The Time Is Ripe: The 1940 Journal of Clifford Odets* (New York: Grove Press, 1988), 334.

2. Quoted in Margaret Brenman-Gibson, *Clifford Odets: American Playwright* (New York: Atheneum, 1982), 216.

3. Clifford Odets, personal paper, 18 May 1932, Lincoln Center Archives of the New York Public Library (hereinafter cited as LCA). All material quoted from the LCA collection is copyright © 1990 by Walt Odets and Nora Odets. Reprinted by permission of the Estate of Clifford Odets.

4. LCA, 26 July 1932.

5. Brenman-Gibson, 218.

6. Telecast interview with Herman Harvey, quoted in Harold Cantor, *Clifford Odets: Playwright-Poet* (Metuchen, N.J.: Scarecrow Press, 1978), 207.

7. *Complete Essays and Other Writings of Ralph Waldo Emerson* (New York: Modern Library, 1950), 279.

8. Ralph Waldo Emerson, *The Conduct of Life* (New York: Dolphin Books, n.d.), 35.

9. *Complete Essays,* 285.

10. Cantor, 51.

11. *The Time Is Ripe,* 343.

12. LCA, 28 July 1932. In November 1937, in an essay published in the *New York Times* entitled "Democratic Vistas in Drama," Odets cited Whitman's complaint in 1871 that American theater was engaged in trivial pursuits and did not truly represent American life or ideals. Odets echoed this concern for his own time but went on to assert that the film industry, in developing a folk drama, had gone at least part of the way to meet Whitman's criticism.

13. LCA, 18 May 1932.

14. LCA, 20 July 1930.

15. LCA, July 1962.

16. As early as 1923, Odets read and recommended Israel Zangwill's *The Melting Pot* (Brenman-Gibson, p. 69), a play dealing with the assimilation of immigrants in America. Interestingly, the immigrant hero, David Quixano, is a Russian-Jewish violinist who had suffered a shoulder injury during a pogrom in his native land. Unable to perform at a high level because of this injury, he turns to composing and is successful at it.

17. W. J. Turner, *Beethoven: The Search for Reality* (London: J. M. Dent & Sons, 1945), 78.

18. Turner, 66.

19. *The Time Is Ripe,* 291.

20. *The Time Is Ripe,* 312.

21. For a discussion of these connections, see my essay, "Clifford Odets's Musical World: the Failed Utopia," in *Studies in American Jewish Literature* 5 (1986): 80–88.

22. *The Time Is Ripe,* 38.

23. *The Time Is Ripe,* 84.

24. *Six Plays of Clifford Odets* (New York: Grove Press, 1982), 31.

25. Hugo, in *Les Misérables,* describes the French aristocracy and bourgeoisie during the post-Waterloo decades in considerable detail. Frequently, when Napoleon is mentioned, he is contemptuously referred to as Buonaparté, emphasizing his obscure Corsican-Italian (rather than French) background. Joe Bonaparte is the son of poor Italian immigrants.

26. Charlie recalls at one point reading Hugo, who had urged compassion and help for the lost and fallen.

27. In Hugo's *Les Misérables,* Jean Valjean reveals his true identity in a court of law. He does so to prove the innocence of a man wrongly accused of a crime after being misidentified as Jean Valjean. As a result, he must give up his position as mayor of a town he has governed successfully and faces the possibility of a lifetime in prison. Odets's plot reversal does much to indicate the extent of Charlie's moral decay.

28. R. Baird Shuman, *Clifford Odets* (New Haven, Conn.: Twayne Publishers, 1962), 131.

Clifford Odets and the Found Generation

MALCOLM GOLDSTEIN

Our machine had been in a smash-up too. But we wanted to remain on the
scene of the accident and see if we could fix it. We thought we could save it.
Instead of a *lost* generation, I guess you might call us a *found* generation. We
found out what was wrong. We were pretty damn sure we'd have something
new out of all this mess that would be better than anything you had before.
—Budd Schulberg, *The Disenchanted*

The death of Clifford Odets in August, 1963, at the age of fifty-seven,
was followed by obituaries in the *New York Times* and *Variety* resembling in
their complaining tone the notices of a play which has not quite come up to
expectations. The playwright, it was recalled, had been recognized in the
thirties as a "writer of promise," the American reviewers' standard description of any new dramatist whose work is tolerable; the question now was
whether in his twenty-eight years of fame Odets had ever passed beyond the
promising state. Two months later NBC television inaugurated the weekly
series of plays on which Odets had spent his last months; the producers' plan
was that he should write a few of the pieces himself and choose the rest from
new scripts submitted by other writers. Although his well-wishers were
hopeful that the series would belie the strictures of the obituaries, the program was too dismal to last beyond an initial thirteen weeks. All the plays
were dull, the two by Odets no less than the others. The most recently
completed and produced work by the playwright before the posthumous
debacle was a 1961 film, *Wild in the Country* starring Elvis Presley.

The thinning of Odets's once considerable talent over the last dozen
years of his life was and is a loss to the American theater. The talent was never
of such magnitude that it could be confused with genius, but it was substantial enough to create at least four plays of broad popular appeal and to leave
traces of itself on passages of dialogue in even the meagerest of the remainder.
Moreover, in number alone the works are impressive: eleven plays produced
on Broadway do not constitute a negligible record. Yet it is true that all but
three were staged between 1935 and 1941 and that the plays of 1949, 1950,
and 1954, though better received than a few that preceded them, are ill-

Originally published in *American Drama and Its Critics*, edited by Alan S. Downer (Chicago: University of
Chicago Press, 1965). Reprinted by permission of University of Chicago Press.

composed. Some of the causes of the decline are likely to remain permanently hidden from readers, if indeed they did not remain hidden from Odets himself. However shrewd our guesses, we cannot confidently account for such symptoms of disorder as the sloth and narrow attention-span that cursed his later years—cannot, that is, know why after 1954 he began play after play with enthusiasm, only to let each drop before completion. But there is much in the troubled, fitful career that is not concealed, and it makes up part of the history of not one playwright alone, but of an entire generation in the theater.

The principal problem for Odets was the difficulty of finding appropriate focal points for his abundant sympathies. Plots came easily, themes did not. As late as 1949 he continued to write the best American plays of the thirties, and nothing else. Much the most skilled of the radical playwrights of the Depression stage, he wrote his first plays of economic injustice with such flair that the political right and left alike acknowledged their theatrical viability. Nevertheless, he was capable of no greater judgment than may be credited to the less intelligent dramatists of his generation; in attempting to develop class-consciousness among the Depression's victims for an attack upon their presumed oppressors, he did not recognize that he was merely substituting one brand of materialism for another. More damaging to the growth of his talent was the inability to free himself completely, as the years passed along, from the materialist theme with which he began his career. His perception of the world around him dimmed with the beginning of the national economic recovery late in the prewar decade, and the mind that should have taken cognizance of the new situation contented itself with after-images of the poverty of the Depression's worst years. It is true that Odets took up other issues in certain works, particularly in his late plays; but whether subsidiary or paramount, class-consciousness is never absent, regardless of the year and the remoteness of his characters' concerns from money worries. Having taken a stand with the destitute proletariat, he could not recognize the fact of a rising employment index. After the first six plays, handsomely brought together in an omnibus volume in 1939, Odets's work dwindled in relevance to the age, until finally, after 1954, he could give the stage nothing at all.

At the beginning, however, it was another matter. Odets's ability and interest revealed themselves in precisely the right place and time. Few would-be playwrights can have been more fortunate in their circumstances than was Odets as a young man. Employed as an actor in the perennially embattled, hard-pressed Group Theater, he received, to be sure, not a scrap more than a living wage, but he was at least secure—secure both economically and emotionally. The Group's historic position as the most seminal organization in American theatrical history was achieved by the determination of its original directors, Lee Strasberg, Harold Clurman, and Cheryl Crawford, to exert maximum effort for the security of the company which they had assembled at the beginning of the decade. In the midst of general economic dislocation, the Group members were assured food and shelter by their directors and were encouraged by their sense of community to give the best of themselves in performance. Their willingness to live as a collective on a slim margin was indicative of their social attitudes. A few—far from enough to control policy—joined the Communist Party; none stood further to the right than the position occupied by the New Deal administration, which the President himself described as being a little left of center. In this society it did not matter that Odets was not a notable actor, since he only accepted inconspicuous parts; on stage and off, each performer used his resources for the benefit of all and took according to his needs. Despite occasional comments to the contrary, all were committed to the ideal of social theater, and it was a rare play that could attract them unless it embodied a cry of protest against poverty, militarism, fascism, or bigotry. With such certainty that it is stunning to contemplate, they knew precisely where they stood, what they wished to achieve for themselves and for the populace in general, and how, as craftsmen, to express their feelings to advantage. When in 1933 Odets began to work on the play ultimately titled *Awake and Sing!*, he wrote with complete awareness of his colleagues' virtuosity and social commitment. Always troubled by a shortage of appropriate plays, they were pleased to discover an effective dramatist in their own ranks.

But for all its theatrical skill, the Group lacked literary discrimination. Of the two dozen pieces mounted between 1931 and 1941, more than half were ineptly written. Often, however, as with Sidney Kingsley's *Men in White,* the company could add out of its own technique the strength missing from the material submitted by an author. Their passion was altogether too strong to allow for good judgment. It is, moreover, conjectural whether greater flexibility on the part of the directors and actors could have affected Odets's work, since he was as eager as they to record with intense heat the new social awareness of his age. His haste resulted frequently in a marked crudeness of construction and the employment of ill-conceived symbols and awkward stage-groupings. In such successes as *Awake and Sing!* and *Golden Boy,* as well as in lesser plays, stretches of bathos fall between moments of lively dialogue.

The zeal and self-righteousness constituting the manner that the Group displayed to the world are present not only in these plays but in *Waiting for Lefty, Till the Day I Die,* and *Paradise Lost.* All are class-conscious, revolutionary plays, and with the exception of *Golden Boy,* a tragedy, all embody elements of *agitprop* (short for "agitation-propaganda"), the optimistic, aggressive dramatic form promulgated after the crash of 1929 by workers' theaters close to the Communist Party. Providing for maximum dynamism and minimum logic, the form posits two forces which clash bitterly on stage in brief but harrowing action. In the first examples of *agitprop,* the forces are groups of industrial overlords—the "bosses"—on the one hand and underpaid workers on the other. Unlike their employers, the workers lack organization at the outset, but with the help of a strong and usually young leader they unite to win their demands. In due course as the form became popular the contentions exposed on stage took place between Communists and fascists, Communist unions and the A.F.L., Negroes and bigoted whites, and the *Daily Worker* and the Hearst press; for broad distribution, many were published in *Workers' Theatre,* a leftist monthly of the early thirties. Odets along with the rest of the Group was aware of this new form and sensitive to its impact; for its second production the company had offered an elaborate work modeled directly on the *agitprop* format: Claire and Paul Sifton's *1931—.* In 1934 two members, Art Smith and Elia Kazan, collaborated on an *agitprop* piece titled *Dimitroff* which presented to American audiences the events of the trials following the Reichstag fire, and Group personnel performed in it to benefit the New Theater League, a federation of workers' and other socialminded troupes. The entire company, and especially those members dissatisfied with the directors' refusal to move further to the left, took a sharp interest in the radical theaters of the city. Some worked in various capacities with the Theater Union and the Theater Collective, new professional troupes organized in the hope of attracting intellectuals as well as workers to programs of social drama. Odets himself gave acting classes to members of the Theater Union. It is understandable that when a few of the Group became dramatists, they should turn to the agitational mode. Having joined the Communist Party late in 1934, Odets composed a play expressing the firmness of his commitment: *Waiting for Lefty,* an *agitprop* drama which took the form to a level of excellence it had never before reached. After an opening night on which the audience in delirium stormed the stage to congratulate the actors, it played across the nation. According to the playwright's count, recorded in *New Theatre* (the successor to *Workers' Theatre*) for January, 1936, it played in 104 cities in eight months of 1935; through the thirties it continued to be performed.

The play is unique among the works of Odets in its over-all adherence to the basic *agitprop* design. Although the strike of the New York taxi drivers, his point of departure, had been settled early in the year, the memory was fresh enough to provide strong pro-labor material. In the approved manner, the play presents a power struggle between opposing classes; since the taxi union officers act as the mouthpieces of management and not as the standard bearers of the men who elected them, they are the oppressors of the honest rank-and-file drivers. The traditional young leader of the poorly organized union dissidents is one Agate, who at the close draws the drivers together for an overwhelming strike vote, despite pressure from the officers to keep them at their work. Agate, however, is the leader only because of the absence of the better-known Lefty—such is the significant nickname of the chairman of the strike committee. As Kazan and others had done before him, Odets strove to give more substance to his play than the short *agitprops* printed in *Workers'*

Theatre had possessed. While waiting for the elected chairman to arrive at their strike-vote meeting, the drivers act out terse scenes commenting on the conditions which brought them to their underpaid occupation and which now make them wish to call a strike. These five episodes, the core of the play, reveal the strength of Odets at his best; from the start he was capable of compounding moving dialogue of homely images. Yet they also reveal him at his worst, for the situations of at least two of the drivers appear, as he reveals them, to be the visions of a man suffering acutely from hysteria. It is difficult to understand why in even the exacerbated climate of 1934 a gifted intern, released from his hospital primarily because he is a Jew, could find no more lucrative or appropriate work than driving a cab. Nor is it quite possible to accept the story of the lab technician, another skilled professional man, that he was asked to write a weekly report on the honesty of his superior, the inventor of a new poisonous gas, and for the sake of secrecy to live inside the plant. A third episode, the tale of an unemployed actor, is no less naïve, though possibly more credible. Unable to make an impression on a hard-bitten producer, the actor reveals his despair to the producer's stenographer, who thereupon offers him a dollar. On hearing his refusal of the gift, she promptly reminds him that with it he can, after all, buy ten loaves of bread. Or, more to the point, he can buy nine loaves of bread and a copy of the *Communist Manifesto.* When preparing the volume of *Six Plays* in 1939, Odets had the delicacy to excise this scene. However, it was present at the first "New Theater Night" performances on Fourteenth Street in January, 1935, and was still present when the Group brought the play to Broadway at the end of March, along with *Till the Day I Die,* a shaky piece on Nazi Germany hastily prepared to fill the bill.

Given the speed under which it was written and the special audience of radicals it was originally intended to reach at leftist benefits—not necessarily the Group's own audience of Broadway customers—*Waiting for Lefty* should be spared criticism. The day is long past when it can be taken seriously. To ignore it, however, is to leave unexplained the distraught, evangelical tone of the plays which followed. *Awake and Sing!* and *Paradise Lost* allegedly present close investigations of the American middle class caught in the confusion of financial disaster from which the entire nation suffered. Like all the Odets plays for the Group, they are in the form of the well-made play; that is, they are constructed on a cautious design to show cause and effect in a logical pattern which culminates in emotion-laden confrontation scenes. To this mode of construction, first used by Ibsen for serious social drama, Odets added an overlay of Chekhov, one of his most admired writers. The Chekhovian influence is evident in the oblique expression of strong feeling, as in Moe Axelrod's first-act curtain line for *Awake and Sing!,* when, his heart breaking for a lost love, he spits out, "What the hell kind of house is this it ain't got an orange!" Like the two European playwrights, Odets reached, after *Lefty,* an audience for the most part middle class. Yet the pull of the revolutionary theater was too strong to be denied, with the result that Odets jeopardized his new plays with hortatory *agitprop* conclusions. That such scenes were neither structurally nor emotionally valid and that they offered scant comfort to the Group audience was, in the passion of the moment, of no importance. In *Awake and Sing!* young Ralph Berger's last-act cry of determination to read Marx, spread the revolutionary word in the warehouse where he works, and "fix it so life won't be printed on dollar bills" at a time when his emotional life is in collapse bears a heavy air of unreality. It was felt by many of the play's first critics, who charged the author with a last-minute revision to render his work revolutionary in its final effect. In a lengthy taped interview printed in two numbers of *Theatre Arts* (May and June, 1963) Odets denied having done so with this play, but admitted tacking revolutionary endings on the others. Although he named none of them, it is most likely that *Paradise Lost* was in his mind, for its revolutionary conclusion is so out of keeping with the rest of the action as to take the play into a kind of fantasy world. Leo Gordon, Odets's spokesman, finds life marvelous to contemplate at the close, despite the bankruptcy of his business, the loss of his home, the death of one son, and the fatal disease of the other: "Ohh, darling, the world is in its morning . . . and *no man fights alone!*" He has lost the paradise of the middle class, but has found a better life among the homeless proletariat. The phrases that he and Ralph trumpet forth in their respective plays are proclamations of self-discovery—that is, each man sees himself as a fighter for a better society. But the scenes, coming after unrelieved calamity, suggest self-intoxication as much as self-discovery. In real life, such indulgence usually results in a hangover of chagrin.

Like his characters, Odets himself soon became something of an *agitprop* visionary in his personal life. Generous with his time and royalties, he took up a position of leadership in the left-wing theater movement. In May, 1935, he provided a brief monologue, *I Can't Sleep,* on the stricken conscience of the American businessman for a performance to benefit the Maritime Workers Industrial Union; it was acted by Morris Carnovsky, one of the best-known Group performers. In the summer he served as nominal head of a Communist Party–backed organization calling itself the American Committee to Investigate Labor and Social Conditions in Cuba. As he later told the Un-American Activities Committee, the investigators fully expected to be arrested on arriving in Havana; they were pleased when, indeed, the incarceration occurred on schedule, since they knew it would receive full coverage in the American press. At some time soon after this incident, Odets gave up his membership in the Party, but on November 19, 1935, he ran the following announcement in the *New Masses,* the Party's cultural organ: "Clifford Odets will be glad to advise DURING REHEARSALS of First Run Production of Any 'Valuable' Play. No Charge." After the closing of *Paradise Lost* the next year, he accepted the offer of a Hollywood contract and, amid his friends' protests of "sellout," left New York. Yet he remained with the Group in spirit; part of his salary came back to support the Group actors, and with *Golden Boy* he attempted to provide the company the glossy material which would draw in the Broadway crowd.

These activities are the evidence of self-consciousness; with his initial success on Broadway Odets had come, it would seem, to sense that he had a certain role to play in life. The result to his new work was an obvious, labored literary quality. Both *Paradise Lost* and *Golden Boy* are burdened with a clumsy system of symbols which, though possibly less evident on the stage than in print, sorts uncomfortably with their class-conscious theme. It is surely no coincidence that Leo Gordon and Sam Katz, the two Depression-hounded businessmen of *Paradise Lost,* are manufacturers of ladies' handbags, items useless, or nearly so, when money is scarce. Another of the play's complaints against the idea of a capitalist society is embodied, awkwardly, in the dying younger son of the Gordon family, a one-time bank clerk now afflicted with sleeping sickness. Such strength as remains to him he uses in making paper profits on the stock market. To his mother falls the task of reporting the barely audible words he speaks before taking to his deathbed in the hospital: " 'United Aircraft'—it's an active stock, he says." In *Golden Boy* the symbols lack such simple-mindedness, but nevertheless create doubt as to the validity of the work as a whole. The life of the spirit is presented in young Joe Bonaparte's love of music and in the violin bought for him by his father. The dangerous, crippling battle for wealth which Odets finds, to his sorrow, inescapable under the capitalist system, is symbolized explicitly by prizefighting. When Joe, believing that money alone will bring him self-respect and general acclaim, turns from music to the fight ring, he acts out a parable of despair which provides the audience with a series of moving incidents. Yet we may wonder about the play. To quarrel with the author's social view at this late date is simply to waste time; but it is possible, even so, to take issue with his presentational means. The professions of fiddling and boxing are separated by so great a gulf of emotional and intellectual distance as to make almost a freak of the man who can perform competently in both; Joe's situation is special pleading on a grand scale. Viewed dispassionately, he is not much less astonishing than the young women encountered occasionally in the newspapers who divide their time between courses in law school and the burlesque stage.

But at the same time that Odets's zeal to reform American society drew him into such errors in judgment, his perception of the problems of the individual deepened. The agitational fury of the first plays inhibits the development of the characters as individual persons with special goals and private problems: Odets tells so little of their anxieties, except for those caused by poverty, that the differences among them appear only in such superficial matters as age and accent. With *Golden Boy* however he began to let his mind speculate at greater range. It is not only the desire for money that goads Joe Bonaparte to the fight ring, but the desire to make up for the indignities he suffered in childhood and youth because of his odd name and strabismic eyes. In his adulthood the old taunts remain in his mind, and he fights to work off the hostility they induce. Again in *Rocket to the Moon,* produced in 1938, rooted dissatisfactions with no economic cause are at work alongside the financial worries. Ben and Belle Stark, a middle-aged dentist and his wife, are unhappy together, and although Ben's lackluster career is one cause of distress, another is that they have never been able to have children. Belle, moreover, cannot tolerate her father and prefers to remain in relative poverty if the alternative is to accept a loan from him. Among the most ingratiating characters in any of the plays is Steve Takis, a boy in *Night Music,* Odets's last Group Theater production, who is also driven by problems of the mind. It is true that he is poor and in danger of losing his job as a minor employee for one of the Hollywood studios, but equally powerful among his griefs is the early death of his revered mother; whenever the worries grow too fierce, he thinks of her. None of these plays is lacking in sociological interest, but in each of them Odets gives equal weight to psychological determinism. It is chiefly through the revelations of the mind which he was willing to vouchsafe his audience that the plays have staying power. This is not to say that Odets was ignorant of inner pain at the start of his writing career, but that before *Golden Boy* he chose not to round out his characters with the kinds of problems from which at one time or another each man suffers privately, the better to stress the problems from which, in his vision of American life, all men suffer in the mass.

Had Odets given more attention to character analysis, the result might well have been rapid growth in the direction later taken by such writers as Arthur Miller and Tennessee Williams, for whom the study of personality is of paramount importance. As it was, he continued to fill up his pages with references to hard times and the problem of maintaining honor and dignity in the economic battle. *Rocket to the Moon* (1938), *Night Music* (1940), and *Clash by Night* (1941) all refer to the scarcity of ready money to lengths extravagant for their day. On having a belated first glance at them, a reader today may forget that the national economy, though nothing like the boom of the fifties and sixties, had changed for the better by the end of the decade and that with the coming of war to Europe in 1939 the American "defense" industries were priming the pump still further. Although he had long since given up his Party membership, Odets continued to write in the querulous Communist style, forswearing reason and magnifying grievances at every turn. In *Night Music* this tactic is particularly oppressive. Written during the period of the Soviet-German non-aggression pact, it makes a plea for American non-intervention, since an American alliance with England and France would mean war against Russia. In his despair Steve Takis contemplates joining the army—one way to make a living—but is dissuaded from doing so by the advice that it is better to work as a civilian for the good of the nation.

In his postwar plays Odets continued, in various ways, to demonstrate unwittingly the perils of his commitment. *The Big Knife,* like *Golden Boy,* is melodramatic tragedy, and once more the theme is class warfare. With an almost intolerable shrillness the playwright demonstrates his conviction that the artist, a worker like any other, is at the mercy of an exploiting class, the men who will use his talent for profit. Charlie Castle, a sensitive film actor, is so baited and affronted by the head of production at his studio that in the end he can escape only through suicide; the bosses, well-organized as always, win the battle even though they lose their star, for they are better off with Charlie dead than Charlie alive and looking for an opportunity to strike back. The play is Odets's gesture of revenge on Hollywood, the lotus land whose easy way of life dulled his flair as a writer. The characters are drawn in the starkest black and purest white, as in a shabby western or *agitprop* diatribe. All that is lacking to take the play back to the early thirties is a way out for Charlie from the trap his studio has cunningly set for him, and perhaps a proclamation of his personal independence. On looking at this play again, the present writer is reminded of the brief sketch of Jean Harlow which the *Daily Worker* printed in lieu of an obituary after the actress's death in June, 1937. The paper had not been able to bear her performances, and had been infuriated by her appearance in an anti-labor film titled *Riff Raff,* but on this occasion a reporter recalled having seen her in a Hollywood drugstore not long before her death and thinking that she looked faded and pinched—a healthy American girl sapped of her vitality by the ruling class, and not such a bad actress after all.

In the fifties Odets came to sense that something was wrong. He was brought forcefully to recognize that times had changed by the flagging of interest in his work. Under pressure in the McCarthy period to make a public confession of his political activities or lose his value to Hollywood, he chose at first to ignore the threat and write a foolproof, money-making play: *The Country Girl.* It is a bland piece concentrating on psychological disorders to the near-exclusion of sociological comment. With great effort, an alcoholic actor is persuaded to return to the stage, and, helped by his vigorous wife and a young, optimistic director, succeeds in the part. But he too has a class enemy: the producer, who wishes the director to fire him lest he turn back to the bottle and ruin the play. The money motive, once more, looms as a destructive force. The play tries for suspense as the audience wonders whether the actor will regain his self-confidence, but the happy outcome is clear enough from the start. Too long trained to work with social motives, Odets could not bring himself to make a thorough-going investigation of the hero's problem; the victory comes about with preposterous ease. To his credit, Odets revealed in *Theatre Arts* (May, 1963) that he was fully aware of the meretriciousness of the piece. In 1952, following the paths of old friends, Odets took the next step indicated by the fall in his fortunes and made the obligatory trip to Washington for a confession of his political past. What he had to say was scarcely new; the names he gave had all been given before by others—actors, directors, and playwrights—who had come to prominence in the thirties. But had he not given in, it is unlikely that Hollywood would have filmed *The Country Girl.* Screened in a slick production, with Odets's name prominent in the advertisements, it became one of the most profitable films of the mid-fifties.

With his last produced play, *The Flowering Peach,* Odets tried to explain to himself and to his public the reason for his appearance before the Un-American Activities Committee. At once moving and amusing, the play is a reworking of the story of Noah and the flood in the idiom of the lower-middle-class Jews of New York. The religious tone, unexpected of the once-rebellious writer, is sustained throughout with no trace of embarrassment, but is set off with mild comedy as Noah protests the burden God has inexplicably placed upon him. A looseness in the second act, however, obscures the shifts in Noah's character and prevents the play from reaching its potential level as the most convincing of all Odets's works. It is as though a scene or passage of dialogue were left out that might bring the play into focus by accounting for God's mercy toward this particular family. Brooks Atkinson, writing in the *New York Times* on September 3, 1963, explains that Odets was aware of the flaw and promised his producer to correct it during the Washington tryout performances, but instead spent the days attending Congressional hearings. Possibly he hoped, by listening to some of the scores of ex-Communists still arriving to make their reports, to understand the motive behind his own willingness to comply. At the close of the play he gives the reason as best he can. It sounds in Noah's decision to make his home, after the landing on Mount Ararat, with Shem, his obsessively materialistic second son. Life in Shem's household will be, in Noah's words, "more comfortable."

Thus too late, and for what many of his audience would take to be the wrong reason, Odets tried to alter the direction of his life and art. With his original subject taken away from him, he wrote without stimulus, and soon his reserves of emotion and energy were gone. For the creative artist the failure to grow always results in disaster. Although he may not regress in his craft, but merely stand still, he *seems* to regress as the current of intellectual life swells and sweeps beyond him; it is an optical illusion affecting the inner eye.

Odets's particular problem, or what we can understand of it, was not his alone; the pages of theatrical histories are filled with the names of playwrights who failed to concern themselves with changes in the values of the world around them, and more will be added as the decades flow on. At present the American theater suffers acutely from the influence of members of Odets's generation—more precisely, of his one-time associates in the Group—who have not grown sufficiently with the times. The two producing units in New York of which much was to be hoped in the sixties, the Lincoln Center Repertory Theater and the Actors Studio Theater, showed every symptom after their first full season, 1963–64, of what may be called the Group Problem.

Both were headed by men trained in that remarkable organization who could not free themselves of the grip of the past.

Of the Lincoln Center company's new plays, both Arthur Miller's *After the Fall* and S. N. Behrman's *But for Whom Charlie* have the stale flavor of the thirties. Miller's play treats candidly the issue of Congressional Clearance of persons with a history of Communist affiliation—an important subject, but no longer fresh, and robbed of its edge by opaque dialogue. Behrman's piece is merely a flashy drawing-room comedy such as would have delighted the well-to-do Theater Guild audiences who saw his *Biography* and *End of Summer;* it is an unbelievable choice for a supposedly dynamic company. Among the Actors Studio productions of the first year were June Havoc's *Marathon '33,* a play attempting to recapture the atmosphere of the Depression, and thus of little appeal to present-day audiences, and James Baldwin's *Blues for Mister Charlie,* a throwback to *agitprop* with Negroes and whites lined up in crucial scenes on opposite sides of the stage, the whites united from the outset and the Negroes gradually coming to see that in union there is strength. For all their shortcomings, the plays by Miller and Baldwin show great skill; what is needed by the writers and producers alike is sufficient lessening of the straitjacket of passion to allow them to recognize the passages of incoherent, overwrought writing. But what is needed even more is the passing of leadership to younger, less self-assured practitioners of the theater arts, along with the proviso that they too will be heeded only as long as their minds are free.

Turning from the Political to the Personal: Clifford Odets and John Howard Lawson

Norma Jenckes

The question of turning from the political to the personal in American drama is a large and a largely unexamined one. The turning has had serious consequences for the life of drama in contemporary America. The two cases on which I focus in order to trace this change are those reflected in the careers of John Howard Lawson and Clifford Odets during the 1930s. My use of the term *political* should not be read as referring to agitprop or a committed polemic. Rather, I use *political* in the sense of the polis; the lives of men and women are shaped by their political realities. No society has existed without politics; it is an essential experience of men and women living in any community. Political concerns exist for me in plays that admit and examine the fact that the private and most intimate moments of the characters' lives have been constructed by, and are under pressure from, the nature of the state they inhabit. It is in this sense that I can find powerful political concerns in the plays of William Shakespeare—not only in *Coriolanus, Antony and Cleopatra,* and *Troilus and Cressida* but also in such personal tragedies as *Romeo and Juliet, Hamlet,* and *Othello.*

My thesis is that sometime in the 1930s a radical rupture appeared between the political and the personal in American drama. By 1940 we had already entered the house of mirrors of the American family—a self-reflecting, no-exit hell of mutual recrimination. It was a territory of the tormented psyche whose dramatic masterpiece, *Long Day's Journey into Night,* was penned in tears and blood by Eugene O'Neill. This rupture has not healed but has been painfully exacerbated by the years of the House Un-American Activities Committee (HUAC) investigations, McCarthyism, the Cold War, the turmoil of the 1960s and 1970s, and the laissez-faire rapaciousness of the 1980s, until today *political* is a dirty word.

The radical rupture between the political and the personal was first perpetrated in the name of "political" drama, even proletarian drama. This bias emerges in comments on the development of Lawson and Odets. Left-

This essay was written specifically for this volume and is published here for the first time by permission of the author.

wing critics hailed Lawson's increased political clarity and greater certainty for the need of social revolution in his work. Odets's play *Waiting for Lefty* was greeted in the 1930s as his clearest and strongest composition because it ends in a call for a strike. The overt insistence on political content was used to minimize the personal conflicts in the drama. Lawson and Odets were both urged, and urged themselves and others, to write with a greater sense of political partisanship and certainty. When the shared sense of that political future faded from the general population, they were left with a drama that could either turn inward in disappointment or resentment, or turn reactionary and recant its faith in revolution, or become dogmatic by insisting that the old verities of the Depression would find an audience in the 1940s. Odets chose to unleash his personal furies; Lawson stopped writing for the stage rather than give up his political doctrine. What neither had produced was a drama that integrated the personal and the political, such as Ibsen's *The Pillar of the Community* or Chekhov's *The Cherry Orchard*. Instead, the false dichotomy of political and personal was enshrined in American dramatic practice.

That the personal is the political was one of the slogans that roused much debate in the 1960s and early 1970s. It was a concept that also came to seem obvious and central to the analysis of the emerging gay rights and women's rights movements. Can the slogan be reversed? Is the political the personal? Why did the equation of political and personal seem radical, whereas now it seems merely to be wordplay, and when did the assumed polarity of those terms surface in dramatizations of human experience? Tellingly, when the two terms are opposed, as most often they are in the consideration of the polarities, a privileging of the personal emerges as the essential and inviolate member of the pain. How does this privileging and polarization show up in drama? Very simply, if a character must make a choice between a personal or a political good, the choices are set up in opposition to each other. The political action diminishes the personal life of the character. For the playwrights themselves, the dilemma is framed as an adversarial one between writing political plays or personal plays; the writer can choose one only at the expense of the other. The idea of a whole vision that combines the personal and the political is ruled out as utopian and romantic.

From the 1930s to the present, American culture has found it necessary to privatize every aspect of experience—to shelter it from public scrutiny and separate the personal and political—to the detriment of American theater. This generalization does not apply to British theater, which had the gigantic figure of George Bernard Shaw insisting on the dialectics of the political and the personal in plays from 1892 to 1946. The British also absorbed the theatrical theory and practice of Bertolt Brecht, and since 1968 an entire generation of post-Shavian, post-Brechtian playwrights, including Howard Brenton, David Hare, Edward Bond, Trevor Griffiths, Caryl Churchill, and Christopher Hampton, have insisted on a political and personal drama. Great theater has always depended on the sense that the most personal decisions reflect political realities and that the political system impinges on the most personal choices. If these two arenas of experience are bifurcated or set at odds with each other, the theater is in trouble.

The two playwrights linked in this discussion were brought together during their lifetimes by circumstances, political allegiance, and cultural heritage. John Howard Lawson and Clifford Odets had more in common than their Jewish identity and Marxist orientation. Their lives overlapped in various ways. Perhaps Odets was more than a little enamored of the older, powerful playwright, who had opened up the theatre in the 1920s with the struggle to dramatize the conflicts of class and race and who had brought from Europe the incentive to develop new, experimental forms beyond the naturalistic stage conventions.

One significant moment that they shared—besides their mutual work in the Group Theatre—occurred in 1935, when both visited the Italian playwright Luigi Pirandello, who had come to New York to praise Mussolini and to defend the war in Ethiopia. In the Waldorf-Astoria Hotel the two American playwrights, whose best work in the theater still seemed to be ahead of them, urged the Italian absurdist to relinquish his nationalistic hero worship of Il Duce. In 1935 they were the two most likely spokesmen for the American stage and the antifascist left; in a short five years, both of their careers in the legitimate theater would be nearly over.

Why did the polarization of the political and personal take place in 1940 at the close of the decade of the Great Depression? The political and economic crisis of the 1930s seemed to demand a drama of economist goals, and the two foremost playwrights of that time responded. Lawson had earlier, in the 1920s—in plays such as *Roger Bloomer*—brought to the United States the experimental theater of Brecht and Piscator, with its sense that revolution in the theater would require new forms as well as new content. He had sought a synthesis of Karl Marx and Sigmund Freud, staged with expressionist techniques.

Odets got caught up in the debate over social realism when, under the tutelage of *The New Masses,* he aspired to give voice to proletarian aspirations. In June 1932 Odets joined the fifty artists who were members of the Group Theatre centered around such figures as Cheryl Crawford, Harold Clurman, and Stella Adler. The young Odets listened avidly to all the discussions of politics and literature; he attended the frequent play readings and soon was himself an understudy to Luther Adler in Lawson's *Success Story.*

Success Story forged more links in the association of Lawson and Odets. A play about a Jew who betrays his political and religious identity for money, power, and marriage to a "Nordic" wife, *Success Story* excited Odets's admiration. He refused to agree with later critical dismissals of Lawson's work; he had found in it a kind of permission from an older, powerful father figure of a playwright to explore questions of Jewish and Marxist loyalties in his own writing. Harold Clurman considered Lawson to be "the hope of our theatre" and characterized *Success Story* as a play about "what happens to an idealistic force when it finds no effective social force to contain it."[1]

Only twenty-five years old and struggling to find a form for his personal and political concerns, Odets was drawn to Lawson, a divided, disputatious, dedicated Jewish intellectual nearing forty. Lawson had been trying for the past ten years to bring expressionistic theater experiments to the American stage. His lectures and lecture notes attest that he was a born teacher. Throughout the summer of 1932, Lawson lectured to Odets, a particularly avid student. A less sanguine observer of those long afternoon sessions described Lawson as "a combination of one-eyed Izzy and a rabbi." Odets was enthralled by Lawson, who seemed to him "like some medieval figure, a Borgia with a good strong chest and great vitality who could write with any sort of noise around him."[2]

Years later, in an interview taped during his 73rd year, Lawson remembers Odets as a serious listener who seemed, by the very intensity of his attention, to be extremely susceptible to Lawson's words and presence.[3] Odets wanted to play the role of Sol Ginsberg in Lawson's *Success Story*. The character is a superefficient Russian Jew from the lower East Side of New York who evolves from fervent pro-Communist revolutionary to rich businessman. He ends with the realization that he has lost his life energy, his heritage, and his identity. In one speech, Sol tells how "this feller Christ took me up to a high mountain and showed me the earth . . . this Christ was a Jew dressed in a rainbow, and He said, 'Do you want the earth, Solomon Ginsberg, or do you want to join me in a cellar, sweating and plotting with a few close friends?' Well, I made my choice and somewhere Christ is in a cellar laughing at me right now—don't I know it?"[4] Odets identified very early with that role and that experience, and he wrote in his diary that "to play that part every day would be a catharsis."[5]

That particular catharsis was denied him, but under the influence of Lawson, Odets developed his own artistic credo. The year 1935 was a kind of annus mirabilis for Clifford Odets. In the short space of one year, four of his plays were produced by the Group Theatre, beginning with *Waiting for Lefty,* then *Awake and Sing* and *Till the Day I Die,* and culminating with *Paradise Lost.* In the next three years he wrote *Golden Boy* and *Rocket to the Moon.* By 1939, in his preface to *Six Plays,* he reminds us that "at the ripe age of thirty-three" he is writing what he thinks is only the first of many prefaces to future collections. He insists that "we are living in a time when new art works should shoot bullets." In fact, the tone of the work is vaguely apologetic for plays "written when it was almost impossible for me to do more or differently with them." In what was perhaps false modesty then, but which rings as an ironic understatement today in the face of his later writing block, Odets affirms, "Let them stand, crudities and all, as a small parade of a young talent discovering and shaping itself."[6]

These six plays, "this small parade" that would be the only one in the field, display an interesting trajectory of growing uncertainty and complexity, moving as they do from external to internal motivation, from public to private dilemmas. The first play, *Waiting for Lefty,* ends with ecstatic, simple certainties: "Hello America Hello. We're storm birds of the working class. Workers of the world—our bones and blood. And when we die they'll know what we did to make a new world! Christ, cut us up to little pieces. We'll die for what is right! Put fruit trees where our ashes are." The last words of the play are those shouted as a call by all on stage: "Strike, strike, strike!!!"[7]

This play and that ending are famous and are often cited in discussions of proletarian literature. *Waiting for Lefty* is often taught in classes as paradigmatic of a certain kind of agitprop drama. It is interesting to compare it with plays by other avowedly radical and communist playwrights, such as George Bernard Shaw, Maxim Gorky, or Garcia Lorca, to name just three. Have any of them ended a play in such a manner? Who declared that this was the way to write proletarian drama? Odets himself never did it again, and certainly his mentor, John Howard Lawson, had never displayed such simplicity or crudity. Yet this was the measure to which Odets and other left-wing playwrights were held in certain circles.

In discussing the two later plays, *Awake and Sing* and *Paradise Lost,* Clurman raises and dismisses the Chekhovian comparison, finding instead that Odets is "active, impulsive and rather lusty." He introduces Sean O'Casey as a closer model, noting that both playwrights share "some of the special tenement tenderness and certain quality of improvisatory spontaneousness."[8] In his 1940 journal Odets agreed in a self-flattering tone that "in a small way I have been influenced in my own playwriting by O'Casey, but it is mostly because we must be similar men: he lives physically, not with the noodle."[9] Writing again in his journal later that year, he worried more honestly about the negative connections and problems of repeating himself as O'Casey had: "A long time ago I noted in Sean O'Casey a certain problem. He wrote a vivid 'parochial' drama at first, proletarian life in Ireland. Naturally he was not content to keep repeating these genre pictures and wanted to move out into the wider world where he would have the opportunity of showing other types and the lives they lead. This shift from one life to another must be watched very carefully, for it is possible that in transit the whole talent may fall off the moving van."[10] Odets believed that this loss of talent happened to both O'Neill and O'Casey, and he worried about his own transitions: "I don't want to continue writing about Jewish life exclusively if I can help it, but great care must be observed while I move to other fields."[11] One of the disheartening things about reading such acutely prophetic passages in Odets's journal is knowing that no matter how much he warned himself about certain tendencies in his own work and life, he could not change the direction and he could not avert the disasters that he himself foresaw. The trend in his writing was larger than his good intentions.

Clurman's comments on *Golden Boy* raise an early warning of the future accusations of selling out that would bedevil Odets: "It has been blamed for betraying Hollywood influence in its use of terse, typical situations, story motifs which resemble that of either popular fiction or movies, and possibly too in its use of an environment (the prize-fight world) that somehow seems unworthy of the serious purpose professed by its author."[12]

Odets's last play in this remarkable group, *Rocket to the Moon,* was described by Clurman as "the first love play the Group has ever done . . . the first love play by a modern playwright."[13] Plagued by a separation from his first wife, Odets wrote and rewrote the third act up until opening night. A surprise meeting at Sardi's effected a temporary reconciliation between the famous couple, probably affected the outcome of the play's plot, and was front-page news. *Rocket to the Moon* is the central text in any reading of Odets's growth as a playwright. It looked like the start of something new for him, but it was the beginning of the end.

Odets ends that play on a bewildered but hopeful note, in a tone that acknowledges ignorance as a kind of new starting point. Stark, a dentist who decides to forego his affair with his assistant and return to his wife, says to his father-in-law: "For years I sat here, taking things for granted, my wife, everything. Then just for an hour my life was in a spotlight. . . . I saw myself clearly, realized who and what I was. Isn't that a beginning? Isn't it?"[14] The curtain drops on his laughing recognition that "what I don't know would fill a book."[15] This ending had the same tone of so many of the entries in Odets's 1940 journal—"I know where I could go wrong—surely I won't." But he did.

It is the woman Cleo in *Rocket to the Moon* who raises the Whitmanian ideal of a wholeness of life that could be discovered elsewhere. "I'll go up all those roads 'till I find what I want. I want a love that uses one, that needs me. Don't you think there's a world of joyful men and women?"[16] She is seeking a unity of being that is denied her in the world run for profit; she brings together the political and personal concerns in the play. Work has become for the dentist a source of alienation that vitiates his emotional and sexual life. Cleo asks, "Must all men live afraid to love and sing? Can't we sing at work and love our work? It's getting late to play at life; I want to live it."[17] This speech echoes a similar one in a play by Lawson, *The Pure in Heart,* wherein a character speculates about the limitations of his present society and conjures a different place: "Maybe someplace it's different—I don't know: where they'd keep busy working, digging, plowing, building cities too, laying one brick on another brick—There's nothing bad with all that stuff. People could be happy, people could build things, work without stealing, love without going crazy."[18]

Odets knew that the problem he faced was integration, not separation, of the personal and the political. He analyzes his predicament in the entry for 7 March 1940 in his journal: "First, there is the problem of keeping in the plays a content full and progressive, radical to the extent that it re-evaluates ordinary daily life around us, giving fresh insight and interpretation to familiar types, both personal and social. Next there is the problem of finding a form for this material, a form which does not exclude the richness of the material, but is as inclusive as the material itself. Finally, there is the problem of adjusting that form so that it is acceptable to a typical American audience—that is, a completely enjoyable and understandable play from start to finish."[19] Still committed to social change, Marxism, and his faith in the Soviet Union, Odets declares on 25 March 1940: "No matter what the detractors of Russia say, it is the new Russia which will lead the world in the road of change. I believe, as I believed five years ago, in the destiny of men and women, the high and flowering destiny, and if I did not believe in it I would not want to live as a good man—then would you see a Caliban."[20] Caliban peeked out when Odets railed before the HUAC on the problem of the left expecting plays with a specific political content.[21] He failed to admit that the work he was doing daily for the Hollywood studios was also writing to their ideological orders. Most tellingly, what his published work reveals (which he faced on his deathbed) is that he had done his best work while struggling to find a way to express the political life of his time and place on the American stage in the 1930s.

The elite-educated and aristocratic Lawson, when confronted with the same constructed imperative of choosing between the personal and the political in his work, moved completely into the political realm and stopped writing for the theater. How much did the two former friends see of each other during those busy Hollywood years of the 1940s—agonizing and frustrating sellout years for Odets and organizing years for Lawson? They both came to their logical conclusions—Odets testifying as friendly witness before the HUAC and naming names, Lawson refusing to cooperate and serving a year in a federal penitentiary in Kentucky.

Odets's biographer, Margaret Brenman-Gibson, gives a searing account of his deathbed despair and sense of failure in August 1963: "At times he extended his arm at full length, shook his fist and shouted, 'Clifford Odets, you have so much to do.' He yelled for several days saying, 'I may fool you all—you know I may live. Then perhaps Clifford Odets will do something to redeem the last sixteen years.' "[22] Sixteen years—Odets himself dated his artistic death to his decision to cooperate with the hateful HUAC.

The tenor of the criticism of such left-wing critics as Michael Gold was harsh. Writing in the *New Masses* on 10 April 1934, he reviews Lawson's career in dogmatic and finally derogatory terms. Gold condemns Lawson's early play, *Processional,* stating that "futilitarianism was the garment then fashionable in the bourgeois studios and gin mills." He claims that although the play had raised hopes on the left about Lawson's promise, "he has written and has produced about a dozen plays since *Processional* and all of them have been stultified by the same painful confusion." He continues, "Ten years have passed and it is fair to ask an author, even one who is a fellow-traveller, 'What have you learned in those ten years?' " Gold goes on to answer his own rhetorical question with more negative and unflattering observations about Lawson: "The answer tragically seems to be, 'Nothing. I am still a bewildered wanderer lost between the two worlds, indulging myself in the same adolescent self-pity as in my first plays. Hence my lack of maturity and aesthetic or moral fusion.' "[23]

Gold was only one voice, but he was an influential representative of the criticism that Lawson received from the left. When he concludes by condemning Lawson as a liberal, Gold uses terms that expose the one-sidedness of his own view: "A bitter strike serves only as a background for a love story with a Floyd Dell happy ending, and to offer the sophomore notion that American can be explained by its jazz. The revolution in the Far East becomes a piece of Ziegfried Orientalism and the background for another unimportant love story."[24] The phrase "unimportant love story," contrasted pejoratively with the idea of a serious treatment of a strike, betrays Gold's notion of where and how radicalization occurs and in what spheres of life oppression is felt. We also read in Clurman's assessments of Odets an insistence on the strike as a central image of progressive drama. The emphasis on the political, thus narrowly defined, vitiates the attempt to show the personal side of experience. Instead of recognizing that if class oppression exists, it is ubiquitous and experienced in every aspect of daily life, Michael Gold desired to see dramatized isolated moments of revolutionary clarity and fervor.

The actual dramatic achievements on the side of revolutionary change integrate the personal and the political. Calderon, Cervantes and Goethe are examples of successful playwrights who have done this; in the twentieth century, the names of Gorky, Shaw, Brecht, O'Casey, and Lorca spring immediately to mind. In that fairly formidable list of great dramatists, not one is an American. Two American playwrights who tried to achieve a synthesis of the personal and the political were berated from the left and the right. When the Depression was over and they could no longer muster the proletarian focus, they retreated to Hollywood. There Odets articulated a narrow personal vision that failed to express his social interest, while Lawson took up a clear political position but went silent as a playwright. Lawson's political commitment deepened in the 1940s, but he could not successfully develop as a playwright in the United States. In 1937 *Processional* was revived for the Federal Theatre project, and *Marching Song* was produced by the Group Theatre. That was the last of Lawson's plays to be produced in the United States. His career in Hollywood blossomed with such screenplay credits as *Blockade* (1938), *Algiers* (1938), *They Shall Have Music* (1939), *Four Sons* (1940), *Sahara* (1943), and *Action in the North Atlantic* (1943).

As early as 1944, Lawson became a target of the Tenney State Legislative Committee on Un-American Activities in California; by 1947 he was one of the Hollywood Ten. *Smashup* (1947) was his last pre-blacklist film script;

in 1948 he was sentenced to prison after being cited for contempt of Congress. While serving his one-year sentence in the Federal Reformatory in Ashland, Kentucky, beginning in 1950, Lawson wrote a book, *The Hidden Heritage,* and a play, *In Praise of Learning,* edited the prison newspaper, and wrote anonymously the screenplay for *Cry, the Beloved Country.* After his release from prison in 1951 he entered into a black-market arrangement: using the pen names James Howard and James Christopher, he completed scripts for a television series and several movies including *The Careless Years* (1957) and *Terror in a Texas Town* (1957). In 1963, a last play, *Parlor Magic,* was produced in the Soviet Union and in the German Democratic Republic. The production utilized a revolving stage, film clips, and expressionistic techniques inspired by Piscator and Brecht.

Clifford Odets, if we are to believe the evidence assembled by his biographer and the testimony of his own journal, dedicated his life and art to the emulation of two towering models—Walt Whitman and Ludwig von Beethoven. They had achieved an aesthetic synthesis of democracy and art, and in his own life and art he aspired for nothing less. Odets identified music, and especially the music of Beethoven, as embodying an ideal of wholeness. He called the composer "the admirable unhappy Beethoven"[25] and credited him with being a "very tough man to have done what he did in his art." What precisely did Beethoven achieve in his art that Odets so wished to emulate? "Beethoven's work . . . represents the deepest expression of man's faith in life which has ever been written by a man. No artist before or since expressed so deeply the will to live and accept every fact of life."[26] Odets hailed Beethoven as "the only man or artist I can think of . . . who never once faltered in this difficult task: he was a fanatic! He hacked and chopped, twisted and tortured, but he did not *EXCLUDE* a drop of his experience from his work; in each phase of his life he found the right form for an increasingly higher and deeper experience."[27]

Both Whitman and Beethoven dared to dream of a world transformed by the impulse of human love. In Beethoven's *Fidelio* we see dramatized a sublime vision of human love transforming and irradiating a political landscape. He dared to imagine a diminished, repressed, totalitarian world defied and finally defeated by the power of human love—the love of friendship, the love of freedom, and the faithful love of two people in ecstatic sexual union. That opera showed no rupture of the political and personal, no tragic renunciation of either, no oblation of whole chunks of either public or private experience.

Odets and Lawson both attempted to dramatize the interpenetration of the political and the personal. That they were forced to choose one or the other defeated them as playwrights who aspired to create great drama. Their defeat reflects the repression of reactionary opinion from the right, which suppresses the political, and also from the "correct left," which disapproves of the personal. The American stage still enforces a vision of these two essential aspects of human experience as being in conflict, even mutually exclusive. American theater still labors under the burdens of this false dichotomy and continues to be impoverished by it.

Notes

1. Margaret Brenman-Gibson, *Clifford Odets, American Playwright* (New York: Atheneum, 1982), 222.
2. Brenman-Gibson, 223–24.
3. John Howard Lawson, taped interview, 1970, University of Southern Illinois Archives, box 16.
4. John Howard Lawson, *Success Story* (New York: Farrar & Rinehart, 1932), 230.
5. Brenman-Gibson, 224.
6. Clifford Odets, *Six Plays* (New York: Random House, 1939), ix–x.
7. Ibid., 31.
8. Ibid., 421.
9. Clifford Odets, *The Time Is Ripe* (New York: Grove Press, 1988), 16.
10. Ibid., 87.
11. Ibid., 87.
12. *Six Plays,* 429.
13. Brenman-Gibson, 521.
14. *Six Plays,* 418.
15. Ibid., 418.
16. Ibid., 416.
17. Ibid., 416.
18. John Howard Lawson, *With a Reckless Preface: Two Plays* (New York: Farrar & Rinehart, 1934), 108.
19. *Time Is Ripe,* 58.
20. Ibid., 84.
21. Testimony of Clifford Odets, in "Communist Infiltration of the Hollywood Motion Picture Industry," part 8, House Committee on Un-American Activities *Hearings,* 19–21 May 1952.
22. Brenman-Gibson, 3.
23. Mike Gold, "A Bourgeois Hamlet of Our Time," *New Masses,* 10 April 1934.
24. Ibid.
25. *Time Is Ripe,* 55.
26. Ibid., 79.
27. Ibid., 78.

[The Family as Theme in Odets's Plays]

Harold Cantor

First and last, the terrain of Odets' plays is the home of the American middle-class family, and the action of those plays almost always arises from the family situation. There is hardly a play in which domestic life does not figure; even the homeless wanderers of *Night Music* face family conflicts in person or in memory, while the legendary travelers aboard Noah's Ark in *The Flowering Peach* become transfigured in Odets' hands into biblical bourgeoisie. The family's dwelling place becomes a battlefield on which the recurring quarrels are fought between father and son, mother and child, brother and brother, a combat that endlessly repeats itself even after the young have moved out and set up homes of their own. Moreover, if we define themes as the abstract concepts or "ideas" dominant in a work of any intention, it is clear that a major theme in Odets' plays is that the middle-class family is a social trap from which the individual must escape to achieve his human potential as a member of the family of man. Yet this idea is consistently refuted by Odets' simultaneous recognition that the family is a viable source of tenderness, love and affection that can be deserted only at the individual's peril. This theme, and the ambivalence that accompanies it, is best dramatized in the early *Awake and Sing!, Paradise Lost,* parts of *Golden Boy,* and in Odets' last play, a kind of coda to his early work, *The Flowering Peach.*

The Berger family in *Awake and Sing!* provides the prototype of this theme, as they do for so much else that is central to Odets' work. In their cluttered Bronx apartment, they sing the blues as they sit down to supper in a familiar ritual of complaint. Ralph, the son, is stuck in a dead-end job as a clerk in a silk house on Fourth Avenue, drowning "in bolts of silk and velour" (III). Pinched on his sixteen dollars a week salary, he sleeps on a day bed in the front room and desperately wants to "be something" and to "get to first base" (I). Hennie, the daughter, as Odets tells us in his Preface Notes, "is fatalistic about being trapped, but will escape if possible." But as the action unfolds she is forced to marry Sam Feinschreiber, whom she pities but does not love, to salvage her mother's sense of respectability and have a father for

Originally published as "Themes and Motifs: The Family Trap," in *Clifford Odets: Playwright-Poet* (Metuchen, N.J.: Scarecrow Press, Inc., 1978). Copyright 1978 by Harold Cantor. Reprinted by permission.

her illegitimate child. Life for Hennie, whom the family nicknames Beauty, becomes bestial—a weary round of diapers, dreariness, and sleepless nights in a hated marital bed.

If the young are trapped, so too are the old. Myron, the father, has been a haberdashery clerk for thirty years and is "heartbroken without being aware of it" (Preface Notes). Jacob, the grandfather, is a student of Marx and an advocate of revolution, but he is "a sentimental idealist with no power to turn ideal to action" (Preface Notes). He is an abject failure—"Every job he ever had he lost" (I)—forced to depend on his children's bounty, and he is treated by Bessie, the mother, like a captious child. Furthermore, he is aware of his own deficiencies, recognizing that he is a talker not a doer, that he "had golden opportunities but drank instead a glass tea" (II, 2).

If all of the members of the family are trapped by "a struggle for life amidst petty conditions" (Preface Notes), it is this same fundamental activity which draws them together and makes them need one another. This ambivalence is not so much a matter of conscious understanding on their part; it is part of the very atmosphere in which they live. At home, they are free to let off steam, to console each other by hooting each other down; they live in a perpetual frenzy of complaint or argument, but quick derision ("Quack! Quack!") and anticipated attacks ("Another county heard from!") are beneficial to the victim as well as the attacker. Sarcasm in this play becomes a mode of familial affection. Yet they are not without moments of mutual love and tenderness. Hennie is a loving daughter as she tries to cheer her parents (and herself) by offering to treat them to a night at the Yiddish theater. Jacob comforts the despairing Ralph with tears in his eyes when it seems as if Ralph has lost his girl at the end of Act II, 1. Myron makes a similar attempt in Act II, 2, in his usual ineffective fashion—"It's an American father's duty to be his son's friend."

Even Bessie, the strong-willed and dominant mother who embodies what Odets considers the ersatz values of bourgeois respectability and pragmatism, is not without her own style of family love. When Schlosser, the janitor, makes an angry remark to Jacob about walking the dog in the hallway, Bessie defends him indignantly: "Excuse me! Please don't yell on an old man. He's got more brains in his finger than you got—I don't know where. Did you ever see—he should talk to you an old man?" (I). Bessie considers herself a realist, but she has been infected by the American dream of success. All of the misery in the play is fueled by her good intentions. It is her conviction that "a woman who don't raise a family—a girl—should jump overboard" (II, 1), and she dreams of the day when Ralph will ride "up to the door in a big car with a chauffeur and a radio" (II, 1), a success like his Uncle Morty. So she tightens the trap around Ralph by opposing his love for Blanche, and virtually strangles Hennie in a net of deceit. All of her actions are justified in her eyes by her fear of poverty and her sense of family loyalty.

Even her rapacious attempt to appropriate Jacob's insurance money is motivated by her feeling that "It belongs for the whole family. . . . A family
needs for a rainy day" (III). But Odets cannot depict such a woman with mere
contempt, and in Act III he allows her more than a villain's measure of
passion and dignity as she defends her conduct:

> Ralphie, I worked too hard all my years to be treated like dirt. It's no law we
> should be stuck together like Siamese twins. Summer shoes you didn't have,
> skates you never had, but I bought a new dress every week. A lover I kept—
> Mr. Gigolo! Did I ever play a game of cards like Mrs. Marcus? Or was Bessie
> Berger's children always the cleanest on the block?! Here I'm not only the
> mother, but also the father. The first two years I worked in a stocking factory
> for six dollars while Myron Berger went to law school. If I didn't worry about
> the family who would? On the calendar it's a different place, but here without
> a dollar you don't look the world in the eye. Talk from now to next year—this
> is life in America.

And a further touch of sympathy comes soon after as Bessie, winding an
alarm clock before going to bed, confesses to Ralph that she, too, has been a
prisoner all her life: ". . . I'll tell you a big secret: My whole life I wanted to
go away too, but with children a woman stays home. A fire burned in *my*
heart too, but now it's too late. I'm no spring chicken. The clock goes and
Bessie goes. Only my machinery can't be fixed." (III).

A similar pattern confronts the Gordon clan in *Paradise Lost;* although
ensconced in Shakespeare Place in a house of their own, they represent a
higher bracket of the middle class than the bourgeois Bergers. With the
Katzes, who rent upstairs, they have long lived on the proceeds of a pocket-
book manufacturing concern and have insulated themselves from the horrors
of the Depression. Moreover, their daughter, Pearl, is a dedicated pianist,
while their older son, Ben, is a star athlete whom they believe has a promising future. But their "paradise" is an artificial one: it turns rapidly to dust
and ashes, as they lose their savings in the bank crash and mortgage their
house to keep the business going. In this play Clara, the practical mother, is
the source of love and tenderness as she welcomes her guests with the tag-
line, "Take a piece of fruit," and proudly boasts: "I raised my whole family on
Grade A milk" (I). Her husband, Leo, is an impractical, foolish dreamer who
"sits with artistic designs" (I) while Sam Katz runs the business, until Leo,
awakening as from a deep sleep, gradually realizes the gravity of his situation
and that of the world conflagration. The feeling of entrapment is imparted
both by dialogue and event: Pearl Gordon tells her boyfriend, Felix, "No, I
have no place to go, Felix. Where would I go?" (I); Ben marries the silly,
pleasure-loving Libby Michaels and, unable to find work, gets sucked into
the rackets of his friend, Kewpie, and dies a gangland suicide; Sam Katz
confesses to his friend and partner why he doctored the firm's books: "A man

like me wants to stand on a mountain. So instead he lays in a grave with dirt on his face. Twenty-four hours a day he eats gall" (II). In the play's most obvious bit of symbolic action, the younger son, Julie, who dreams of a killing on Wall Street and follows the stock market pages, lies dying of sleeping sickness, while his mother reads to him from a book of biblical legends of Moses' terrible anger at the worshipers of the Golden Calf. Though *Paradise Lost* is a very different kind of play from *Awake and Sing!*, it shares with the earlier work a vision of a middle-class family facing extinction in an economic holocaust (but in this play because of its own naiveté, ineptitude, and lack of social awareness), yet sustaining itself by tenderness and mutual loyalty as the disintegration begins.

By the time he wrote *Golden Boy* (1937), Odets' interest had centered on the world outside the family; however, the protagonist's home continues to figure importantly in the play as a different sort of trap. Here we are given a sentimental and idealized version of middle-class family life whose spokesman is Joe's father, a character so saintly, wise, and folksy that he is hardly credible. The function of Joe's home is to serve as polar opposite to the ruthless, competitive fight world; it is characterized by the plaster busts of Mozart and Beethoven and the cage of lovebirds that adorns the combination dining-living room where Mr. Bonaparte and his skeptical Jewish friend, Mr. Carp, sip beer and, as the son-in-law Siggie puts it, "slice philosophical salami" (II, 3). Joe Bonaparte rebels against this "natural" background of wedded bliss, music, and love (and adopts the "unnatural" competitive world of sports) because family life seeems to him a dead end. As the shrewdly pessimistic Mr. Carp remarks of Joe's violin case: "It looks like a coffin for a baby" (I, 2). Though Joe's father benignly states, "Whatever you got ina your nature to do isa not foolish" (I, 2), he is ambitious for his son and is secretly convinced that Joe's "nature" is to be a violin virtuoso. But Joe takes the way of the fist instead of the fiddle because he is impatient for success: ". . . Every birthday I ever had I sat around. Now'sa time for standing. Poppa, I have to tell you—I don't like myself, past, present, and future. Do you know there are men who have wonderful things from life? Do you think I like this feeling of no possessions? Of learning about the world from Carp's encyclopaedia. . . . You don't know what it means to sit around here and watch the months go ticking by! Do you think that's a life for a boy my age? Tomorrow's my birthday! I change my life!" (I, 2).

Joe makes good on his promise but never loses his affection for his father. When at the end the love-lined trap proves to have been the better option, Mr. Bonaparte says of his dead son: "Come, we bring a him home . . . where he belong . . ." (III, 3).

Japheth, in *The Flowering Peach,* has a loving attachment to both Esther, his mother, and Noah, especially the latter with whom he shares deep affinities. Odets in his Preface Notes to Scene 2, calls them "two outcasts in the more competent and fluent world." But Noah is a stubborn traditionalist who insists on doing things his way—"Disrespect to a father is disrespect to God!" (3)—and he orders his sons about highhandedly. Noah and his troup of "assorted clowns and acrobats" (2) become a comic equivalent of the earlier bourgeois families, and the closed-in ark becomes a metaphor for the family trap as quarrels erupt among the brothers, wives, and parents. Japheth's quarrel, however, is mainly with God. He feels compelled to protest against the cruelty of the divine decree and states, "Someone, it seems to me, would have to protest such an avenging, destructive God!" (2). Despite his father's anger, when his conscience tells him that he can work no longer for "this brutal God" (3), he decides to leave his vital role in the construction process. But he is only gone overnight and, after a tussle in the town, returns to ask his father's blessing and explain: "The ark can't be built without me. For your sake, Momma, and Poppa's, that's why I came back—for the family, not for God" (4).

Over and over, Odets' characters struggle with their divided feelings toward their families. Sometimes, as in *Night Music,* the conflict is expressed simplistically in terms of the generation gap and rebellion against the ennui of middle-class existence. Many a participant at Woodstock or Watkins Glen might echo the credo of Fay, the fledgling actress, as she refuses to return to "a secondhand life" and confesses that she loves her parents but doesn't care for their ideals. "Every relative I have tells me I'm a criminal. But I think *they're* criminals. Because they don't live—because their alphabet's from A to B—because their lives are narrow, petty and small!" (I, 3). Fay, in this atypical comedy, does not return home, but often the more serious characters do: Ben Stark returns to "A life where every day is Monday" (I) in *Rocket to the Moon;* and Ernie Mott—in Odets' best screen play, *None But the Lonely Heart*—returns to the hated junk furniture shop, which will make him both victim and victimizer when he learns that his mother is dying of cancer.

How to break out of the family trap is a central concern of Odets'. In his plays he explored different ways of doing so: running away from bondage; social commitment; the search for independence and power; even death as a means of release. It is important to examine some of these attempts to understand how essential the break-out motif is to Odets' worldview. In *Awake and Sing!* there are three attempts to break out: Jacob's, Hennie and Moe's, and Ralph's. Jacob sees in Ralph "his new life" and a means of symbolic resurrection, and warns Bessie that rather than allow her to mold Ralph in her image he would die first, in this subtle foreshadowing of the event: "Bessie, someday you'll talk to me so fresh . . . I'll leave the house for good!" (I). Presumably, his sense of outrage at Bessie's treatment of Ralph's girl friend, his humiliation when Bessie smashes his Caruso records, his desire to transcend his useless existence with some meaningful act of protest, his wish to give Ralph a chance to realize "the possibilities of life" (II, 1) with the proceeds of his insurance policy (an ironic motive in such an idealist)—all these motives contribute to his suicide in Act II, 2. There is, perhaps, an even more important motive for Jacob's sacrifice (not noticed by most critics) which I shall note in my section on the motif of treachery. Despite the critical bromide that Odets is a facile optimist, death as a way of breaking out of the *existential* trap occurs in *Till the Day I Die, Awake and Sing!, Golden Boy, Clash by Night,* and *The Big Knife.*

The break-out of Hennie and Moe, however, is more directly applicable to the family trap. Moe is a cynical hedonist who has lost a leg in the war and who believes "It's all a racket—from horse racing down" (II, 1). But his love for Hennie is genuine. He confesses that he, too, has struggled to escape a hellish environment, and he urges Hennie: "Make a break or spend the rest of your life in a coffin." The imagery in which he clothes his vision of their future life is Edenic: "Come away. A certain place where it's moonlight and roses. We'll lay down, count stars. Hear the big ocean making noise. You lay under the trees. Champagne flows like—." At this point a phone call from Sam interrupts his lyrical appeal, but he continues relentlessly: ". . . Paradise, you're on a big boat headed south. No more pins and needles in your heart, no snake juice squirted in your arm. The whole world's green grass and when you cry it's because you're happy" (III).

Moralists have objected to Hennie's decision to leave her husband and child, and have confused Ralph's approval of her action with Odets'.[1] Hennie is swept along by her passions, and decides to ignore the human cost and leave a life founded on lies and hypocrisy in a desperate bid for happiness. We do not know whether her break-out will succeed or not; it may be that her guilt about the vulnerable Sam Feinschreiber or the thought of her child left to Bessie's ministrations will bring her back. Odets has merely presented one of the possible options; in Axelrod's words, "The doctor said it—cut off your leg to save your life!" (III).

But "breaking out" for many of Odets' characters most often occurs at the moment when they become politically aware and when, in a moment of flashing illumination like St. Paul on the road to Damascus, they cast their lot with the rest of mankind (e.g., the working class) in the revolutionary struggle. This is particularly true in the early plays, and Ralph in *Awake and Sing!* sets the tone of lyrical optimism which critics, both in 1935 and 1974, find so difficult to accept[2]:

> Sure, inventory tomorrow. Coletti to Driscoll to Berger—that's how we work. It's a team down the warehouse. Driscoll's a show-off, a wiseguy, and Joe talks pigeons day and night. But they're like me, looking for a chance to get to first base too. Joe razzed me about my girl. But he don't know why. I'll tell him. Hell, he might tell me something I don't know. Get teams together all over. Spit on your hands and get to work. And with enough teams together maybe we'll get steam in the warehouse so our fingers don't freeze off. Maybe we'll fix it so life won't be printed on dollar bills (III).

There are several ways critics have reacted to such speeches: one is to regard them (as Odets did in retrospect) as reflections of the political pressures within the Group Theater and from outside intellectual circles for playwrights of the period to end plays with a Chorus for Survival which would parallel the International in tone if not in tune.[3] Admittedly, these speeches are excrescences on Odets' plays, since they do not develop logically out of the characterizations and seem tacked on.[4] Perhaps, if Odets had had the "know-how" and commitment which he ascribed to Communist functionaries[5] and which he conspicuously lacked, he might have had Ralph join a Communist cell and invent ways to hasten the death of a doomed capitalist system. But, even in *Waiting for Lefty,* he does not go that far. Ralph chooses to remain at home and, convinced that he has turned an ideological corner, works within the system for some vague and unspecified social reform. From this perspective one can regard these speeches as reflections of Odets' own uncertainty and political naiveté, the kind that brought him frequent lectures from John Howard Lawson[6] and bad notices from the Left-wing press.[7] Another possible critical reaction is to see them as the mystical yearnings of an idealist to escape the trap of solipsism and achieve transcendence; William Gibson felt that his friend's theme "had always been the liberation of the soul from its social shackles."[8] From this perspective, even Leo's closing speech at the end of *Paradise Lost,* so bitterly attacked by James T. Farrell,[9] acquires religious and visionary overtones:

> . . . Everywhere now men are rising from their sleep. Men, men are understanding the bitter black total of their lives. Their whispers are growing to shouts! They become an ocean of understanding! *No man fights alone.* Oh, if you could only see with me the greatness of man. I tremble like a bride to see the time when they'll use it. My darling, we must have only one regret—that life is so short! That we must die so soon. (CLARA *slowly has turned from* JULIE *and is listening now to her husband.*) Yes, I want to see that new world. I want to kiss all those future men and women. What is this talk of bankrupts, failures, hatred . . . they won't know what that means. Oh, yes, I tell you the whole world is for men to possess. Heartbreak and terror are not the heritage of mankind! The world is beautiful. No fruit tree wears a lock and key. Men will sing at their work, men will love. Ohhh, darling, the world is in its morning—and *no man fights alone!* . . . (III)

Yet somehow the rhetoric does not ring true. It is not simply that the tone of optimism seems naive, for, as Gerald Weales points out, it is "certainly no more so than the automatic existential despair that has characterized the last fifteen years."[10] Rather it fails because it does not proceed from the play's structure. *Paradise Lost,* unlike *Awake and Sing!,* is patterned on *break-ins* rather than *break-outs,* break-ins such as the visit of the shop delegation, Ben's death, the appearance of the two homeless men at the end, which invade the suffocating atmosphere of the Gordon family trap and impinge on Leo's muddled, seeking consciousness. The break-ins succeed in awakening him from his sleep, but they should logically bring despair—not hope. There is no reason for Leo's curtain speech except the willed optimism of the author.

In later plays, the break-out by social commitment tends to become muted in articulation, or it is placed in the mouths of subordinate characters. Lorna's appeal in *Golden Boy* (III, 2) is simply a yearning for a romantic utopia, and A. L. Rosenberger in *Night Music* (III, 2) debases the theme by turning it into a youth cult and urging the lovers to join a "Party-to-Marry-My-Girl!" It seems clear that as Odets matured he saw the difficulties of holding to a collective ideal in a competitive society and in a culture whose values were both individualistic and materialistic. [11] He never lost hope entirely; Noah, in the covenant scene of *Peach,* says: "Now it is in man's hands to make or destroy the world" (8), but Odets had no formula for social cooperation that he knew would work. His characters hover on the verge of an unrealized ideal. The only successful break-out by social commitment is that of Frank, Joe's brother, a CIO organizer, in *Golden Boy.* But he serves only as a foil and contrast to Joe, and the thrust of the play belies his self-satisfaction.

Odet's understanding of the middle-class trap was at its most profound when he was dealing with those who made no attempt to escape, with the forces that kept the bourgeoisie content and passive in its family coffin. Though not an astute political thinker or sociologist, as a dramatic poet, intuitively, Odets has extraordinary insight into what kept his characters from achieving the revolutionary goals he espoused. His knowledge is so precise and uncanny that one suspects that—down at the roots—he, himself, was affected by the forces of inertia he wished to destroy. In a real sense, the strength of his plays lies in his portrait of the submerged and paralyzed American will.

Foremost among the forces that keep the middle class entrapped are the mass media—movies, radio, the newspaper, comics, the sports page—all the purveyors of popular culture. Odets' interest in satirizing the movies is evident in *Waiting for Lefty:* Edna tells her amorous husband, "Do it in the movies, Joe—they pay Clark Gable big money for it" (I); Fayette, the industrialist, comments on how consumers have their buying habits shaped by Hollywood: ". . . just let Mrs. Consumer know they're used by the Crawfords and Garbos—more volume of sales than one plant can handle" (II). In "The Young Hack and His Girl" episode, Sid and Florence play-act a scene of a wealthy, glamorous lovers' meeting ". . . like in the movies" (III). Florence refers to Queen Marie of Rumania, who had recently made a highly publicized tour of America from which she profited by endorsing beauty products and writing a woman's column. [12] Sid ends the scene by miming the "nose camera" bit from Paramount News—"The Eyes and Ears of the World."

But, unlike *Lefty,* in the family plays the myths of America as conveyed by the mass media are not merely satirized; they serve as both anodynes and stimuli for the emotional life of the middle class. For the young, like Ralph in *Awake and Sing!,* they are standards of measurement for one's self-image. Ralph says, "Who am I—Al Jolson?" and, "What do I do—go to night clubs with Greta Garbo?" and, derisively, he snorts, "I'm flying to Hollywood by plane—that's what I'm doing" (I). Since they are tantalizingly out of reach, the myths underscore the lack of progress of the young. For the old, however, they are comforting—proof that America is indeed the land of opportunity and that the poverty in the streets is a temporary aberration. Bessie says: "We saw a very good movie, with Wallace Beery. He acts like life, very good," and acidly comments, "Polly Moran too—a woman with a nose from here to Hunts Point, but a fine player" (II, 2). For Myron the movies provide an escape from harsh reality; he tries to remember "the great Italian lover in the movies. What was his name? The Sheik. . . . No one remembers?" and, two minutes later after leaving the room, he returns to announce: "Valentino! That's the one!" (I) For failures like Myron, and Gus Michaels in *Paradise Lost,* the movies are a necessary dream factory because they make life bearable. When Ben takes Libby (another ardent movie fan) to see Marlene Dietrich, Gus remarks, "Marlene—she's the intellect and artistic type," and "Marlene—I got her in the harem of my head" (I). Then he tells Clara Gordon that he often thinks of committing suicide, but laughingly confesses, ". . . I turn the radio on instead of the gas" (I). Jacob in *Awake and Sing!* diagnoses the appeal of the movies astutely: "He [Ralph] dreams all night of fortunes. Why not? Don't it say in the movies he should have a personal steamship, pyjamas for fifty dollars a pair and a toilet like a monument? But in the morning he wakes up and for ten dollars he can't fix the teeth" (II, 1).

Jacob's theory draws laughter from Uncle Morty, the successful businessman of the play. His mockery illustrates still another function of Hollywood— to turn life into a cartoon and dissipate the social malaise by suggesting that life is fundamentally ridiculous and animalistic. In his Preface Notes, Odets says that Uncle Morty "sees every Mickey Mouse cartoon that appears," and Morty's worldly wisdom and scorn for Jacob are garnished with cultural tidbits from Popeye the Sailor, the funnies (Ignatz and Boob McNutt) and Charlie Chaplin comedies. Uncle Morty uses the popular media only to reenforce his crudely stereotyped thinking, but Odets was aware that in a symbolic sense the world of Disney was an ironic paradigm of American values. In *Paradise Lost,* there is a striking scene (which I suspect influenced Ralph Ellison in *Invisible Man*) in which Ben, unable to find work, returns home with a box containing a Mickey Mouse Drummer Boy, a mechanical toy which he buys for nine cents and sells for fifteen on street corners. Ben identifies with the toy: "Poor Mickey Mouse!" (II); the all-American hero has been reduced to "a mechanical, capering mouse" (I), as Charlie Castle in a later echo describes himself in *The Big Knife.*

Long before *The Hidden Persuaders*, Marshall McLuhan, and the Yippie media freaks, Odets was aware of the potent forces that could lure the common man into creating a fantasy life more real than reality, and of the none-too-subtle manipulations by means of which the poor could be made to accept their status quo in the capitalistic system. In *Clash by Night*, Joe Doyle denounces the use of the media as an opiate: ". . . Earl, Jerry, Mae, millions like them, clinging to a goofy dream—expecting life to be a picnic. Who taught them that? Radio, songs, the movies—you're the greatest people going. Paradise is just around the corner. Shake that hip, swing that foot— we're on the Millionaire Express! Don't cultivate your plot of ground— tomorrow you might win a thousand acre farm! What farm? The dream farm!" (II, 2).

Odets has some of his characters protest directly; in *The Big Knife*, Charlie Castle says, "The whole movie thing is a murder of the people" (III, 2). But more often he shows us how the media insinuate themselves into the lives of those enclosed in the family trap, drugging their sensibilities against pain, offering a tablet of success to lull and tranquilize them. There is Myron in *Awake and Sing!* reading "a thing the druggist gave me. 'The Marvel Cosmetic Girl of Hollywood is going on the air. Give this charming little radio singer a name and win five thousand dollars. If you will send—' " (II, 2). And there is Gus in *Paradise Lost* thinking about putting in "a complete line of radios," and recalling what "a certain party in the American Tel and Tel" told him—"He says television's comin' in, sure as death" (I). Is it accidental that Myron's leaflet came from a druggist or that Odets associates the coming of TV with death? The symbolism is on target, though it is not as explicit here as in the climactic scene of *Clash by Night,* in which Jerry Wilenski murders Earl Pfeiffer as we listen to the movie dialogue of "a typical Hollywood 'product' " (II, 3), which Odets tells us is "so stupid and cruel, so *fraudulent* in the face of the present reality."

In his plays Odets constructs a further linkage between the phony fantasies of Hollywood and the popular press and the images of power and prestige puffed up by ad men for American industry. In *Golden Boy*, Gary Cooper's fourteen thousand dollar car pictured in the paper inspires Joe Bonaparte to buy the Deusenberg in which he dies. In *Paradise Lost*, in the scene in which the newly married Ben and Libby are interviewed by the press, Odets has the family posing in front of Gus's shiny, highly decorated motorcycle. 'Put Greta Garbo on the handlebars" (I), suggests a newsman. In *Night Music* (II, 4), the backdrop of the New York World's Fair (commercialism mixed with patriotism) is made to seem equally fraudulent as it presents to thousands a phantasmagoria of progress from which the poor are excluded.

Another force which seems temporarily to loosen the bonds of the family trap, ultimately to knot them even tighter, is nostalgia for the past: man's natural tendency to look back on a Golden Age when confronted with an untenable present. Myron, in *Awake and Sing!*, survives by ignoring the facts of the Depression—"Life is an even sweet event to him, but the 'old days' were sweeter yet" (Preface Notes). Nearly everything Myron says or does harks back to the past: his admiration for Teddy Roosevelt; his treatment of Hennie as though she were still a little girl—"Where you going, little Red Riding Hood?" (III); his conviction that "people aren't the same. N—O— The whole world's changing right under our eyes" (I). He takes solace in his recollections of Nora Bayes singing "at the old Proctor's on Twenty-third Street," and in idly boasting about his two years of law school and his job as a jewelry salesman on the road before he married. Even the weather will launch him on a voyage into yesterday: "There's no more big snows like in the old days. . . . I was a little boy when it happened—the Great Blizzard. It snowed three days without a stop that time. Yes, and the horse cars stopped. A silence of death was on the city and little babies got no milk . . . they say a lot of people died that year (II, 2). Odets' ironic technique in such reminiscent passages is to juxtapose the shadow of the present on the speaker's haloed memory, as he places the speech above just before Jacob's suicide.

Since the forces of the mass media and the pull of the past conjoin to seal the family trap, we may wonder what happens to those who remain and attempt no break-out. For the most part, we have adumbrated their fates already: either they become hapless victims of social forces they cannot control or a kind of walking dead, like Myron and Julie. But the analysis would be incomplete without noting still another Odetsian motif—that of mendacity or hypocrisy—which both affects those who remain in the trap and motivates those who would flee. The Moloch-god of materialism corrodes the family's moral values, and each play usually contains a pivotal scene of deceit which shows the trap closing on an unanticipated victim. This can best be illustrated by examining three key moments from the family plays.

In Act II, 2, of *Awake and Sing!,* Sam Feinschreiber comes to his in-laws' home disheveled and excited. He has had a fight with Hennie, and his wife has told him in a burst of anger that the baby is not his. Humiliated, ashamed at being "a second fiddle in his own house," he blurts out the incident to Jacob and Ralph, then repeats it to Bessie and Myron when they return home. Sam feels the remark "like a knife in his heart" and wants to know the truth. Hennie's parents, sensing that he wants consolation more than candor, attribute the remark to their daughter's "nerves." They butter up Sam's ego outrageously.

Sam is pathetically eager to snatch at the bait, soothe his wounded vanity, and return home to the wife and child he loves. But the point is not that Bessie and Myron connive to dissipate the fears of their son-in-law, but that Jacob, the idealist, *joins* them in the conspiracy. In a moment of crisis for the family, for all his lofty moral idealism, Jacob cannot suppress his feelings of family solidarity. He lies, and a few moments later—when Myron blurts out the truth—it becomes apparent to Ralph that his grandfather has participated in the trap laid for Sam from the start. Ralph's disgust is unbounded.

This exposure as a moral hypocrite, in combination with the other motives I have mentioned, prompts Jacob to take his own life shortly afterwards. A close reading of the text will, I believe, confirm that it is the decisive factor that leads to his death. In this scene, not only is Sam Feinschreiber a victim of mendacity; Jacob is destroyed by it.

While *The Flowering Peach* has been regarded by some critics as a softening of Odets' critical attitude toward the family,[13] I find evidence that his basic outlook had not changed. It is true that the Noah legend as set forth in the Bible dictated a more conciliatory spirit at the play's conclusion, but the old conflicts still rage before and during the voyage of the ark. The motif of mendacity is still present, in comic form, at a crucial moment in Scene 6; after 41 days of drifting, exploitation already exists on the ark. Shem, the business-minded son, is bribing Ham with liquor to do his work for him; Noah finds evidence of lechery and backbiting; but what sends him into a towering rage is his discovery that Shem has been hoarding "dried manure briquettes," fuel which this entrepreneur hopes to sell to his family when they reach dry land and thus begin a new capitalistic hegemony. Previously, Noah had insisted, "On the ark nothing will be for sale, no investments, hear me? Money is unholy dirt on the ark—" (4); he had forced Shem to return to the tax collector the money from his last-minute sale of his land. Now, while the ark is tipping perilously from the weight of Shem's fertilizer, Esther makes an artful defense of her son's action:

ESTHER: If you made it to sell, Shem, you're a low dog! But if you made it for the family—

SHEM   (*picking up the cue*): But, Momma, that's what I did—I made it for the family!

ESTHER   (*pretending surprise*): You hear, Noah?

NOAH   (*suspiciously*): Esther, you shouldn't take his part, hear me?

ESTHER: But if it's for the family, why throw it overboard. . . . ? (NOAH *looks at her, aware that she is putting something over on him; he turns away with tight lips, hands behind his back.* ESTHER, *stolidly*): Shem made a useful thing from nothing, yeh? Why kill the man with brains? No. make him use if for the *family!* (*Innocently*): I said it right, Noah. . . . ?

NOAH   (*mutteringly*): Go 'way from me. . . . (6).

Noah, who had wanted the ark to be "a holy place," is cajoled into starting the new world literally with *merde*. Esther's hypocrisy may be practical—indeed, that trait is the essence of her character—but her deceit not only dismays Noah but must surely have an injurious effect on the idealistic son, Japheth, who remains silent.

The motif of mendacity begins with bourgeois rationalizations like Esther's; its more serious implications can be seen at the end of Act II of *Paradise Lost,* when another mother makes a plea for her son. Leo has been paid a visit by Mr. May, a business-like arsonist, brought to the Gordons' home by Leo's partner, Sam Katz. May is proud of his record of 53 fires set for "respected citizens" who cash in their insurance policies to save their foundering businesses. Indignant at the illegality, but more shocked by the man's inhumanity, the idealistic Leo ejects him from his home. There follows a terrifying showdown with his partner, in which Katz is revealed as an impotent, twisted deceiver; not only has he lied to his friend about the firm's books, but he has placed the blame for his sterility on his wife, deceiving the whole world. After this moment of Sam's exposure, mendacity claims still another victim. Clara Gordon finds the card which Mr. May has left behind and learns of his profession.

There is something chilling in this transformation of the gay Clara who, in Act I, said, "I never worried a day in my life," into a creature so bedeviled by anxiety for her dying son and family misfortune that she is tempted to commit a criminal act. Clara does finally tear up the card, but Odets has shown that no inhabitant of the family trap is untouched by moral hypocrisy.

So the vicious circle completes itself. Those who remain in the family trap become its victims. Aged idealists like Jacob or Noah become corrupted or compromised. Loving mothers like Bessie, Clara, and Esther become moral hypocrites. Sons and daughters may be docile victims, like Pearl and Julie Gordon, or they may writhe and pull like Ben, Ralph, Hennie, Japheth, or Joe Bonaparte, in an attempt to break out. Most of these attempts, as we have seen, are failures. But Odets, who is interested primarily in his characters' humanity and only secondarily in their ideology, insists that there must be a way out. Outside the closely knit family circle looms a world of strangers, of fierce competition and external pressures, of economic dangers and, in some plays, global cataclysms. But the idealist cannot rest content in an island of mendacity, nor can he be lulled by media myths and nostalgia. He is driven forth by his conscience to meet the world's body, seeking a link with the rest of mankind and a chance for self-fulfillment.[14] For if death, running away, and social commitment do not work, there is another way out of the family trap, and that is to accept society on its own terms temporarily, to strike out for independence and power that will put you on top rather than keep you bottom-dog. This is a second major territory Odets explores as he moves from the family trap to the societal, from the world of blood relations to the bloody world outside.

Notes

1. "For Ralph, moreover, to applaud his sister's abandonment of her child and flight with Moe as an awakening does not speak well for his own awakening." John Gassner, "The Long Journey of a Talent," *Theatre Arts,* 33 (July 1949), 28. "The incongruity of the situation is enhanced by Ralph's approval of Hennie's elopement, an act which in purport is precisely

the opposite of his own plan to fight it out at home." Malcolm Goldstein, *The Political Stage* (New York, 1974), p. 96. For an argument that Ralph is merely calling for action for its own sake, not because he believes the break-out will succeed, see Shuman, p. 64.

2. See summary of Michael Blankfort's review from *New Masses,* 5 Mar. 1935, in Morgan Y. Himelstein's *Drama Was a Weapon* (New York, 1963), p. 167, and Goldstein, pp. 96–97.

3. Quoted above, p. 21. Wagner, "How a Playwright Triumphs" (Sept. 1966), p. 73. See also HUAC Hearings, May 19–21, 1952, "Communist Infiltration of the Hollywood Motion-Picture Industry, Part 8," pp. 3475–6.

4. Moe's comment on Ralph's speech, "Graduation Day!," seems particularly inept, since it comes from a cynical racketeer. The only explanation for it is that Moe admires Ralph's fighting spirit and tone; but it sounds almost as though Odets was patting himself on the back for a rousing curtain speech.

5. HUAC, p. 3468.

6. Lawson, *Theory and Technique of Playwriting and Screenwriting* (1936; rpt. New York, 1960), pp. 249–64, *passim.*

7. Himelstein, pp. 166–69.

8. William Gibson, Introduction to *Golden Boy* (musical version, New York, 1966), p. 9.

9. James T. Farrell, rev. of *Paradise Lost, Partisan Review and Anvil,* 3 (Feb. 1936), 28–29.

10. Weales, "The Group Theatre and Its Plays," in *American Theatre,* Stratford-Upon-Avon Studies 10 (New York, 1967), p. 72.

11. Weales, p. 69.

12. Robert Warnock, ed., *Representative American Plays* (Oakland, N.J., 1952), p. 564.

13. See Michael J. Mendelsohn, "Clifford Odets and the American Family," *Drama Survey* III (Fall, 1983) p. 242; and Shuman, *Clifford Odets,* p. 136.

14. Shuman, "Thematic Consistency in Odets' Early Plays," *Revue des Langues Vivantes,* 35 (1969), 418–19.

[*Waiting for Lefty*]

GERALD WEALES

When *Waiting for Lefty* was published in *New Theatre* it carried the subtitle, "A Play in Six Scenes, Based on the New York City Taxi Strike of February, 1934." It has been customary in general comments on the play to repeat the easy label, one that gives a suggestion of historicity without the need to be specific. The 1934 taxi strike however, was a somewhat complicated one, likely to place Odets's play in an oblique light.

It began on February 2 in a quarrel over the dispensation of a five-cent fare tax which had been declared unconstitutional. Fiorello LaGuardia, then mayor, had suggested that the five-cent charge remain and be given to the drivers whose tips had dropped after the tax was put on; the companies suggested a 60-40 split in their favor. Within the week (February 8), the drivers settled at 50-50, but the strike was far from over. The taxi men had no organization when they went out but from the strike itself emerged the Taxi Drivers Union of Greater New York, a confederation of drivers' groups from the various boroughs. A second demand, for the recognition of the union, was not granted in the first settlement. It was this demand that triggered the second strike, March 10, although the ostensible cause was the firing of a driver by the Parmelee System.

By this time, there was a fight within the TDU between the men who had run the February strike and the new leaders, of which Samuel Orner, head of the Manhattan union, and the organizer, Joseph Gilbert, were the most important. Burnshaw's review of *Lefty* reports that, at the second performance, Gilbert stepped from the wings "to say that just such a meeting as Odets presents took place last March when the members of the Union met in the Bronx and overwhelmingly voted to strike." Not that Sam and Joe, as they were called in *New Masses* (line drawings of them accompany Joseph North's "Taxi Strike" in the April 3 issue), ever had the full support that a theatre "STRIKE" cry implies. For the moment dominant, they called a general strike on March 17, but it was not nearly so effective as the February strike had been. The situation was further complicated by the formation of a Parmelee company union (headed by "Mr. Irving 'Rat' Robbins," as North

Originally published as "already the talk of the town below the Macy-Gimbel line," in *Odets: The Playwright* (London and New York: Methuen). Reprinted by permission of Methuen, London.

called him) and, as the trouble spread, similar organizations in the other companies. Violence began, according to the New York *Times,* when one thousand striking drivers marched through midtown, wrecking cabs that were still in service. While LaGuardia's office and the Regional Labor Board tried to work out a plebiscite on union representation (which no one—the companies, their house unions, the TDU—seemed to want), the violence continued.

There were charges of gangsterism on both sides. LaGuardia warned the strikers that there were gangsters among them and implied that the companies were using "Chicago strong-arm men." Orner had earlier denied that he was using "guerillas": "The drivers are pretty good with their fists and know how to use them, I have found. We don't need any gangster to help us." North, celebrating the ingenuity of the striking hackies, described "the Education Committee . . . which is a guerilla picket line well adapted to the needs of a big city strike of this sort . . . the scab finds his car doorless or even in flames." One of North's hackies said that the scabbing taxis were driven by "Chicago gunmen wit' soft hats," and there was apparently some truth to the charge. In *I Break Strikes!,*[1] Edward Levinson mentions casually, as though everyone knew, that Max Sherwood's Eagle Industrial Associates— one of whose hoods was called Taxi Murray—helped break the 1934 taxi strike.

The taxi strike was broken. The TDU accepted defeat. Orner tried to put a brave mouth on it, promising a stronger union to come, but he and Gilbert, among others, were expelled from TDU, accused of "conducting the strike for the benefit of the Communist party, rather than for the union membership and of having caused the loss of the strike by this action." This thumbnail history of the taxi strike indicates the distance between the simple, black-and-white world of the propaganda play and the gray reality which it presumably reflects and certainly serves.

In answer to a direct question at the HUAC hearing about whether *Lefty* had been based on the strike, Odets answered, "That is what they[2] say. But it is just something I kind of made up. . . . I didn't know anything about a taxicab strike. . . . I have never been near a strike in my life." In an oblique way what he is saying is probably true, even though, when *Lefty* was new, he was quoted in the *Daily Worker,* "The play was written out of admiration for the boys who fought along with Joe Gilbert and Sam Orner against LaGuardia's cops and the taxi-company's scabs." I suspect that it was not the strike, but Joseph North's article on it, which gave rise to the play; Odets's direct borrowing, minimal as it is, suggests that. North uses, almost as an epigraph, a long paragraph identified as "Hackie's Fable," in which the wife demands—as Edna does in the first scene of *Lefty*—that the driver choose between her and the company. Agate's identification of the Communist salute with the "good old uppercut to the chin" at the end of Odets's play comes directly from North ("His left fist—a huge affair—goes up in a sort of short uppercut"), although North goes Odets one better at the tough meta-phor game by letting his Pondsie call it "The left hook." Of course, Odets may not have been aware of his debt to North by the time he put words on paper. All of his plays are full of echoes—quotations, songs, taglines, some-times identified, sometimes not—which suggest that his was a kind of flypaper talent, pulling ideas and phrases out of the air. That I recognize "Come out in the light, Comrade," the line that ends the actor's scene, as a variation on the Black Man's "Come into the light, comrades, come into the light" from *Newsboy,* the play that Gregory Novikov made from a V. J. Jerome poem, does not mean that Odets consciously used *Newsboy,* even though (since the Workers Laboratory Theatre was acting it in 1934 and Jerome was a kind of cultural commissar for the Party) he probably knew the play. Even if Odets had used this material deliberately—patting a bit of North into place here, a touch of Jerome there, a whisper of Alfred Kreymborg (I think I hear echoes of the "Poor couple" scene from *America, America!* in the Joe-Edna quarrel) elsewhere—it would have been perfectly legitimate; in the context in which art is a weapon rather than an individual investment, this is not literary cannibalism but the proper use of existing tools.

Waiting for Lefty says a great deal less about the actual taxi strike of 1934 than it does, by implication, about the general labor situation of the time. The assumption, on the Left, was that the working man was being victimized not only by his employer but by a combination of politicians (headed by President Roosevelt) and dishonest labor leaders (the AFL as a gigantic company union). "We suppose that the supporters of the New Deal will admit that its purpose is to save American capitalism" (*New Masses,* March 1934). The NRA was seen as a first step toward fascism and the reigning assumption (as in Sid's big speech in *Lefty*) was that there was always a capitalistic war ready to chew up the workers when they were no longer usable on the production line. The cover of *New Masses* for August 1933 shows the NRA Eagle with a worker crushed in one claw, guns in the other; a good strong working-class arm is reaching onto the page, wringing the bird's neck: WE DO OUR PART. The network of villains might not be quite so wide outside the Communist press; but, at a time when militant unionism was pushing into new industries, upsetting not only the companies but the old labor status quo, its sympathizers—as the labor reporting in *Nation* and *New Republic* shows—shared the same general frame of reference. For this reason, Odets is able to use simple indicators, knowing that this audience will respond as he himself does to "textile strike" or "the man in the White House."

His Harry Fatt is conceived as the most obvious kind of corrupt union leader; his description ("A fat man of porcine appearance") leans heavily on the standard cartoon stereotype. If this were not immediately clear when the audience saw him (Russell Collins, who played Fatt originally, does not fit the description at all), it would be apparent as soon as he begins to speak, trying to persuade his own union that this is not the time to strike. "Look at the textile strike—out like lions and in like lambs." The textile strike had ended in September 1934 with none of its demands granted, and Frank Gorman, the AFL strike leader who had refused left-wing aid, was already becoming the villain in what the *New Masses* called the "super-super-super strike sell-out." "Take the San Francisco tie-up—starvation and broken heads." This is a reference to the maritime strike, but attitudes toward it can be seen in *Nation's* report on the three-day sympathy general strike which took place when "patriotic A.F. of L. members . . . stirred by the fiery appeals of Harry Bridges and other ardent strike-leaders of the I.L.A., bolted from the control of their usual masters, the reactionary labor leaders." "The steel boys wanted to walk out, too, but they changed their minds." In "The Steel Strike Collapses," Louis Adamic explained that the conservative labor leaders, in order to forestall the Communists and the radicals, started an organization drive of their own and held out a possibility of action, only to take shelter in William Green's call for mediation and to kill the expected strike. In each of these lines, Fatt says, look, strikes fail, and the audience hears, corrupt leaders sell out the workers. So, too, with the rest of his speech. Fatt's reference to Roosevelt ("looking out for our interests") suggests the remark of "one of the dubious leaders of the taxi men" whom Joseph North quotes: "that Great Humanitarian in Washington who won't let us suffer injustice." When Fatt calls a heckler "you damn red," the audience recognizes it as a too familiar tactic. "Our officials yelled 'Reds' at us, just like the police," complained a mill worker in still another *New Masses* article on the textile strike. Fatt's catalog of Russian crimes—endangering both Christ and virtuous womanhood—could have come directly from the Hearst papers; as Ferdinand Lundberg indicates in *Imperial Hearst,* the publisher initiated a particularly strong anti-communist campaign in late 1934.

In Fatt's first speech and throughout the play, Odets pulls his references out of the recent headlines (as he often does in later plays), but their use in *Waiting for Lefty* depends on a particular response rather than simple recognition. Given this pattern, it is surprising that more people did not call him out on the strike about which he was ostensibly writing. Some reviewers, like Percy Hammond of the *Herald Tribune* and Richard Lockridge of the *Sun,* did consult a taxi driver or two, convincing themselves that Odet's figures ("six-seven dollars a week") were wrong,[3] but it took Bill Shulman on the *Socialist Call* to question "the facts . . . since as history bears out, the leaders themselves were communists, who called the strike prematurely." Odets's crowd would presumably answer that it was not bad tactics, but a combination of liberal politics, big business and labor stooging that broke the strike. Shulman, of course, did not speak out of simple objectivity. His and other Socialist reviews displayed an understandable distrust of the Communists, since it was only recently (a *New Masses* drama review on November 27, 1934 praised a "First United Front" event) that the Communists had decided that maybe, after all, the Socialists were not their chief class enemy. Joseph T. Shipley in the *New Leader* added this qualification to his praise of *Lefty:* "It is guilty of the frequent Communist playing into Fascist hands, in its picture of the labor leader as a capitalist rat." The *New Leader*—compared to the *Call*— was a conservative Socialist voice, and it was in its pages that the oddest political response to *Lefty* appeared. Gertrude Weil Klein, deprecating "the wild acclaim of the self-appointed Bolshevik interpreters of the working class," attacked the play and did so by dipping into reminiscence, recalling or inventing a "Cliff Odets" who used to hang around Greenwich Village and to whom she attributed the remark, "The workers stink." The protests were so immediate and so loud (from Odets, the Group, *New Theatre*) that the *New Leader* printed an apology although, as the *Daily Worker* pettishly said, it was in "an inconspicuous corner." The Socialists were having internecine trouble of their own at this time, a split between the Militants, who wanted to work with the Communists, and the old-line Socialists. Given that situation, the Odets character who says, "The MILITANT! Come out in the light, Comrade," might appear to be doing something more than attempting to awaken the apolitical actor, might seem to be meddling in a private quarrel. Since none of the Socialist reviewers mentioned this point and since Odets was not the kind of theoretical Communist who played the hair-splitting ideational games so popular in the early 1930s, the use of MILITANT to balance "the meek" may be no more than one of the echoes I talked about earlier.

It was, of course, only in the leftist press that Odets's play got the kind of attention a propaganda play might be expected to elicit. Whether the uptown reviewers responded for or against the play politically, it was a reaction to the generalized radical thrust of the play rather than to the specific nuances. Once the play got to Broadway, the audiences—even though they were generally sympathetic to the play's message—could hardly have been as sensitive to the implications of "San Francisco" or "steel boys" as the special audiences for which it was presumably written. As the decade wore on and *Lefty* remained a favorite for amateur production, the references certainly lost their immediate meaning as well as their emotional freight. *Waiting for Lefty* was obviously created by the political-labor-theatrical context of 1934, but it was also created by a playwright, which may explain why it turned out to be so much hardier than the others of its breed—all as ephemeral as the daily paper. It had (perhaps still has) a dramatic vitality that can be understood only by taking a close look at how it was put together.

In the "Notes for Production" originally published with *Waiting for Lefty,* Odets said, "The form used is the old black-face minstrel form of chorus, end men, specialty men and interlocutor." More than twenty-five years later, he was still insisting that the minstrel show was his structural source, although he admitted that the play "took its form necessarily from what we then called the agit-prop form." Except for the fact that a circle of performers sits on stage and that now one, now another steps out of that circle to do an act of his own, the minstrel analogy is very tenuous. *Lefty* is more obviously an agitprop. Ben Blake, in his pamphlet *The Awakening of the American Theatre* (1935), explained that agitprop became popular with workers' theaters around New York in the early 1930s. The Prolet-Buehne, a German-speaking group, introduced the form as early as 1928, and the Workers Laboratory Theatre (founded in 1930) developed a similar kind of program on its own; eventually the two groups made contact and by the time the first National Workers Theatre Conference was held in 1932, the agitprop was the accepted dramatic weapon. Blake, thinking of the Prolet-Buehne's *Scottsboro,* called the agitprop "a new, chanted type of play," but the unsigned preface to the drama section of *Proletarian Literature in the United States* (a collection that Granville Hicks, *et al.* put together in 1935 for International Publishers) differentiated between works like *Scottsboro* ("This was the mass chant, consisting of a simple factual story, or a poem, which builds to a direct agitational appeal") and another kind of short play "written generally in doggerel, with stylized characters representing the boss, the worker, the militarist, the imperialist nations . . . really an animated cartoon, with a specific political message, delivered in schematic form." Perhaps the two can be seen as representing the two sides of the generic name (agitation and propaganda), but the forms (like the name) never remained separate; chants and cartoons alike had a way of pulling the audience, verbally at least, into the action. The function of the agitprop, after all, was to manipulate the audience, to elicit a particular response, one that hopefully would persist after the audience left the theater. A report on that first national conference outlined one of the basic tasks of the workers' theater: "to arouse the workers for the defense of the Soviet Union, against the coming imperialist attack." The issue of *Workers Theatre* for June–July, 1932, contained a typical collection of early agitprops that illustrate both the crudity of the form and the implementation of the task quoted above. *15 Minute Red Revue,* by John E. Bonn of the Prolet-Buehne, ends with its eleven performers asking, in unison, "Where is your future?" and then crying out, presumably joined by the audience, "FOR THE SOVIET UNION!!!" Both the anonymous *Vote Communist* ("An Election Play for Street Performances") and Nathaniel Buchwald's *Hands Off!* ("An Election Agitprop Play for Indoor Performances," translated from the Yiddish of J. Shapiro) end with the cry "VOTE COMMUNIST!" A sophistication of the form can be seen in the Smith-Kazan *Dimitroff* ("A Play of Mass Pressure"). Bad as it is, it is far superior to something like *Hands Off!* It builds to the usual audience chant, but it does so by using brief scenes—sometimes slapstick, sometimes serious—that give a cartoon account of the burning of the Reichstag and the subsequent attempt to place the blame on the Communists.

Odets may not have known the 1932 agitprops mentioned above, but he was certainly familiar with *Dimitroff.* He may even have acted in it. *Waiting for Lefty* is, of course, a great advance over the Smith-Kazan play, but the influence of *Dimitroff* and the agitprop in general can be plainly seen—in the characters, the ending and the relationship between performers and audience. Joseph Wood Krutch's complaint, "The villains are mere caricatures and even the very human heroes occasionally freeze into stained-glass attitudes," is an accurate criticism. Yet it is misleading because it assumes that Odets is mainly concerned with psychological depth, which is not the case. His characters are not thin realistic figures but thickened out agitprop cartoons. This can be seen in his use of significant names: what are "Fatt" and "Lefty" but labels?[4] The primary function of the scenes, for all the praise they received, was pedagogical; each had a point to make (the same point: the situation is unbearable, refuse to bear it) and, within the total context of the play, that point is more important than the incidental pleasures of character and dramatic action.

As for the ending, Lefty's "STRIKE, STRIKE, STRIKE!!!" is obviously one with the cries that brought the other agitprops to a close. In one sense only. Ideally the manipulation in agitprops is both artistic and political. The final cry is the inevitable result of the play itself, but it, in turn, is a new beginning. One not only shouted "VOTE COMMUNIST!," one presumably went out and did so. One not only shouted, "Free *Torgler!* Free *Thaelmann!*," one did what one could about it; an introductory note to *Dimitroff* said, "It should lead directly into the present mass-struggle to force the release of Thaelmann and Torgler." One not only shouted, "STRIKE, STRIKE, STRIKE!!!" but . . . what? The taxi strike was over; no new one was being planned; even if it were, the audience—except perhaps on the night of the taxi driver's benefit—would not directly be involved. We can assume, as Frederick A. Pottle did when he reviewed the published play, that the final shouts "refer to no mere cab-drivers' revolt," that the play ends "in a lyric proclamation of the proletarian revolution." In fact, we should so assume. *Lefty* is a call to action, but the action is amorphous, the revolution is metaphorical. The direct line between play and political action breaks down. The final STRIKE cry is a cousin to Aristotelian catharsis, a fulfilling of the audience, a moment of community that substitutes for direct action and makes it unnecessary. *Lefty* fails as agitprop because it succeeds too obviously as a play.

The last shout is only the most overt example of the way *Lefty* breaks down the conventional separation of audience and performers. The audience has a role to play from the beginning. It is the union meeting, being harangued from the stage, and there are plants in the auditorium—hecklers, the man who runs on stage in the "Labor Spy Episode"—to help give the whole thing verisimilitude. Helen Deutsch, in charge of publicity for the Group, explained in the New York *Herald Tribune* that the production used only five actors in the audience "but occasionally they seem like twenty, because so many persons are seeing the play for the second or even third time that they know all the answers, and lift their voices to help response." For

John Mason Brown this was "an old Reinhardt trick," and a number of
reviewers invoked Pirandello. Miss Deutsch herself pointed out that audience
plants had been used in the Theatre Union production of *Peace on Earth* by
George Sklar and Albert Maltz, and in John Galsworthy's *The Skin Game.*
Since the nonrealistic staging of *Peace on Earth* was abandoned in rehearsal (so
Morgan Y. Himelstein says in *Drama Was A Weapon,* and the reviews seem to
bear him out) and the Galsworthy play, which did plant bidders in the
audience in the auction scene, had been performed in 1920, when Odets was
still a schoolboy, I like to think Miss Deutsch was joking. In fact, she was
probably simply doing her PR job, helping to keep *Lefty* on the drama pages,
but her examples might be a way of saying *what is all this nonsense about
Pirandello. Lefty* is a revolutionary play, but Odets was certainly not involved
in an aesthetic revolution. Aside from *The Cuban Play,* which was never
produced, *Lefty* is the only play in which Odets abandoned the conventional
realistic form. He did so, however, without abandoning convention. The
play does not destroy the proscenium arch because, in its proper setting,
there would be no proscenium arch. *Lefty* was written to be performed by
small groups, in union halls, schoolrooms, anywhere. It was only chance—a
play that good emerging at a time so congenial to propaganda—that it ended
up on the stage of the Longacre Theatre, looking like one of Pirandello's
progeny. In its use of the audience—much more than its characters, which
keep slipping out of their cartoon origins, or its ending, in which agitation is
infected with art—*Lefty* is most obviously an agitprop.

The central action of *Waiting for Lefty* is not the waiting itself but the
struggle that takes place for control of the union meeting. As the play opens
Harry Fatt—with his gunman lolling down left, making an occasional threatening gesture—appears to be in control of the situation. Although his
opening speech is designed (by Odets) to turn the audience against him, he is
so sure of himself that he can taunt the members of the committee, can even
indulge them: "Sure, let him talk." Joe's speech turns into his scene with
Edna, but the audience has never left the union hall. "The seated men are
very dimly visible in the outer dark," the stage direction says, "but more
prominent is Fatt smoking his cigar and often blowing the smoke in the
lighted circle." There is a photograph of the original production which
indicates very clearly how the flashbacks are made to exist both in the past
that they are remembering and in the present of the meeting. Ruth Nelson
(as Edna) can be seen in her own shaft of light, but the committee is more
than "dimly visible;" a light behind has turned the sitting figures into
silhouettes, unmistakably if inactively part of her scene. The meeting once
again takes center stage in Episode IV when Fatt introduces "Tom Clayton
from little ole Philly" to warn them against going out on strike. There had
been a taxicab strike in Philadelphia, a bloody one, at the beginning of 1934,
but, unlike the New York strike, it ended with the recognition of the union.

Although knowledge of that successful strike adds an irony to Clayton's appearance, the scene is much more conventional than that subtlety suggests. The unmasking of the spy was practically mandatory in a labor play; *Peace on Earth,* which Odets would have known, had such a scene in 1933, but it was a standard before that (see *Gods of the Lightning,* the 1928 play by Maxwell Anderson and Harold Hickerson). Odets's variation (perhaps an unconscious throwback to all those Civil War stories in which brother met brother on the battlefield) lets the spy's brother expose him. If the play were taken as unbendingly realistic, one would have to assume that Clayton was on the agenda before the meeting began, that Fatt intended to use him in any case, but Odets's realism is only as real as the immediate dramatic demand allows it to be. Fatt obviously introduces Clayton at this point because he senses that the meeting is slipping away from him and Odets lets him do so to remind the audience, who has presumably been moved by the first three scenes, that the struggle is not over yet. At this point, it might be a good idea to look at those scenes.

The two most successful episodes, as miniature plays, are the first ("Joe and Edna") and the third ("The Young Hack and His Girl"). Both are domestic scenes. The former is simply a family quarrel which follows a familiar pattern. The wife, unable to persuade her husband with words, threatens to leave him, and thereby wins the argument; such a scene tradition-ally ends with an embrace and so does this one—although it is Joe's embrace of the cause. The other is a lovers-parting play, poured into the Depression mold. Although Irv warns his sister that she must give up Sid, it is economic conditions, not the family, that come between them. This situation—the impossibility of marriage in a world where poverty turns love sour (see Edna's "Do it in the movies, Joe—they pay Clark Gable big money for it," when she refuses to let him touch her in Episode I)—is one of the reigning clichés of the 1930s. Group audiences already knew it from the Siftons' *1931—.* It is based on the very real fact that marriages fell off when the Depression was at its worst. By the time Odets got around to using it, however, it was less a reflection of fact (there were more marriages in 1934 than in 1929) than a sentimental indicator of a world out of joint. It was a favorite with Odets. It recurs in *Awake and Sing!* and *Paradise Lost* and—long after it seems appropriate—in *Night Music* and *Clash by Night.* That Odets was aware that it was a variation on an ancient dramatic situation can be seen from his first use of it in *I Got the Blues,* the early version of *Awake and Sing!;* there, as though he were unsure that it was enough to let the economy come down on the shoulders of Ralph and his girl, he made her a Catholic and let Bessie worry about her being a *shikse* as well as a poor orphan. The economic situation may be the ultimate subject of Episode III, but its dramatic heart is the farewell itself. Sid and Florrie play at being movie lovers, a game that collapses under their distress. Unlike Adam and his girl in *1931—,* whose farewell scene follows their making love, Sid and Florrie remain pure (he gallantly refuses her offer), an instance in which Odets's romanticism becomes a device that lets his two characters remain vulnerable children. Since both these scenes follow standard patterns, their distinctive quality lies in the characters and their language, the way in which they use words connotatively (Edna's "Get out of here!" means "I love you") and jokes as protective devices (Florrie answers Sid's "What's on your mind?" with "The French and Indian War").

At first glance the second scene, "Lab Assistant Episode," might seem out of place between these other two. It introduces the first of the middle-class characters, about whom John Howard Lawson said, "One cannot reasonably call these people 'stormbirds of the working class.' " It does not dramatize the conditions which are pushing the taxi drivers to strike as the two domestic scenes do; instead, it shows the moment in which Miller loses his job and, thus, explains how he came to drive a taxi. In that way, it resembles the fifth and sixth episodes, which may be the reason the scene was dropped when the play was printed in *New Theatre* and *Proletarian Literature in the United States*. Yet, Episode II belongs with the first group because it, too, is a standard dramatic situation. The propaganda content of the scene, the pacifism that looked back to World War I (Miller's lines about his dead brother) and forward to the next war ("The world is an armed camp today"), masks a simple worm-turns situation. Clean-living Miller (he neither drinks nor smokes), conventionally subservient to those above him, finds himself, line by line, acceding to Fayette on matters about which he really does not agree (that the victims of World War I "died in a good cause," that the making of poison gas is necessary); he finally reaches his breaking point when Fayette asks him to spy on his superior. A good American boy, conditioned not to snitch on his buddies, his sense of honor forces the whole industrial structure into a new perspective, and, like the doting schoolboy who discovers that the basketball star is a bully not a hero, Miller hits Fayette in the mouth. "Fatt, of course, represents the capitalist system throughout the play," Odets says in the "Notes," and although the text does not specifically call for doubling—as it does later with the producer in Episode V—Russell Collins played Fayette as well as Fatt in the original Broadway production. The audience, recognizing Fatt in Fayette, will not, then, be watching the scene to see *what* will happen; it is the *when* that holds them, and the punch in the mouth is the fulfillment of audience expectations.

Although the three episodes contain direct propaganda statements, particularly in the speeches of Edna and Sid, the scenes are designed to work conventionally, to elicit audience sympathy, thus unloosening Fatt's hold on the meeting. Hence, his need for Clayton in Episode IV. After the failure of that ruse, the next speakers attack more directly, the scenes—"The Young Actor" and "Interne Episode"—become more sermons than dramatic scenes. It is true that Episode V is a comic turn of sorts in the caricature of the producer as businessman and there is a whisper of plot in the humiliation and rejection of the actor, but the main thrust of the scene lies in the exhortations of the secretary, her giving the actor a copy of *The Communist Manifesto* and inviting him to come into the light. The scene was dropped when *Lefty* was reprinted in *Six Plays* because it was "too untypical," a product of the immediate professional concerns of Odets and his fellow actors; or so Odets told Mendelsohn. I can think of at least one other reason why it might have been pulled. It is the most unequivocal statement of the play's Communist position. Even Agate's speech at the end works in metaphor (the uppercut) and allusion ("STORMBIRDS OF THE WORKING-CLASS"). If this is a correct guess, it is not simply a matter of the Odets of 1939 withdrawing a little from the Odets of 1935. The cast list suggests that the actor's scene had disappeared from *Lefty* by September 1935, when the play reopened on Broadway. In that case, it may be a matter of Odets, the Broadway playwright, withdrawing a little from Odets, the Communist playwright.

Episode VI, which today might be called a spin-off of *Men in White,* is a simple revelation scene, in which Dr. Benjamin learns that he is being fired because he is a Jew and the two doctors learn that the charity patient has died at the hands of an incompetent but well-connected intern. The meat of the scene is in the speeches of Dr. Barnes, who is old and corrupted by society, and can only ask Benjamin to act for him ("When you fire the first shot say, 'This one's for old Doc Barnes!' "); and in Benjamin's decision not to run to Russia but to stay and "Fight! Maybe get killed, but goddam! We'll go ahead!"

When we return to the meeting at the end of the play to hear Agate's speech, to learn that Lefty is dead, to answer the call to strike, we find that the previous two scenes have completely routed Fatt. He and his gunman are reduced to a show of violence, and even that is ineffective as the committee members step between them and Agate. Lawson, criticizing the development of *Lefty* as a play, says that the emotional intensity comes not from the action but from "the increasingly explicit statement of revolutionary protest," but he is working out of a too conventional idea of drama. Surely the growing explicitness is the motivational force in the action, the persuasive power that lets the committee convince themselves and finally the meeting (the audience) that the power in the hall (the theater? the country?) must pass to them. Lawson calls the play "a study in conversions," and, indeed, the scenes do detail past conversions (I, II, V, VI) or the situation out of which conversion will come (III); but these scenes become converting mechanisms thamselves, turning the committeemen from simply followers of Lefty to active strike leaders. That is why the news of Lefty's death is introduced at the end, almost an afterthought; it is the immediate trigger to the strike call, but it is not an important motivating event in the creation of a climate in which the cry of "STRIKE!" becomes possible. Lefty's absence provides an occasion, but his death is only an emotional fillip; the play has already reached its conclusion when the committeemen stop Fatt's attack on Agate.

All that remains is for the audience to ratify that fact which—this being an agitprop—they do not by applauding, but by shouting "STRIKE!"

Today *Waiting for Lefty* is considered little more than an historical artifact, and so it is. Yet its position as a representative propaganda play of the period rests in great part on the fact that, for all the crudities inherent in the form, it is an impressively made play, tailored to do a specific job. It is also the play in which the Odetsian style first burst on an unsuspecting public, but I prefer to consider that style in the next chapter, the discussion of *Awake and Sing!* which—despite the accident of production—is really Odets's first play and his best.

Notes

1. Levinson's book is primarily about the techniques of Pearl L. Bergoff, self-styled "King of the Strikebreakers." The line in *Lefty* about "that Bergman outfit on Columbus Circle" is probably a half-remembered reference to Bergoff, who once had offices at 2 Columbus Circle and who would certainly have been one of the villains in any strikelore.

2. This is presumably the same *they* who appears in the contest disavowal I quoted earlier. Odets's use of the pronoun in his testimony suggests a disengaging *otherness.*

3. An NRA report quoted in the New York *Times,* March 13, 1934, suggests that Odets was not far off.

4. This use of names—which was a way of working out character traits for Odets, as Lewis Milestone's article in the October 1936 *Stage* indicates—remained a favorite device for the playwright, even after he began to work in a more conventional realistic form. From Mr. Carp in *Golden Boy* to the ironic Buddy Bliss in *The Big Knife,* Odets continued to use names as indicators.

[*Awake and Sing!*
and *Paradise Lost*]

C. W. E. BIGSBY

Awake and Sing (1935) . . . represents a move away from the methods and assumptions of *Waiting for Lefty* and the simplicities of *Till the Day I Die*. Since it predates both plays it constituted another pole in Odets's work, an opposing approach to the agit-prop sketch and the episodic or collage plays of the Left. These had stood as revolts against bourgeois realism. They had sought to reduce the gap between life and art not merely by the choice of subject matter, nor even by the use of street theatre, the pursuit of new audiences, the creation of a collective protagonist or a collectivist approach, but by foregrounding theatricality, by undermining illusionism, by insisting on the factitious nature of the theatrical moment.

Distrustful of their own articulateness, fearful of stressing the individual component of experience, left-wing groups, particularly in the early 1930s, saw some virtue and integrity in a flight from realism. But in *Literature and Revolution* (1924) Leon Trotsky defended both the need for art and the necessity for retaining realism: "Art, it is said, is not a mirror, but a hammer: it does not reflect, it shapes . . . But . . . if one cannot get along without a mirror, even in shaving oneself, how can one reconstruct oneself or one's life, without seeing oneself in the 'mirror' of literature?" He distrusted the abandonment of a psychological drama, asking, "What does it mean to 'deny experiences,' that is, deny individual psychology, in literature and on the stage?" replying that "This is a late and long outlived protest of the Left wing of the intelligentzia against the passive realism of the Chekhov school and against dreamy symbolisms." But, he insisted, "If the experiences of Uncle Vanya have lost a little of their freshness—and this sin has actually taken place—it is none the less true that Uncle Vanya is not the only one with an inner life. In what way, on what grounds, and in the name of what, can art turn its back on the inner life of present-day man who is building a new external world, and thereby rebuilding himself? If art will not help this

Originally published as "The Group Theatre and Clifford Odets," in *A Critical Introduction to American Drama, Volume One, 1900–1940* (Cambridge: Cambridge University Press, 1982). © Cambridge University Press, 1982. Reprinted with the permission of Cambridge University Press.

new man to educate himself, to strengthen and redefine himself, then what is it for? And how can it organize the inner life, if it does not penetrate it and reproduce it?[1]

Odets's Berger family is trapped, in a mental no less than a physical world. The limits are partly those imposed by an urban setting which itself has been shaped by a history of speculation and exploitation, and partly by a mental geography which they regard as implacable as a physical terrain. Most of the family accept as unyielding what is mutable, constructing their own prisons out of economic fiats to which they give metaphysical authority. The primary space which they surrender is the crucial territory within which the self defines its own possibilities. Dreams are mistaken for visions and vice versa. The harsh realities of economic life are allowed to deform the moral imagination. The falsehoods of public mythology become the falsehoods of private life. The social lie, which proposes the inevitability of success and which accounts for failure by locating it in the weakness of the individual or the incorrigible wilfulness of a particular group, becomes the private lie, which demeans by forcing the individual to respect externalities, to allow a dangerous gap to open up between appearance and reality. The Berger family are on the verge of the middle class and as such are especially vulnerable. To deny the reality of the American dream is ostensibly to condemn themselves to permanent deprivation. The constant image is one of flight, escape. They look to escape the reality of their situation through marriage, through luck, through a desperate commitment to political or social myths, through a sardonic humour, through self-deceit, or even, most desperately, through suicide, albeit a suicide which, like that which was to send Willy Loman to his death in *Death of a Salesman,* is designed to liberate the next generation.

All the material is there for a social play which indicts a brutal and brutalising system. Certainly it is possible to make money. Bessie Berger's brother does so by dint of caring nothing for anyone, remaining blandly unaware of others' suffering and evidencing the crudest intolerance. Otherwise, it is really only the gambler and the cynic who can survive, and they do so by taking society on its own terms. But Odets is less interested in offering an indictment of capitalism than he is with asserting the need for a morally improved world, for the individual to wake up to a failure which is as much private as public. Odets was now a Communist Party member, but the mood of *Awake and Sing* is much closer to Roosevelt than to Marx. The awakening with which the play climaxes is very much that moral regeneration for which Roosevelt had called and which he was to continue to call for in his Second Inaugural, where he was to assert that:

Old Truths have been relearned; untruths have been unlearned . . . We are beginning to wipe out the line that divides the practical from the ideal; and in so doing we are fashioning an instrument of unimagined power for the establishment of a morally better world. This new understanding undermines the old admiration of worldly success as such. We are beginning to abandon our tolerance of the abuse of power by those who betray for profit the elementary decencies of life . . . Shall we pause now and turn our back upon the road that lies ahead? Shall we call this the promised land? Or, shall we continue on our way? For "each age is a dream that is dying, or one that is coming to birth."[2]

Awake and Sing recounts the personal growth to a kind of maturity of Ralph Berger and, ostensibly, of his sister Hennie. Condemned to play their required roles in the social drama which their mother has formulated from shreds of American pietism and capitalist propaganda, wedded to the lower middle-class insecurities of immigrant life, they are caught between her pretensions and the constraining power of their far from genteel poverty. Having failed to win her own place in the sun, she relies on her children to justify her and is implacable in the zeal with which she seeks to mould them. By the end of the play they have apparently learnt the need to break free, though the suicide of their grandfather offers an exemplary warning of the futility of a commitment and a vision not rooted in practical action.

Clifford Odets is an urban writer. The pressure which his characters feel is that of the city. The collapse of personal space, the closing off of social possibilities, the erosion of familial cohesion, the betrayal of moral values, the loss of transcendent vision, are the product of a world which is seen as essentially urban. The Bergers live in a tenement building. Their dog is exercised on the roof; their son sleeps in the living room; the different generations are crowded together, making the ironies of lost lives inescapable. Lost opportunities, denied hopes, frustrated plans, are ruthlessly exposed. Nothing can be concealed. The loss of space is the loss, too, of privacy, the exposure of failure and weakness. The transformation of this circumstance by simple ideological shift is not credible nor presented as such by Odets. Jacob's communism is a fantasy, rooted neither in knowledge nor action, while Ralph's personal liberation is drained of ideological content. Indeed that lack of ideological content emphasises the individual nature of that transformation, and its slender foundation. The ambiguity of this conversion is an indication of some of the play's more disabling contradictions. Odets delineates with care the pressures which destroy personal relations, individual conscience and communal values; he is less capable of identifying the source of regeneration which survives in language but not in action. Hennie's pursuit of personal fulfilment at the expense of her child, whom she abandons at the end of the play, is ostensibly endorsed by Ralph, suggesting a concern for self at the heart of his own bid for freedom which stains it with an egotism at odds with his language, and with the logic of the play which suggests a movement towards a self-realisation linked to national recovery.

Odets's is a world in which language is warped by circumstance. The language of familiarity cloaks a fundamental estrangement. The pressure of the city erodes the word, insinuates a space between language and meaning.

Jacob's romantic radicalism is born out of a desire to bring word and referent into some kind of dialectical relationship, to close the space opened up by time and the loss of an environment in which such a relationship would be possible. The pathos of Jacob is clear. He dies without closing that space and, worse than that, he dies with a kind of betrayal. In plunging to the sidewalk from the rooftop he offers his life to buy his grandson a future by leaving him $3000. It is a gesture which denies the life that he has constructed in his mind. It is a bribe offered to the world he thinks he holds in contempt. It is a gift which will taint the young man; which, if accepted, will pull him down into the material world, which will locate him with the forces he affects to despise. Like Willy Loman, in *Death of a Salesman,* he offers a dubious inheritance. The proof of Ralph's maturity lies, like Biff's, in his realisation that it is an inheritance which has to be refused. But where Willy Loman prides himself, no matter how self-deceivingly, on his success, desperately trying to relate to the public myths of America, Jacob consoles himself for his failure by condemning that society. In doing so, he inevitably defuses Odets's own indictment of the system. In both cases the weakness lies as much in the individual, wilfully self-blinding, vacillating, visionary without cogent perception, as it does in society. It is a weakness which blunts the social critique.

By the same token Ralph's decision to hand the money over to his mother and stay in the tenement leaves him in a social world unreconstructed except by his new version of a world which he now believes, without any evidence, to be susceptible to his transforming imagination. But that imagination is too insubstantially rooted to carry conviction. The density of the city, the accumulated evidence of loss, betrayal and surrender, is too great for his new perception to sustain the weight which Odets would place on it. What is presented as a triumph, as perception transmuted into action, is invaded by an irony generated less by his own weaknesses, though these are plain, than by the subversive power of a social world whose force lies more in its demeaning materialism than in the capitalist injustice. The play's action implies a determinism scarcely neutralised by a quixotic gesture, a commitment to transformation pushed not simply into the future and hence untested in action, but into a spiritual world which is perhaps indistinguishable from the fantasy which had animated his grandfather.

In the context of *Awake and Sing,* in which disillusionment, the blunting of aspirations and the slow depletion of energy are demonstrable facts of personal and public life, there is a terrible symmetry in Ralph's decision. The naive enthusiasm which he feels in the closing moments of the play is indistinguishable from that with which Moe Axelrod had gone off to war, Bessie had married her now dispirited husband and Jacob had responded to the images of human solidarity which had filled him with sufficient energy to purchase, but not read, a library of radical texts. There is a logic established which cannot be neutralised by simple rhetoric. He exchanges one dream for another; the vaguely-felt social commitment which now engages him. As he puts down the telephone, following the ending of a brief, but apparently passionately-felt affair, he announces, "No girl means anything to me until . . . Till I can take care of her. Till we don't look out on an air shaft. Till we can take the world in two hands and polish off the dirt."[3] The extent of the rationalisation seems clear, though it threatens the integrity of his new commitment. Indeed his failure to sustain that personal relationship in the face of opposition, the collapse of will which leads him to sacrifice her to her vindictive relatives, is of a kind with his sister's willing sacrifice of her child, abandoned so that she can seek happiness unencumbered. It cannot be viewed unambiguously and it must be presumed to have implications for his new faith, which is expressed with precisely that enthusiasm which he had previously reserved for his private world.

And the risk clearly exists that for Ralph the future will become a kind of crystalline myth, as the past does for his father. Teddy Roosevelt and Valentino define the parameters of his fantasy world, as Marx and Lenin do those of Jacob. The present is evacuated. It contains the threat of uncontrolled emotion; it demands a human response. It is Jacob who is described by Odets as being "a sentimental idealist with no power to turn ideal into action" but it is not clear why this should not also prove an adequate description of Ralph.

For Odets, the change in the lives of Ralph and Hennie, at least, though minor in origin and in immediate effect, was to be a public act. To newspaper interviewers he asserted that "The play represents an adjustment in the lives of the characters, not an adjustment of environment . . . just a minor family turmoil, an awakening to life of the characters, a change in attitude . . . But today the truth followed to its logical conclusions is inevitably revolutionary. No special pleading is necessary in a play which says that people should have full and richer lives."[4] When Jacob is particularly depressed or harassed he plays a recording of Caruso singing "O Paradiso" and explains that "a big explorer comes on a new land—'O Paradiso' . . . You hear? Oh paradise! Oh paradise on earth!"[5] This, presumably, is the America, now destroyed by greed, which must be redeemed.

The family, central to American mythology, becomes, if not the source of corruption, then its most obvious evidence. Jacob's comment, "Marx said it—abolish such families," is a genuine reference to the Communist manifesto, which does indeed assert that the bourgeoisie have made the family relationship into a financial relationship. This is exemplified here not merely by Bessie's willing sacrifice of moral value to financial security but also by the legacy left by Jacob. It is a temptation which has to be resisted. And yet the family is not to be abandoned, or, as in Hennie's case, not to be abandoned without moving into a dubious moral world. It is to be transformed by changing the nature of the society in which it is located. But this merely serves to underline the inadequacy of Ralph to the task which he wishes to take on. "Get teams together all over. Spit on your hands and get to work," he insists, "And with enough teams together maybe we'll get steam in the warehouse so our fingers don't freeze off. Maybe we'll fix it so life won't be printed on dollar bills."[6] But the agency for this transformation, the process whereby he will move from perception to action, is unclear.

The play's final speech signals his private rebirth in his own mind, but the link between that and a public act of reconstruction is dubious while the tone of the speech is scarcely different from that in which he had earlier announced his love-affair. At the beginning of the play he had explained that "I'm telling you I could sing . . . We just walked along like that, see, without a word, see. I never was so happy in all my life . . . She looked at me . . . right in the eyes . . . 'I love you,' she says, 'Ralph.' I took her home . . . I wanted to cry. That's how I felt."[7] At the end of the play it is an abstract cause rather than a girl, but the tone and indeed the language are the same: "My days won't be for nothing . . . I'm twenty-two and kickin'! I'll get along. Did Jake die for us to fight about nickels? No. 'Awake and sing,' he said . . . The night he died, I saw it like a thunderbolt! I saw he was dead and I was born! I swear to God, I'm one week old! I want the whole city to hear it—fresh blood, arms. We got 'em. We're glad we're living."[8] For Odets, his was an affirmative voice, just as below what he acknowledged to be the "dirty lie" implicit in Hennie and Moe's escape to Cuba he could bring himself to assert that "I do believe that, as the daughter in the family does, she can make a break with the groundling lies of her life, and try to find happiness by walking off with a man not her husband."[9] The flouting of convention is offered as itself adequate evidence of rebellion, but it is difficult to sustain this interpretation given Hennie's weakness and her casual abandonment of her child, and given Moe's strategy of neutralising the crude immorality of society with his own homeopathic corruption. Marx did not propose adultery as a solution to capitalism, nor the exchange of one failed capitalist paradise for another. But the confusion does not only operate in Odets's mind; it is endemic in the play. A drama of praxis requires both the possibility of change and characters capable of imagining and sustaining that change. Neither Hennie nor Moe has this imagination. They gamble on the future, on a radical change in Moe's personality for which there is no evidence; on the existence and desirability of a static world of romantic delight which will make no demands on their sensibilities or their consciences. Odets is caught between a social play of public revolt and a private drama of personal rebellion. The two are never successfully welded together except at the level of language.

There is perhaps an explanation of sorts in the fact that *Awake and Sing* had originally been deeply pessimistic. Indeed Clurman had called it "almost masochistically pessimistic." In an early version Moe is arrested before his proposition to Hennie; Bessie is a cruder figure, drained of what sympathy attaches itself to her in the final version. The changes may explain something of the obvious tensions in a play whose realism of dialogue and character was not matched by a coherent dramatic or social vision. Clurman described Odets's work well when he said:

> There was in it a fervor that derived from the hope and expectation of change and the desire for it. But there was rarely any expression of political consciousness in it, no deep commitment to a coherent philosophy of life, no pleading for a panacea. "A tendril of revolt" runs through all of Odets's work, but that is not the same thing as a consistent revolutionary conviction. Odets's work is not even proletarian in the sense that Gorky's work is. Rather it is profoundly of the lower middle class with all its vacillation, dual allegiance, fears, groping, self-distrust, dejection, spurts of energy, hosannas, vows of conversion and prayers for release. The "enlightenment" of the thirties, its efforts to come to a clearer understanding of and control over the anarchy of our society brought Odets a new mental perspective, but it is his emotional experience, not his thought, that gives his plays their special expressiveness and significance. His thought, the product chiefly of his four years with the Group and the new channels they led to, furnished Odets with the more conscious bits of his vocabulary, with an occasional epithet or slogan that were never fully integrated in his work. The feel of middle-class (and perhaps universal) disquiet in Odets's plays is sharp and specific; the ideas are general and hortatory. The Left movement provided Odets with a platform and a loud-speaker; the music that came through was that of a vast population of restive souls, unaware of its own mind, seeking help. To this Odets added the determination of youth. The quality of his plays is young, lyrical, yearning—as of someone on the threshold of life.[10]

Paradise Lost (1935), begun in 1933 and completed when the play was already in rehearsal two years later, was designed to be a work in which "The hero . . . is the entire American middle class of liberal tendency."[11] It is certainly concerned with indicting a group whom he wished to accuse of complicity in the collapse of the very moral values to which they had historically laid claim. Clurman responded to it because it reflected his own sense of a disintegrating social and moral world. Returning from the Soviet Union in which he had been impressed by the sanity of the people whom he had met, he was struck by the fact that "Wherever I went it seemed to me I observed an inner chaos. People hankered for things they didn't need or really want, belied their own best impulses, became miserable over trivialities, were ambitious to achieve ends they didn't respect, struggled over mirages, wandered about it in a maze where nothing was altogether real for them. *Paradise Lost* seemed to me to reflect this almost dreamlike unreality and, in a measure, to explain it.[12]

The play, presented in December 1935, takes place in the home of Leo and Clare Gordon. Leo is the somewhat vague and idealistic partner of Sam Katz. Together they run a small business manufacturing handbags, which Leo designs and Sam makes. But times are bad. Unbeknown to Leo, his partner has been systematically defrauding him, and at one point proposes that they should employ a gangster to burn their business down so that they can claim on the insurance. Under the pressure of a deteriorating financial situation criminality is presented as a constant temptation. Leo's son, Ben, an Olympic runner who discovers that public success as a sportsman is of no value to him in the job market, turns gangster and dies in a hail of police bullets. Another son, Julie, is dying, while a daughter, Pearl, abandoned by her lover, plays a piano all day long, finding that musical accomplishment is of no practical use to her. And the same mark of disaster is apparent in virtually all of the play's characters. A delegation of workers protest the inhuman wages and conditions to which they have been subjected by Sam. Leo's daughter-in-law is an empty-headed nymphomaniac. Through the Gordon apartment troop homeless men, corrupt politicians, bored newspapermen. Odets crams his stage with evidence of collapse and decay.

The characters are all dreamers. Pearl looks for a concert career. Ben confidently, and with no justification, expects "a swell berth" in Wall Street. Like Biff, in Miller's *Death of a Salesman,* he believes that athletic success necessarily leads to business success—that achievement is a matter of personal magnetism. And where for Miller the symbol of Biff's delusive dreams is the golden football helmet, for Ben it is a gold athletic figurine. And lest the significance of this should be lost on the audience Odets has Clare recount the story of the making of the golden calf, the false idol which the Israelites preferred to the worship of the true God. And this is a play about false gods, about the pre-eminence of money, the failure to distinguish between the real and the ersatz, about the betrayal of basic human values, about the collapse of American idealism into pragmatism. In other words, in many respects it is another version of *Awake and Sing,* but Odets attempts to paint a broader canvas.

It is a sprawling mess of a play, with a series of cameo portraits which suffer from the violence which he does to character. But beneath the level of melodramatic action, of trite plot, of painful caricatures, there is a real sense of pain and of an abandonment which goes considerably beyond the fact of financial collapse. His targets are various but indefinite. They are those who betray themselves for money, the system which has failed everyone, the distant fascists, and those, closer to home, who seem to be preparing the way for a new war. They are the persistent failure to learn from experience, the capitulation to despair and the reaching for dreams which are dangerous in their power to distract from a real world of human need and positive action. As Leo remarks, "We cancel our experience. This is an American habit."[13]

But there is an attempt to root these views in character no matter how much character itself is seen as a product of social reification. Thus Mr Pike, the furnace man, is given a speech which is ostensibly concerned with denouncing warmongers (a woman on the radio is heard celebrating Armistice Day by pledging American motherhood to sacrifice another generation for the maintenance of a system exposed by the rest of the play as fraudulent and deeply inhuman) but which, in its incoherences, offers a striking and even lyrical sense of a man reaching for a language which can contain experiences which can only be diminished by that language:

PIKE: . . . they have taken our sons and mangled them to death! They have left us lonely in our old age. The belly-robbers have taken clothes from our backs. We slept in subway toilets here. In Arkansas we picked fruit. I followed the crops north and dreamed of a warmer sun. We lived on and hoped. We lived in garbage dumps. Two of us found canned prunes, ate them and were poisoned for weeks. One died. Now I can't die. But we gave up to despair and life took quiet years. We worked a little. Nights I drank myself insensible. Punched my own mouth. Yes, first American ancestors and me. The circle's complete. Running away, stealing away to stick the ostrich head in sand. Living on a boat as night watchman, tied to shore, not here nor there! The American jitters! Idealism! (*Punches himself violently*) There's for idealism! For those blue-bellied Yankee Doodle bastards are making other wars while we sleep . . . No logic . . .

LEO: But what is to be done?

PIKE: I don't know . . . I mean I don't know . . .

LEO: I will find out how to do as I think.

GUS   (*drinking and laughing*): We're decayin', fallin' apart minute by minute.

PIKE: All these years one thing kept me sane: I looked at the telegraph poles. "All those wires are going some place," I told myself. Our country is the biggest and best pigsty in the world."[14]

The Pike who speaks of the solitary, piano-playing Pearl as "alone in her room with the piano—the white keys banked up like lilies and she suckin' at her own breast"[15] is not the simple radical the others would wish to make him. He represents not only the need to work for the transformation of his society—a need in which he is himself deficient—but also the necessity to create space for beauty. He is, in a sense, an expression of Odets's own amalgam of romanticism and radicalism.

It is once again clear who the enemy is. The local democratic politician is concerned only with votes, and when the Gordon family is dispossessed and their furniture placed on the street outside, his only thought is to have it removed lest it interfere with the "prosperity party" which he wishes to hold. In the face of sixteen million unemployed the politicians are presented as powerless and self-contained. But again all that Odets has to offer is the need to abandon fantasy, a world in which "in the end nothing is real. Nothing is left but our memory of life,"[16] and to wake up to the reality of a world which is no longer susceptible to pieties derived from an American idealism negated by the present realities of unemployment, corruption and despair. Again the whole weight of Odets's faith rests on the play's final speech in which Leo, content up to this time to remain uninvolved, declares his conviction that the time has come to take a stand, to abandon illusion and acknowledge responsibility.

> There is more to life than this! . . . the past was a dream. But this is real! To know from this that something must be done. That is real . . . we searched; we were confused! But we searched, and now the search is ended. For the truth has found us . . . Everywhere now men are rising from their sleep. Men, men are understanding the bitter black total of their lives? Their whispers are growing to shouts! They become an ocean of understanding. *No man fights alone.* Oh, if you could only see with the greatness of man. I tremble like a bride to see when they'll use it . . . I tell you the whole world is for men to possess. Heartbreak and terror are not the heritage of mankind! . . . the world is in its morning . . . and *no man fights alone!* Let us have air . . . Open the windows. [17]

In the context of the play such a speech should be ironic. It is clearly not offered as such. Brecht was amazed that Odets apparently saw such middle-class businessmen as worthy of sympathy, but this is a characteristic of Odets's plays. The bourgeoisie may have been in some respects the heart of the problem but to Odets they were also the class capable of articulating the dilemma; they were the class with its roots in American idealism.

Odets presents his capitalists as sexually impotent. Indeed the play transposes the social into a sexual dimension. The embezzler is impotent. The children of his partner are denied sexual relations (Pearl loses her lover; Ben is cuckolded). Kewpie, the gangster, is sexually as well as financially avaricious. It is a familiar conceit. Hemingway, Fitzgerald and West each offered a sexual correlative for their sense of a lost harmony between the self and society. But here, as in Hemingway's *To Have and Have Not,* it is rather too casual a gesture to sustain conviction. The symbol becomes an alternative to analysis.

In common with others Odets's imagination was caught by the forces which so manifestly press on the sensibility and physical existence of individuals for whom individuality had become problematic. Liberalism itself had undergone a profound redefinition. The novel had registered a collapse of faith in liberal individualism which was a product, in part, of the shocks of late nineteenth-century life—the determinism engendered by urbanism, industrialisation, the disturbing new realities exposed by Darwin and Freud—and in part of the bewildering brutalities of the First World War. For Hemingway, liberal language and the abstract virtues had been destroyed by an ineluctable facticity; for Fitzgerald liberal individualism was inherently ambiguous, dangerously allied to romantic egotism. The old liberal virtues—individualism, self-improvement, laissez-faire economics—had effectively been taken over by conservatism. Politically, liberalism re-emerged as a corporate reformist philosophy. For many the logic of that was that this line should be projected in the direction of Marxism. But in the case of many Americans, more especially writers, the Marxism they embraced was less ideological than spiritual—it was an image of human unity, a conviction that capitalism had run its course (by which, more often than not, they seem to have meant that money should no longer be a defining factor, that war was simply a product of capitalist imperialism). But in truth the model which Odets, no less than Steinbeck, treasured was closer to that embodied in Jefferson. What they looked for was a sense of spiritual and moral renewal. The rhetoric was often Marxist, the content essentially concerned with the need to restore an idealism which was recognisably American. They were against a life "printed on dollar bills," saw business as potentially a form of gangsterism, proposed a model of history with clear edges, saw America as waking up to its own betrayals. It was to be a new Great Awakening.

The realist texture of Odets's work itself implies rejection—a rejection of fantasy and dream. His characters have to be weaned from their self-conceits, from the myths to which they pledge their lives, because, ostensibly at any rate, it is that tactile world which has to be reforged, shaped so as to contain the freedom they would claim. And yet there is a problem here for Odets in so far as he is himself a visionary. He rejects the myths with which society has sought to validate greed and self-concern, but wishes to endorse the potential sentimentality of love and to parade his own visionary ideas. It remains true that for him the crucial transformation is within, a conversion which will radiate outwards from the self to the context within which it operates. If realism, as René Wellek implies, was a polemical weapon against romanticism, for Odets this opposition was only of limited validity. Certainly he saw himself as opposing the dangerous and facile illusions paraded by society (the glory of war, the significance of externals, the value of status) but he was drawn to the romantics' view of art as a central moral force, as in some senses an expression of a rebellious sensibility as well as of a visionary experience. And if he clearly replaces one romanticism with another, then Wellek was prone to do much the same.

The vagueness of the commitments to which his protagonists awake is striking. They turn their backs on poverty, injustice and violence, to be sure, but the world to which they turn their faces is a simple blur of light. It is negatively defined; it is everything the old world was not. And yet the characters who set out towards that light as the curtain falls are themselves imperfect—if the plays' action is to mean anything. They have learned the need for conversion but there is no agency for that conversion, no object of worship, no regulated life for the convert, no creed (beyond the brotherhood of man), no sacraments, no icons, no mechanism to turn the moment of conversion into a dedicated life. The Party, which for many provided all this, is for the most part nowhere to be seen. They are apparently reconverted to American idealism but an idealism historically stained, subverted by time and by human nature which Odets had presented as implacable but now wishes to believe is redeemable. Against all evidence, perfection is proposed as a realisable objective in *Awake and Sing* and in *Paradise Lost.* Dealing in absolutes he thus had nowhere to go in *Golden Boy* and *The Big Knife,* when he was forced to acknowledge the inadequacy of his characters to the task which they glimpsed. The irony is that the real energy of the plays is not contained in the unlocked fire, the spiritual regeneration, but in the cluttered plot, the dense human matter, the wit, the overlapping, energetic self-displays. This may be the energy of a culture in decline but it is compelling in a way that the new world which he welcomes at the end of the play is not. The debate between the rights of the individual and those of the collective are contained in the form of the plays which pitch the resistant self against the density of social experience and the sheer volume of incident. This is the central strategy of Odets's work.

Notes

1. Leon Trotsky, *Literature and Revolution* (Ann Arbor, 1968), pp. 137–8.
2. Clarke A. Chambers, *The New Deal at Home and Abroad, 1929–1945* (New York, 1965), pp. 71–2.
3. Clifford Odets, *Six Plays by Clifford Odets* (New York, 1979, originally published 1939), p. 96.
4. Gerald Weales, *Clifford Odets* (New York, 1971), p. 68.
5. Odets, *Six Plays,* pp. 50–51.
6. *Ibid.,* p. 97.
7. *Ibid.,* p. 47.
8. *Ibid.,* pp. 100–1.
9. Weales, *Clifford Odets,* p. 72.
10. Clurman, *The Fervent Years,* pp. 150–1.
11. Weales, *Clifford Odets,* p. 92.
12. *Ibid.,* p. 166.
13. Odets, *Six Plays,* p. 191.
14. *Ibid.*
15. *Ibid.,* p. 199.
16. *Ibid.,* p. 224.
17. *Ibid.,* p. 229.

[*Awake and Sing!*]

R. Baird Shuman

The basic social unit with which Odets deals in *Awake and Sing!* is the family. He has been quoted as saying that the family is "society's basic biological cell . . . strong and organic." The Bergers, who represent in many ways a typical American family of the 1930's, are of the working class and are struggling to rise above this status. Ralph, the idealistic son, is just ". . . looking for a chance to get to first base," as is the rest of the family. But the play leaves one wondering whether in a capitalistic system, the sensitive and intelligent youth, Ralph, will ever be able to succeed.

The signs of success presented in the play in the persons of Uncle Morty and Moe Axelrod are not encouraging. Uncle Morty, a clothing manufacturer, has flouted labor's cause, "has risen out of its ranks to exploit it. Morty is a sensualist. He lives well, drives a big car and contributes the sum of five dollars a week toward the support of his father whom he baits as a 'nut.' "[1] Uncle Morty is insulated against any tender emotions which might tend to weaken him in his business dealings. We are told in the description of characters which is given before the play that "something sinister comes out of the fact that the lives of others seldom touch him deeply" (38).[2] His philosophy is well summed up in his words, "In the long run common sense is thicker than love" (65). Though successful, Morty is a victim of the capitalistic system which, in the view of the play, deprives a man of all personality. He recognizes this lack in himself when he says, "Business don't stop for personal life" (89), but there is little he can do to remedy his situation; and it is unlikely that he would choose to remedy it if it were in his power to do so.

The other financially successful figure in the play is the embittered Moe Axelrod, a boarder in the Berger household, who lost one leg in the war and who, because of this injury, has the security of a government pension. A petty racketeer, his realistic view of life is: "It's all a racket—from horse racing on down. Marriage, politics, big business—everybody plays cops and robbers" (71). Moe is another product of a world order in which war is condoned as well as what Anita Block in *The Changing World in Plays and Theatre* calls the oppression and contrived insecurity of the worker.

From *Clifford Odets* (New York: Twayne, 1962). Reprinted by permission of R. Baird Shuman.

It is important to note that both of the successful characters in this play are deformed: one, spiritually and emotionally; the other, physically and emotionally. If one is to accept Albert Hunt's theory that Odets deals entirely in symbols,[3] and this writer has a great inclination to do so, then Uncle Morty and Moe represent the compromise which one must make in order to succeed in a capitalistic system. Each is warped and crippled in his own way; each has made the adustment within himself which success demands.

Ralph and Hennie represent the younger generation in the Berger household. Theirs is ". . . the struggle of the younger generation to get away from the sordid realities created by their parents, which bind them hand and foot," as Miss Block points out. But in winning their own struggle, they create for the succeeding generation sordid realities which, in the moral code of their society, are far more difficult to face than those created for them by their parents. When Hennie runs off with Moe Axelrod, leaving her husband and her child, she is creating a situation for that child which is essentially much less favorable than any which she ever had to face in her childhood. Anyone reading the play knows just how unfavorable a situation Hennie's child is left in because Odets, in the character descriptions before the play, says, of a minor character, Schlosser, that he "is an overworked German whose wife ran away with another man and left him with a young daughter who in turn ran away and joined a burlesque show as chorus girl. The man suffers rheumatic pains. He has lost his identity twenty years before" (39). This description of a character who has only three small speeches in the play is indefensibly prolix unless it has some additional relationship to the play. The purpose of it is to point to the sort of situation which Hennie is creating for her child and husband.

In a way Hennie has actually had a much pleasanter existence than a girl in her circumstances might be expected to have. Bessie Berger, her mother, has had a sincere concern for her family, albeit an overconcern. But Bessie was ". . . not only the mother, but also the father. The first two years [of my marriage]," she says, "I worked in a stocking factory for six dollars a week while Myron Berger went to law school. If I didn't worry about the family who would?" (95). There is nothing of the dreamer about Bessie; her concern is with the here and now; her fundamental quest is respectability. When she admonishes her father, who is giving Uncle Morty a haircut, not to get any hair on the floor because "I like my house to look respectable" (59), it is obvious that she is stating the aim of her whole life. By the time she utters this statement, she has shown that her desire for respectability is the chief motivating force in her life, for she has already forced the pregnant Hennie into a marriage with a man whom Hennie does not love; Bessie does this in order to save face for the family, little realizing that she is forcing upon the family the ultimate deterioration which is evident at the close of the play. When Ralph discovers what his mother has done, he is completely appalled; he is even more shocked by the indifference of Jacob, his grandfather, who is an idealist and a Marxian, for having permitted Hennie to marry Sam Feinschreiber, who is to be deluded into thinking that Hennie's child is also his child. Ralph says to Jacob:

> I suppose you knew about this, Jake?
> JACOB: Yes.
> RALPH: Why didn't yo do something?
> JACOB: I'm an old man.
> RALPH: What's that got to do wth the price of bonds? Sits around and lets a thing like that happen! You make me sick too. (84)

In these few lines it is evident that the older idealist, Jacob, is not a man of action. He can only say, "This is a house? Marx said it—abolish such families" (55), but he cannot rise to action and he realizes this shortcoming in himself; indeed, it is very largely this realization which leads to his suicide. He is aware of the fact that his life has been a waste; his hope for the future is in Ralph and he gives him advice which he has never been able to follow himself: "This . . . I tell you—DO! Do what is in your heart and carry in yourself a revolution. But you should act. Not like me. A man who had golden opportunities but drank instead a glass tea" (78). This advice, of course, suggests a solution to social ills which is so generalized, so vague and tenuous, that it is really not a solution at all.

After Jacob has spoken his words of counsel, there is a pause during which the mail plane from Boston flies above the house. The mail plane is very much connected with the depiction of Ralph's psychological constitution. It represents a vague, anticipatory hope analogous to the dreamy hope in Ralph's lines at the beginning of Act II which read, "When I was a kid I laid awake at nights and heard the sounds of trains . . . faraway lonesome sounds . . . boats going up and down the river. I used to think of all kinds of things I wanted to do." Implicit in the transportation theme is the sense of going somewhere and to Ralph it is a sort of wish fulfillment; Ralph wants to think that he is going somewhere, that he is accomplishing something, that life has meaning and that *his* life specifically will be meaningful.

The mail plane is also to recur as a *leit motif* when the meaning of Jacob's life and thought finally becomes clear to Ralph in the last act:

> RALPH: I see every house lousy with lies and hate. He said it, Grandpa—Brooklyn hates the Bronx. Smacked on the nose twice a day. But boys and girls can get ahead like that, Mom. We don't want life printed on dollar bills, Mom!
> BESSIE: So go out and change the world if you don't like it.
> RALPH: I will! And why? 'Cause life's different in my head. Gimme earth in two hands, I'm strong. There . . . hear him? The air mail off to Boston. Day or night, he flies away, a job to do. That's us and it's no time to die. (95)

Whereas, just days before, Ralph had belittled his grandfather's statement that "never a young man had such opportunity like today. He could make history" (76), he now gives his approval to it. He realizes the importance of action; and in this speech as well as in his aforementioned speech at the beginning of Act II, the accent is on the word "do." And this word, of course, is the essence of Jacob's advice to Ralph. Through his grandfather's death, Ralph has been reborn. Moe Axelrod had said, in the last minutes of the play, ". . . cut off your leg to save your life! And they done it—one thing to get another." Now this statement echoes as Ralph vows, "My days won't be for nothing. . . . I'm twenty-two and kickin'! I'll get along. Did Jake die for us to fight about nickels? No! 'Awake and sing,' he said. Right here he stood and said it. The night he died, I saw it like a thunderbolt! I saw he was dead and I was born! I swear to God, I'm one week old!" (100).

This speech is most dramatic, but it appeals more effectively to one's sense of drama than to one's logic. As John Howard Lawson points out, the audience is merely *told* that Ralph has undergone a change. The change is not effectively or convincingly presented through any development in his character as the play progresses. Essentially Ralph is left at the end of the play with the same situation that faced him at the beginning of it—with one exception: He has had the chance to change the situation and did not.

At any rate, Moe Axelrod's statement, "One thing to get another," sums up much of Odets' philosophy here; the suicide of Jake, who was constitutionally unable to rise to social action, Odets would have his audience believe, has precipitated the rebirth of a man who could rise to such action. Jake's hope had always been in the future; he had used the past only in order to be sure that he was building towards a better future, as Ralph implies he will do when he comes to Jake's room with an armful of the old man's books. One cannot be sure that Ralph will be any more successful in attaining his ends than Jacob was, because Odets does not give one evidence that Ralph is a man of action, but rather suggests the contrary; he has shown some signs of being willing to rebel, but he demonstrates an inability to rebel in a situation so commonplace as that involving his relationship with Blanche, the young woman with whom he has fallen in love. He does appear to strike out against his mother when she tries to come between him and Blanche, and his speech in this regard is stirring, but he does not follow it up with action. He says to Bessie: "I been working for years, bringing in money here—putting it in your hand like a kid. All right, I can't get my teeth fixed. All right, that a new suit's like trying to buy the Chrysler Building. You never in your life bought me a pair of skates even—things I died for when I was a kid. I don't care about that stuff, see. Only just remember I pay some of the bills around here, just a few . . . and if my girl calls me on the phone I'll talk to her any time I please" (66). But when Blanche most needs Ralph's help, he does not give it. He hesitates to go to take her away from her unsympathetic uncle merely because he knows that her uncle is muscular and he doubts his own physical strength. Finally, when he has within his reach the legacy which Jacob has left him and when he might finally marry Blanche, he finds excuses and says to Moe, "No girl means anything to me until . . . I can take care of her. Till we don't look out on an airshaft. Till we can take the world in two hands and polish off the dirt" (96).

Hennie, as well as Ralph and Jacob, tends to live in the future; but she envisions a future of escape to a land of heart's desire as described to her by Moe, a place ". . . where it's moonlight and roses. We'll lay down, count stars. Hear the big ocean making noise. You lay under the trees. Champagne flows like—" (98). But Hennie is the antithesis of Ralph and Jacob, for to them it is important that "life should have some dignity," while to Hennie this is unimportant. She wants to be comfortable physically and materially. Jacob has always stressed the value of love, but Hennie is incapable of loving either her husband or her child. She would willingly leave them in order to find an easier life with Moe, a man whom she does not love either.

This presentation of Hennie has caused many people to level unfavorable criticism at Odets' values; however, it seems evident that he is diagnosing one of the major ills of society; he is stressing the fact that circumstances can completely nullify one's ability to love and that Hennie's behavior is inevitable in the light of the circumstances which have been so much a factor in the development of her personality. Hennie lacks understanding and is utterly unable to face life realistically. Romance has replaced reason in her. She has utterly no understanding of or interest in the ideological positions of Ralph and Jacob; she cannot strive towards the new world which they envisage, so she strives towards the only hopeful goal within her reach. The point of Hennie's action is only that of emphasizing the moral chaos which Odets saw about him as a result of the Depression and, by extension, of the capitalistic system.

Hennie would agree with Uncle Morty that "to raise a family nowadays you must be a damn fool." This sentiment, already seen in *Waiting for Lefty,* is the sentiment of an age, and Uncle Morty is Odets' representation of the practical capitalist. However, Uncle Morty's statement does not go unchallenged, for Bessie Berger, speaking for her particular segment of Jewish society, answers, ". . . a woman who don't raise a family—a girl—should jump overboard. What's she good for?" (62). Bessie represents nothing so fully in the play as she does stolid plodding and continuance. She lives from day to day; but through the most trying situations Bessie continues to maintain her family. Hennie expresses what the audience comes to feel about Bessie when she says of her mother, "She'll go on forever" (100).

Bessie is fully aware that the margin between having a home and some degree of security and family stability and not having these things is very narrow. More than once she refers to people who have been evicted from their homes and this thought is nightmarish to her: "They threw out a family on Dawson Street today. All the furniture on the sidewalk. A fine old woman with gray hair" (43). This is the sort of situation with which Bessie feels an extreme empathy, especially in view of her emphasis on maintaining a front of respectability. If Bessie has dominated her family to such a point that her husband has lost all semblance of self-respect and her children find her hard to bear, she has done so in order to preserve the family as a physical unit. She cannot agree with Jake that family should be abolished any more than she can agree with Uncle Morty that "to raise a family nowadays you must be a damn fool." Bessie, despite all of the problems which the family causes her, enjoys her role of mother which she has turned into the role of martyr.

Myron, her husband, has been a clerk for thirty years. He has never known success, but he cannot entirely admit defeat either. He lives almost exclusively in the past, nurturing his hero worship for Theodore Roosevelt, a man who stands in polar opposition to him temperamentally. Myron's gullibility makes him blind to the social injustices which trouble Ralph and Jacob. Myron has yearned for success, but he does not realize that "all the cards of the social structure . . . were stacked against him."[4] Instead of despairing, he puts fifty cents into the Irish Sweepstakes and hopes for sudden, dramatic success; or he bets on a horse, winning just often enough so that he does not lose hope and will continue to place his bets regularly; or he enters a contest to name a beauty who is going on the air to advertise cosmetics. When Moe says that Myron still believes in Santa Claus, Myron answers with naive faith, "Someone's got to win. The government isn't gonna allow everything to be a fake" (87).

This is perhaps the most telling statement that Myron makes in the entire course of the play. It reveals what his life has been—a fake. The sum total of his existence adds up to zero; he has grown so used to frustration that he accepts it as commonplace in his life. Only a miracle can alter Myron's existence, so there is no reason for him not to believe in miracles. Without this hope, life would be utterly meaningless and hopeless to him. Petty gambling, in his life, fills the need which Marxism fills in the lives of Jake and Ralph. All three are basically interested in materialistic betterment in life: Myron, on an individual basis; Ralph and Jake on a level which would affect all of society. But, despite Ralph's philosophical solution to the ills of society, one cannot help comparing his statement, "I pay some of the bills around here" (66), with Uncel Morty's statement to Jake that ". . . without rich men around you don't have a roof over your head" (72). Both men, despite the extreme cultural and philosophical gap between them, are using a baldly economic standard as a means of self-assertion.

It is obvious that Odets is concerned in this play with what he calls "general fraud." This he defined in an interview for *Time Magazine* as ". . . the Cinderella approach to life, the American success story." It is because of his concern with "general fraud" that he emphasizes Hennie's interest in the movies; it is her one easily obtainable means of escape. This theme of basing one's dreams on Hollywood standards is recurrent in the play and is blasted by Jake, who, instead, dreams of something which he feels is within the reach of the masses. In talking about "success," Jake says that American youth dreams all night of fortunes: "Why not? Don't it say in the movies he should have a personal steamship, pyjamas [*sic*] for fifty dollars a pair and a toilet like a monument? But in the morning he wakes up and for ten dollars he can't fix the teeth. And millions are worse off" (71–72). It is with such juxtapositions that Odets achieves his highest level of social dynamism. This, to Odets, is the great American lie. This is the sort of thing to which Ralph refers when he says, "I see every house lousy with lies and hate" (95). The lies spawn the hatred which grows from ". . . the persistent and many-sided rebellion of human nature against everything which thwarts it," as Joseph Wood Krutch points out in *The American Drama Since 1918*.

The only real point of communication between the various members of the Berger family is that each wants something desperately and that each is thwarted in his quest. The family, dominated by Bessie, becomes an instrument of unjust coercion; its boredom leads Hennie to have an affair which results in her pregnancy. Bessie, more vitally concerned with respectability than with the ultimate good of her daughter, arranges a marriage which cannot succeed in doing anything more than giving legitimacy to an unborn child. She does all this because she is so sensitive to the pressures of public opinion, because she is weighed down by what Odets considers to be a set of obsolete social values. The effect of this marriage is far-reaching: Not only is Hennie to find herself in a situation which she cannot endure, but Jake and Ralph are completely nonplused by the basic immorality of what Bessie has done to Hennie and to the likeable, naive Sam Feinschreiber.

There is little fully developed situation in the plot of *Awake and Sing!* The play is sustained primarily through character development, and the characters, with the possible exception of Jake and Ralph, are examples of people with a great spiritual lack. This deficiency is sharpened, as Edith Isaacs noted in *Theatre Arts Monthly,* "by an immediate economic crisis, which has made them morbid, frustrated, decadent." Odets is writing from the inside out; he is able to do so because he is emotionally akin to the people about whom he is writing.

If there is anything recognizable as hope in the conclusion of *Awake and Sing!*, it is hope with a bitter aftertaste. As the play reaches its end, Ralph urges Hennie to go off with Moe: ". . . do it, Hennie, do it!" he exhorts her. This is Ralph calling for action, but he wants this action merely for its own sake, not because it represents any overall good. He is urging her on towards a course which is totally irresponsible and unrealistic. What happens to Hennie just before the conclusion of the play is almost a metaphorical commentary on what happens to mankind in the social situation. Moe asks Hennie to go off with him:

HENNIE:	Leave the baby?
MOE:	Yeah!
HENNIE:	I can't . . .
MOE:	You can!
HENNIE:	No . . .
MOE:	But you're not sure!
HENNIE:	I don't know.
MOE:	Make a break or spend the rest of your life in a coffin.
HENNIE:	Oh God, I don't know where I stand.
MOE:	Don't look up there. Paradise, you're on a big boat headed south . . . and when you cry it's because you're happy.
HENNIE:	Moe, I don't know . . .
MOE:	Nobody knows, but you do it and find out. When you're scared the answer's zero.
HENNIE:	You're hurting my arm. (99–100)

And with this Hennie capitulates. This has been Hennie's whole life: capitulation, compromise, uncertainty, regret. Circumstances have been "hurting her arm" for as long as she can remember, and she has had no control over this.

Myron, as the play concludes, brings out with poignancy another bit of grim irony which has from time to time run through the action. Early in the play Moe rants because there is not an orange in the house, just an apple. And in the last moments of action Myron says, "No fruit in the house lately. Just a lone apple" (100). This, of course, serves to emphasize once more the utter lack of luxuries in the Berger household. But it goes beyond that to suggest rather dismally what man's future might be. Continuance and endless recurrence are the fruits of man's frailty as it is depicted in the Judeo-Christian concepts of the creation of man. Myron goes off paring his apple as Ralph says, "When I look at him, I'm sad. Let me die like a dog, if I can't get more from life" (100). The looming question is whether Ralph and succeeding generations *will* get more from life. there is no overwhelming call to action as at the conclusion of *Waiting for Lefty*. Rather, the audience is left with a very faint hope and with the thought that the play's title must be ironic. The decision of what man's destiny will be is placed in the hands of an audience left pondering, not shouting.

Notes

1. Anita Block, *The Changing World in Plays and Theatre*, p. 288.

2. Page notations throughout this chapter refer to the Modern Library Edition of *Six Plays of Clifford Odets*.

3. Albert Hunt, "Only Soft-Centered Left: Odets and Social Theatre," *Encore*, VIII (May–June, 1961) p. 10.

4. Block, *op. cit.*, pp. 286–87.

[Odets and Tragedy:
Golden Boy and *The Big Knife*]

GABRIEL MILLER

In *The Fervent Years* Harold Clurman wrote that "for Odets . . . Hollywood was a sin." To a large extent this was true, for until the end of his life, Odets had difficulty reconciling his attraction to Hollywood with his need to produce significant art for the theater. It is certainly easy to read *Golden Boy* as a metaphor for that division in Odets and *The Big Knife* as a highly subjective apologia as well. But this is merely to skim the surface, for in both these plays Odets managed to transform his personal conflicts into explorations of broader issues related to his constant themes: the soul's difficult journey on earth, and its need to find a haven, a home. As Charlie Castle says in *The Big Knife,* "We're homesick all our lives," and this human dilemma is ultimately more important than the discovery of personal reference in the writer's work. In both plays Odets was able to project aspects of contemporary American experience into the realm of tragedy, exploring the dividedness of the spirit in two distinctive protagonists living in different times and in very different worlds.

Golden Boy is a different kind of play than *Awake and Sing!* and *Paradise Lost,* for in writing it Odets was experimenting with new techniques, baffling the critics, who apparently expected him to continue in the same vein as his earlier work. His desire to break away from the realistic / naturalistic mode of *Awake and Sing!* was evident in *Paradise Lost,* where he imposed a symbolic framework within the play, involving the characters of the Gordon children and, to a certain extent, Sam Katz. This device, unfortunately, weakened the play's thematic unity, and while *Paradise Lost* is among Odets's richest works, its awkward structural duality ultimately defeats the characters' emotional interplay.

Golden Boy, on the other hand, works best as a symbolic play. Odets clearly intended it as an allegory; indeed, he subtitled an early draft *An American Allegory.* Yet it is Odets's particular accomplishment in *Golden Boy* that his characters are so vividly presented as to transcend their allegorical functions and propel their personal conflict into the realm of tragedy. In

Originally published as "The Tragic Vision," in *Clifford Odets* (New York: Continuum, 1989). © 1989 by Gabriel Miller. Reprinted by permission of the Continuum Publishing Co.

order to stimulate a tragic apprehension, dramatic characters must engage an audience's sympathy and passion more fully than can be done either in simple allegory or in the realistic, slice-of-life antidramas of Odets's early career. *Golden Boy* thus represents a departure from his previous practice, for, instead of attempting to minimize theatrical involvement and impact, here Odets exploits the conventions of theater to heighten the formal eloquence of his story.

This play's most obvious conventional feature is the introduction of broad theatrical types; suddenly Odets peoples his stage with readily identifiable heroes and villains. At the center of the play stands Joe Bonaparte, a larger-than-life, emotionally engaging protagonist whose aspiration to be *somebody* in America at length leads to his death. Joe's is a story of thwarted potential, unfolding within an overriding mood of doom. It follows the classic tragic formula of an individual's rise to power and subsequent fall, precipitated by the recognition of irreparable error committed in the use of that power; for this he suffers and dies, having exhausted all the possibilities of his life. Odets moves his hero toward an action that causes great suffering, and then by exposing the consequences of the deed reveals to him the true nature of his ambition. The actions of other characters are related closely to various stages of this hero's passage. Joe's story, however, is more than a tragic study of the danger of courting success in America, for Odets is again exploring herein his favorite theme, the soul's yearning for a secure haven in this world. At this level *Golden Boy* reaches beyond the quintessential American dilemma that supplies its plot, attaining a dimension of universal significance in its symbolic progress.

This play also departs from Odets's past practice in its utilization of space. In the first two plays the characters are confined to the living area of the home, as Odets demonstrates their spiritual and emotional entrapment by contriving a sense of physical constraint. This closed setting also conveys Odets's suspicion of the family itself as a kind of trap that the individual must escape if he is to achieve personal fulfillment. The impulse to escape, however, remains an ambivalent one, since the family home represents also the striver's ultimate goal, as the source of emotional support and place of belonging that is the soul's prime object.

In *Golden Boy* Odets opens up the stage to encompass various settings: Moody's office, the Bonaparte home, the park, and the dressing room. Joe, who is Odets's first major protagonist, cannot be confined to the living room; he needs to go out into the world and see what is there. Accordingly, the audience's sense of possibility expands as Joe moves about the stage, extending its space until it becomes its own world, rich in imaginative potential. The proscenium, emphasized in the earlier plays, seems to disappear here, along with any suggestion of permanent walls, thereby transporting character and action beyond real space into metaphysical space, and this liberation of setting heightens the audience's sense of exhilaration in Joe's journey of discovery.

Joe himself is initially introduced in a deliberately theatrical manner: rather than entering prosaically, he seems to materialize on stage at a significant moment, as if summoned by dramatic necessity. The play has opened upon Moody, a fight manager, arguing with his girlfriend Lorna about her decision to leave him. Tired of waiting for Moody's wife to divorce him and evidently determined to force the issue of their relationship, Lorna feels trapped but is afraid to leave Moody. Like *Awake and Sing!*, *Golden Boy* thus begins on a characteristic Odetsian note of movement and stasis, involving a character's need to break out and frustrating inability to do so. Moody, too, is trapped, not only by his wife's demand for five thousand dollars as the price of a divorce, but also by his failure to find a boxer who can revive his managerial career. As for any hope that his current mediocre fighter, Kaplan, might win him some money, Lorna remarks, "It's the twentieth century . . . no more miracles." Regretting this lack of miraculous potential in the present, Moody, like many Odets characters, reverts to the past, the twenties, when he was successful and there was plenty of money. Lorna undercuts his reverie by mentioning that her mother died in 1928, and this exchange provides the first of many instances of the linkage of success and death, a dominant thematic concept in this play. Then, when Moody kisses Lorna, promising to give her anything she wants, Joe appears. Odets's stage direction is significant: "Suddenly a youth is standing at the office door. Lorna sees him and breaks away." Moody's reaction is, "Don't you knock when you come in an office?"

Joe's entrance is reminiscent of Hilda Wangel's in Ibsen's *The Master Builder*. The protagonist of that play, Halvard Solness, is introduced as a man preoccupied with youth, lamenting his own waning creative powers and a marriage that has trapped him. His longing for youth and love is answered just as he is thinking of it, when, in a marvelous theatrical coincidence, Hilda (youth) comes knocking at his door and changes his life. Moody's line, thus, is Odets's acknowledgment of a debt to Ibsen. On a literal level, Joe functions in the same way as Hilda. Moody longs for a miracle, a winning boxer who will reverse his professional decline and personal fortunes, while Lorna wants love and the sense of family lost at her mother's death, and Joe will answer both their longings. Lorna instantly recognizes this, for when she sees him, she moves away from Moody.

Joe's mode of theatrical entrance becomes a motif in the play, a stylistic device that confirms his story's symbolic thrust. In act 1, scene 2, which takes place in the Bonaparte home, Joe's brother Frank and his father are discussing him, and again he appears unnoticed, this time "in the shadows." Odets's use of lighting here underscores visually Joe's estrangement from the home image, for he has committed himself to Moody's world in scene 1. In act 2 scene 3, he once more appears as Moody and Lorna are kissing, after Lorna has again threatened to leave, this time because of Joe. When Joe enters he is followed by Eddie Fuseli, a gangster who serves as the embodiment of the shadow from the earlier scene; Eddie is the epitome of Joe's worst self. Joe's final "appearance" is in act 3, scene 2, when Fuseli is threatening Lorna with a gun, and once again his sudden entrance is timed to break up another man's confrontation with Lorna. The repetition is significant, for it is Joe's movement toward Lorna that comprises the symbolic progress of the play.

Odets's treatment of the hero typifies his adherence to the Nietzschean tragic system, whereby the playwright designates action and character to function as metaphysical complements to the physical world. Nietzsche's theory, in *The Birth of Tragedy* appropriately, draws upon Schopenhauer's definition of music as a universal language, the "immediate language of the will." Nietzsche explains that music, which he associates with the Dionysian strain, stimulates the imagination to embody the immaterial world: "Image and concept . . . gain a heightened significance under the influence of truly appropriate music . . . music incites us to a symbolic intuition of the Dionysiac universality; [and] it endows that symbolic image with supreme significance." Music, then, is Odets's metaphor for the soul, the immaterial, that mode of exaltation that Joe strives after but cannot attain. The energy of this creative inspiration, represented in his violin playing and his love for Lorna, supplies the play's Dionysian dimension.

The Apollonian element, in Nietzsche's words "the transcendent genius of the *principium individuationis,*" inheres in Joe's desire for more material success, his will toward individuation, which is metaphorically embodied in his determination to become a boxer. The need to break free of the spiritual anonymity and poverty arising from his immigrant status and to revenge himself on those who have excluded him—his family name and his cockeye are emblematic of past pain—makes Joe a readily sympathetic figure. However, if the Nietzschean tragic pattern is to be realized, the hero must "deliver us from our avid thirst for earthly satisfaction and remind us of another existence and higher delight." Ultimately Joe, too, must comprehend the error of his pursuit of success and revenge and then willingly embrace his own death; thus, in Nietzsche's words, he realizes himself "not through his victories but through his undoing."

Odets, moreover, seeks to superimpose this tragic model of a contemporary story in order to articulate the distinctive American experience. In an essay entitled "Democratic Vistas in Drama," published in the *New York Times* after *Golden Boy* opened, Odets quoted Whitman's complaint about the lack of an authentic American drama:

> In his essay "Democratic Vistas" written in 1871, Walt Whitman wrote: "Of what is called the drama or dramatic presentation, in the United States, as

now put forth at the theatres, I should say it deserves to be treated with the same gravity, and on a par with the questions of ornamental confectionery at public dinners, or the arrangement of curtains and hangings in a ballroom. . . .

"I feel with dejection and amazement that among writers and talented speakers, few or none have yet really spoken to this people, created a single image-making work for them, or absorbed the central spirit and the idiosyncrasies which are theirs—and which, thus, in the highest ranges, so far remain entirely uncelebrated and unexpressed."[1]

Agreeing with Whitman that the modern theater had failed to express the American spirit, Odets then advanced a rather bold claim for the time, that the movies had, at least partially, supplied the lack:

Let us, for once, give the movies some credit. They have spoken to this people. The movies have explored the common man in all of his manifestations—out of the Kentucky mountains, out of the Montana ranch house, out of the machine shop, from the docks and alleys of the great cities, from the farm, out of the hospitals, airplanes, and taxicabs.

The movies are now the folk theatre of America. But they are still not what Whitman asked for in 1871. . . . Hollywood producers will tell you gladly that they are not interested in presenting their themes "significantly." They are not interested in interpretation or criticism of their material. Their chief problem, they contend, is the one of keeping the level of human experience in their pictures as low as possible. They keep to primary colors with the expected result: The good will be rewarded, the wicked punished; success lurks around every corner; love is only a matter of the right man looking the right girl in the eyes; and so on and so on and so on.[2]

The movies' treatment of theme therefore remaining "puerile in every respect," Odets concluded with the suggestion that the theater adopt the movies' themes but "tell the truth where the film told a lie." The playwright committed to this high cultural calling could thus become in Whitman's term a "celebrator and expressor" of the American experience.

In pursuit of this calling, Odets utilizes in *Golden Boy* a cinematic scene format that, as mentioned earlier, diverges sharply from the tightly knit structure of the earlier plays. The later play's succession of brief scenes and multiple settings was undoubtedly influenced by Odets's recent Hollywood screenwriting experience. This important technical innovation also represents a probably deliberate imitation of the basic form of the gangster film, which became, in the early thirties, a significant expression of the popular culture, uniquely suited to dealing with the traumatic societal upheaval of the Depression years.

Like *Golden Boy* the gangster film typically features an aggressive, violent protagonist of immigrant descent, whose obsessive rise to prominence in the mob is played against scenes of (usually idealized) family life. Odets echoes this pattern, only substituting a devoted father for the widowed mother more common to the family model of the movies, and the change more likely reflects Odets's own troubled relationship with his father than any conscious variation on the film genre. In the play as well as in the movie versions, the nurturing family functions as a counterpoint to the characteristically violent success story. Consequently, the destruction of the family, and often, the substitution of a false family for the real one become recurrent themes in these films; likewise, in *Golden Boy* Joe rejects his family / father for successive surrogate fathers in the fight game, and this betrayal of the values of home eventually leads to his undoing.

The most meaningful affinity between the ganster film and Odets's play is to be found in their makers' corresponding rejection of the demands and essential rewards of modern life: Robert Warshaw claims that the gangster film rejects "Americanism itself."[3] In making this rejection the film genre offers no alternative, either political, social, or economic, to the bleak picture of corruption and degradation conveyed in its narrative. Neither does Odets, and this is consistent with his attitude in the previous plays, where criticism of the system is implied, but no blueprint for the future is offered. Here, however, Odets provides a central character who, unlike Ralph, Jacob, or Leo, recognizes the moral emptiness of his society, and this rejection moves *Golden Boy* into the realm of authentic tragedy.

Like tragedy, the gangster film insists that man is a being capable of success or failure. The gangster fiercely pursues his finite goal and succeeds, in Warshaw's words, in "emerging from the crowd," defying the anonymity of the city. Nevertheless, like any "tragic" hero, he must be defeated at last, often dying alone in the street. The gangster figure has asserted himself as an individual, but he must die because of it. The genre thus echoes the conventions of tragedy but finally falls short of it: whereas tragedy chronicles a protagonist's doomed struggle with necessity and forces him (and the audience that views his story) to acknowledge the inevitability of his fate, it also celebrates man's need to give meaning to his fate. The gangster film, on the other hand, ultimately offers no real meaning, no sense of nobility to account for the ambition and the downfall of its protagonist. If the Apollonian sense of individuation is celebrated, the Dionysian, musically symbolic connection with the infinite, that which "breaks the spell of individuation and opens a path to the maternal womb of being" is missing. In the character of Joe Bonaparte, however, Odets not only gives expression to the human condition in the American city of the 1930s, but also celebrates a broader human experience as well. For if this fighter and Apollonian individualist pursues the finite goal of success and fails, his complementary aspiration toward the infnite imparts nobility and meaning to his struggle and his fate.

The first act reveals the three major settings of the play: Moody's office, the Bonaparte home, and the park—each locale representing an alternative in Joe's struggle to come to grips with himself and the conflicting possibilities offered to him. The Bonaparte home is a kind of haven, a nourishing paradise where—unlike the Berger house of *Awake and Sing!*—it is possible to grow and produce "fruit." In the second draft of *Golden Boy,* Odets gave Mr. Bonaparte this speech, which was eliminated from the final version: "I think sometimes in terms of a citrus grove. I like to think to raise such trees and distribute to a world of children the fresh, natural juices of the fruit."[4] In this impulse Mr. Bonaparte is related to Jacob in *Awake and Sing!* and Leo Gordon in *Paradise Lost,* all kindly, moral men who "love to slice philosophical salami," though unlike them, he seems unconcerned with the economic situation or even his own poverty. He is in love with life and his children and external troubles seem unimportant in comparison. Joe's ambition for material success does not impress him, for he feels "a good life 'sa possible," achievable in an attitude of self-acceptance and contentment with the simple pleasures of living: "You say life'sa bad . . . well, is pleasure for you to say so. No? The streets, winter a' summer—trees, cats—I love a them all. The gooda boys and girls, they who sing and whistle—very good! The eating and sleeping, drinking wine—very good! I gone around on my wagon and talk to many people—nice!"[5] Even Mr. Carp, his best friend, cannot convince this amiable man that his philosophy has no place in modern-day America.

Carp is the serpent in the Edenic garden of the Bonaparte home, countering Mr. Bonaparte's native optimism and his hopes for Joe's career in music with gloomy cynicism: "In the end, as Schopenhauer says, what's the use to try something? For every wish we get, ten remains unsatisfied. Death is playing with us as a cat and her mouse!" (p. 249). The reference to Schopenhauer is important, for Carp proves to be prophetic in his assessment of Joe's pursuit of the American dream. Briefly, Schopenhauer posited that conflict between individual wills is the cause of continuous pain and frustration, and the world is thus a place of unsatisfied wants and unhappiness. Man's intellect and consciousness are mere instruments of the will, while music, the ultimate expression of the soul, provides a means of momentarily transcending the conflict, investing human life with higher significance. Odets's reference to Schopenhauer through Carp confirms the Nietzschean tragic model in the play, for Carp's discussions with Mr. Bonaparte provide in themselves harmless instances of the clash of opposites that causes conflict.[6]

The fateful significance underlying the two friends' contrasting outlooks is emphasized most powerfully in scene 2, when Mr. Bonaparte shows Carp the violin that he has bought for Joe's twenty-first birthday; Carp comments that "it looks like a coffin for a baby." (The coffin image recurs in scene 3, when Moody, disgusted with his ex-wife's constant demands for money, declares, "If I had fifty bucks I'd buy myself a big juicy coffin.") Carp's remark, then, not only prefigures Joe's death but also taints the redemptive music motif with a suggestion of abortive effort. Again, the transcendent impulse seems linked, in Odets's world, with a movement toward renunciation and death.

Joe, unlike Ralph Berger or any of the Gordon children, is a strong, decisive character capable of achieving success; in so doing he rejects his father's home, where he learned music and was encouraged to develop his talent. For Joe, a boy growing up in America, the old-world values of Europe, represented by his father, are not enough—one of many thematic motifs in *Golden Boy* is the generational conflict between the European immigrant and his son. In this context music represents an extension of the European sensibility that cannot survive on the streets of America. Joe, like many first-generation Americans, must reject the ways of the father completely, although in embracing the values of the new land and its ethic of "making it," he risks losing his soul. Joe's rejection of his home suggests that Odets felt the temptations and pressures of the American economic condition were undermining the nurturing influence of the family; certainly his immigrant families, torn between the conflicting demands of two cultures, find little peace or sustenance in the new world.

Joe replaces his father with two successive surrogate fathers who seek to advance his career as a fighter: Tom Moody, his manager and chief rival for Lorna, and Eddie Fuseli, the gangster who eventually comes to dominate Joe's career. Moody serves as a kind of transitional figure here, his values falling somewhere between those of Mr. Bonaparte and his antithesis, Fuseli. Odets even demonstrates a certain affection for Moody, a man down on his luck and in need of a good fighter to revitalize his career as a manager. Joe appears, as discussed earlier, as if in answer to this need, and his declared allegiance works to rejuvenate the older man's spirits. Moody is also in need of a divorce from his wife so that he can marry Lorna, a much younger woman, and so he sees Joe not only as his economic salvation, but a "spiritual one as well." In act 1 Moody longs for the twenties, when the economy was booming and he was successful; he is like the country itself, decimated by the Depression, nostalgic for a former glory and hoping for some miraculous, youthful talisman to revive him. But Moody does not know what to do with the two young people who seem ready to perform this miracle for him: he wants only to exploit Joe's talent, regardless of his best interests or of the spiritual dilemma that troubles Joe, and, when the need arises, he exploits Lorna as well. When Joe seems doubtful as to whether to continue fighting, Moody uses Lorna, along with the promises of fame and fortune, to seduce him back to the ring. In consequence, he eventually loses both Joe and Lorna.

Jealous of Moody's hold on Lorna and increasingly impatient for greater success, Joe gravitates toward Eddie Fuseli, Odets's first truly loathsome character. Basically an outgrowth of the gangsterlike Moe Axelrod and Kewpie, but without any redeeming characteristics, Fuseli is clearly the villain of the play, and when Joe adopts him as his manager, his fall is complete.

A strong link between the two is established in the manner of his first entrance: he comes onstage unnoticed, interrupting a conversation betwen

Moody, Tokio, and Lorna. Shortly after saying hello, he "drifts out of the scene on his cat's feet." A few minutes later, when Joe joins the conversation, he appears "unseen by others" and listens. Thus Odets is emphasizing that Fuseli, like Joe, is a figure of the theatrical world, a poetic double who will figure prominently in the drama of the soul that will unfold.

A significant element in Fuseli's resemblance to Kewpie involves the homosexual overtones with which Odets characterizes the two gangsters' relationship to the young men they befriend. There is in *Paradise Lost* some suggestion of such an attachment between Kewpie and Ben, and in *Golden Boy* Odets provides similar hints about Fuseli's attraction to Joe. When they first meet, the stage directions read, "curiously Eddie is almost embarrassed before Joe"; later Moody calls him a "queen." In addition, Odets associates Fuseli with a cluster of phallic images. After his initial appearance, Lorna comments, "What exhaust pipe did he crawl out of?" Later in the play he threatens her with a gun until Joe appears to stop him. The exhaust pipe image, further, links Fuseli to the Dusenberg that Joe buys and that eventually becomes his "coffin," as he rides it to his death. The gun and the car are two of the central iconographic images of the ganster film, and their prominent use here indicates that Joe's embracing of Fuseli constitutes another Odetsian indictment of the success ethic of America.

Other image patterns are equally suggestive. Just before Fuseli's entrance Moody is complaining to Lorna about getting Joe away from the influence of his home; he employs a vivid simile to express his concern: "We can't afford no more possible bad showings at this stage of the game. No more apparitions, like suddenly a fiddle flies across the room on wings!" (p. 274). After Fuseli appears, Moody once again waxes poetic: "Every once in a while he shoots across my quiet existence like a roman candle!" The images are similar but with widely differing connotations: Joe is described in transcendent terms, Eddie in phallic, violent ones. Once more, in the reiterated flight image, the linkage of music with death is reinforced.

These two image patterns become fused in the final scene of act 2 that takes place in a dressing room before a fight. Here the disparate elements of Joe's world converge, as Mr. Bonaparte, Lorna, Moody, and Fuseli all appear in the scene. Mr. Bonaparte's dissociation from this setting is emphasized in Lorna's greeting to him "What brings you to this part of the world?" and when Joe confronts his father he irrevocably breaks with his true father: "I have to fight, no matter what you say or think: This is my profession! I'm out for fame and fortune, not to be different or artistic! I don't intend to be ashamed of my life!" (p. 298). Shortly before this, he has remarked to Moody, "Eddie's the only one who understands me." Having thus rejected both his father and Moody, he tells Tokio, his trainer, "Now I'm alone. . . . When a bullet sings through the air it has no past—only a future—like me." The image pattern thus echoes Moody's twin similes and confirms Joe's new spiritual allegiance to Fuseli. The act ends when Joe has knocked out his opponent. Returning to the dressing room, his "eyes glitter" and his hands are broken; this changed Joe exults, "Hallelujah! It is the beginning of the world!" Odets's stage directions are significant: "Joe begins to laugh loudly, victoriously, exultantly." He seems almost demonic, and Fuseli, Odets writes, "watches with inner excitement and pleasure."

However, Joe's most important relationship in the play is with Lorna Moon. Her name has overt symbolic overtones, but she functions effectively as a realistic character as well. On one level she feels that she is a "tramp from Newark," survivor of a rough childhood, and she looks to Moody, a man old enough to be her father, to make her respectable. She is impatient for Moody to get a divorce from his wife and marry her because, like Kewpie and Moe, she is anxious for a home. In Moody she is looking for a combination father and husband; Lorna wants what Joe seeks to escape.

When she meets Joe, however, her values are overturned, as she responds to the young man's tenderness and artistic aspiration. She is that familiar movie type, the cynical city girl who was really waiting for true love to rescue her from herself. In her two scenes in the park with Joe, her symbolic function is established, and they are the most expressionistic scenes in the play. Odets emphasizes carousel music and the changing colors of the traffic lights, seemingly projecting his characters into a world apart, where their true inner selves can be revealed. In act 1, scene 4 Lorna compares herself to a butterfly, a traditional symbol of the soul, and Joe literalizes the image when he asks her, "What does your soul do in its perfumed vanity case?" In the next scene, which takes place in the Bonaparte home, she reveals that she was once an airplane hostess, and Odets repeats the airplane image from *Awake and Sing!* again conjuring up the dream of leaving the earth behind in aspiration for a better life. Here Lorna seems to become a personified spirit of the music with which Joe needs to identify himself; he even explains this spiritual need to her in personal terms: "With music I'm never alone when I'm alone—Playing music . . . that's like saying, 'I am a man. I belong here. How do you do world—good evening!' When I play music nothing is closed to me. I'm not afraid of people and what they say. There's no war in music" (p. 263). In this scene, however, Lorna is trying to persuade Joe to pursue his boxing career, though she will intuit the error of her ways by the end of the scene. Joe, too, despite his obvious attraction to Lorna, leans toward the other world, and he moves from this discussion of music and the soul to his desire to buy a car, which is "poison" in his blood.

Lorna's name supplies the most obvious symbolic undercurrent in Joe's attraction to her. The moon was a popular symbol among the Romantic poets, particularly Wordsworth and Coleridge, as the ultimate inspiration of poetic reverie and heightened imaginative consciousness. An effective example is found in Wordsworth's short poem, "A Night-Piece," where a glimpse of the moon affords the poet, "whose eyes are bent to earth," a glimpse of the infinite:

> He looks up—the clouds are split
> Asunder—and above his head he sees
> The clear Moon, and the glory of the heavens.
> There in a black-blue vault she sails along,
> Followed by multitudes of stars.

The moon again appears in a climactic scene in *The Prelude,* where viewing it, Wordsworth has a glimpse of "the soul, the imagination of the whole." Clearly, then, Joe must move toward this moon figure in the play, toward a reconciliation with the Dionysian spirit of the eternal. Lorna's name is not, as Margaret Brenman-Gibson writes, a symbol of the "cool, inhospitable, unattainable woman" for Joe has the ability to attain her if only he could resist the Apollonian ambition and understand his true nature.

Lorna, too, will be worthy of Joe when she recognizes her salvation in him and not in Moody, and she does so in act 2, scene 2, the second and last park scene. She is no longer trying to keep Joe away from music; Joe even compares her to his music: "You're real for me the way music was real." He wants her to teach him love and to be his family, his new life. The music in this scene is provided not by a carousel, but by a whistling duet that Joe and Lorna perform. After trying to resist him, even struggling with herself, Lorna admits to Joe that she wants him: "I've been under sea a long time! . . . Take me home with you."

Joe finally unites himself with Lorna after killing the Chocolate Drop in the fight ring. Now he understands how he has violated his own nature: "What will my father say when he hears I murdered a man? Lorna, I see what I did. I murdered myself, too! I've been running around in circles. Now I'm smashed! That's the truth. . . . But now I'm hung up by my finger tips— I'm no good—my feet are off the earth!" (p. 315). Lorna then declares her love for Joe and consoles him: "We have each other! Somewhere there must be happy boys and girls who can teach us the way of life! We'll find some city where poverty's no shame—where music is no crime!—where there's no war in the streets—where a man is glad to be himself, to live and make his woman herself!" (p. 316). Obviously she is referring to death, for no such place can exist in the real world. Joe understands this, realizing that in order to salvage his soul he must separate it from his body, and the language of his declaration strangely echoes Wordsworth's "A Night-Piece": "We'll drive through the night. . . . You're on top of the world then. . . . That's it— speed! We're off the earth—unconnected!" (p. 316). After the poet has been inspired by the moon, as noted before, Wordsworth likewise emphasizes speed:

> There in a black-blue vault she sails along,
> Followed by multitudes of stars, that, small,
> And sharp, and bright, along the dark abyss
> Drive as she drives: how fast they wheel away.

The play concludes in the Bonaparte home where Frank announces the deaths of Joe and Lorna to Mr. Bonaparte, Moody, and Fuseli. The play's final words, "Joe . . . come, we bring-a him home . . . where he belong," are spoken by Mr. Bonaparte, and they recall Joe's description of music to Lorna in act 1, scene 4 as well as the ending of O'Neill's *The Hairy Ape*. Odets labored over the ending, changing the final speech a number of times before settling on this rather elegant coda. In one draft Mr. Bonaparte flatly says, "Let us go there . . . and bring the bodies home." In another draft the conclusion is even less satisfying, as Frank cries, "What waste, what waste . . . what ugly [foul] waste." The final version, in contrast, conveys an acknowledgment that the true closure of the soul's longing comes only in death—perhaps it is the only true paradise. Or possibly, as Odets demonstrates here in his compelling tragic vision, paradise must rather be sought in the transcendent power of art to unify and pacify the conflict of wills that undermines the human condition.

Odets began writing *The Big Knife* in 1948, copyrighting it as "A Winter Journey." He changed the title, it seems, late in 1948, having extensively revised the play a number of times. In explanation, Odets said that the earlier title implied "a difficult passage in one's life," whereas the new one alluded to "a force that moves against people." This comment, in fact, illuminates an unresolved problem in the play, for one title emphasizes character, the other exterior forces operating on character. Much of the criticism of the finished play would focus on the protagonist, Charlie Castle, as an insufficiently developed character who was seemingly swallowed up in Odets's vitriol against Hollywood. The early drafts confirm that Odets was struggling to balance the exploration of character with the representation of forces operating from outside it.

When *The Big Knife* opened on Broadway in 1949, it was Odets's first play there in eight years. The critics were not kind, as was generally the case for the plays after *Golden Boy;* even Harold Clurman and Joseph Wood Krutch, always supporters, dismissed *The Big Knife*. The play has fared no better with more recent critics of Odets, and it has rarely been revived.

Much of the disparagement centers on the play's biographical parallel, the critics complaining that Odets, who worked in Hollywood for many years after the collapse of the Group Theatre, was protesting too much. Having made a great deal of money there, now, it seemed, he was suddenly offering an extended bombastic apology for having abandoned his art and the "serious" work of the theater. Clurman criticized the play as defeatist and suggested that Odets was attempting to project his own sense of guilt onto society. More recently, Gerald Rabkin, in his study *The Drama of Commitment*, questioned the protagonist's climactic "act of faith," and unfavorably comparing the play to *Golden Boy,* wrote that *The Big Knife* presents no social alternative as does the earlier play.[7] Some of this criticism, particularly the biographical issue, is beside the point. Readings such as Rabkin's are more disturbing and need to be answered, for *The Big Knife* remains one of Odets's most widely misinterpreted and yet most compelling plays. (Only Edward Murray has attempted to deal with it in detail.)

Both Clurman and Rabkin imply that in this play Odets tried to write a serious tragedy, in a sense, to duplicate the strengths of *Golden Boy,* and simply failed. However, despite its many similarities to that earlier success, *The Big Knife* is sufficiently different in structure and technique to indicate that Odets was attempting here to convey his tragic vision in a very different mode. *The Big Knife* is, in fact, closer in form to *Awake and Sing!* and *Paradise Lost* than to *Golden Boy,* its action confined to a single set, "the playroom" of Charlie Castle's house in Beverly Hills. The sense of entrapment is made even stronger, for if the stage space of the two early plays was shared by family and friends, now it is a lone protagonist's space. Charlie remains at the center of the play, onstage continually until he goes upstairs to kill himself at the end. Other characters enter and leave this space, but no one stays for very long; it is as if everyone has access to the world outside the stage except Charlie, who is confined to the Hollywood castle that his own name betokens.

This intensive, and thematically significant, use of setting provides a strong resemblance to Ibsen's *A Doll's House,* a play that shares various motifs with *The Big Knife,* among them the exposure of a fatal secret from the past. Like Charlie Castle, Ibsen's Nora is confined to the drawing room of her home, and during the course of the play various characters, including her husband and children, become part of her world and then leave. She is the devoted wife and mother, nothing more, and while the others have access to the world outside the drawing room, Nora does not. Ibsen's point is that Nora, as a woman, is trapped in her society, just as she is trapped in her room, without scope for realizing any wider potential. Until she takes her life into her own hands and decides to transform herself, she remains a doll in a doll's house, neither a woman nor a human being. Her walking out at the play's end provides not only a spiritual release but a physical one as well, for by that time the audience has begun to feel as confined as Nora.

While the structures of the two plays are thus alike, the circumstances of the protagonists' captivity are quite different. Plainly, Nora is victimized by her society, locked into a box by the social dictates of her world; her conflict, then, is between herself and her husband and the larger world that her husband represents. Nora is a person who is acted upon, and until the end of the play she does not react to oppose or escape the restraining conventions of her situation. Charlie Castle, on the other hand, is trapped in a predicament primarily of his own making. Formerly a man of deep political conviction, a talented actor, and a loving husband, he is now a wealthy studio star playing endless variations of the same superficial role, estranged from his wife and son, and extremely dissatisfied with himself. The central issue of this play, as in *Golden Boy,* involves the protagonist's conflict of identity, here polarized in Charlie Castle's sense of his true self, represented by his real name Charlie Cass, and the corrupt self represented by his stage name Charlie Castle. Again, life has posed contrasting opportunities, entailing self-defining choices, and again the terms of choice require a dedication either to idealism or to materialism. The Hollywood environment exerts pressure on Charlie to surrender to his worst impulses, but Odets makes clear that this society, however flawed, is not the primary culprit, and that his protagonist, unlike Ibsen's, is and always was free to make his own choices. Charlie Castle's sense of detainment in the playroom that is Hollywood results from his belated recognition of the falsity of the values he has chosen to act upon in life.

Nevertheless, the Hollywood setting is important to the play's thematic design. In an interview before the Boston opening of the play, Odets declared:

> The big knife is that force in modern life which is against people and their aspirations, which seeks to cut people off in their best flower. The play may be about the struggle of a gifted actor to retain his integrity against the combination of inner and outer corruptions which assail him, but this struggle can be found in the lives of countless people who are not on the wealthy level of a movie star. I have nothing against Hollywood per se. I do have something against a large set-up which destroys people and eats them up. I chose Hollywood for the setting for *The Big Knife* because I know it. I don't know any other company town. But this is an objective play about thousands of people, I don't care what industry they're in.[8]

This, of course, is rather disingenuous, for Hollywood is, as Odets was aware, more than a conveniently familiar "company town"; the very name of the place serves as perhaps the primary symbol of those cultural forces that endanger the "integrity" of the idealist in America. Edmund Wilson wrote, "Everything that is wrong with the U.S. is to be found there in rare purity." Certainly that is the basic premise of the most literary representations of the Southern California scene; and the aspect of Hollywood most pervasively emphasized in the literature is its artificiality, as in Nathanael West's memorable image of a rubber horse at the bottom of a swimming pool in *The Day of the Locust*. For writers this falsity of environment underscores the betrayal of the promise of America: those who succeed in Hollywood learn that such material success is empty, while those who fail only see the chasm between dreams and reality all the more clearly.

Two prominent thematic motifs in *The Big Knife* are the abuse of sexuality and the meaninglessness of work, both problems commonly attributed to the hedonistic life-style of the moviemakers' society.[9] Sexual freedom was a prime component of the Hollywood image, at least until the lurid sex scandals of the twenties; by the midthirties Hollywood literature had replaced the orgiastic tone with one of either sexual revulsion or indifference, suggesting that the revelry of the past had given way to disillusionment and exhaustion. Similarly, the wild energy that had fueled the growth of the film industry had given way, in its heyday, to a complementary attitude toward the work itself. The work ethic, always a basic component of the American experience, was somehow betrayed in Hollywood, where the rewards were excessive, and the stories of people, especially writers, paid enormous sums for not working became legendary. The work, moreover, has always been seen as trivial, nonfulfilling, and debilitating.

Odets's characters and dialogue build upon these connotations of the Hollywood setting. The atmosphere of unreality is pervasive: Charlie's "play-room," where all of the action takes place, is itself a false front for the man he is not, for the piano and the paintings by Maurice Utrillo, Georges Rouault, and Amedeo Modigliani embody an artistic pretension that is belied by the movie industry and Charlie's films themselves. Even Charlie's professional name, Castle, is a glibly regal substitute for the more mundane Cass. In one of the play's most vivid exchanges, Charlie sums up Hollywood's affectation for his neighbor, Dr. Frary, explaining that "we all wear these beautiful expensive ties in Hollywood. . . . It's a military tactic—we hope you won't notice our faces."[10]

Another such façade of success and respectability is discredited in the portrayal of the various marriages in the play. The destructiveness of sexuality in its divorce from love and commitment has concerned Odets in earlier plays; here it becomes obsessive. Charlie Castle and his wife are separated when the play begins. As Charlie says, "The place is hell on married life!" Charlie hopes for a reconciliation with her, but the depth of their estrangement is revealed when, in act 2, Marion tells him what Hollywood has done to him and their relationship: "You've taken the cheap way out—your passion of the heart has become a passion of the appetites! Despite your best intentions, you're a horror . . . and every day you make me less a woman and more the rug under your feet!" (pp. 62–63). Meanwhile Charlie is indulging in an affair with the wife of a close friend, Buddy Bliss, who is likewise struggling to save his marriage. Charlie also has had an affair with Dixie Evans, who was with him in the car on the night of the accident in which a child was killed, and the concealment of this incident has fused the implications of sexual infidelity with the betrayal of friendship (Buddy Bliss was blamed for the accident) and the reckless, hit-and-run destruction of life. Near the end of the play when the studio fears that Dixie will talk about the incident, it is suggested that Charlie marry her to prevent her testifying against him in court. The dispassionate calculation of this proposal only reinforces the emptiness of the marriage bond in this Hollywood society.

The prime exemplar of Hollywood values in the play is the studio head, Marcus Hoff. In a lengthy speech in which he tries to persuade Charlie not to listen to Marion's plea that Charlie leave Hollywood and not sign a fourteen-year contract with the studio, Hoff delivers the industry's basic business pitch, based on the priority of moviemaking over the personal commitments of love and family. Feigning emotion for effect, he complains of his own wife's suicidal neurosis as an unpardonable interference in his business life:

> One day, in my office—Smiley was there—Frank Lubner, a pioneer in the industry—I drank a light scotch and soda and I began to cry. I don't think I wept like that since I was a boy. Because I saw, by a revelation of pain, that my wife had determined, in her innermost mind, to destroy me and my career out of wilful malicious jealousy! You ask me why? I ask you why! But from that day on I realized an essential fact of life: the woman must stay out of her husband's work when he's making her bread and butter! The wife of a man in your position should have the regard and respect to advance his career! . . . Because sometimes it becomes necessary to separate our-selves . . . from a wife who puts her petty interests before the multiplicity of a great career! (p. 41)

Charlie's own dissipated life-style is in part a by-product of his disgust with his work, which he considers trivial and beneath contempt. In his films he plays a variation of the same role again and again from a series of proper-ties that the studio buys for him. Charlie has, in effect, become a studio property himself, and by the time the play opens, this mechanization of his life and his art has become intolerable, although he continues to enjoy the money and the luxury of star status. Unlike Joe Bonaparte, or any other Odets protagonist, Charlie Castle is not aspiring toward material success when introduced; he has already achieved it and accepted it, and now he must deal with the implications of that acceptance. Charlie has seemingly realized the American dream, but the painfully divided consciousness resulting from his recognition of the various betrayals involved in the achievement make Charlie a tragic protagonist comparable to Joe Bonaparte in the exploration of the corruptibility of the American ideal.

Odets makes occasional oblique references to *Golden Boy,* both to empha-size the connection and to separate this new play from it. While talking to his best friend, a writer, Hank Teagle, Charlie observes:

CHARLIE: When I came home from Germany . . . I saw most of the war dead were here, not in Africa and Italy. And Roosevelt was dead . . . and the war was only last week's snowball fight . . . and we plunged our-selves, all of us, into the noble work of making the buck reproduce itself! Oh, those luscious salmon eggs of life!

HANK: If you feel that deeply . . .

CHARLIE: Get out of here? Does the man in your book get out of here? Where does he go? What, pray tell, does he do? Become a union organizer? Well, what does he do?

HANK: Charlie . . . I can't invent last-act curtains for a world that doesn't have one. You're still an artist, Charlie. (p. 111)

The Big Knife, then, represents a world that differs from Joe Bonaparte's more deeply than in its wealthy setting. *Golden Boy* was set in a period when the seeds of World War II were being planted; now the war is over, leaving behind it the postmodern world, wherein people's hopes for the future have been drastically reduced. Charlie's reference to becoming a union organizer is a direct reference to Joe's brother Frank in *Golden Boy,* where Frank represented an alternative to the success world of boxing. But the implication here is that Frank's idealism and activism are now out of place and only another pipe dream.

The loss of a kind of innocence is this fallen world is indirectly evoked in the beginning of the play as well, when the gossip columnist Patty Benedict speaks of Charlie's killing "that child in your car." In the context of the *Golden Boy* parallel, Odets is referring symbolically to Joe's essential youth and idealism—he, too, was killed in a car—and possibly to Ralph and the Gordon children as well, inhabitants of another time and another place. Charlie seems to be related to these characters and yet somewhat beyond them. There is an aura of hopelessness about him that did not figure in the earlier plays, although Odets, again, does not allow the implication that this man's life holds no possibilities. Hank's protest, "You're still an artist," implies that the artist still possesses some power in society and may still act on his principles.

Charlie Castle is thus carefully differentiated from Joe, and he is also a more complex character. *Golden Boy* ends with Joe's realization that materialism will not make him happy and that the pursuit of it has tainted his soul. But Charlie is partly in love with his success, and he has been capable of sacrificing most of his integrity to it. Joe kills himself after he murders the Chocolate Drop, but Charlie manages not only to live with a killing, but even to let his friend go to jail in his place and then to sleep with that friend's wife. He does, however, stop short of deliberate murder: when the studio boss hints that Dixie Evans may be killed in order to ensure her silence about the accident, Charlie at last rebels against the cold-blooded evil of the business and his own implication in it.

Like other Odets drafts, the early version of *The Big Knife* is overly long and very preachy; in final form, its action is more compact and suggestive, and the forward movement more direct. The basic story outline remains the same, but Odets eliminates certain characters and cuts the parts of others in order to focus more narrowly on his central figure. Charlie's business manager, Harold Waterman, has an extended scene in the first draft but is only an offscreen presence contacted by telephone in the final version, while the character of a publicity agent named Jerry White is simply incorporated into Buddy Bliss. In the early drafts Buddy is an actor who knew Charlie when they were young men struggling to find work in New York. Still struggling, he has become Charlie's stand-in. In the final version the youthful association is retained, but Buddy's function changes.[11]

Odets's most revealing cuts and changes, however, relate to the character of Charlie Castle himself. In the early drafts Charlie is an incessant whiner and complainer, constantly moaning about what a terrible place Hollywood is while at the same time enjoying all of its rewards. Most unfortunately, he seems to blame the place and not himself for the moral surrender he has committed there. By the end of act 2, as a result, his suicide comes as rather a relief, which is clearly not what Odets had in mind. This early Charlie is also endowed with a more detailed past than the final version, but the detail only serves to simplify him, turning him into a typical agit-prop character from the thirties, an effect Odets wanted to move away from by 1948. The overt politicization of his character is apparent early in the play when Charlie speaks to the gossip columnist Patty Benedict about the death of his parents: "They were both killed in the Ludlow Massacre in 1912. That's one of the great scandals of what they call 'the History of the American Working Class.' Federal troops wiped out a whole tent colony of miners and their families who were striking for a better wage." Meanwhile, Charlie's abandonment of his past is emphasized by his wife's identification of the symbol of what he has become: "You're debased. . . . Like the currency. In fact you're currency itself—every gesture and word modulated. Every real human impulse made negotiable."

Odets also introduces the subject of anti-Semitism in the early versions, which is interesting in itself, for although he was Jewish, this subject is rarely addressed elsewhere in his work. Charlie mentions that he was raised by his aunt and uncle after his parents' death. His aunt was not Jewish and, although married to his uncle, she was not, according to Charlie, fond of Jews. Later, when Charlie quotes his uncle, Patty remarks, "That's a very Jewified remark." Charlie replies, "I have nothing against Jewified remarks." Odets apparently seeks not only to allude to anti-Semitism in Hollywood, but also to associate Jewishness with the more moral aspects of Charlie's nature, from which he has distanced himself. This association extends also to the studio head, Marcus Hoff, a man of no moral fiber, whom Charlie calls an "apocalyptic beast" (a remark that was removed in the final draft), and Nat Danziger, Charlie's agent, who, despite a sweet nature, tends to look the other way for the sake of business. At one point utterly repelled by Hoff, Nat cries, "That a man like you is now a Jew to shame and harm my race!" This and all other references to Jewishness were also cut, as distractions from Odets's focus.

The Charlie of the early versions is obviously too completely an idealist, his change too simplistic. The final version exhibits little of this background, retaining only the information that Charlie was raised by an aunt and uncle and was once a stage actor in the East. This pared-down portrait is more suggestive than the original, not reducing Charlie or society to convenient stereotypes, but implying that the main flaw resides in Charlie, as Charlie himself is to some extent aware. He is an exceptionally imaginative man, and his qualities as an artist are attested by those around him. Odets emphasizes both that Charlie is (or at least was) an artist and not just another pretty face, and that Hollywood is fatal to Charlie because there is something within him that responds too readily to its lure. At the same time Hollywood represents the larger world, and when he surrenders to it, he becomes entangled in a web of fate. The play, indeed, unfolds as a series of circumstances that work to enmesh this protagonist in a horrific nightmare of his own making. Perceptive about his own ambition and the stimulation he receives from power and success, Charlie is also disgusted by his capitulation and remorseful about ignoring the dictates of his better self. At last his conscience overwhelms him as his imagination confronts him with the image of a damnable man. In an early draft he remarks, "To myself I am not an institution—I'm a weak, self-disgusted, very human man, very ordinary, guilty, . . . lonely . . . trapped."

Near the end of the finished play Charlie remarks to Nat Danziger, "It's too late, from *my* point of view. I can't go on, covering one crime with another. That's Macbeth. . . . Macbeth is an allegory, too: one by one, he kills his better selves" (p. 135). Clearly, Odets had *Macbeth* in his mind when he wrote *The Big Knife;* in an interview he referred to Dixie Evans as "Banquo's ghost." Like Macbeth, Charlie Castle is an extremely tormented character, perhaps the most suffering character in Odets's canon. In Edward Murray's words he is a character, "sickened by compromise and driven to self-destruction in an effort to expiate his sins." *The Big Knife,* therefore, is more than a simple attack on Hollywood, because Charlie's dilemma results as much from the divided nature of his own soul, torn between conflicting values and unable to reconcile them, as from the moral emptiness of his environment.

The early versions, in fact, display a number of references to *Macbeth* that were cut from the final. Near the play's end, for example, Charlie says to Marion, "Macbeth doth murder sleep." He then alludes to a web of deceit and hints at his suicide: "Burnham wood is moving up. I hope you know Shakespeare." There are also a number of references to blood, images of which permeate Shakespeare's play. In a scene later cut from the early portion of the play, Patty says to Charlie, "Blood's more saleable than water, sweetie. A thimbleful of blood is relished now and then by the best of readers." After Charlie's suicide, his butler comments, "All that blood, all that blood and water. . . . Ain't no blood left in him." Most important is Charlie's description of Hollywood: "I'm afraid of Hollywood because it's a tough, desperate world. They play for keeps here. It's as deadly as anything you read in Shakespeare, plots, intrigues, revenge, and cynicism—it's here, including corruption, intimidation, suicide and murder for succession."

In the tragic career of Odets's Macbeth figure, Hollywood, epitomized in the character of the producer Marcus Hoff, plays the role of Shakespeare's witches, tempting Charlie with wealth and fame undreamed of when he was a poor boy growing up in Philadelphia. There he read the authors in his uncle's library—Jack London, Upton Sinclair, Henrik Ibsen, and Victor Hugo: "Hugo's the one who helped me nibble my way through billions of polly seeds. Sounds grandiose, but Hugo said to me: 'Be a good boy, Charlie. Love people, do good, help the lost and fallen, make the world happy, if you can!' " (p. 9) Having elected, instead, to pursue the promise of riches and power conveyed in Hoff's visions of moviemaking glory, Charlie now feels imprisoned by compromise and a life that violates his better nature. The burden of guilt generated by the fatal accident and its tangled consequences only objectifies the deeper sense of self-ruination that plagues him in the recognition that his success is hollow, that he has subverted his idealism and wasted his art for an ignoble goal. Marion voices this sense of spiritual loss in her complaint about the man Charlie has become:

> Charlie, you're half asleep right now! I haven't seen you sparkle since the day Billy was born! You used to take sides. Golly, the zest with which you fought. You used to grab your theatre parts and eat 'em like a tiger. Now you act with droopy eyes—they have to call you away from a card game. Charlie, I don't want you to sign that contract—you've given the studio their pound of flesh—you don't owe them anything. We arrived here in a pumpkin coach and we can damn well leave the same way! (p. 22)

Charlie, however, knows that in his case no such fairy-tale exist is possible, for he has become too far embroiled in the ugly business of faked glamour and casual destruction. Throughout act 1 he agonizes over whether or not to sign the new fourteen-year contract with Hoff's studio; his compliance is at last extorted when Hoff threatens to expose Charlie's part in the hit-and-run accident. Critics have argued that this early capitulation robs the play of its dramatic tension, when its effect, rather, is to deflate the melodrama of Charlie's predicament, focusing the remaining action instead upon the emotional disintegration caused by his entanglement. Charlie's own sense of fatal incrimination is reflected in Smiley Coy's remark, "Just keep in mind that the day you first scheme . . . you marry the scheme and the scheme's children," which supplies a clear analogy to Macbeth's lament, "I am in blood stepp'd in so far that, should I wade no more, returning were as tedious as go o'er" (act 3, scene 4).

Odets's central thrust in the play is to bring Charlie to a final awareness of what he has become. Already in act 1 he seems to be aware of the falseness of his position, but he is not yet ready to accept fully his personal implication in the corruption he sees around him. Macbeth, too, knows his crimes, but only at the banquet scene does he reach his breaking point, when the true horror of his own nature is exposed to him. Charlie, likewise, proceeds toward his breaking point, remarking his progress of enlightenment in act 3, scene 1: "Murder is indivisible, Smiley. I'm finding that out. Like chastity, there's no such thing as a small amount of it. I'm finding that out" (p. 62).

Finally, in act 3, scene 2, when he says to Marcus Hoff, "Now . . . I realize what I am," his understanding echoes Lady Macbeth's in a prior scene:

> Nought's had, all's spent,
> Where our desire is got without content:
> 'Tis safer to be that which we destroy
> Than by destruction dwell in doubtful joy. (act 3, scene 2)

At last he recognizes that in subverting his better self he has destroyed his family as well, that the comfort and joy he enjoys is very "doubtful" indeed.

Charlie's internal conflict is revealed primarily through his conversations with Hank Teagle, a close friend and a writer who has decided to renounce the Hollywood life-style and return East to work on a novel. Teagle is Marcus Hoff's opposite number, a kind of Banquo figure, reminding Charlie of what he once was and what he could do if only he could regain his youthful idealism. Teagle has even proposed to Marion, vowing to take her back to New York, to a more normal and fulfilling life; like Banquo, he will have the "heirs," whereas the wasted potential of Charlie / Macbeth will ultimately yield him nothing.

During a central conversation between the two friends Teagle tells Charlie about the book he is writing, "I still try to write out of Pascal's remark: 'I admire most those writers who tell, with tears in their eyes, what men do to other men.' This book is about a man like you" (p. 109). Explaining why he wants to take Marion away from the Hollywood environment, Hank expands the Hollywood metaphor to encompass an entire contemporary state of mind:

> Marion's future interests me deeply. No. I don't think she'll be happy here with you! I don't want Marion joining the lonely junked people of our world—millions of them, wasted by the dreams of the life they were promised and the swill they received! They are why the whole world, including us, sits bang in the middle of a revolution! Here, of course, that platitude carries with it the breath of treason. I think lots of us are in for a big shot of Vitamin D: defeat, decay, depression, and despair. (p. 109–10)

Finally, he charges that Charlie is destroying himself trying to choose between moral values and success, sarcastically recommending that he simply yield to the Hollywood ethic: "Your wild, native idealism is a fatal flaw in the context of your life out here. Half-idealism is the peritonitis of the soul—American is full of it! Give up and really march to Hoff's bugle call!" (p. 110). When Hank leaves, Charlie is still torn, unable to act. Only when the studio pushes him to acquiesce in the murder of Dixie Evans does Charlie decide to take his fate into his own hands.

The conclusion of *The Big Knife* is in certain respects similar to *Golden Boy,* as Charlie breaks with Marcus Hoff and so makes himself a Hollywood outcast. When he tells his agent Nat and then Marion that he now recognizes his own culpability and the degradation of his life, Odets employs an Ibsenian stage device to reinforce the suggestion of clearing sight, of startling enlightenment. As in *A Doll's House,* Charlie twice turns on a lamp in act 3, scene 2, once as he says, "Now I realize what I am" (p. 134). The second time, when he says good-bye to Marion, he observes, "Keep meaning to put larger bulbs in these lamps" (p. 139). In his farewell Charlie also remarks, "Aren't the times beyond us, cold and lonely? Far away as the stars." The image echoes Odets's use of the moon in *Golden Boy,* at once a death image and a romantic symbol of aspiration that moves the lovers beyond the bounds of the physical world. Embracing Marion, he pledges to her a better future, then goes up to the bath to slash his wrists. For Charlie, as for Joe Bonaparte, death represents the only way out of a spiritual dilemma.

Charlie's suicide is discovered by Smiley Coy and Marion when they notice a water spot behind the stairs, ominously recalling Lady Macbeth's inability to remove the blood spots from her hands during her mad scene. Charlie's suicide here precipitates Marion's madness, for after viewing the body, she begins screaming "help," the word that concludes the play. Odets's final stage directions read: "Hank has his arms around her, but the word does not stop and will never stop in this life" (p. 147). It is Odets's most devastating ending, indicating a tragic loss so profound that Marion, unlike Lorna, is unable to comprehend it.

The loss of Charlie Castle attains the dimension of tragedy because the man has come to recognize the futility of his worldly success as well as his own implication in the sordid business of maintaining it. Like Macbeth, he is guilty of a series of crimes committed in the pursuit of an ephemeral glory and in defiance of his own higher nature. Yet, like Shakespeare's overreacher, he is consistently portrayed as a man of stature, clearly superior to the Hollywood types who surround him, and commanding the love and loyalty of Marion and Hank Teagle, the two most sympathetic characters in the play. Just as Macbeth's preeminence as a soldier is established by the wounded soldier at the play's beginning, and his personal virtues attested by his wife and by Duncan, Charlie Castle's integrity and potential are indicated by the deference and affection of his friends and confirmed in the extraordinary perceptiveness he displays in judging his own actions. The weighty catalog of his sins is thus matched by the nobility of his spirit. Ensnared at the last in a mounting calamity of his own making, he destroys himself as "a final act of faith," a victim, like Macbeth, of the dagger of his own ambition.

Notes

1. Clifford Odets, "Democratic Vistas in Drama," *New York Times,* 21 November, 1937, sec. 11, p. 1.

2. Ibid.

3. Robert Warshaw, "The Gangster as Tragic Hero," in *The Immediate Experience* (1962. Reprint. New York: Atheneum, 1974), p. 130.

4. This early draft of *Golden Boy,* dated 1937, is in the Billy Rose Theatre Collection of the New York Public Library at Lincoln Center.

5. Clifford Odets, *Golden Boy* in *Six Plays of Clifford Odets* (New York: Grove Press, 1979), p. 247. All further references to the play are from this edition and are cited in the text.

6. Carp's quotes from Schopenhauer are more extensive in the earlier versions of the play.

7. Gerald Rabkin, *Drama and Commitment* (Bloomington: Indiana University Press, 1964), pp. 197–98.

8. Quoted in Edward Murray, *Clifford Odets: The Thirties and After* (New York: Frederick Ungar Publishing Company, 1968), pp. 160–61.

9. For a full discussion of the characteristics of Hollywood fiction, refer to Carolyn See, "The Hollywood Novel: The American Dream Cheat," in David Madden, ed., *Tough Guy Writers of the Thirties* (Carbondale: Southern Illinois University Press, 1968), pp. 197–217.

10. Clifford Odets, *The Big Knife* (New York: Random House, 1949), p. 106. All further references are to this edition and are cited in the text.

11. All quoted material not in the published version of *The Big Knife* is from "A Winter Journey, First Draft" dated 1948, in the Billy Rose Theatre Collection of the New York Public Library at Lincoln Center.

[Rocket to the Moon]

Margaret Brenman-Gibson

We must not lose sight of the fact that the creative process is not finally consummated until the artist's experience—given form on paper, on canvas, or in stone—has reached an audience. Most particularly, the dramatist, that most topical of artists, must feel that he has succeeded in obliterating boundaries and established a union with the group assembled to watch his play.[1] Proceeding from this assumption, the position of *Rocket to the Moon* in 1938—in Odets' personal history as well as in the history of American drama—is pivotal. While, to be sure, even in so manifestly agitational a play as his early and slight strike play, *Waiting for Lefty,* Odets' characters and dialogue are already characteristically vivacious, electric, and original, the shift from the emotional currency of economics and politics to that of psychology first becomes evident in *Rocket to the Moon.* This cogwheeling of an artist's personal themes with those of his society determines (aside from the size of his gift) his success or failure in his lifetime. It is not unusual that there is a lag in either direction.

The manifest spine of the play *Rocket* is no longer politically messianic: unlike Odets' early plays, addressed to the oppressed international proletariat, pleading with them to "awake and sing" in economic liberation; the appeal is, rather, for creative liberation. Odets told director Harold Clurman it was about "love and marriage." On the one hand, this shift clearly reflects Odets' own struggles with the crisis of intimacy. But that is not all. The cogwheeling turn of history was changing his audience: those who in 1935 had looked for ultimate salvation in the theory of Marx, the activities of the "working class," and the model of the Soviet Union were becoming progressively cynical and wary. The peaceloving Russian comrades—hitherto embraced by idealistic Americans as apostles of the realization of individual potential and dignity—had lately made a pact of mutual defense with "imperialist" France, and, worse, had begun the systematic extermination of their own domestic enemies. The barbarous Moscow trials of these "enemies" were leaving an increasingly bitter taste, straining the loyalty of even the most

Originally published as "The Creation of Plays with a Specimen Analysis," in *Psychoanalysis, Creativity, and Literature,* edited by Alan Roland (New York: Columbia University Press, 1978). Copyright © 1978 Columbia University Press. Used by permission. Only a portion of the essay is reprinted here.

devoted of American fellow travelers. In short, there no longer existed so credulous an audience as the one that had risen in joyous unison at the close of *Waiting for Lefty* to shout, "Strike!"

The major critics dimly understood Odets' shift away from the manifestly political as a "landmark in his growth." Those writing for the communist press—missing entirely the point of the play: a plea for the liberation of creativity—mourned that he had given over his "magnificent flair for character study and dialogue" to such bourgeois concerns as "love and marriage." Of the first-line critics, only the sagacious Joseph Wood Krutch, writing for *The Nation,* understood the nature of Odets' evolution as a playwright and the resultant shifts within himself, and, accordingly, the nature of his transactions with an equally changing audience: "The tendency still persists to make of Clifford Odets and his plays a political issue. That, I think, is a pity from any point of view now that the facts are becoming increasingly clear. Whatever his opinions may have been or, for that matter, may still be, those opinions are shared by many, while Mr. Odets reveals a gift for characterization and a gift for incisive dialogue unapproached by any of his Marxian fellows and hardly equaled by any other American playwright."[2] Another central point made by Krutch was that Odets—and correspondingly his audience—had gradually shifted from the manifestly political to the psychological arena.

Keeping in mind as scaffolding Erikson's new perspectives on the dream as well as his fourfold complementarity (that is, the writer's history and his present stage of life plus the present state of his society and *its* history), I proceed to our play specimen.

Odets' first jottings for *Rocket to the Moon,* made in 1937 when he was thirty-one, outline a play whose sensory quality and affective atmosphere are immediately reflected in its wasteland setting: in sharp contrast to the play's title, the space is tightly, even suffocatingly, bounded. People and flowers alike thirst, are dead, constricted, manifestly allowing little room for locomotion, "play," or growth. With fewer characters than ever before, he gives these again neutral "American" names of indeterminate national origins.

His earliest scribbled notes indicate Odets' conscious intention to create as the protagonist of *Rocket to the Moon,* a frightened, ineffectual, submerged little dentist named Ben Stark, a man in a "mid-life crisis," torn between his controlling, sterile wife and his juicy, aspiring secretary, and bitterly disappointed in his creative aspirations. Initially, it appeared the central *action* of the play would be his. The fourth, and perhaps the richest character is his wife's father, Judah Prince, a man of the world, determined to "have love" before he dies. A man who prides himself on knowing "how to talk to a headwaiter," he is the dentist's rival for the girl. The idea for this play had come to him, Odets said, when he was sitting in a dentist's chair looking at the equipment and the water cooler, and wondering what kinds of emotional life were concealed behind the numb routines of this office and behind the constricted face of the meek little dentist himself. Early notes, written by Odets at a time when he began to be in conscious conflict over his marriage, indicate the central theme would be *"about love and marriage in America."*

By way of this specimen play analysis, I will provide data which illustrate the two major hypotheses: first, *that a play always deals at some level with the playwright's view, conscious and unconscious, of the nature of the creative process itself,* and secondly, *that the playwright's distribution of himself (of his identity elements), constitute the cast of characters,*[3] their conflicts and resolutions reflecting the playwright's effort via Form to bring these dualities into harmony, restoring wholeness where there was conflict.

Over a year had elapsed after his first notes for *Rocket,* at the end of which time Odets' own efforts at a faithful intimacy were reaching a bitter climax in the crumbling of his marriage. In response to his coldly detached reply to her telegraphed announcement from Hollywood that she was pregnant, his wife had aborted their first and only child. Odets had fled with the company of *Golden Boy* from New York to London, and in the fall of 1938, now thirty-two, he drove alone to Canada, carrying with him, in addition to the few notes written the year before the "dentist play," the manuscript of his labor play, as well as the play about the Cuban revolution. It is evident his necessity is to work, preferably on material manifestly tied to the ongoing historic upheavals. In his "General Notes," from 1938, he had written: "The invasion of Prague, from news dispatches. Crowds of thousands stood, weeping silently, and then spontaneously broke into their national anthem! A policeman outside the city hall tried desperately to direct traffic but was too blinded by his tears. Many of the Czechs covered their faces with their hands and turned away at the first sight of the German troops. Well, can a writer write in the face of these things? Yes, he *must* write in the face of these things!"[4]

It troubled him, however, that a formal vessel by means of which he might explicitly unite these large and somber historic events to his own emotional urgencies continued to elude him. Finally, he stopped work on the manifestly "social-historical" plays—all of which took as their theme the beginning of the end of the American Dream—and concentrated instead on what appeared to be the strictly "personal" struggles of three ordinary and lonely people, with Ben Stark, the passive, submerged dentist, trying to find sufficient courage to "take life by the throat" by having an affair with his childlike, attractive, and aspiring secretary, Cleo Singer.[5] It is implied that his stifled growth—his generativity—will thereby be given new impetus and he will escape the feeling he has "blown it."

In the playwright's original outline, written only a few weeks after his wedding, and during the first of many separations, the dentist's secretary succeeds in detaching Stark from his wife. After a year of intense emotional negotiation, Odets' own marriage all but finished, he found as he was rewriting this play that the character, Cleo, had begun to take center stage away from Ben and to evolve as the "identity element" by now familiar to me from his earliest juvenile writing: the aspiring, unformed, even damaged, artist, or—as he liked to call her—"the moral idealist," whose growth is in steady jeopardy of becoming fraudulent, or crippled by a premature restriction of options, manipulated by the seductive and worldly American businessman whose own innocence and idealism, like that of America, has long since disappeared.

The dentist, Stark, a "second-class professional," is a man who reads Shakespeare, but who would—according to Odets' notes—be frightened even to get a passport and who "plays it safe" in his own work. He is in competition for this girl Cleo (that is, for the identity element we can call Odets' Muse) with his father-in-law, who decisively proclaims, with no trace of his son-in-law's shame and doubt, "*I want what I want!*" This is the polarity between that aspect of Odets' identity structure which (like his mother's) is deadened by a fearful, proper, and obsessional paralysis, and his insistence on a full, joyful, and maximal experience of life which would "exclude nothing," and which he thought would therefore be "disobedient" and "evil."

Advising the meek Ben Stark he is an iceberg, healf-dead, who excludes so much from awareness and action that there is no "play" in him, the older man recommends to the younger that he regain elbow room, leeway, and, thus, vitality before it's too late: "You'll be dead soon enough." Judah Prince concludes with an extraordinarily bold, locomotive proposal which in 1938 was synonymous with saying, "Undertake the visionary, the impossible." He says to the only half-alive dentist, "Explode, take a rocket to the moon!" supplying here the title for the play eagerly awaited by director Harold Clurman and then-actor, Elia Kazan.

The other pole of Odets' conflict is jotted in a "production note" in the margin: "Motto: 'You don't easily give up a home if you have been an orphan.'"[6] This caution issues from a person terrified to make a great leap lest he fall into an abyss.

So delighted were the Group Theatre actors that Odets had finally brought his new play that they swallowed their disappointment that he had completed only two acts. All agreed the three major characters were among his best and most mature yet. Director Clurman found himself, however, unsettled by what appeared from these two acts to be a significant shift away from the original plan of the play about a constricted man who stops "playing it safe" and who bursts *his* bonds by a union with a liberating young *anima,* the girl Cleo. "Awakened" by his love for this girl, Odets had said, he would undergo a ravaging depth of experience which, despite the girl's childish self-absorption, would increase his stature as a man and propel the growth hitherto blocked. As Clurman now listened to Odets read his first two acts, it appeared to him that subtly, the play's center—without sufficient psychological justification in Odets' development of her character—had shifted to the girl Cleo and that the play's focus had radically changed from that of a man torn between two women to a girl freeing herself from two men.

Moreover, with a new prominence for the worldly Prince (a man who recommends himself as someone who "don't look foolish before authority"), quite a different triangle had been created, with the aspiring girl instead of the frightened dentist at its apex. The play's theme had originally centered on the question of whether the timid and dependently vulnerable man could break through the enveloping, dead wasteland of his static and submerged existence by an explosive and creative thrust (a "rocket to the moon") toward a fresh, young (amorphously talented), girl in quest of both love and of self-expression. It had been conceived as the man's play, and the struggle was to be his. Now, the theme appeared to have moved from him to the girl even as Odets had moved from his failed struggle for intimacy with his wife to the broader issues of his own creativity or generativity: Carrying the responsibility for the recent destruction of his first unborn *biological* child, he deeply feared that his stagnation would extend to his "brain-children" as well. The character, Cleo, his Muse, now bore the burden of reestablishing his generativity. It was disquietingly clear to director Clurman that something significant in Odets' emotional life had intervened between the first outline of this play and the present two acts, throwing out of kilter the formal dramatic structure. He devoutly hoped the still unwritten third act would dispel his fear that the character, Cleo, had run away with the play, confusing its formal structure sufficiently to sabotage both its aesthetic unity and its commercial success.

An interesting question for study here is: how had an experienced playwright of great skill begun with one play and ended with another?[7]

For over a year, Odets had been seriously blocked in his work, had had a dismaying *sense of loss of emotional connection to his wife and of creative connection to the growing crisis in the immediate events of world history*. He sensed only dimly that the deeper connection in his current work to the unfolding of history lay in its reflection of an increasingly urgent conflict between the values of salesmanship and an innocent creativity. His notes suggest he was seeing both his wife and his father as "the enemy," while finding it increasingly difficult to identify "the enemy" as a simple, political-economic order with which he could do battle as he had in the past. The references in *Rocket* to the villainy of the economic system are perfunctory and hollow.

Now that his marriage was coming to an end, it must have appeared to him that, despite his loneliness and shame at this failure, he had a second chance, a fresh start in his *primary*—his most "real"—self-identity as an honest artist, if not as a husband or father. His *anima* (Cleo) says, "*It's getting late to play at life: I want to live it . . . something has to feel real.*"

It is as if Odets falls back to an earlier stage in his development and hopes this time for a firmer resolution at least of his work identity and for a renewal of his generativity as playwright. He will find the "real reality" in his brain-children, a safer fatherhood, he felt, than of a flesh-and-blood baby.

In *Rocket to the Moon,* for the first time in his life, Odets was writing a play which does not culminate in some kind of crippling or catastrophe: injury to his creative "hands," suicide, or death. A key tragedy of his childhood, it will be recalled, was the "abandonment" of him by his mother in favor of his crippled sister. It is this personal sense of disinheritance which had cogwheeled with the collective sense of disinheritance in the Depression era. *Rocket* is a desperate turn to a psychological instead of an economic deliverance. It is an adumbration of the reach in American cultural history—three decades later—toward self-actualizing (inner) values. In *Golden Boy,* written by Odets the year before, Joe Bonaparte, who has irrevocably lost himself as a violinist by crippling his hands in a prizefight, cries out in a climactic, locomotor defiance of gravity, "We're off the earth!" and—while the "money-men" are dividing shares of him—the speeding automobile incinerates Joe and his girl in Babylon, Long Island. It is the paradigm of the price paid for the machines and the worldly values inherent in the American dream.

Here, while there recurs the image of an escape from the constricting pull of a "Mother Earth," it is in a rocket, a machine even more powerful than an automobile and this time with the intrepid thrust of a confident citizen of a virile, technological world-power. The emotional tone of the rocket image is not suicidal but freely adventurous and open; of a man still on an explosive American frontier. With the impulsive surge of personal liberation from the constrictions of immigrant terror, the image is of a twentieth-century American conquistador planting his flag in unmapped territory (the feminine moon). Wholly different from the apocalyptic locomotor image which closes *Golden Boy,* or even from that of a businesslike astronaut, a "rocket to the moon" is filled with hope, initiative, and even a promise of a peak experience of freedom.

I wish there were space to discuss *Rocket to the Moon* "beat by beat." Only by following each of its dramatic moves in microscopic detail is it possible to see the specificity with which the data support the two working hypotheses I propose. I will try here to state the essentials.

With a pace and a focus of intent rare in dramatic literature, Odets manages in the first distilled "beat" of the very first scene to get into the heart of the play's conflict and its *apparent* theme: there is an immediate confrontation between the frightened, isolated dentist, Ben Stark and his scolding wife, Belle.[8] Their conflict commences in a sensory web of heat and claustrophobic *imprisonment.* He wants to "specialize," to grow, and she, like Odets' father, gives practical reasons against it, reasons which stifle his growth. By a most economic exchange, the playwright ends the first round, with the controlling wife, Belle, the victor. Indeed, she has won even before the play opens and when she concludes the opening beat with, "Any day now I'm expecting to have to powder and diaper you," she has established herself as the parent, the boss, the *obstacle* in the path of the aspiring Ben Stark's creative growth. As the play opens the conflict between these two—husband and wife—appears to be its theme.

The connective tissue of the play, as in a musical fugue, derives from fragments of this announced theme: Belle says her husband must not simply agree to *do* as she says; he must also "see that I am right," play it safe, and not try to expand his practice and creative work. He, who was once a "pioneer with Gladstone in orthodontia" (in making straight and whole that which is crooked) has already lowered his creative sights to tooth pulling and to cultivating petunias in a flower box, and his income to one-tenth of what "men with half my brains and talent are making." "If he had to go get a passport, it would become a terrific event in his life."[9] The fact that he is a dentist, not a doctor, is already a comedown in the "good prototypes" of Jewish middle-class life. But Belle does not approve his creative collaboration with Gladstone in dentistry, any more than did Odets' father approve of Harry Kemp or his wife Luise Rainer approve his association with Clurman in the Group Theatre. Even Ben's last-ditch attempts to nurture (to generate) his sadly drooping little flowers which his secretary calls his "orphan babies" are immediately revealed in the first few minutes as fumbling and inept:

STARK: I wanted to do something . . . what was it? not a drink . . . Oh, the flowers! (He fills a paper cup, puts his pipe between his teeth and tries without success, one hand full to fill a second cup.)

BELLE: Try one at a time, dear.

STARK: (Coolly) One at a time is a good idea. (At the window, right, he pours the water on a window box of drooping petunias. As he turns for more water he faces Belle who has brought him a second cupful.) Thanks.

BELLE.   (Smiling) Anyday now I'm expecting to have to powder and diaper you.[10]

In these few lines between the initial major player and counterplayer, the husband and wife, there stands a distilled illustration of the way a playwright juggles and adjusts the conflicts and the "moves" of his internal "gallery of characters"—that is, of his own identity elements and fragments—to the external masks of the people in his past and present worlds.

In this short exchange much is reflected: Odets' conviction at that time that his wife—like his father—chronically wished to criticize, denigrate, and control him and his work (Ben's petunias), as well as to convert, reform, and direct him. There are reflected other paradigms as well. Odets has condensed in the dentist's relation to his controlling, depressed wife not only his own responses to his father's tyranny, but also to the mood of his melancholy mother and the steady (internalized) combat between his parents. Were it not for the fact of Odets' own struggle between his longing to surrender, abdicating all autonomy, initiative, and responsibility (as he had long ago sat obediently for hours on his little chair, waiting), and his impulse to "explode," there would be no conflict and no play. In his production notes,

Odets wrote of Stark, "He is a man who suffers because he can't make important decisions easily . . . fears scenes and fights. . . . If he feels it is a matter of principle, he can stand up, otherwise, he may cave in. . . . Principle is a shield where the self can be forgotten."

Ben Stark's physical ineptitude, his indecisiveness, an expression of Odets' own sense of incompetence, like his mother's, takes its contemporary external shape, however, from Clurman's clumsiness in practical undertakings. It was a steady source of banter in the Group Theatre that Clurman—like Ben Stark—could scarcely open a package of cigarettes, was unable to use a can-opener, and would say "Hello" without picking up the telephone receiver. Odets often said, "Gadg Kazan is Harold's muscle and his legs."

Odets, himself, consciously thought of Ben Stark's meek obedience to his wife's disdainful will ("You win, you win," he says to her wearily) as simply a literal copy of Clurman's compliance with the powerful Stella Adler. Not so. These characters are all configurations and subconfigurations of identity elements with Odets' own self, organized long before he met Clurman or Stella Adler. Such are the complexities of joining an inner gallery of characters with the playwright's actual contemporaries from whom he is said to have "taken" his cast of characters.

This is a good example of how misleading it is to make a one-to-one biographic correlation between the playwright as protagonist, and the people in his life as "supporting cast." To be sure, those in the playwright's life space, most especially members of a family, or even of a gifted acting company like the Group Theatre, call out his own internal "gallery," providing the masks for the characters who people his play. It is no accident, for example, that actor Morris Carnovsky always played the "spiritual" parts in Odets' plays, while Kazan was usually cast, as Odets put it, as the "original getahead boy." Odets regularly used each of the Group Theatre members as a mask for his own warring identity elements and fragments, and was actually helped to create whole persons (lovingly and fully) by reason of the independent existence of these excellent actors.

As the play moves on through this first act, with the playwright keeping the polyphonic conflicts alive while offering expository material, minor characters, crackling dialogue, and lovely jokes, we see reverberations not only of Odets' struggles with his wife and of his grief about their aborted child, but also of his own earlier trail of dead or aborted children, creative as well as biological. This is a play in which the people steadily reveal themselves. Belle Prince Stark, ironically calling herself "your terrible wife," as Odets' wife, in fact, often had—says, in Luise Rainer's actual words, "You have to love me all the time . . . a woman wants to live *with* a man, not next to him," adding she has been "blue all morning," thinking of their dead baby.

Throughout this first act of *Rocket to the Moon,* it is evident that the playwright initially intended the central question to be: Will this frightened individual summon the courage to break his bondage and fulfill his life by a love affair or will he play it safe, abdicate his growth, and be like the enslaved immigrant who continues to the end (in the words of Bob Dylan, born Robert Zimmerman) to "passionately hate his life and likewise fear his death?"

After the initial victory in the first scene of the wife (Belle) over the husband (Ben), the girl (Cleo) enters, and the play appears ready again to move forward. We are forewarned, however, of the increasing imbalance in the play's structure by the fact that the protagonist (Ben Stark) is, from the beginning, the least interesting character. He is the quiet observer, the static center, and, if the playwright had maintained him as the central character, the play would never have moved forward. Moreover, we have seen early hints that the new triangle is building, with the two men competing for the girl. While it is difficult to care what will happen between Ben and the sexy, stockingless Cleo Singer,[11] dressed in "angel-skin satin," the interchange between the passionate old man and this girl is from the outset arresting, enlivening, and involving. Clearly it is in *their* relationship that the playwright sees the formidable threat to the American artist: in the struggle between worldly and creative values. To the extent that it was difficult for the audience to see Cleo as a symbol of creativity, to that extent was the play a failure.

Obviously unsuited to her job and as inefficient in it as Odets in his youth had been in all of his, Cleo is like him, an insecure name-dropper and fabricator; she lies that her mother was an opera *singer* (her surname) in Europe and that "I come from a well-to-do family . . . I really don't need this job." Later, Ben says to her, "Everyone tells little fables, Cleo. Sometimes to themselves, sometimes to others. Life is so full of brutal facts . . . we all try to soften them by making believe." Cleo, the storyteller—the artist—becomes now (psychologically) *the central identity element in the play, though not yet the central character in its formal structure.* The fables she tells are the effort to make life bearable by "making believe." Precisely this is the work of a playwright: to make himself and other people believe in a reality he creates. Manifestly, however, at this early stage of the game, Cleo appears to be no more than a shallow rival to the oppressive Belle Prince Stark who is simultaneously patrolling many beats, strengthening her hand not only against the girl in this first triangle but on all those who are making her husband's office "inefficient." She is calling everyone to heel and trying to hold her barren fort in a status-quo position. As she leaves the office, we are introduced to the play's third major character, Mr. Judah Prince. Odets describes him in terms clearly recognizable as belonging to his father, L. J. Odets, yet with more affection and empathy than usual. Consciously, he thought he had modeled this character after Stella Adler's father, tragedian

Jacob Adler, attorney Max Steuer, and the Yiddish actor, Tomashevsky: "He is near sixty, wears an old panama hat, a fine Palm Beach suit of twenty years ago and a malacca cane. There is about him the dignity and elegant portliness of a Jewish actor, a sort of aristocratic air. He is an extremely self-confident man with a strong sense of humor which, however, is often veiled. He is very alive in the eyes and mouth, the rest of him relaxed and heavy" (p. 339).[12]

His daugher no longer speaks to him because of the dreadful life he had given her dead mother, a punitive silence to be meted out much later by Odets to his own father. "I am the American King Lear," says Mr. Prince, whose dreams of self-realization—like the secret aspiration of the senior Odets to be a writer—have come to nothing: "In our youth we collect materials to build a bridge to the moon," Stark comments, "but in our old age we use the materials to build a shack."

The charged excitement between the sensual, worldly old man and the aspiring young person (read, artist)—as so often in an Odets play—is immediate and unmistakable; as it was between the equivalent characters of Moe and Hennie in *Awake and Sing!* or gangster Eddie Fuseli and fighter-musician Joe Bonaparte in *Golden Boy.* Structurally, it is clear something new is starting here: The old man tells the girl he likes her honesty and that "everything that's healthy is personal." He adds (as Odets' father often said of himself and his son) that he and she are identical. She aspires to being a dancer and he, *"without marriage"* could have been, he thinks, "a great actor." He was also once, he tells her, an idealist. In all of this, the old man is clearly making a move toward the girl. Structurally, by dint of this move, the play has shifted ground: alongside the original triangle of husband, wife, and aspirant girl there stands now a new one: that of husband, aspirant girl, and father-in-law. Prince, like Odets' father, announces he has been made to "play safe" by *his* wife even as Belle (his daughter) now urges Ben, her husband to do. ("A housewife rules your destiny," says Prince to Stark, adding he had "disappeared in the corner with the dust, under the rug" and lives a dull life "where every day is Monday.")

Although Judah Prince boasts that he still earns money, he bitterly asks to whom shall he leave it all, "to Jascha Heifetz?" Addressing himself, and simultaneously his son-in-law, he asks, "Is this the life you dreamed?" The answer is no, he thinks, for both of them and the path to salvation is clear:

PRINCE: (Suddenly turning, hand on door knob, pointing his cane at Stark and lowering his voice to a near whisper) Iceberg, listen . . . why don't you come up and see the world, the sea gulls and the ships to Europe? (Coming back into the room) When did you look at another woman last? The year they put the buffalo nickel on the market? Why don't you suddenly ride away, an airplane, a boat! Take a rocket to the moon! Explode! What holds you back? You don't want to hurt Belle's feelings? You'll die soon enough. . . .

STARK: I'll just have to laugh at that!

PRINCE: Laugh . . . but make a motto for yourself: "Out of the coffin by Labor Day!" Have an affair with—with—this girl . . . this Miss Cleo. She'll make you a living man again. (p. 350)[13]

By making himself one flesh with an innocent, growing girl, Prince assures Ben he will be creatively activated by sex, a formula often alternated by Odets, in his own frenzied life, with sexual abstinence. It is as if (some of the time) he regarded the feminine aspect of himself as the source of his generativity which would be brought to life by sexual union. This element is in conflict with that of the worldly American businessman who, though magnetic, is ruthless, exploitative, senses-bound, self-centered, lonely and fundamentally out of touch with his own creativity, with the "play" in himself. By reason of his richness, this character, Judah Prince, threatens to "run away" with *Rocket to the Moon,* as does his equivalent character in so many of Odets' plays.

Act One closes with the inhibited Ben Stark looking out at the "Hotel Algiers," modeled after the seamy Columbus Circle Hotel of Odets's youth (a symbol to him of sexual vitality and forbidden freedom). At the windows of this teeming place, he used literally to peep at "real life," in order, he reasoned, to gather material for his plays.

As Cleo leaves, she reminds Ben of his dreary coffin of an existence: "Your wife expects you home at seven." It is not these routines Odets fears, rather it is that in the "real" intimacy of marriage he will disappear as an artist. ("A man falls asleep in marriage," says Ben.) Thus Odets, on some level, is convinced that a continuing intimacy with a woman threatens his creativity.

The second act of *Rocket to the Moon* opens in sharp contrast to the first: the girl, Cleo is offering Ben cool water to comfort him in the hellish heat of this summer.[14] Unlike his wife, who wants him to play life safe, she does not deprive him, fight him, seek to reform, and ultimately to possess and control, him as though he were her lost baby. Indeed, Cleo expresses her own reassuring determination never to marry: "It's too sordid," she says.

By now, it is becoming apparent to Mr. Prince that his obsessive son-in-law—whose mentor for a fuller life he has tried to be—will not leave his wife, nor even seek to renew himself by having an affair with Cleo. Accordingly, he makes his own dramatic "move," and, in a richly ornamented (indeed brilliant) scene of power and restraint, he is on the seductive attack. Like Odets himself, he is a "student of the human insect," flirting, teasing, and promising. He tells her she is "talking to a man with a body like silk" who "possesses the original teeth, every one" (*he* has no need for a dentist!), and "in all the multitudes of your acquaintanceship you won't find a man with younger ideas than your present speaker." True, he wears high-heeled shoes because "I don't like to be so small," but if she will put herself in his hands, he will help her to learn and to grow.

Just as in *Awake and Sing!*, where the powerful racketeer Moe Axelrod offers Havana on a silver platter to the girl Hennie, or in *Golden Boy* where gangster Eddie Fuseli promises fame and fortune to the violinist-fighter Joe, and the gangster Kewpie, a soft life to Libby in *Paradise Lost*, so now does Mr. Prince offer Cleo not only his money but his deep understanding of her needs ("My girl, I studied you like a scientist"). This same identity element would assume the form of the Hollywood film executive in Odets' later play, *The Big Knife*. The price, in each play, for material power (that is, attachment to the sense, not to money) is surrender of one's integrity and freedom.

Cleo, like an identity element of Odets himself, is naive, quick to take offense, frightened, fragile, and unsupported. She fears ridicule for her yearning to become a dancer (a clear echo of L. J. Odets' taunts to his son when he aspired to being an actor) and is convinced no one loves her: "Millions of people moving around the city and nobody cares if you live or die." She will, in revenge (as Odets had often, in fact, contemplated) "fall down on them all," from a high building.

It takes courage, says the girl, a courage she is not sure the dentist has, "to go out to things, to new experiences," to seek an expansion, an intensification of life: of one's consciousness and expression ("Don't you think," she says, "life is to live all you can and experience everything? Shouldn't a wife help a man do that? . . . your wife broke up your courage.") Cleo clearly speaks Odets' struggle to establish himself as the "center of awareness in a universe of experience," unfettered by arbitrary inner and outer restriction. It is an innocent expression of Erikson's description of the very nature of "I-ness."[15]

A minor character cries, "Diphtheria gets more respect than me . . . why can't they fit me in, a man of my talents?" The nineteen-year-old Cleo replies, "Just because you're sad you can't make me sad. No one can. I have too much in me! . . . I have a throat to sing with, a heart to love with! Why don't you love me Dr. Stark?" Ben, like Odets, smiles when he can't meet a situation. As this first scene in Act Two ends, Cleo announces that not Stark "or any other man" deserves her. This statement turns the central theme of the play from an inhibited dentist's struggle over whether to have an affair, to the aspiration of a young, unfulfilled artist. Taking this initiative, her answer to the question "how should one live?"—boldly or timidly—is unmistakable:

CLEO: (Shyly) I'll call you Benny in a minute! (after a throb of hesitation) Ben! Benny! . . . (They are standing off from each other, poised on needles) Don't be afraid. . . .

STARK: . . . No? . . .

CLEO: Love me. . . . Love me, Ben.

STARK: . . . Can't do that. . . .

CLEO: (Moving forward a step) Put your arms up and around me.

STARK: Cleo. . . . (Now they move in on each other. Everything else gone, they are together in a full, fierce embrace, together in a swelter of heat, misunderstanding, loneliness, and simple sex.) (pp. 379–80)[16]

The initiative *must* come from the girl; had Odets left it to the paralyzed identity element represented by the character of Stark, nothing would happen. Cleo, like Odets, always afraid of repudiation, is for the moment confirmed, and Ben Stark is breaking his long sleep to give rein to his impulse, with this girl. Perhaps, he dreams, it will restore his "power for accomplishment" lost through "unhappy marriage." A man who "don't get much personal satisfaction out of his work . . . is a lost man."

Another minor character who functions psychologically as a negative identity fragment in the play "glistens with arrogance." He, too, is trying to seduce Cleo, whose "jingling body" is a magnet. She is impressed by this man whose very name suggests a smooth, shiny surface: Willy Wax. "A man who gets his name in the paper so often," she says, "must be important to some people" (p. 382). Willy Wax is a caricature of the sexual predator who is at the same time a Spurious Artist. This is Odets' unconscious fear of what he could become were he to accede to the worst of his father within himself. Group Theatre actor Sanford Meisner, cast in this part, recalled him with utter distaste, a man "with no redeeming feature." "Movies," says Wax, "started me off on my path of painless perversion" (p. 386). Director Clurman told the cast about this character, "*He plays with his talents. His adjustment is a constant perversion of himself,*" and Odets has added in the margin of the production notes, "He likes to astound and impress . . . actually he is worn out, alienated." Not yet thirty-three, Odets' terrified vision of his future lay tucked into this distasteful minor character.

It is not accidental that the play's motion has been taken from the middle-aged, imprisoned dentist, Ben, and given to the nineteen-year-old *anima*, Cleo. Odets finds himself at this time in a new edition of his central—essentially unresolved—adolescent identity crisis: whether to play life safe and to become the kind of stereotyped householder his father wanted him to be, obediently writing advertising copy for the Odets Company, and rearing a family; or in the style of a priest (or a romantic artist) giving first priority, before everything else, to the creation and communication of *his* vision of life. This was, of course, not a conscious, voluntary decision when he was nineteen, nor is it now at thirty-two. Art deals not in a deliberate choice among a number of possibilities, only in necessities. The "necessity" in *this* play is reflected first in the creation of the submerged dentist as the central character. He is a man who has abandoned his creativity. But, it emerges, Odets could not emotionally "afford" to open up this static man and risk a violent confrontation with the powerful Mr. Prince.

In the discussion which followed the original presentation of this material, playwright Arthur Miller said:

. . . There is a terror underneath (this play), which stopped it from being written . . . my own feeling about the play (is that) there is a phantomlike quality about it, which was one of the things that always drew me to Odets. I could never understand how he was equated with realism, naturalism, or even social drama, after *Waiting for Lefty*. I think he is dealing with phantoms. . . . In this play, he is raising conflicts which he never engages in. There is a projection of myself into this, but that's the way it is. . . . This play is a measurement—not in a moral sense, but in another sense—of values, life values . . . and it seems to me that the showdown, the climax, the unveiling which he is always promising, will have to engage a real knockdown fight, between the dentist and that old man. . . . Now there is a conceivable end to his play where the *Life Force* escapes all of them, and they are left in effect with no Force. Cleo, ridiculed, with her make believe and lying, a fairly pathetic creature, walks out and with her walks out (ironically enough) all their lives, because she somehow embodied their aspirations. There is a fear which is probably very complicated, of just the conflict he proposed . . . which is a very common thing in playwrights.

Miller continued: "It would involve some disaster which is too great a price to pay, and consequently the conflict is aborted before it got started. Of course, he can let her [Cleo] be free because her struggle is not a menace to him, that's a free-flowing thing—he can create enough distance towards it to allow it to happen. But these other two—he has too much of an investment in, and they would really knock him to pieces if he would allow them to come to blows, and *there would be nothing left of him.* [Italics mine.] That's the kind of terror that casts a pall over the vividness."[17] The biographic data of Odets' life support Miller's impression of an overload of anxiety attached to the *unconscious aspects* of Odets' conflict among the identity elements, experienced as the "corrupt" materialist (Prince), the innocent "idealist" (Cleo), and the obsessively blocked intellectual (Stark).

Faced with this emotional dilemma, Odets tried thus in midstream to find a safe *structural* solution by placing the heart of the play into the hands of the identity element, Artist, trapped in a family where they laugh at her wish to be a dancer. Here, he runs no risk of an unmanageable confrontation. However, it is precisely in this shift of focus that the play's structure becomes confused, and for most critics (representing most audiences), difficult to follow. The playwright does not quite succeed in persuading his audience that Cleo is the identity element representing their unconscious longing for creative fulfillment. The audience has not been sufficiently prepared for so large a responsibility to be put on the shoulder of a stockingless girl who wears "angel-skin satin."

With the Aspiring Artist Cleo at the center of the action, she is wooed by all the men in the play: Odets' Muse is torn between the sybarite Mr. Prince (Artist Manqué), the safe Ben—who has sacrificed creativity for security—and the Corrupt Artist Willy Wax who warns her she is "living in the city of the dreadful night" wherein a "man is coarse or he doesn't survive." As for Cleo, ". . . even her breasts stand at attention. Alas, she is not yet wise in the ways of the world" (p. 384).

When the dentist's controlling wife—who counsels security—suddenly appears in his office, Ben is touched—as Odets had often been by his own wife—by her loneliness and by her efforts to stir his jealousy. But her offer to *replace* Cleo as his assistant is an intolerable invasion, exactly like Odets' experience of his wife's efforts "to help" him in his work and to make a mutual career of their marriage. ("A man's office is his castle," says the dentist.)

His compassion and his tolerance come to an end as she states her suspicions. Finally he blazes out: "Will you stop that stuff for a change! It's about time you began to realize there are two ends to a rope. I have needs, too! This one-way street has to end! I'm not going to stay under water like an iceberg the rest of my life. You've got me licked—I must admit it. All right, I'm sleeping, I don't love you enough. But what do *you* give? What do you know about my *needs?*" (p. 393).

Now, in a duplication of many such dialogues Odets had had with his wife, Ben continues: "It's like we're enemies. We're like two exposed nerves! . . . These scenes go on . . . we're always worried. We're two machines counting up the petty cash. Something about me cheats you— I'm not the man to help you be the best woman it's in you to be" (p. 395). The internal subconfiguration here is the struggle between the passive, deadened, and demobilized identity element of Ben Stark—which oppressed Odets' mother and does now him—and his Muse, Cleo Singer, the "radium girl" who gives off heat, light, and creative energy. The inner war is between the playwright's wish to be a "safe" householder and an adventurous Creator.

The second act closes with the dentist making a declaration of love to Cleo; he is now desperately jealous of both his rivals: the urbane Prince as well as the Spurious Artist, Willy Wax. He says, "You're more important to me than anything I know Cleo, dear," and her closing plea is, "Don't let me be alone in the world, Ben . . . don't let me be alone" (p. 397). The girl is using all power at her disposal to force the relationship with the dentist into an overt sexual affair. Here again these externalized relationships mirror the internal struggle.

If this exchange is understood solely on its manifest level—as it was by the critics in 1938—it is baffling what it is that has moved the dentist to the conviction that this storytelling, naive child who is steadily "making believe" has become "more important than anything I know" in Ben's life. If, however, we assume the identity element of the innocent Cleo to be Odets' *anima,* the Aspiring Artist, rather than simply the "jingling body" of a lovely girl, his capitulation to her makes sense. The confusion of these two levels of meaning has issued in many baffled discussions in drama textbooks.

The third act opens with the dentist and his wife silent, "each one revolving in his own tight little world." She is ready in her desperation to "forget" his affair with the girl if he will agree "it was only a thing of the moment." Impulsively ("anything to blot out this pale ghost before him") he cries, "Yes, yes!" but immediately finds himself twisting and saying, "It can't be settled in a minute, Belle. . . . I have a *responsibility*." He cannot agree to his wife's scream, "Your first responsibility's to me! You hear that?" Again, unless we seek a meaning beyond the manifest level, Ben's statement is baffling.

The key to this mysterious exchange lies in the word "responsibility." On the surface, it makes no sense that a man uses this word to his wife to describe his duty to a nineteen-year-old paramour. If, however, we ask what is the latent meaning—the underlying structure—of the word "responsibility" here, it begins to hang together. If refers to Odets' *allegiance to his own talent* ("Talent must be respected," he said). Their heated exchange sums up the position of an artist battling for his creative life. The struggle is only manifestly with his wife's demand that he give up the girl.[18]

Unaware that his underlying dilemmas in the play issue in part from his own current struggles with intimacy and generativity, Odets has his protagonist, the dentist (who is almost forty and yet "feels like a boy"), ponder what people get out of life "anyway" when he asks Frenchy, a bachelor chiropodist,[19] if he does not want marriage and children. In their ensuing dialogue on the nature of love and the difficulty of discovering it "in this day of stresses," this "nervous time," Frenchy declares happy marriages are rare "like the dodo bird" and sternly advises his friend to be practical, "leave the morals out. . . . Never mind the shame and guilt":

FRENCHY: (With extreme seriousness) Love? Depends on what you mean by love. Love, for most people, is a curious sensation below the equator. . . .
STARK: You're that good, you think?
FRENCHY: (correcting him): That *bad*, Doc! She'll have to be the good one. This is why: Love is a beginning, a jumping-off place. It's like what heat is at the forge—makes metal easy to handle and shape. *But love and the grace to use it!*—To develop, expand it, variate it!—Oh, dearie me, that's the problem, as the poet said!

Frenchy now offers a definition of love singularly close to Erikson's view of the developmental achievement of intimacy:

FRENCHY: Who can do that today? Who's got the time and place for "love and the grace to use it"? Is it something apart, love? A good book you go to in a spare hour? An entertainment? Christ, no! it's a synthesis of good and bad, economics, work, play, all contacts . . . it's not a Sunday suit for special occasions. That's why Broadway songs are phony, Doc!—Love is no solution of life! *Au contraire,* as the Frenchman

says—the opposite. You have to bring a whole balanced normal life to
love if you want it to go!

What Odets called his "slow exhaustion, this shame" over his failed
marriage and his fear of precisely the kind of intimacy he has just described is
promptly retracted in Frenchy's next words, which would be a pleasure to
any member of a contemporary women's liberation front:

FRENCHY: In this day of stresses I don't see much normal life, myself included.
            The woman's not a wife. She's the dependent of a salesman who can't
            make sales and is ashamed to tell her so. . . . (p. 404)

Odets thus tries to understand his marital failure, his isolation, and the
nature of his creative struggles in terms of the "stresses of the time." He is, of
course, both right and wrong.

As the cynical chiropodist leaves this scene with the injunction that the
dentist must choose between the girl and his wife—reviving the manifest
conflict which opened the play—the latent meaning is once again underscored: the playwright must choose between his own development as an artist
and the demands of a "normal, married life." His (partly unconscious) dilemma lies in whether he is wedded to the "real" world of relationships with
other living humans or to a constructed world, peopled by the characters into
whom *he* breathes life, who are, of course, the distribution of *himself.* It is a
world he hopes to control. When Belle, his wife, pushes him to make this
choice, it is more on the basis of a moral obligation than a mutually nurturant
relationship. Moreover, real children, unlike brain-children, "break too easy,"
he says, and become (in Bacon's words) "hostages to fortune."

At this point, the other major threat to Odets' creativity reappears:
Carrying an umbrella with a "fancily carved dog's head of ivory" for a handle
("A quiet dog always bites," he says, smiling smoothly), Mr. Prince, calling
himself "King Midas,"[20] confidently announces *his* intention to marry "Miss
Cleo." Having dreamed the "secret of the world," namely, that "It is not
good for Man to live alone," he is determined to capture his prize by offering
her "maturity and experience in everything—love, what to eat, where, what
to wear, and where to buy it—an eye turned *out* to the world!" Translation:
The identity element which is flooded with desire for sensual and material
fulfillment and power competes now with creative aspiration: *the eye turned in.*

When the dentist says, "And you dare to think you'll buy that girl?
You're a damned smiling villain!," Judah Prince replies with a remarkable
and passionate speech which signaled the by-now bewildered critics that the
play's theme was "man's search for love":

PRINCE: Listen, a man in the fullness of his life speaks to you. I didn't come here
           to make you unhappy. I came here to make *myself happy!* You don't like

MARGARET BRENMAN-GIBSON ♦ 213

it—I can understand that. Circumstances insulted me enough in my life. But *your* insults I don't need! And I don't apologize to no man because I try to take happiness by the throat! Remember, Dr. Benny, I want what I want! There are seven fundamental words in life, and one of these is love, and I didn't have it! And another one is love, and I don't have it! *And the third of these is love, and I shall have it!* (Beating the furniture with his umbrella.) *De Corpso* you think! I'm dead and buried you think! I'll sit in the long winter night with a shawl on my shoulders? Now you see my face, Dr. Benny. Now you know your father-in-law, that damned smiling villain! I'll fight you to the last ditch—you'll get mowed down like a train.[21] I want that girl. I'll wait downstairs. When she returns I'll come right up, in five minutes. I'll test *your* sanity!—*You,* you Nobel prize winner! (He stops, exhausted, wipes his face with a large silk handkerchief, does the same to the umbrella head and then slowly exits). (p. 408)

The identity element embodied in Mr. Prince is not simply the negative aspect of Odets' partial identification with his salesman father. Indeed, when this many-faceted character protests he *will* have love, it is Odets' own passionate statement that he cannot live a life without human intimacy. ("I love your needs!" Prince says to Cleo.) But this longing for intimacy wars with his wish to be a self-sufficient artist responsible only for what he generates on the stage, and not for a flesh-and-blood wife or their children. Just as Prince is more interesting than Ben Stark precisely because he harbors many strong polarities, so is *Rocket to the Moon* a more interesting play than the "political" *Waiting for Lefty,* where one end of a conflict is ploughed under, leaving a cast of simple characters in a simple play, all on one note.

There occurs now a short interlude between the dentist and the Spurious Artist, Willy Wax. The latter, just come from his own unsuccessful attempt to seduce the girl, says, "Your little Neon light splutteted right in my face," adding she is old-fashioned and "belongs somewhere in the last century."[22] This is Odets speaking not so much of a sexpot as of the virtues of integrity and of creative conscience. Ben Stark pleads with Wax, here representing artistic prostitution, not to corrupt the aspiring girl, to "keep away from her," as she is "young, extremely naive. . . . You might warp her for life. . . . She's a mere mechanism to you." This sentence expresses Odets' steady fear that his own identity fragment (Spurious Artist) could seduce him into an abdication of his gift, and into the film industry. Cleo, however, turns in a fury on this would-be seducer, Wax, saying, "Mr. Wax, we don't want you around this office. You make love very small and dirty. I understand your type very well now. No man can take a bite out of me, like an apple and throw it away. Now go away, and we won't miss you" (p. 411).

When she turns back to the helpless dentist, a man as "mixed up as the 20th Century," she finds him evasive, collapsed, on the point of tears, and unable to leave either his wife or the "prison office" of his life. He can say to her only, "Help me."[23] Only the small voice of that fragment of himself represented by the chiropodist, Frenchy, asks the opposite question, "What can I do for the girl, Cleo? What will she be in ten years *with my help?*"

The indomitable old man makes one last strong bid for the girl. She, in turn, asks the dentist if he will leave his barren wife, and he—consumed with fear and guilt—can say nothing at all. He is chained and sterile. The dentist's "decision" occurs by default; it is helplessly passive, not active. With the character of Stark having clearly gone beyond his emotional depth, and unable to handle the "mistake" of his intimacy with the girl, he is inarticulate. When Cleo asks, "What do you say, Ben?" Odets writes, "Stark (lost): Nothing. . . . I can't say. . . . . . nothing."

Here is a good example of the reflection in the play's overburdened structure of the playwright's inner fractures. Given the premises of the opening of the play (a man who will be forced to a choice between a wife and a mistress), the closing climax *should* be Ben choosing between Belle and Cleo. But, as we have seen, there slowly emerged on this initial triangle a superimposed one, among Ben, Prince, and Cleo, and the play took on the fuzziness of a double exposure, with the playwright emotionally unable fully to loose the players and counterplayers into the struggle in either triangle. Thus, with Ben (the character originally at the play's center) immobilized, it falls to the characters of Cleo and Prince to propel the play to its end. Prince says of Stark, "He won't leave her. That needs courage, strength, and he's not strong."

Cleo makes a last stab at passing the initiative back to the evasive, lost Ben. His response is soft and defeated: "Listen, Cleo . . . think. What can I give you? All I can offer you is a second-hand life, dedicated to trifles and troubles . . . and they go on forever. This isn't self-justification . . . but facts are stubborn things, Cleo; I've wrestled with myself for weeks. This is how it must end" (p. 415).

When Judah Prince asks Cleo what she'd have to lose by a union with *him,* she replies, "Everything that's me." The underlying meaning here is Odets' conviction that the core of his identity lay in resisting his father's bids to surrender to him and to his values (arising from power hunger and sense satisfaction), and to become instead an honest artmaker.

As in the closing of Odets' earlier play, *Awake and Sing!* (equally confusing to the critics), the powerful older man, identity element of Odets' father, moves in, making a real "pitch" for the girl: "And I offer you a vitalizing relationship: a father, counselor, lover, a friend!" In *Awake and Sing!* the "equivalent" girl Hennie—mother of an illegitimate child and subsequently married by a weak man called Sam Feinschreiber (fine writer)[24]—succumbs and runs off with another old sybarite called Moe (roughly the equivalent of Judah Prince).

In *Rocket to the Moon,* however, the Aspiring Artist (Cleo) makes the final *active* statement of the play. Manifestly, she is "looking for love," but

Prince sees beyond this: he tells her she will never get what she is looking for, namely a life with the purity of an aesthetic creation: "You want a life like Heifetz' music—up from the roots, perfect, clean, every note in place. But that, my girl, is music!" (p. 416).

In other words, says the playwright, only in that transcendent distillation of experience we call Art can there be found the precision, the intensity, the confident joy and serenity, and above all, the integrated and liberating wholeness she seeks.

When Prince says to her, "You'll go down the road alone—like Charlie Chaplin?" Cleo's response and Prince's rejoinder finally clinch the hypothesis that this girl represents for Odets the identity element, Aspiring Artist:

CLEO: Yes, if there's roads, I'll take them. I'll go up all those roads till I find what I want. I want a love that uses me, that needs me. Don't you think there's a world of joyful men and women? Must all men live afraid to laugh and sing? Can't we sing at work and love our work? It's getting late to play at life; I want to *live* it. Something has to feel real to me, more than both of you. You see? I don't ask for much. . . ."

PRINCE: *She's an artist.* [Italics mine] (p. 416)

Whereas Odets' initial, conscious intention had been for the character of Ben to emerge with greater stature and confidence from the overwhelming experience of his love for this girl, it is now in fact Cleo who announces such growth: "Experience gives more confidence, you know. I have more confidence than when I came here. Button my coat, Ben" (p. 417). It is *she* who escapes the airless constriction of the dental office, not he. It is clear he will *not* return to "creative orthodontia," whereas her future is open-ended.

Prince says, "Yes, you love her. But not my iceberg boy, we have both disappeared."

In these two short sentences, there stands distilled a paradox filled with grief. On the one hand, the identity element I have called Aspiring Artist determinedly walks away, free alike from the vacillating, timid dentist lacking self-esteem, *and* from the sensual, worldly predator, *both of whom have abandoned their creativity.* Manifestly, Prince is saying both men have lost their chance for "love" (". . . we have both disappeared"). Beneath the surface, however, Odets is saying that he stands now in mortal dread that if this Muse escapes him—as Cleo does in the play—he will be left only with the internal war between the elements of a weak, constricted, and guilt-ridden indecisiveness and a strong, aggressive, and commanding sensuality. In their actual lives, *both Odets and his father* consciously felt themselves to the end of their days to be artists manqués, from whom their creativity had somehow slipped away.

Stark, in a desperate postscript, eyes flooded with tears, says, "I insist this is a beginning. Do you hear?—I insist. . . . For years I sat here, taking things for granted, my wife, everything. Then just for an hour my life was in a spotlight. . . . I saw myself clearly, realized who and what I was. Isn't that a beginning? Isn't it? . . . And this is strange! . . . For the first time in years I don't feel guilty. . . . But I'll never take things for granted again. You see? Do you see, Poppa?" (p. 418).

The play closes with Stark "almost laughing," confessing his ignorance of life: "Sonofagun! What I don't know would fill a book!" The final image is of an empty room, lit only by the lights of a hotel (where real—forbidden—life is lived) the locale of so much of Odets' actual peeping and listening: "Prince exits heavily. Stark turns out the last light, then exits, closing the door behind him. The room is dark, except for red neon lights of the Hotel Algiers and a spill of light from the hall . . . Slow curtain" (p. 418).

This last stage direction distills Odets' sense of the playwright as "witness," the man who, like all artists, cannot help distancing himself and watching his life's experience—and transposing it by way of Form—even while he lives it.

> In making art one is free from inhibition and masking of emotions and fear of encounter. One ranges freely, taking *painlessly* all sides. Inactive, incapacitated, passive, arid and sterile, aware but unable and helpless—in art one becomes freely a man of action and all is possible!
>
> In this world, one may always be the hero—loved, pitied, magnanimous, stern, strong, successful against men, women and dragons; one may forgive and even pity others—it is something god-like and absolute that the artist becomes with the exercise of what is usually his only talent. . . ."[25]

Although there is evident strain and self-doubt in Ben Stark's triumphant announcement that his identity has been significantly illumined and integrated by the play's events (". . . for an hour my life was in a spotlight. . . .") it does affirm that aspect of Odets which *takes nothing for granted* (a creator). Ben declares, moreover, that "For the first time in years I don't feel guilty." While neither of these affirmations of enlightenment and freedom is persuasively buttressed in the play, we can decode the playwright's latent wish: he is saying (defensively) for the first time in any of his plays that he is determined not to surrender his creativity to the other pulls within him: the identity element of his Muse (Cleo) rejects not only the weak identity element which has fearfully abdicated created powers (Ben), but also those which have "sold out" to the vulgarizations of Art (Willy Wax) and to worldly fulfillment (Judah Prince). Moreover, he is here liberated from the guilt evident in all his work (even in an adolescent novel wherein the career of a promising young pianist is "cut short by an accident to his hand") and later in all his plays, wherein the moral idealists—after compromising themselves in their creativity—commit suicide, are murdered, or meet violent death.

Odets was always plagued by a lack of "aesthetic inevitability" in this play, and wondered if his wife had been correct that the seeker, Cleo, should after all surrender to the rich old sybarite, as Hennie had done in his *Awake and Sing!* Displacing his creative discontent, he would remain forever resentful on several counts: that director Clurman was so "full of ideas as to what my play was about" and had never raised the production money; that he had no leeway in which to rework the play, that he was always under emergency pressure to provide the Group Theatre with a brain-child which they would immediately gobble up; and finally, that he could not even protect his newborn progeny by directing the play himself. Almost three decades later, the memory of this time and his anger toward Clurman still fresh, he provided rich data illuminating the creative process:

> He finally got to think that I was kind of like a cow who dropped a calf, didn't know anything about it. I think he still thinks that. He still thinks that when I write a play I have no idea what's in it. That I'm some kind of mad genius who just sort of drops a calf. Because this is what happened in the Group Theatre and I was very resentful of it. I dropped this calf and some people would rush up and grab it, wipe if off and take it away, and I would be left there bellowing. And while they were hustling this calf around you'd think that I had no relationship to it. I let them, too. I would let them do it, but with a great deal of resentment. I never would have let any private producer do anything of this sort. They'd go to work on it, and this one would be assisting Clurman. All the time I wanted to direct the play myself. But in order to direct the play I would have to have at least some decent distance between myself and the play. Well, that never happened. They had to have those veal chops on the table. For the next week or so everybody would go hungry. So in a certain way this gifted calf that I'm talking about, that I dropped, was also veal chops for everybody to eat.[26]

It was Odets' conviction that Clurman, together with this "sturdy crutch" Elia Kazan and the Group business manager, "ran everything, had all the fun, all the excitement and I would just stand there on my legs, like a bellowing mother cow who couldn't locate that calf I just dropped."

If this playwright's image of himself as a "bellowing mother cow," unable to locate her newborn child—the metaphor of pregnancy and an anxious delivery—were an isolated instance, or peculiar to Odets, we could not make much of it. However, the image of creation as a birth followed by the eating of "the child" (or of the forbidden fruit) occurs over and over not only in Odets' writings, but in those of a variety of creators as well as in folk legends, myths, and holy scriptures.[27]

This image appears to be one of the archetypes of the general argument I have been setting forth: this is the way a new "wholeness" emerges: by integrating the contrarieties, including feminine and masculine identity elements. Thus is a new organism created (be it a theory, a scripture, or a play), an organism that simultaneously "feeds" its originator and its audience.[28]

This originator is not far from the image of a Lord of Creation who gives manifest, concrete form to the eternal, the boundless, who breathes life into an Adam and creates an Eve from a fragment of him, who in turn instigates the eating of the forbidden fruit from the Tree of Knowledge or, as it is sometimes called, "The Tree of Life." That this player and counterplayer are then together banished from the innocent joy of trusting, unashamed celebrant children playing in Paradise, to the suffering toil of self-conscious Man—whose "plays" are now "works"—reflects a writer's witness to the vicissitudes, the joys, and the penalties of his own creativity.

Notes

1. In the contemporary theater, where alienation has for some time been the guiding theme, the improvisers (or writers) express on the surface their indifference—even their contempt—for the audience. But even here, the acting group is bitterly disappointed when no audience—from whom they can estrange themselves—appears in their theater, "closing down" their "play."

2. Joseph Wood Krutch, "Review of *Rocket to the Moon*," *The Nation*, December 3, 1938, pp. 600–1.

3. Margaret Brenman-Gibson, "Notes on the Study of the Creative Process."

4. Clifford Odets, Personal Notes, "General," March 15, 1938 (unpublished).

5. In the character of the pathetically aspiring Cleo Singer, there is distilled the symbol of the exhausted American artist, still yearning to realize her creative potential and steadily—like L. J. Odets—verging on fraudulence: she lies pretentiously and is tempted by the fame and fortune held under her nose by the minor character, Willy Wax. The beginning of the dissolution of the Group Theatre was already now evident as only one of the many casualties of the end of the American Dream. Three decades later (a wink in history), the protagonist of the film *Easy Rider* would cry out in despair, "We blew it." On his deathbed, Odets had pleaded with singer Edie Adams, "Don't blow it as I did." Given the fact that all civilizations have a "dream" which rises and falls, it is important for us as observer to note that this playwright conceives this play at a time when his own creative "descent" is more or less in "synch" with that of his culture.

6. Clifford Odets, Personal Notes, "General."

7. In the discussion which followed my presentation of this paper, both playwrights present (Arthur Miller and William Gibson) agreed that such a "distribution of the author" as I am hypothesizing here, in the form of identity elements, does indeed exist in every play. They agreed also that during the writing of the play these elements are seen only dimly, if at all, by the playwright. Miller commented, "When I'm writing the thing, it's as if somebody else is writing those notes. And I think that balance is crucial . . . because if you *know* something, something you *really* solve, then writing the whole play becomes unnecessary" (Brenman-Gibson 1971). The restorative function of the creative act is evident in this observation.

8. These names reflect a variety of identity fragments and elements: Odets took the name, Ben, from his lively Tante Esther's "ordinary" son, a man whose life was indeed in Odets' view "a long forgetting." The word "Stark," according to Webster's, means "desolate, bleak, unadorned or rigid, as in death." The wife's maiden name "Belle Prince"—as with Bessie Berger in Odets' *Awake and Sing!*—condenses the word "belle" (beauty) with the name of actress Stella Adler (Odets had scribbled "Stella, Bella, Belle, Bessie" when making notes); she was seen as a Jewish princess in a long succession of actors in the royal Adler family, and like Ben's wife, a powerful, even tyrannical figure. The conflict, as in a dream, is densely overdetermined: it is simultaneously between a controlling parent (or wife) and a child (or husband).

9. Clifford Odets, *Rocket to the Moon* Production notes, October 26, 1938 (unpublished).

10. Clifford Odets, *Six Plays of Clifford Odets* (New York: Modern Library, 1939).

11. Her name, Cleo Singer, combines that of a sexually irresistible young "Queen of Sheba" (Cleopatra) for whom men would well lose worlds, and Odets' image, steadily drawn from music, of the artist (a *singer* like his Uncle Israel). "Clio" is also the name of the Muse of poetry and history. Odets says, "Whitman is half songbird, half alligator," and the gitka, a mouse, in Odets' last play, *The Flowering Peach,* has a high, sweet singing voice, but having no mate, commits suicide. Also *Cleo* = Cl. Odets: Odets had, in adolescence, often put an "L" in his signature as a middle initial, doubtless after his father's name, "Louis." Again, the products of creative transcendence, akin to dreams.

12. Clifford Odets, *Rocket to the Moon,* Production notes.

13. Clifford Odets, *Six Plays of Clifford Odets.*

14. Cf. Kenneth Burke on Odets in his classic essay, "Ice, Fire, and Decay," in *Philosophy of Literary Form* (New York: Vintage Books, 1941).

15. Erik Erikson, "The Nature of Psycho-Historical Evidence . . ."

16. Clifford Odets, *Six Plays of Clifford Odets.*

17. Margaret Brenman-Gibson, "Anatomy of a Play: With Specimen Play-Analysis."

18. Dynamically, this is identical with Elena's position in Gorky's *Country People.* She, a wife-mother, is however tolerant of her husband's sexual affairs in order, she says, "not to put obstacles in the path of his beautiful inner life." In Gorky's play, thus, the "affairs" are more obviously the artist's journeys into himself. In Pinter's *The Homecoming,* the wife's otherwise mystifying role is similarly illuminated if again we see her as the playwright's creative *anima* in danger of becoming a whore.

19. All his life, Odets had steady trouble with his feet, his hair, and his teeth. Continually seeking help for these difficulties, he came to see them as representing his steady sense of disintegration.

20. This appellation serves to highlight the struggle throughout between material and spiritual values.

21. This is a playwright's gift for eccentric metaphor: the content of Prince's threat reflects Odets' unconscious fear and guilt in competing with this powerful father.

22. In a play he would never finish, *An Old-Fashioned Man,* Odets expressed his yearning for the traditional values in art and in life that his world was steadily losing. Erikson has observed that the steady identity confusion in American life gives it chronically a somewhat adolescent quality (personal communication).

23. Profound issues of the polarities of activity and passivity as well as initiative and guilt are here condensed. Compare this with Odets' later play, *The Big Knife,* which closes with a despairing repetition of the word, "Help!"

24. This image expresses Odets' fear that *all* his creative children are "illegitimate."

25. Clifford Odets, Personal Notes, "Romantics," October 1957 (unpublished).

26. Arthur Wagner, "Interview with Clifford Odets."

27. I have presented in another place data from this rich vein of investigation to illustrate the archetypal level of meaning which exists alongside the idiosyncratic and the representative (historical) levels. (Brenman-Gibson 1976). See also William Gibson's *A Season in Heaven* (1974).

28. William Gibson, *The Seesaw Log* (New York: Knopf, 1959); Gibson, *A Season in Heaven* (New York: Atheneum, 1974).

[*Night Music* and Homelessness]

WINIFRED L. DUSENBURY

In one sense Americans are so used to moving that they are never homeless and may speak of a casual hotel room as home, but in another they are forever homeless, because "home" is not the place where they live, but the place where they lived as a child. The popular song of December, 1954, whose subject is "There's no place like home for the holidays," typifies American ways by explaining: "I met a man from Tennessee, and he was heading for Pennsylvania. . . . From Pennsylvania folks are headin' for Dixie's Southern shores. . . ." The American is not at home where he lives. His "home town" is his parents' home.

Thomas Wolfe, recognizing that to return to one's former home is impossible, entitled a novel *You Can't Go Home Again.*[1] The American can move forward but not back except in memory. What lonesomeness Americans suffer, with a sentimental attachment to a past home but no hope of regaining it in any practical form. Recognizing homelessness as an aspect of modern life likely to be understood by their countrymen, three playwrights have made it an integral part of the theme of loneliness in their artistic medium: Clifford Odets in *Night Music* (1940), John Steinbeck in *Of Mice and Men* (1937), and Eugene O'Neill in *Anna Christie* (1921).

Clifford Odets' *Night Music* is a drama of homelessness[2] very different from his earlier social problem plays. The story is of a boy and girl lost in New York. The boy, who is taking some trained monkeys back to Hollywood for a producer, is arrested when one of the monkeys frightens the girl. He misses his plane and loses his job. The play in which the girl was acting has closed, a failure. Each has as a home merely a tiny, unpaid-for room in a cheap hotel. The actual homelessness of the two main characters is, however, as Odets conceives it, what might be called the Platonic reflection of the *idea* of homelessness. The boy is antagonistic toward the girl from a deep inner feeling of being so lost that contact with another human being is hopeless. Only Steve's guardian angel, the fat detective Rosenberger, saves him and the girl from complete desolation, presumably by providing a place to sleep, but in reality by providing some inner confidence. "You love this girl? And you

Originally published as "Homelessness" in *The Theme of Loneliness in Modern American Drama* (Gainesville: University of Florida Press). Reprinted by permission of the University Presses of Florida.

mean it? Then fight for love! You want a home?—Do you?—then fight for homes" (III, i). George Kernodle says that Odets in this play "sees man's problem as purely a problem of the inner spirit."[3] No menacing industrialists are responsible for the boy's despair. The social scheme may have something to do with his situation, but it is only within himself and through contact with a guiding spirit that he can find happiness. The boy becomes convinced that joining the army is no panacea. The real war of the world is not on the battle front, but on the home front.

Suitcase Steve, as he calls himself, moves through a dozen scenes—from such locations as a New York police station and a stage door to a hotel lobby, a restaurant, and on to Central Park and the World's Fair—among many minor characters who are almost all as impermanent as he. Clurman says that Odets has made homelessness "part of every character, of every scene, almost of every prop. It is not a thesis, it is the 'melody' that permeates the play."[4]

The sense of security which is associated in mankind with home cannot be fortified in Americans by permanent settlement on a family homestead. Rather, the American must learn to carry his home within himself. Odets' attitude is much more hopeful than Wolfe's: "You can go home again—within yourself." Although Thomas Wolfe may be trying to discover that "the way home is the way forward,"[5] Odets is certain that the way forward is the way home.[6] The stolid detective Rosenberger, in bitter pain from advanced cancer, remarks upon learning of someone else with the disease, "These higher-class diseases are universal, like music." Stressing the universality of this theme with such analogous references to the likeness of all mankind, Odets has written a distinctly realistic drama, which with its choppy dialogue and intermittent movement from place to place gives the impression of the search of all men for security and a home and love, in a world in which the people are transient and the environment unfriendly, or at least indifferent.[7] Suitcase Steve and his girl are part of the lonely crowd. It is not until each finds a home in himself that he can communicate with the other and find peace in a hurried world.

Criticism of the play, both when it was first presented by the Group Theatre in 1940 and when it was revived by the Equity Library Theatre in 1951, centered on the unnecessary belligerency of the main character. Whether or not this is the main weakness[8] of the play, about the fact of Steve's belligerency there can be no question. Early in the play he confronts Fay outside the theater with: "Hey, wait a minute, you!" and later, "Look, I'm an eighty octane guy—Ethyl in my veins—and I'm sore as hell!" At another time, after she has tried to help him, he berates her with, "This makes *four* dirty things you done on me." Steve responds to the information that dogs test everything with the nose, babies with the mouth, by announcing, "I test with the fists." With equal acrimony he proclaims to Rosenberger, "I'm an ice-cold feller. . . . I'm a member of the Steve Takis Club. It's a one-man club an' I like it!" When the thoughtful detective sends up some egg sandwiches and coffee to the hungry boy and girl, she gratefully bites into one, but Steve scornfully refuses with the charge, "I say he's a creep!"

Steve, in these instances and many others, evinces a hard exterior, which makes it appear that he is solidly caustic or at least completely self-centered, but both Fay and Rosenberger sense that the belligerency has another cause. At one time, she chides, "You're not that bad, Steve." At another, she says of him: "He's sweet—sweet . . . like a hard-boiled Easter egg." Rosenberger likewise recognizes that Steve's impoliteness is bravado to hide his quaking heart. At the end Steve himself senses that his superior air may be a compensation for his lack of faith in himself. As they are about to part at the airport, Fay speaks of how the monkeys brought them together, and he adds, "An' they showed me what I am. . . . They're not with me. I travel with them! They got the big future. . . . This is petty cash tryin' to be a mint!" When Steve claims he wants to join the army or resign from the human race, Rosenberger says, "You resign too easy, young man. Army? . . . Your fight is here, not across the water. . . . Who told you not to make a new political party? Make it and call it 'Party-to-marry-my-girl!'" (III,ii). Finally moved, the hitherto irascible youth, with "a spreading, wonderful smile" picks up his suitcase, extends his arm to Fay, and utters the surprising words, "Thanks. . . . Thanks, Fatso," to Rosenberger, as the three exit together.

It is not at all illogical that a man—homeless and lonely in New York—should react to his situation as Steve does. Perhaps a weakness of the play, however, is that Steve's bitter hostility remains constant through so many scenes—his sudden conversion coming only at the very end. If the play is not an unqualified artistic success from the point of view of the development of the main character, Odets has composed a drama in which the theme of loneliness because of homelessness is harmoniously carried out through a large number of characters. The most important of these is the girl, Fay, who finds a cheap hotel room preferable to the home of her stuffy Philadelphia family. She heartens the boy by her unresentful attitude toward her plight and her calm optimism toward life. As the playwright's mouthpiece in his explanation of his title, she observes, "Crickets are my favorite animals in all the world. They're never down in the mouth. All night they make their music. . . . Night music. If they can sing, I can sing. . . . We can sing through any night" (II, iv).[9] It is not what she says, however, but what she is, that finally breaks down the wall between her and Steve, for her conversations with him are short and unimportant. In the Chekhovian tradition, in which each character speaks his mind without reference to the others, she does not expect answers from him. According to Eric Bentley this device of short soliloquies "is perhaps Chekhov's most notorious idea. It has been used more crudely by Odets and Saroyan . . . to express the isolation of people from one another."[10] The technique appropriately reinforces the theme of loneliness by emphasizing the separateness of each character from the others.

Rosenberger himself is a lonely individual. After one of his somewhat oratorical speeches he says, "Excuse me. I live alone and sometimes it makes me talk too much." Although he is reconciled to it and not overcome by it, even the raisonneur for the play suffers from his isolation.

Besides Fay and Rosenberger are other characters who appear for a short scene or two to enhance the melody of loneliness which runs through the play. Homeless Man (Roy Brown), whistling "The Prisoner's Song" on a park bench, is going to join the army in order to get three squares a day and a place to sleep. The second time Roy passes across the scene he is described as "a specter, an image of Steve's war thoughts." He is the same age as Steve, and homeless like Steve, and represents that part of Steve which tends to seek an easy solution to his situation. Fay is worried when Roy appears, for she recognizes in Steve's glance at the young recruit a haunting desire for security at the price of imprisonment in army life.[11] Another character, Mr. Nichols, constantly calls out for nickels for the telephone booth. More nickels obviously won't help him to reach somebody, but he is obsessed with the idea that through a call he can make contact with another human being. An actress, departing from an unsuccessful play, has taken with her the curtains which she always puts up in her dressing room as a psychologically fortifying suggestion of home.

Besides these characters and others who appear momentarily, an important semihumorous theme which reinforces the action of the play, "to find a home," is the suitcase theme. From the first scene to the last, suitcases are important properties. In the opening scene in the police station, a policeman sets Steve's suitcase beside him with an obvious, attention-getting flourish. After some time the boy picks it up with the words, " 'Suitcase Takis' is on the street again," and exists with it several speeches later. In the next scene Steve converses with a chorus girl, who leaves the theater with her suitcase, followed presently by a number of actors and actresses, each carrying a small bag or suitcase, and finally by Fay with her suitcase. As Steve stands talking to her, a thief makes off with his suitcase; he becomes irate at her for not noticing the theft until too late. Rosenberger catches the thief and returns the suitcase. Toward the end of the scene Steve orders Fay to carry his suitcase; bewildered, she starts to pick it up, whereupon he takes it, along with hers, as they exit.

With ironic reversal of the idea that a suitcase signifies homelessness, it is made clear to the sailor who is trying to get a hotel room that he cannot do so without some luggage. He is homeless, but, for him, a suitcase might insure a room for the night so he could be with his girl. When Fay and Steve get adjoining rooms in the hotel, the two suitcases are motivating properties for some movement between rooms, and then, toward the end of the scene, Steve repacks his angrily and later stalks out, forgetting it completely. Fay picks it up and runs after him to the park. After sleeping all night on the park bench, "two lonely pathetic creatures, needing a home," they return to the hotel in the morning with Steve's suitcase, to find her father waiting for them with steely glances at the offending object.

The next episode takes place at the World's Fair, where the young couple have run into Roy Brown again, who must quickly get his suitcase uptown before joining the army. In the last of the suitcase series, Steve packs his bag in his hotel room, preparatory to taking the plane back to Hollywood. An attendant at the airport puts it on the plane, and as Steve, having had last-minute orders to remain, stares at the sky, thinking his suitcase now has wings, Rosenberger, like a faithful dog, trots in with the battered object, thus completing the suitcase theme and also the detective's service to Steve.

On a different level of seriousness the suitcase serves the purpose in *Night Music* that the cherry trees do in *The Cherry Orchard*. A symbol of the transiency of Americans, as the cherry trees are of the old regime of Russians, the idea suggested is ever-present throughout the play because of the tangible object upon the stage. As in Chekhov's play, there are connotations beyond the symbolism, which in *Night Music* extend to include the unsettled condition of the mind and emotions of the characters because of the impermanency of their lives. If Gertrude Stein is a reliable judge of national character, the transiency of Americans has an effect upon their way of thinking and is a cause of their being, unlike the British, unsettled in mind as well as in body.

> Think of the American life as it is lived, they all move so much even when they stay still and they do very often stay still they all move so much. They move so much because in moving they know for certain they can know it any way but in moving they really know it really know as certain that they are not daily living in their daily living. The English just in the other way even when they are travelling are not moving, they do move no one can move who is really living in any moment of their living their daily living.[12]

Odets' play assumes to some extent the lack of "daily living" by Americans because of their always moving in mind as well as in fact. Odets nevertheless rejoices in the American spirit that overcomes the debilitating effects of the social and economic conditions which modern America inflicts upon its people.

A transition play of Odets between those of social protest and *Night Music* is *Paradise Lost*, 1936, in which a man is being dispossessed of the home in which he and his family have lived for seventeen years. But with the furniture on the sidewalk, and the curious crowd trying to peer through the closed windows, Leo Gordon is not shattered by his homelessness. He insists upon giving away some bills, which have been left for him, to two "Homeless Men," who are among the crowd outside. One of the two makes fun of Leo: ". . . millions are homeless and unhappy in America today. . . . You have been took like a bulldog takes a pussy cat!" But Leo replies defiantly: "There is more to life than this! . . . Men, men are understanding the bitter black total of their lives. . . . They become an ocean of understanding! *No man fights alone.* . . . For the first time in our lives—for the first time our house has a real foundation" (Act III).

As in *Night Music* the cry is for courage to face the fact of material homelessness without allowing spiritual homelessness to destroy all hope, either with the help of a guiding spirit or the indomitable faith of a Leo Gordon. *Paradise Lost* is aptly titled, for Leo loses everything which might seem to make his land a heaven, but a sequel would certainly have to be titled "Paradise Regained," because he acquires a faith in the brotherhood of man and declares at the play's end: "*No man fights alone!*"

Four years after *Paradise Lost* Odets made a concentrated effort in *Night Music* to present one cause of the lonesomeness of Americans. The purpose of the play is served by the setting, characters, incidents, and dialogue. The numerous settings afford a visible reminder of the movement of the large array of characters, who engage in their isolated activities in dialogue frequently addressed partially to themselves. The form of the play accents homelessness, for, of the twelve scenes of the play, ten end with the forthright exit of the main characters for other destinations. The scene curtains fall on movement, not static stage pictures. The fifth and last scene of Act I is a contrast to the first four in that Fay and Steve sleep side by side on a park bench, and the fifth and last scene of Act II shows them in a momentary embrace in the hotel room. In all the other scenes they are "on their way" as the curtain falls. Thus homelessness is accented by Odets by every possible dramatic device, and the play is artistically created toward the end of portraying the American's loneliness because of it.

Notes

1. Anson Page in his review of the Hamilton Basso novel, *The View from Pompey's Head,* in *New York Times Book Review* (October 24, 1954), says, "Usually the homeward call is largely irrational; the home town would seem to have little to offer the voluntary exile except what is sometimes called 'the indefinable' and sometimes 'roots.' . . . The pattern has been that the hero either can't go home again or can do so only at the expense of falling into outgrown habits of mind. . . ."

2. In the "Introduction" to *Night Music,* p. viii, Harold Clurman says, "Whether or not *Night Music* is the best of the Odets plays I cannot say, but I am sure that among his longer plays it is the most integrated in its feeling and the most completely conceived. The play stems from the basic sentiment that people nowadays are affected by a sense of insecurity; they are haunted by the fear of impermanence in all their relationships; they are fundamentally *homeless,* and whether or not they know it, they are in search of a home, of something real, secure, dependable in a slippery, shadowy, noisy and nervous world."

3. "Patterns of Belief in Contemporary Drama," in *Spiritual Problems in Contemporary Literature,* ed. Stanley Romaine Hopper, p. 202.

4. Introduction to *Night Music,* p. ix.

5. Stanley Romaine Hopper, in *Spiritual Problems,* p. 161.

6. In speaking of her home in Philadelphia Fay calls it "a dead place." According to Steve, "The place where you live is always dead." Both realize they can't go home again.

7. Kernodle, who sees allegory in *Night Music,* says of Rosenberger, "Compassion as a guardian angel seems to me definitely a religious concept," in *Spiritual Problems,* p. 202.

8. If Walter Kerr is right, the lack of action may be the cause of the play's poor success. He believes that the modern theater is hostile to the idea of activity. "What happens next," he says, has been thoroughly discarded. "Killing Off the Theater," *Harper's Magazine,* CCX (April 1955), 55–62.

9. Since the cricket is frequently associated with the hearth, Fay may be unconsciously expressing her desire for a home in this speech, but the playwright does not make this point explicitly.

10. *In Search of Theater,* p. 356.

11. Roy considers himself imprisoned by loneliness, as is evidenced from the song he hums on the bench.

12. *Narration,* p. 11.

Night Music and *Clash by Night:*
Clifford Odets and Two Faces of Modernism

FRANK R. CUNNINGHAM

Near the conclusion of Odets's curious middle-period drama, *Night Music* (1940), as the young lovers seem about to part forever at the airport, the playwright's setting and stage directions suggest both a somber, mechanistic ambience and the promise of an era in which Steve and Fay, feeling "tense, uneasy and out of place,"[1] must fight for lives in which they can create meaning and value: "The airport on a brisk windy day. Overhead are the rich sounds of airport traffic coming and going. In the field left, beyond a wire fence, a transport plane is warming up: twentieth-century music" (219). A little later, as the play ends to the "zooming and singing" (237) of the modern age's most representative machines overhead, the mystically ever-present detective, A. L. Rosenberger, exhorts the young people, "I'll tell you both a secret: no old man can rest if you don't use your health to fight, to conquer disease and poverty, dirt and ignorance. Go back to the city. . . . You had the wisdom and fore-sight to be born in the twentieth century. Go, go with love and health—your wonderful country never needed you more . . ." (236).

The director of the Group Theatre's February 1940 production of *Night Music,* Harold Clurman, in his introduction to the published play, com-mented on the drama's themes of "chaos" and a "wilderness of uncertainty which is the modern world" (x): "The play stems from the basic sentiment that people nowadays are affected by a sense of insecurity; they are haunted by the fear of impermanence in all their relationships; they are fundamentally *homeless,* and, whether or not they know it, they are in search of a home, of something real, secure, dependable in a slippery, shadowy, noisy and nervous world" (viii). Clurman's observations imply that while Odets is certainly a more complex writer of dramatic literature than his early categorization as a 1930s proletarian writer of social problem plays would indicate,[2] he writes also as an artist firmly in the modernist tradition. Insufficient consideration has been given to Odets's stature as a modernist writer[3] and to modern American dramatic literature's connections with the modernist tradition.[4] In

This essay was written specifically for this volume and is published here for the first time by permission of the author.

assessing Odets's place among the significant modernists of the first 40 years of the present century, it is helpful to examine an important thesis held by Richard Ellmann and Charles Feidelson, Jr., who have discerned at least two levels of the modern: disconnection and liberation.

> Modernism strongly implies some sort of historical discontinuity, either a liberation from inherited patterns or, at another extreme, deprivation and disinheritance. In an essay on "The Modern Element in Modern Literature," Lionel Trilling singles out a radically anti-cultural bias as the most important attribute of the modern imagination. Committed to everything in human experience that militates against custom, abstract order, and even reason itself, modern literature has elevated individual existence over social man, unconscious feeling over self-conscious perception, passion and will over intellection and systematic morals, dynamic vision over the static image, dense actuality over practical reality. . . . Interwoven with the access of knowledge, the experimental verve, and the personal urgency of the modern masters is, as Trilling also finds, a sense of loss, alienation, and despair. These are the two faces, positive and negative, of the modern as the anti-traditional: freedom and deprivation, a living present and a dead past."[5]

Odets's early plays reveal the thematic amalgam of liberation and alienation typical of modernist writers discussed by Ellmann and Feidelson. Further, the dramas from *Waiting for Lefty* (1935) through *Rocket to the Moon* (1938) manifest technical attributes of the modernist style, emphasizing the dynamic, the fragmentary, and the subjective, which with the two conceptual faces of modernism are also evident in *Night Music* and *Clash by Night*. In *Waiting for Lefty* Odets's working man and women struggle against an unfair, mechanistic social system, ultimately finding after several disconnected episodes some nascent liberation from spiritual imprisonment. In *Awake and Sing!* Odets gently satirizes modern materialism and implies that an escape route from it for modern humankind may lie in Moe Axelrod's courageous confrontation of modern incoherence: "Nobody knows, but you do it and find out. When you're scared the answer's zero."[6] Odets demonstrates a sometimes farcical tone toward serious sociopolitical themes in *Till the Day I Die,* in which Ernst Tausig suffers as an isolated victim of early mass-media manipulation. In *Paradise Lost* Leo Gordon's (and by implication America's) dream is lost to the underside of the modern century's preoccupation with success as various characters, both tragic and comic, meditate on the passivity and the consequently inevitable depression of modern man. In *Rocket to the Moon* Ben Stark loses his precious Cleo because of such passivity—the personal vacancy which in Odets's late plays dooms Charlie Castle in *The Big Knife* and nearly destroys Frank Elgin in *The Country Girl*. In *Golden Boy* Joe Bonaparte's gradual disconnection from organic influences similar to those that sustain Noah in *The Flowering Peach* is accompanied by Carp and Lorna's realization of the increasing mechanization and depersonalization of the era.

The confusions and ambiguities in the modern world were echoed by similarly unsteady events in Odets's life as a new decade approached. *Rocket to the Moon* had not fared well among audiences and critics, Odets's marriage to actress Luise Rainer was on a shaky foundation, and the Group Theatre would soon dissolve. In his wistful romance *Night Music* and in the following dark psychological tragedy *Clash by Night* (1942), the dramatist reveals in theme and form a continuing awareness of the twentieth century as a frag-mented, inconclusive time in which people endeavor to resist the period's institutionalization and dehumanization, searching for meaning and coher-ence in an attempt to replace the vanished stabilities and consistencies of the past. In the words of an astute critic of Odets's work, the dramatist in *Night Music* set himself the task of creating, "within a panoramically historical sweep, richly alive people who would tell both a generational and a personal story."[7]

The first scene of *Night Music,* in which the policemen wrestle with Steve's two lively monkeys, suggests the modern incoherence that is a motif throughout the play. Steve's unbelievable story, the truth of which matters not to the police, keynotes the atmosphere of unexpected zaniness that will typify the action: "An hour ago I'm standing on the corner, mindin' my business. I'm waitin' for the traffic lights to change, to get to the bus. Here's what happens: Otto, the monkey, reaches in my pocket and throws out my wallet. (Acting all this out) I reach down to retrieve this wallet an' Freddy, the other monk—he reaches out and grabs her locket . . . an' she screams. Then this Dick waddles up . . . here I am" (12).

Before the feisty young rebel is released, the cynical lieutenant can only admonish him, "Be silent, boy—there's only wind and smoke in the world" (17). A little later, near the stage door of the Dover Theatre, Steve meets Mrs. Scott, the small-part actress who always puts up curtains in her dressing room in an attempt at creating a sense of permanence. She sadly tells him that their show is closing after three performances: "They fall like sparrows. My husband sensed this wouldn't last" (26). Throughout the second scene, this sense of indeterminacy is heightened by the stagehands passing through with moving scenery; at one point the somber atmosphere of this continually shifting world is underscored by the appearance of a beggar, who "speaks with that dragging voice so often heard in the mendicant, which comes from a sense of defeat before the battle is begun" (28). At another point the odd, hurrying man suddenly appears with his stolen fur piece and just as quickly tries to steal Steve's suitcase. As the scene ends, the pugnacious Steve is knocked down by a stagehand who then, like the world, mocks him.

In the third scene, in the small lobby of the Hotel Algiers, many aspects of the city's fragmented experience combine to create a seriocomic atmo-sphere. The shrewd bellboy's pockets "are full of amatory supplies" (49). There is the saucy Dot, surrounded by the jazz-record machine; the solitaire-playing Lily; and the inebriated man in the telephone booth, who says cynically of the impatient sailor, "he's the guy who wanted two girls. I remember him. It's all in the mind—two girls he wanted . . . People are so ordinary . . ." (53). Lily, dejected because of a man who "promises to call and twice he don't" (55), trying to deflect Dot's professional's status, rejects her "cold expertness" with, "I can't stand it. If it's over, I'll dry up and blow away" (56).

Odets continues to reinforce the fractural nature of the modern world in the Central Park night scene (1.5), with the sudden appearance before Fay and Steve of Mr. Watson, who sighs, "The zero hours are comin' . . ." (93) before discoursing on his wife, the astrologer Madame Rheba, in whose arts he does not believe; it's merely "a way to make a livin'. I give out the cards . . . Have a card?" (95). Ironically the owner of a construction company, Mr. Watson (identified throughout the scene as the "Little Man"), who actually builds nothing, echoes the modern era's slide toward alienation: "I used to have a motto for myself, 'Fifty and Nifty!', but it don't work no more. . . . I'm sixty now. . . . When you think about it, the old days were best. . . . Eggs two for a cent. . . . Free liver for the dog. Uptown was just a wilderness in the old days. Now the *whole* town's a wilderness. . . . I'm the man nobody knows . . ." (95–97).

As the second act opens in Central Park on Fay and Steve, with Odets's stage directions indicating that "Self-esteem is not exactly lurking around the corner for them" (111), Steve discovers again that little is what it appears to be in the flux of the modern world: the apparently Sinister Man staring at Fay is really blind. In the fourth scene, at the World's Fair, the evanescent Ray Brown reappears, "his pockets even more loaded with newspapers than the night before" (164), but then once again disappears into the crowd. And in the play's final scene at the airport, while Steve is dumped by Mr. Gilbert and left with nothing but bus fare, Fay's words are drowned out by the roar of airplanes. Their mechanistic power showers the lovers "with a miniature typhoon of dust, gravel and dead leaves, a final indignity" as Steve laments that he is "ready to resign from the human race" (232–33).

But if the modern condition is frequently one of discontinuity and deprivation, its formlessness also encompasses dynamism and energy, as Rosenberger reminds Steve during the play's fine final interchange (236). Earlier in Central Park, when Fay had asked him if the old days had been the best, the wise detective had replied, "I am a relic of the old days . . . it was not good. . . . Take the word of an expert. Ignorance, poverty, very unsanitary conditions. . . . Today is better, in my humble opinion. I am like you, Miss Tucker . . . I am in love with the possibilities, the human possibilities . . ." (104–5). He adds, "Everything remains to be seen," before bidding her good-bye with the significant image, "I'll see you in the morning" (106). Ever interested in the opportunity ceaselessly offered in the modern age, Rosenberger, during the scene in the restaurant with Fay's stodgy father and former fiancé, attempts to disperse their custom-laden atmosphere with an invitation to the vitality of the World's Fair. It is there that the play's central symbol of organicism, the crickets' night music, is discussed by Fay and Rosenberger, and there that the detective judges Fay's optimistic words "a very human thought. . . ." "Night music," meditates the girl. "If they can sing, I can sing. I'm more than them. *We're* more than them. . . . We can sing through any night!" (160). Backgrounded by the statue of George Washington (specifically, by his sword), Fay prefigures the feminist era, defying Steve's often thoughtless and dominating behavior with, "You told me 'don't take it' and I won't!" (175). Rosenberger urges Steve out of his essentially passive cynicism: "But you won't die so soon. Fix it, make it, change it" (181). Rosenberger continually functions as the drama's symbol of dynamic flow, as opposed to a static concept of reality. In the final scene of act 2, back at the hotel, after his lazy brother Al lets slip the gravity of Rosenberger's disease, the detective scorns this admission as "immaterial and irrelevant" (187) to a concern with Steve's hostile pathology. Then, in one of his finest speeches, he says quietly to the guilty boy, "There are two ways to look, Mr. Takis—to the past or the future. We know a famous case in history where a woman kept looking back and turned to a salt rock. If you keep looking back on a mean narrow past, the same thing can happen to you. You are feeling mad. . . . You think you have to tell me it's a classified world? . . . But your anger must bear children or it's hopeless. . . . You have the materials to make a good man. But stop breaking things with your fists. Look ahead, Mr. Takis. . . . God gave you a fine head—use it, dear boy" (189).

Typically, undercutting his own seriousness with irony, Rosenberger concludes with, "Sincerely yours, A. L. Rosenberger, your old Dutch Uncle. . . ." The exchange with Steve soon has the desired effect, at least momentarily, for Steve's mood becomes more adventurous as he happily repeats "Great Expectations!" to his girl. And Rosenberger's words animate Fay, too, for at the end of the play, she is filled with renewed vitality. She summarizes the lovers' talents for survival by proclaiming *"Taking chances doesn't frighten me!"* (228) and, moments later, recognizes the inevitability in a difficult decade of open-endedness as well as struggle: "It's war to make a living, to keep respect, to be in love!" (234).

Such a forward-looking, dynamic posture entails a price, of course; many modernist characters are lonely people, necessarily alienated from conventional systems of thought and behavior, which sustain men like Fay's father and Eddie Bellows. Fay comments about Mr. Watson, "I'd die if I thought I'd get like that," and refers to her parents as "living in a pot of lye and they don't know it" (98). Even the soceiety of good-hearted men like Al, who is always "bored" (130), offers little consolation to the protagonists of *Night Music.* Expressing love for her father, Fay adds that "I draw the line when they insist that I must live the same lives they live. I can't admire their way of living and I don't care for their ideals" (146).

Odets, like other modernist writers, emphasizes the individual, subjective experience as superior to that of the customary, the usual. The three central characters of *Night Music* are socially marginal rebels from static cultural norms. Of course, their disconnection from old values is in part due to the appalling economic conditions of the 1930s. Steve is so frequently absorbed in his own consciousness that he can only truly communicate his feelings for Fay through his clarinet (as Odets indicates in a stage direction, "Whatever his pride and fear of repudiation prevented him from saying to the girl he is now able to express in his music" [198]).[8] But Steve learns from the experience of the man of the road, Ray Brown, the "prime spitter" (85), as well as from his own emotional disinheritance from his sister and her husband (88–89). Rosenberger's own separateness from family gives him the liberating opportunity to become "a partisan of the pursuit of life, liberty and happiness" and to attempt to free Mr. Tucker with the wisdom that "the function of the parent is to make himself unnecessary. Unfortunately, only animals and birds know it" (154–55). Rosenberger understands that Steve's alienation has produced the potential for a renewing freedom: "You know," he says to Fay, "with all his noise he still makes a good impression. He's not like your father—he understands that life is no half-way business. He's not ripe, but he's got a future. . . . Only the living can cry out against life. . . . Excuse me, I live alone and sometimes it makes me talk too much" (167–68).

Clurman has indicated that the importance of Abraham Lincoln Rosenberger, the wisest of the play's subjective, solitary rebels, derives from his awareness that in the acceptance of life's required struggle "without bitterness, malice, or self-pity" (x) lies the possibility of a significant life. As much a mythic character as a successful one on the literal level of the work, Rosenberger, dying of cancer, engages himself in a quest for the modern world's latent coherence and stability, attempting to reestablish a meaningful unity from the world's bewildering diversity. It is rare in modern dramatic literature that such a deeply good man as the detective emerges as a probable, interesting literary creation. Integrated well with the play's modernist settings and its nonlinear, episodic structure (he is at once celebrated as a crime solver and detailed to the Balkan Queen [60]), silently present but stylistically implicated in Fay's fine demolition of the coquettishly obtuse Eddie ("I know, all the great men are dead and you don't feel so well" [183]), Rosenberger orchestrates the city's fragments into a dynamic whole. Trying to free Steve from his cage of self-concern, the old man counsels, "You got a weekend here, in New York, the greatest city in the world. You are ready for a crisp adventure, like a toasted sandwich. Go and enjoy yourself" (19). He remembers all, from Mr. George's former great baseball career ("You were a real artist of the people") to Lily's solitaire hands (64); he sends the youths food and watches over them, appearing suddenly, as if godlike, during their weekend in the city. Wise in people's needs and weaknesses, he gives movie tickets to brother Al when the latter's sad, boring life threatens to spill out of control, and renders Al and the young lovers unsentimentalized surrogates for the biological children he lacks. Patient even with Fay's odious father, Rosenberger is yet capable of the famed Odetsian clunking line: "Then let me throw out a suggestion then. We'll all eat breakfast together and something will suggest itself. . . . I hear the little pork sausages calling 'yoo hoo' " (139). Most crucial to the new generation, however, is his example and his courage in a dark time; at the World's Fair he says to Fay, "To fall, Miss Tucker, is permitted. But to get up is commanded" (157). Unlike the psychologically impoverished Jerry Wilenski, an exponent for the value of the autonomous life, Rosenberger is, as Brenman-Gibson has wisely noted, "the vessel both for generational continuity and for what Erickson has called 'generativity' " (587).

Jerry in *Clash by Night* is an esteemed carpenter yet can make nothing of value to hold his life together; unlike Rosenberger, he possesses a wife and child, yet has none of the detective's wisdom and self-understanding and thus can generate meaning neither within nor beyond his life. Odets's relentlessly pessimistic tragedy reminds us that modernism is conceptually an outgrowth of late nineteenth-century naturalism, as it is of earlier romanticism. If *Night Music* contains elements of romantic purposiveness and organicism, *Clash by Night,* with its Arnoldian epigraph, confronts its audience with a similarly fragmented modern world, but a world met with passivity by most of its inhabitants, and thus another paradise lost. For Jerry certainly, but also for Mae, Earl, Kress, and Jerry's father, any search for meaning must be doomed by their very approach to it. For in *Clash by Night,* the working class is ground down not so much by material poverty as by ignorance, by a failure of personal responsibility and maturity. The despicable Kress is correct concerning them all in his indictment of the drunken Tom: "No manhood in the boy!"[9]

Odets's settings and structure convey the play's concern with modern impermanence and confusion. The events retrogress from a soft summer night on the Wilenskis' porch to the apocalypse in the projection booth, and the intervals between actions decrease as events speed to their inevitable course. In the ostensibly benign pavilion Jerry first learns of the drowning of the little girl, which will increasingly occupy his thoughts as his life unravels. There Mae initially confides to Earl her fears of declining energy at age 34 and also laments to him, "I guess I'm a hold-over from another century! Didn't there used to be big, comfortable men? Or was it a dream? Today they're little and nervous, sparrows! But I dream of eagles. . . ." (78). In Act 1, scene 4, in the empty kitchen of the Wilenskis' "house . . . as still as death" (115), with the tolling of the distant bell buoy in the background, the frightened Peggy confides to her fiancé, "It's a nervous world, a shocking world. I don't understand it, I just don't understand. . . . I had some sort of dream when I was a child. . . . I remember words like 'nobility, generosity, courage. . . .' I want to admire something, someone—!" (122–23).

While Peggy and Joe meet the present and future with courage, the buoy bell must toll for the emotionally fragmented final occupants of the projection booth, which is described as a veritable mechanistic hell, its "interior . . . lighted with a typical bluish glare; the projection machinery hums and buzzes . . ." (226). There, surrounded by the incessant dialogue of the Hollywood machine, "so stupid and crude, so *fraudulent* in the face of the present reality" (239), one isolated man tries to kill another with a metal tool and is instead strangled by hands that are mere mechanical appendages of a driven man.

Clurman's discussion of Odets's themes of insecurity, chaos, and homelessness in *Night Music* are also pertinent to *Clash by Night,* which presents through its four major characters an even starker picture of the "wilderness of uncertainty which is the modern world." Even Jerry's father, their link to a more integrated past, plays on his concertina, in Jerry's nostalgic words, "a Polish song . . . about the little old house, where you wanna go back, but you can't find out where it is no more, the house . . ." (10–11). Jerry's pathetic encouragement of Mae and Earl's friendship, his frequent obsequious catering to Mae's every mood, are unconsciously motivated by his feelings of intense aloneness, by his desire to bridge her increasing remoteness from him; sadly, he is too naive to understand that his own behavior causes his deepening isolation. The wise Joe Doyle understands that Jerry's insecurity impels him into "buying your approval" (48), and late in the play Mae stays too long in the house because she fears that the unemployed Jerry will return to "an ash heap" (170). With real compassion she tells him, "You mustn't have false hopes. . . . Jerry, yes I know how you feel. Everyone's so goddam lonely! We can't escape that, how we need the other one. Life's so senseless without it . . ." (188). Like Kress, Earl suffers feelings of separateness: the scenes of his and Mae's tentative groping toward one another are some of Odets's finest. At one point, Earl responds to Mae's inquiry about the causes of his sleeplessness, " 'Cause I'm always outside looking in! Because I wanna get in somewhere! Someone has to need me, love me. . . . I'm not a barge goin' down the river! How do people go on this way? Tell me that—how do they do it? The blues for home . . . but where is home?" (105).

At the end of the first act, Odets creates one of his great stage images to represent Earl's isolation: after Mae goes into her bedroom, "shutting him out," Earl returns to the center of the empty room and picks up a teddy bear whose "doleful 'Momma, Momma' " (163–64) symbolically comments on his isolation (as well as Jerry's) as he holds and bends it, before the sound of the bell buoy accompanies his walk to another, smaller, empty room.

Clash by Night is weakened dramatically by protracted, melodramatic action in its final third and by Kress, a villain too Iago-like to sustain probability in a realistic drama. But Jerry's boozing, lecherous, and ultimately murderous uncle is motivated by feelings of insecurity (64) and passivity, which effectively dramatize the play's concerns with the moral destructiveness emanating from abdication of personal responsibility. Balancing his disintegrative influence are Abe Horowitz, the psychologically integrated projectionist, and Peggy Coffee and Joe Doyle, the latter sometimes a particularly didactic spokesman for Odets's theme of the necessity for consciousness in humans' unending struggle for an authentic life. Abe counsels Earl, "Make a plan. Have respect—do your work with respect" (230), and Joe, facing unflinchingly the economic realities of the era, says to Earl that he will indeed probably marry Peggy "when I become a decent human being" (87). Mae senses that Joe "knows his address—who he is and what he is, I mean. Some of us don't, you know" (110). Before marrying Peggy, Joe insists that they must know, that moral toughness inheres in "understanding what's happening to us" (119). In the drama's welter of spiritual alienation and deprivation, much of its scant liberation stems from Joe's effort at self-knowledge and realistic assessment of the world. In contrast to the continual miscommunication between Jerry and Mae, Joe speaks frankly about the realities of marriage: "Marriage is not a convent. It's not a harbor—it's the open world, Peg. It's being out at sea in a boat" (121). Joe's scorn for the popular culture's sentimentalizing of an illusory, commercialized American Dream symbolically predicts the accompaniment to Jerry's final carnage in the projection booth: "Where does that end? In violence, destruction. . . . Paradise begins in responsibility" (217).

But "Flies time!" (69–70), as Earl and Mae repeat as they fumble toward each other in mutually destructive need. Odets implies that the modern world's pace is so destructive because Joe's wisdom is so little attended. Writers famed for Marxist content supposedly are little interested in the psychoanalytic contexts of conflict and suffering, but Odets makes ample use of this staple of modernism in his treatment of the three main characters. Earl's ignorance of Jerry's signs of change is the death of him, and his fondling of the teddy bear is perhaps predicted in his choosing to stay to drink with Kress, though somewhat aware of the older man's destructive nature. Ignorant of his deep need for external props, Earl, perhaps not consciously, says early in the play, "Sit down a minute, friends—relapse!" (20). Soon after, he admits to Mae, "I like anyone who likes me" (34). His jokes on Peggy and Joe as "Coffey and Cream" (66) mask resentment of Joe's secure address, as revealed in his self-destructive remarks (69–70, 80, 103–4) and his response to Mae's charge that Jerry is a "momma's boy": "Who isn't?" (74). Mae, alone of the three central characters, comes to a measure of awareness of shared responsibility for the final horror as she calls to the crazed Jerry "with a thousand years of awful patience" (242). Through much of the action, however, she is as disconnected as her men, yearning for "comfortable men," passively allowing Jerry over the years to utilize her emotionally as a prop for his undeveloped ego, and staying with him for security rather than for opportunity and emotional fulfillment (67, 96).

Jerry, a "Polish Apollo" (25) whose emotional fragmentation allows him to bring no illumination to his world, ends "buried in incoherent prayer" (242). His destiny is an inevitable outcome of his holding to childish, irrational values, including a sentimental relationship with the natural world (3, 38) and an equally naive dependence on his religion (62) to ward off the uncomfortable fact of the child's drowning. Equally irresponsible is his addiction to installment-plan buying in a parlous economy; he has swallowed the American Success Myth that men like Edison "make all the people happy" (185). When confronted with the fact of Mae's affair, he tries to repress his father's information, and he can finally only rely on simplistic cliché: "You're bad, both bad" (162). Instead of hearing Mae's plea for respect and for intimacy, "You have to hold your woman!" (160), Jerry can only cry out to his father, "Poppa . . . I know what that song means you play. . . . We had these Christmas cards when I was a boy—a little warm house in the snow, yellow lights in the windows . . . remember? It was wonnerful . . . a place where they told you what to do, like in school. . . . (Beginning to cry) I wished it was like on the Christmas cards again, so nice and warm, a wonnerful home. . . . No, I wished I never grew up now!" (223).

But like Charles Foster Kane's illusory security, Jerry's shatters into a thousand pieces through his failure of dynamic vision, his incapacity to understand the bases of his beliefs. As the modernist tradition has frequently implied, with Arnold's epigraph to *Clash by Night,* lacking Rosenberger's and Joe Doyle's liberating courage and intelligence, what may appear to be a land of dreams contains but chaotic fragments that promise, of themselves, no "certitude, nor peace, nor help for pain. . . ."

Notes

1. Clifford Odets, *Night Music* (New York: Random House, 1940), 219. All further citations are from this edition; page numbers are noted parenthetically in the text.
2. See R. Baird Shuman, *Clifford Odets* (New York: Twayne, 1962). Subsequent critics who have concentrated upon Odets's artistic complexity include Edward Murray, *Clifford Odets: The Thirties and After* (New York: Ungar, 1968) and Harold Cantor, *Clifford Odets: Playwright-Poet* (Metuchen, N.J.: Scarecrow Press, 1978).
3. Elements of Odets's modernist themes are discussed in Frank R. Cunningham, "Clifford Odets," in *American Writers,* suppl. 2, ed. A. Walton Litz (New York: Scribners, 1981), 529–54—particularly with regard to *Waiting for Lefty* (531–33) and *Paradise Lost* (538–39).
4. Joseph Wood Krutch has expressed his discontents with modernism's influence in *"Modernism" and Modern Drama* (Ithaca: Cornell University Press, 1953). C. W. E. Bigsby has traced among representative playwrights social and metaphysical alienation resultant from modern materialism in *A Critical Introduction to Twentieth-Century American Drama, Vol. 1, 1900–1940* (Cambridge: Cambridge University Press, 1982).

5. Richard Ellmann and Charles Feidelson, Jr., eds., *The Modern Tradition: Backgrounds of Modern Literature* (New York: Oxford University Press, 1965), vi.

6. Clifford Odets, *Six Plays* (New York: Random House, 1939), 99.

7. Margaret Brenman-Gibson, *Clifford Odets, American Playwright: The Years from 1906 to 1940* (New York: Atheneum, 1981), 583. Brenman-Gibson, a psychoanalyst, records that in *Night Music* Odets "tries to re-create and to master his recent as well as ancient sense of deprivation, guilt, estrangement, and hopelessness" (585). Her thorough account of this period includes Clurman's reminiscence of Odets' insistence that *Night Music* be housed at the large Broadhurst Theater rather than in the more appropriately intimate Lyceum and his belief that this contributed to the play's failure. "It seems he didn't want to be . . . Jewish, he didn't want to be the child of immigrants, he didn't want to be ghettoized. Somehow he thought if his lovely little play were . . . on that street of success he would be in 'the class of the Robert Sherwoods, the Sidney Howards'! In the same way he had to buy a big car and hang around those lousy places like the Stork Club and the 21, places where he shouldn't have been. He really had a better time eating knishes at Moscowitz' . . ." (583–584). Brenman-Gibson attributes Odets's insecurities to his premature birth: both "Odets and his wife, Luise, had both . . . weigh[ed] in at three and a half pounds!" (584).

8. Psychoanalytic themes are of course a staple of modernist art, and Odets several times refers to Steve's various repressions—for example, on pages 59 and 119.

9. *Clash by Night* (New York: Random House, 1942), 61. (All further citations are from this edition; page numbers are cited parenthetically in text.) There was apparently little consciousness behind the casting of Mae or other production matters. Gerald Weales offers an interesting account of the play's commercial failure in *Clifford Odets: Playwright* (New York: Pegasus, 1971), 145–46.

The Country Girl

Edward Murray

The Country Girl is a two-act play. (The title page of the published text erroneously describes it as "A Play in Three Acts.") There are five scenes in Act One and three scenes in Act Two. The time-sequence covers about two months. In "How The Country Girl Came About," Odets says: "I write fluently, but to combine a certain linear drive of story with psychological drive is the real problem. I don't know anyone who can do it, who ever did it." This is a typical Odetsian exaggeration. Many plays combine "linear drive" and "psychological drive"—indeed The Country Girl itself combines the two drives. Which is to say that the play, though not without its faults and limitations, is much better than its creator believed.

In Act One, Scene One, Bernie Dodd, a young director, offers the alcoholic actor Frank Elgin a role in a Broadway show. Frank, who has a morbid lack of confidence in himself, is reluctant to accept the assignment. In Scene Two, Georgie, Frank's wife, is prepared to leave her husband, but when Frank resolves to take the part in the show she decides to give him one more chance. The point of attack occurs, then, when Frank accepts responsibility for himself. He informs Georgie of a dream he had the previous night:

> A big sign—now get this—a big banner was stretched across the street: "Frank Elgin in . . ." I couldn't make out in what. . . . I'm going to take that part, Georgie! You don't have to tell me not to drink—haven't I been a good boy all summer? . . . This morning I got up early—that funny laughing dream. And I was thinking about our lives—everything—and now this chance! Don't you see that all those people in the dream, they wish me luck. I won't fail this time! Because that's what counts—if the world is with you—and your wife! (He looks at her, earnest, boyish, and questioning, appealing for her support.)[1]

Several important dramatic questions are posed here: Will Frank stay sober and make a success of himself in the role? Will Georgie stay with Frank permanently? What is the nature of the bond that unites the couple?

From Clifford Odets: The Thirties and After (New York: Frederick Ungar Publishing Co., 1968). Reprinted by permission of Edward Murray.

238

Complications develop in the following scene. Frank is secretly dependent on Georgie, but he pretends to others that his wife is really the neurotic partner in the marriage. The early action of the play suggests that, in spite of Bernie's resentment and suspicion of Georgie, the two young people may eventually grow attracted to each other. Frank's two-faced attitude causes many problems; characteristically, however, he allows his wife to correct matters. One of these incidents occurs near the end of Act One, with the result that Frank and Georgie quarrel:

FRANK: Boy, I'll never understand your moods, and that's the truth! A man can't be right can he? Two strikes against him before he opens his mouth! (*Sullen and offended, he goes back to his dressing. She sits, stiff, cold, and wordless.*) Now my stomach's all in a whirl again. That's what you wanted, isn't it? (*He sits at the make-up shelf; there is silence and distance between them.*)

GEORGIE: One day soon . . . we'll see what I want. . . . (p. 72)

Which line looks forward to the resolution of the play.

During Act Two Frank struggles with the demands of his role, and also with his increasing desire to escape anxiety by means of the bottle. Eventually Frank's neurotic inner pressure reaches an almost unbearable level of intensity—and he succumbs to temptation. When Georgie discovers that her mate has been furtively drinking there is another, more violent, quarrel:

GEORGIE: Oh, the hell with it! . . . I'm going back to the hotel—do what you want! Sometimes I think you're plain out of your head!
(*She exits without more ado, slamming the door hard.* FRANK *whirls around; he glowers bitterly, snorting and mimicking her tone, walking in circles before he snatches his tie off a hook*)

FRANK: Out of your mind! Do what you want . . . plain out of your mind! . . . That's right walk out on me! Typical! Typical! (*He is down at the pier glass now, angrily snapping the tie into a knot, muttering to himself.*) Forget I'm alive. Take their part and forget I'm alive! Helpmate, real helpmate. . . . (*He dribbles off, his attitude abruptly changing. He stops and then tiptoes to the closed door and listens. Then he goes to the trunk and from the bottom drawer brings out a full bottle of cough syrup. He uncaps it, takes a swig, and throws the cap away over one shoulder. The bottle plopped down on the chest in front of him, he continues with the tie and collar. His tone is less intense but as bitter.*) Helpmate! Sweetheart! Country girl! (pp. 95–96)

This is the turning point of the action because Frank's decision to get drunk will force Bernie to make a counter decision regarding the actor's part in the show. Similarly, Frank's action will compel Georgie to render a decision about the future of the Elgin marriage.

The crisis arrives in the next scene. Bernie finally discovers that Frank is a pathological liar, and that Georgie, far from being the villain of the piece, is the show's best hope in the joint effort to preserve the star's sobriety.

BERNIE: Dammit, listen to me! You're knocking all the apologies out of my head! (*He has pulled her in close to him and is holding her by both arms.*) Now, *listen,* Lady Brilliance: you have to stay—he doesn't play unless you stay! It's a time for promotion, not more execution! But I can't take the chance *if you don't stay!*
(*A quick tense moment follows.* GEORGIE *is frozen in his arms, her hands against his chest.*)

GEORGIE: Why are you holding me? (*Pushing*) I said you are holding me!
(*Abruptly, not releasing her, he kisses her fully on the mouth . . .*)
. . .

BERNIE: . . . I deserve anything you say—no excuses, no excuses. . . . (*His manner changes.*) Now I need your answer. For Frank's sake, I want you to stay.

GEORGIE: Wanting, wanting, always wanting!

BERNIE (*humbly for him*): I'm asking . . . Will you stay?

GEORGIE (*after a pause*): Yes.
(*He starts for the door, his face rigid. She stops him.*)

GEORGIE: You kissed me—don't let it give you any ideas, Mr. Dodd.

BERNIE (*quietly*): No, Mrs. Elgin.
(*He walks out, quietly closing the door.* GEORGIE *stands for a full moment, as if listening, an air of impenetrable unreality about her. Her hand slowly moves up to her face. Her fingers touch her lips.*) (pp. 108–110, italics in original)

The scene ends with Georgie's final decision suspended, with Frank's success in the show still uncertain, and with the future of Bernie and Georgie in doubt.

The climax, which Odets skillfully plays down in order to avoid the appearance of melodramatic contrivance, follows in the final scene of the play. Frank's success in his role prompts a new self-confidence in him, and as a result he asks Georgie for her decision:

FRANK: . . . Don't leave me, darling. Give me a chance. I love you. . . .

GEORGIE: Frank . . . I married you for happiness. . . . And, if necessary, I'll leave you for the same reason. Right now I don't know where I stand.

FRANK (*humbly*): You don't . . . ?

GEORGIE: . . . No. Because neither of us has really changed. And yet I'm sure that both our lives are at some sort of turning point. There's some real new element of hope here—I don't know what. But I'm certain . . . and you, Frank, have to be strong enough to bear that uncertainty.

FRANK (*hushed*): I think I know what you mean. . . . I—I don't know how to say this, but no matter what happens, you have saved me, Georgie— you and Bernie. . . . I think I have a chance. (pp. 121–122)

But it remains for Bernie Dodd to reveal the future better than Georgie herself knows: "You'll never leave him," he informs her. Then—after kissing her "lightly on the lips"—he exits. The play concludes as Georgie *"slowly walks out of the room with* FRANK'S *robe across one arm"* (p. 124).

As the title of the play suggests, Georgie, not Frank, is the protagonist. True, Frank's decision launches the point of attack; and it is again Frank's action that brings about the turning point. Thereafter, however, the resolution largely depends on Georgie. Actually, it might be argued that the play is not as "well made" as most critics would have it. The reviewers—Margaret Marshall, Walter Kerr, Harold Clurman and others—all commented on the "smooth" craftsmanship of the piece. Similarly, in *American Drama Since World War II,* Gerald Weales says that Odets' play is, "extremely well structured (*slick* is the word that comes to mind, but it would have to be used as a compliment). . . ." In "How *The Country Girl* Came About," Odets remarks that the play went through various drafts, and that Georgie evolved from a "destructive bitch" dying from cancer to the much more admirable woman of the final version. According to Odets, Georgie is the main character. It seems possible that in his final treatment of the play Odets failed to unify the structure completely, for analysis suggests some confusion of focus in motivation. Certain details in the play reveal that the dramatist, consciously or unconsciously, was aware of problems in construction.

The point of attack, for example, is framed by Georgie's decision to leave Frank and by her later postponement of that leavetaking. Although Frank is responsible for the turning point, Georgie is made the innocent cause of his decision to get drunk. Which is to say that Odets seeks to make Georgie the active force, or protagonist. For the remainder of the play the focus is steadily on Georgie. In the last scene Frank is a success in his part, but the action takes place off-stage and the spotlight is on Georgie. As already noted, there are no fireworks in the last scene; Odets plays down the climax. The first question—will Frank be a success?—is answered almost at once. The second question—Will Georgie marry Bernie?—is not left in much doubt, for the crisis ends with Bernie kissing Georgie but calling her "Mrs. Elgin." In spite of what Georgie says at the climax, the audience is made to feel that she will stay with her husband, and consequently there can be little surprise in store when, at the conclusion, Bernie confirms the permanence of the Elgin marriage. It seems a fact worth noting that Odets had a tendency to shift the focus from his male protagonists to his female leads late in the action of some of his best plays; witness the displacement of interest from Ralph to Hennie in *Awake and Sing!,* from Ben to Cleo in *Rocket to the Moon* and from Frank to Georgie in *The Country Girl.* (This inclination was perhaps rooted in psychological conflicts in Odets, a problem which lies outside the scope of the present study.)

In order to show how *The Country Girl* is much more complex than a discussion of its logical structure suggests, it is necessary to discuss "the play-within-the-play" device in Act One, Scene One, and also to analyze some of the "external" techniques Odets employs to unify the action. One critic objected to the use of "the play-within-the-play," but investigation reveals that this rather long enactment of Frank's reading for the role is far from inconsequential. The dialogue of "the play-within-the-play" foreshadows subsequent developments in the "real" play and exposes the character traits of Frank and Bernie. Thus, Frank enacts the role of the rather corrupt Judge Murray; Bernie reads the part of the young "reformer" who wants to marry the Judge's grandchild, Ellen. The two characters struggle over Ellen, as Frank and Bernie are later to struggle over Georgie. The Judge's moral decline parallels Frank's alcoholism and emotional sickness. Bernie, who calls himself an Italian-American (p. 31), is identified with the "Wop bastard" who aspires to Ellen's hand (p. 16). During this audition Bernie is guilty of a "slip of the tongue"—a slip that is not without its Freudian significance—and calls the Judge "Frank." Similarly, Frank calls Bernie "son" (p. 18). When Bernie taunts the Judge that Ellen has already deserted him, the older man proudly proclaims his former and future greatness, and stresses the belief that he is a long way from being beaten. The younger man, however, is unrelenting in his attack. "*Soon* [BERNIE] *is pacing around* FRANK, *like a bull fighter around a helpless animal, which is the impression* FRANK *gives for the moment*" (pp. 17–18). Clearly then, the opening sequence has an integral function in the dramatic action and casts much light on both character and theme.

In his short story "The Gambler, the Nun, and the Radio" (1933), Hemingway deals with some "opiates of the people." Each of the opiates mentioned in the piece is a form of escape from the self; thus the protagonist plays his radio all night long in an effort to forget his pain. Odets employs the same device in *The Country Girl*. In the opening sequence, for example, Bernie is disturbed by a radio blaring while he is talking to Frank:

BERNIE (*abruptly calling off to the left*): Hey, "Props"! Shut off that radio or close the door! (*Gently, to* FRANK) Read the part, Frank. (p. 15)

There are a couple more references to sound in this scene (p. 13 and p. 17). When Scene Two opens Odets says: "*Loud music comes out of a small radio*" in the Elgin apartment. Bernie knocks on the door, but Georgie mistakenly thinks it is a neighbor complaining about the music. After turning off the radio, Georgie finally opens the door for Bernie (p. 25). The radio, then, is identified with Georgie. In the first scene Bernie's anger at the radio noise and his gentle approach to Frank prepares the audience for the coming struggle between Georgie and the director over the alcoholic actor. Georgie's listening to the radio, like her voracious reading, underlines her loneliness and sexual frustration. "When you think about it—so many plays and books, so much reading in the stillness of the night," Georgie remarks at one point,

"—and for all of it, what?" (p. 74). In Act One, Scene Five, Georgie and Bernie have one of their numerous arguments over Frank: "[BERNIE] *looks at* [GEORGIE] *carefully, with a polite charm masking a certain scorn, then leaves. Despite her awareness of his good sense,* GEORGIE *is somewhat disturbed by him. Thinking, she turns on a small radio. She looks up as* FRANK *enters*" (p. 61). After a brief exchange, Frank barks: "Shut the radio off!" (p. 62). In other words, both Bernie and Frank "turn off" Georgie, which is to say, they frustrate her need for love.

When Act Two opens Georgie is once again listening to the radio and talking to the playwright, Unger. After the latter praises Bernie to Georgie, he asks: "Does my typing bother you?"; to which Georgie replies: "No. Does the music?" (p. 75). Georgie's radio and Bernie, then, are again juxtaposed. Later in the same scene Georgie indulges in some revealing play acting: "*She takes off her glasses and looks at herself [in a mirror]. Something poignant reaches out from image to reality. The radio has begun playing a waltz.* GEORGIE *begins to sway to its rhythm, and in another moment she is waltzing alone, almost as if it were possible to waltz herself back to a better time. What she is murmuring to herself we cannot hear. Then she stops abruptly. A sardonic* BERNIE *stands in the doorway*" (pp. 82–83).

Immediately Georgie dons her glasses again—and shortly afterward snaps off the radio (p. 84). When Bernie later remarks that Georgie is "as phony . . . as an opera soprano," she slaps his face (p. 87). However, when Bernie finally kisses Georgie, Odets says: "*She seems to come out of sleep*"—and then the hostility vanishes (p. 109). Bernie, instead of continuing to "turn off" Georgie, now loves her and hence "turns on" the woman. There are no more references in the play to the radio.

Off-stage noises become identified with Frank's success in the show, and with the new sense of command he exercises. In the last scene, for example, he barks: "Close that window!" (p. 117), and his resemblance to the Bernie of the first scene is plain. Finally, the director realizes that he "can't escape [Frank's] voice" (p. 114), and decides to give up his hope to possess Georgie. It is interesting to note that the image of Bernie as a bull-fighter stalking Frank, the "helpless animal" at the start, merges with the radio device I have just analyzed. When the opening curtain goes up a radio is playing "*a popular Mexican song. . . . [And]* BERNIE *. . . is softly whistling with the song*" (p. 11). The reference to Bernie's "whistling" foreshadows his loneliness and his openness to Georgie's charm, which will persist beneath the cynical crust of his opposition to her. The Mexican motif is carried through when, right before the crisis, Georgie informs Bernie: "I'm going back to New York, to the fiesta of a quiet room" (p. 108). Bernie then kisses her, and the "fiesta" explodes in the dressing room in Boston.

The most impressive feature of *The Country Girl,* however, is Odets' brilliant psychological characterization. Critics seem not to have noticed how deeply the dramatist probes into Georgie, Bernie and Frank. For one thing,

244 ◆ EDWARD MURRAY

it is quite apparent that Odets has depicted a symbolic oedipal triangle in *The Country Girl*. Frank is fifty years old (p. 14), Georgie is over thirty (p. 82), and Bernie is thirty-five (p. 14). Indeed, Frank openly refers to himself as "Poppa" (p. 71), and calls Bernie and Unger his "sons" (pp. 30, 46 and 76). The first time Bernie sees Georgie he exclaims: "You're even younger than I thought . . . you act like an old lady and you're not" (p. 27). Later Georgie informs Bernie: "Frank's brought out the mother in me" (p. 47). There is not, it should be noted, much sexual life in the Elgin marriage. Although Georgie stands for the "mother" her age would seem to make her more ideally suited to Bernie than to Frank. In Scene Two, Georgie complains of a toothache and a chill: "It's cold out," she tells Bernie. "The summer collapsed so abruptly, didn't it? You could fall asleep here and not wake up till they called you for the Judgment Day . . . I have a bad toothache. All of autumn's in this tooth. . . . My hands are numb. . . . What time is it? . . . Three clocks, a radio, and never know the time" (pp. 26–27). This theme is repeated later in the play in an exchange between Georgie and Frank:

GEORGIE: I haven't felt like a woman in ten years.
  FRANK: . . . I suppose that's my fault.
GEORGIE   (*lightly*): Summer dies, autumn comes, a fact of nature—nobody's
          fault. (pp. 52–53)

Directly before the curtain falls ending Act One, Georgie declares: "I really must . . . get these teeth fixed" (p. 71). Clearly, Georgie's "toothache" is Frank and the unsatisfactory life he has given her. The "cold autumn rain" represents Georgie's premature sexlessness. Georgie is half-dead; she doesn't know "what time it is"; even her hands are "numb." She is like a fairy princess asleep in the midst of life. In *The Big Knife* Marion Castle says: "I believe the fairy tale is a lie. In real life no one ever comes to wake us up" (p. 34). In *The Country Girl,* however, Bernie Dodd kisses Georgie, and she comes "*out of her sleep*" (p. 109). Viewed in these terms the crisis of the play is "the Judgment Day," and the verdict rendered is that Georgie is renewed and ready to go on with Frank: "*For a moment* [GEORGIE] *wears a sad and yearning look* [*after* BERNIE]; *finally a towel in her hand calls her back to reality*" (p. 124).

Why did Georgie marry Frank? Evidently she was lonely, even as a child. "My father was always away on tour," she informs Unger. "My mother was off with gardening and hobbies" (p. 73). As a result, Georgie read a lot of books—"too many," she says—and became excessively romantic (p. 105). Note that Georgie's father, like Frank, was in show business. Which suggests that Frank is a father image to Georgie. Moreover, Georgie believed that Elgin, like her father, was a strong man:

GEORGIE: You mystify me, Frank, your sense of guilt and insecurity. Take a
          lesson from my father, the late Delaney the Great. He didn't care what

people thought of him, no matter what he did. Played every vaudeville house in the world. Didn't show up at home but twice a year—and those two times he was down in the cellar perfecting new magic tricks.

FRANK: Oh, sure you'd love that—seeing me only twice a year!

GEORGIE (*whimsically*): My mother didn't mind it as much as I did—it orphaned me. Might not have married you if I'd had a father. But he *believed* in himself, I mean—you don't. That's cost you plenty . . . it's cost me as much. . . . (p. 53, italics in original)

Georgie later explains to Bernie that she "had such a naïve belief in Frank's worldliness and competence" (p. 105). It is certainly worthy of note that Georgie refers to Bernie as "Bernardo the Great" (p. 54). Like "Delaney the Great," Bernie is a "magician" to both Georgie and Frank (p. 113). Part of Bernie's attraction for Georgie, then, derives from his image as a strong father figure.

But Bernie, like Frank, is not as strong as he pretends. "I don't know," he admits to Georgie at the end of the play, "maybe a magician *does* live in this frail, foolish body, but he certainly can't work wonders for himself!" (p. 124, italics in original). Bernie calls himself "frail" here, a word which Georgie previously used to describe Frank (p. 105). Much of the psychological motivation in the piece involves the problem of whether Frank or Bernie will assume the final father role. Although Bernie, like Frank, refers to himself as "Poppa" (p. 59), the older man retains possession of Georgie. Furthermore, the "magic" associated with Georgie's father appears to be left in Frank's keeping: "A man like Elgin, giving his best performance," says Bernie, "—he has the magic to transform a mere show to theater with a capital T!" (p. 103). Bernie's interest in Frank, however, seems to depend on more than merely a business arrangement.

Like Elgin, the elder Dodd was an alcoholic (p. 22). Whereas Frank simply attempted suicide in the past, though, Bernie's father succeeded in destroying himself (p. 90). For Bernie then—as for Georgie—Frank stands in the place of the father. There is a strong element of latent homosexuality in Bernie's attitude toward Frank. From the opening of the play, Bernie reveals a hostility toward women. For example, he barks: "Don't come in here, Nancy—we're busy" (p. 12)—a line which reflects Bernie's contempt for women, and his desire to keep them out of his life. "Does he like women?" Georgie asks Frank after meeting Dodd (p. 51). Bernie is recently divorced, and consequently he is extremely bitter toward women: "*My* wife was so twisted"—says Bernie, apparently identifying himself with Frank and the former Mrs. Dodd with Georgie—" 'I hope your next play's a big flop!' she says. 'So the whole world can see I love you even if you're a failure!' " (p. 45, italics in original). During the play a number of references are made to Georgie's knitting, and at one point Georgie sews a loose button on Frank's coat (p. 53). Later in the action Bernie informs Georgie: "I was married to one like you. . . . It took her two years—she sewed me up!" (p. 85). If Odets is presenting a "negative oedipus complex" here, the roles in the original relationship are reversed; for Bernie is the more active and aggressive one, Frank is the more passive and dependent one. At the end of the play, of course, Frank steals the "magic" and becomes "Poppa" again. On one level then, *The Country Girl* represents a struggle between Georgie (the wife-mother) and Bernie (the friend-son) for possession of Frank (the husband-father). Thus, Bernie warns Georgie: "I'm going to fight you as hard as I can for this man!" (p. 85). "I'll think about you," Bernie tells Frank, "if you take this job. I'll commit myself to you—we'll work and worry together—it's a marriage!" (p. 31). (The reader will recall that Odets used the same approach in *Golden Boy,* where homosexual symbolism underlined Joe Bonaparte's loss of his true nature. In *The Country Girl,* however, Odets fails to extend the symbolism beyond the psychological realm.) "Nobody wants to get your goat, Mrs. Dodd," Bernie assures Georgie (p. 32)—which in the light of the present analysis takes on significance when Frank remarks: "You know Poppa—walks like a mountain goat—never slips" (p. 77). Bernie is convinced that Georgie is "jealous" of him (p. 91), and the reader may feel that she has good reason for her jealousy.

Bernie's unconscious attraction to Frank originated in the past. At the beginning of the play he says: "Twelve years ago I saw [Frank] give two performances that made my hair stand up—(*Abruptly he calls offstage:*) Close that door and keep it closed!" (p. 13). Here we see Bernie's admiration for Frank juxtaposed to the radio noise outside, which symbolizes Georgie. (Since "hair" represents male potency—witness, for example, the Samson and Delilah story—the reference to Bernie's "hair" standing up is suggestive.) The unconscious sexual symbolism is rationalized, however, into mere hero worship: "You and Lunt and Walter Huston," Bernie tells Frank, "—you were my heroes" (p. 30). That Bernie regards Frank as a father is plain from Odets' manipulation of the word "kid." In the audition scene Bernie, reading the play with Frank, says: "Look at me! I'm a fresh kid—I wanna marry your grandchild and you don't want me to" (p. 17). The following exchange occurs in Act Two between Frank and Bernie:

FRANK: . . . Why kid around? It's all my fault—I'm no good.

    . . .

BERNIE: You're guilty as hell! But I want you to do something for the kid—

FRANK: What kid?

BERNIE: *This* kid! Stop being naïve: stop protecting her!

    . . .

BERNIE: . . . If we go on together, you move in with me for the duration! (p. 102)

There is an element of irony here, for in the audition scene Bernie played the "kid" who wanted the mother surrogate (the "virginal" Nancy-

Ellen seems to be a disguised maternal imago), but now his desire is fixed on the father figure, Frank. After "marrying" Frank, however, Bernie, like Georgie before him, is rudely jolted into seeing the truth about the man. As a result of his disillusionment, Bernie's love for the mother in Georgie returns and Frank becomes a rival for the woman's affection. Actually, the negative oedipus complex was only a smokescreen concealing Bernie's deeper desire for the mother.

Twice in the play Bernie calls Georgie "Mrs. Dodd" (p. 104 and p. 107). The form of address is ambiguous. Is Bernie unconsciously confusing Georgie with his ex-wife whom he detests? Or is he expressing an unconscious desire to make Georgie "Mrs. Dodd"? It is also possible, considering the symbolic triangles of the play, that Bernie is transforming Georgie into his mother, for the latter would also be "Mrs. Dodd." After Bernie kisses Georgie, however, he calls her "Mrs. Elgin" (p. 110). Why? Is Odets suggesting that Georgie is no longer, for Bernie, either an ex-wife or mother? Or is the playwright merely foreshadowing Bernie's final renunciation of the forbidden woman? Perhaps we do not have an "either-or" situation here but a "both-and" construction.

Bernie Dodd is one of a long line of characters in Odets' plays who are in search of a "home." It is part of Bernie's grudge against modern women that they "don't want a home: the only piece of furniture they'll touch is the psychoanalyst's couch!" (p. 44). At the end of the piece, Bernie bemoans his fate: "A job is a home to a homeless man. Now the job is finished—where do I go from here?" (p. 113). Georgie's character, though, has impressed itself upon Bernie, and as a result he is no longer a misogynist. The good mother in Georgie has inspired a new appreciation in the director for women. Hence, he informs Georgie: "You are . . . steadfast. And loyal . . . reliable. I like that in a woman!" (p. 124). Odets suggests, by the way, that Bernie may not be entirely homeless in the future. At one point in the play, Georgie and Nancy gaze together into a mirror and Nancy remarks: "Look at you—we could be sisters!" Immediately Georgie begins to dance, and then Bernie enters (p. 82). If Georgie and Nancy "could be sisters," perhaps the one could be replaced by the other in Bernie's affections. After Frank strikes Nancy during a performance in the final scene, Bernie soothes the girl with a kiss (p. 116). It seems quite possible, then, that Bernie may eventually find a home with the "virginal, which is to say untried and initiatory" Nancy (p. 37).

In his characterization of Frank Elgin, Odets projects an accurate portrait of an orally regressed neurotic. Some recent psychoanalytic theory places an increasing emphasis on the oral level of development, and regards disturbances in this area as being the decisive factor in neurosis. The oedipus complex, in this view, is merely a later "rescue station" from a basic oral regression. Such an explanation of neurotic motivation seems especially meaningful in the case of an alcoholic, who clearly substitutes a bottle for a breast, but whose solution to the infantile conflict is ultimately self-destructive. For the oral neurotic is a psychic masochist inwardly fixated on the bad cruel mother that he has himself imaginatively, and unconsciously, constructed. Significantly, the oral neurotic spends his life denying his neurotic attachment by erecting a number of defenses, such as pseudo-aggression, displacement of blame for his allegedly unprovoked suffering onto a mother-surrogate, and alcoholism. Originally, so the theory goes, the infant believes that the mother's breast is part of his own organism; and when the infant is in any way frustrated during breast feeding he is consumed by intense aggressive feelings. He comes to feel that bad Mother, whose independent existence he slowly awakens to, is sadistically refusing him. Since the infant cannot act out his rage, however, the aggression boomerangs, and in the process produces severe guilt feelings in the infant. Furthermore, since every organism seeks pleasure and avoids pain, the unpleasant guilt feelings and aggression become "libidinized," that is, they are converted into "pleasurable pain." The alcoholic, according to this approach, denies that he wants to be refused by the mother, and consequently he seeks to establish what the late Edmund Bergler called a "liquid pseudo autarchy." By drinking excessively the alcoholic proves that he can take care of himself with "milk" (alcohol), but in addition he indicates—unfortunately with self-destructive results—that all one can get from Mother is "poison." This intrapsychic process is further complicated by the alcoholic's identification with the mother. Thus, he not only "poisons" himself—an expression of masochism—but he also incurs guilt by "poisoning" Mother. Marriages involving oral neurotics are distinguished by defensive pseudo-aggression, self-provoked suffering, and general "injustice collecting." My description of the oral neurotic is necessarily sketchy, but perhaps enough has been said in order to analyze and interpret Frank Elgin.

That Frank represents what the psychoanalyst would call an oral neurotic seems clear. Whenever Frank feels expansive, for example, he turns to food. "Let the wind blow down the street," he informs Georgie happily, "—the oysters and lobsters are delicious!" (p. 51). "Guess what I'm in the mood for?" he asks his wife later. "One of those one dozen oyster stews. . . . Oh, boy, what that'll do for my stomach!" (p. 70). Whenever Frank's unconsciously provocative behavior prompts Georgie to reach with resentment toward him, however, the neurotic actor at once assumes a conscious self-pitying pose: "Now my stomach's all in a whirl again. That's what you wanted, isn't it?" (p. 72). And he then commences to drink with a vengeance. Georgie tells Bernie that Frank "has to be nursed, guarded, and coddled!" (p. 107). At one point Odets refers to Frank as a "child" (p. 92). Even Frank's acting is described in oral terms by Bernie: "my problem," the director informs Georgie, "is to keep him going—overflowing. The longer I keep him fluid and open, the more gold we mine" (p. 60). *Consciously,* Frank wants people to like him (p. 67); *unconsciously,* though, he prompts rejection through his drinking and lying. In order to appease his unconscious conscience, however, Frank must vociferously deny that he wants to fail; he must place the blame elsewhere: "They all want me to fail!" he tells Georgie. "And you want me to fail, too! You don't love me!" (p. 95).

There are times in the play when one feels that Georgie is a psychic masochist, too. Her consciously expressed reason for marrying Frank—namely, that he resembled her father—may have been merely a rationalization for a deeper orality. For Georgie knew that Frank was a drunkard when she married him. And there is something masochistic in Georgie's remaining with Frank over the years. "I don't know who's punishing who anymore!" she tells Frank in one scene (p. 92). The Elgin marriage appears to thrive on quarrels. Numerous references are made to Georgie's oral propensities. When Frank asks her why she married him, Georgie replies: "That's easy: you always had a box of Chiclets in your pocket" (p. 79). And she informs Bernie that her one aim in life is "to buy the sugar for my coffee!" (p. 108). Georgie, like Frank, consciously maintains that she wants to get "milk" (gum, sugar), and not be refused; yet her capacity for suffering seems suspiciously inexhaustible. (There are likewise repeated references to Bernie's overindulgence in smoking—another oral practice.)

In "How *The Country Girl* Came About," Odets says: "I never wrote a play that didn't tell a story. The only thing is that I usually verbalized the implications. It may be that in *The Country Girl* I didn't verbalize them—things like what makes a man like Frank Elgin a drunkard." When *The Country Girl* was filmed a scene was added which showed the Elgins' child killed by an automobile, supposedly as a result of Frank's carelessness. In the play, however, Georgie tells Bernie: "There's no one reason [for Frank's drinking]. . . . I'd say bad judgment started him off. He had some money once, but you don't know my Frank—he wanted to be his own producer—eighty thousand went in fifteen months, most of it on two bad shows. . . . A year later we lost our little girl. It was awesome how he went for the bottle. He just didn't stop after that. (p. 74)

Earlier in the piece, though, Frank traces his difficulties back to the couple's days in California: "I knew it then—on the coast—I lost my nerve! And then, when we lost the money, in '39, after those lousy Federal Theater jobs—! . . . Whatever the hell I did, I don't know what!" (p. 33). As noted, however, Frank drank *before* he met Georgie; consequently, the basic motivation for his self-destructive tendencies must be said to lie farther back in his past.

One might note that psychic masochists, not surprisingly, are notoriously prone to "bad judgment" (p. 74). Similarly, oral neurotics unconsciously create their mates in the image of the bad cruel mother of the nursery. As previously noted, Odets started with the idea of making Georgie a "bitch," but later he changed his mind and transformed her into the "good mother." The original conception of Georgie as the "bitch" (that is, the bad mother) has existence in the finished play solely as a fantasy creation of Frank and Bernie. "Lady," Bernie tells Georgie, "you ride [Frank] like a broom! You're a bitch!" (p. 69). Georgie accuses Frank: "You have a real conviction of woman's perfidy, don't you?" (p. 52). When Georgie threatens to leave her husband and return to New York, Frank fumes: "Who's in New York? What pair of pants are you looking for?" (p. 95). Frank is capable of casting Bernie in the role of the bad mother, too. At the crisis of the play, for example, Bernie says to Frank: "Sit up! Don't act as if I'm beating you up! Don't make me the victimizer! Sit up!" (p. 102). Unconsciously, Bernie seems to be saying: "Don't cast *me* in Georgie's role; that is, the role of the bad cruel mother—the role, incidentally, that I myself cast women in. Let me play the good mother to you, Frank!"

Although Odets did not, as he put it, "verbalize" the reasons for Frank Elgin's alcoholism, he would seem to have presented sufficient material on which a psychological interpretation could be established. With its conscious motivation, unconscious oedipal symbolism and unconscious oral symbolism, *The Country Girl* surely represents Odets' most complex approach to character. It might be objected that the ending is unsatisfactory. Thus, Gerald Rabkin asserts that Frank "might well have gone on another bender and failed to achieve his theatrical triumph," that the "element of hope" for the future is unconvincing, and that "Frank's theatrical triumph does not arise out of the fact of his coming to terms with himself." In 1949 Odets told Russell Rhodes: "Chekhov was the ideal playwright—all character and nothing happens. But people crave excitement and movement." And somewhere Chekhov says that the beginning and end of plays are almost always dishonest. Given the depth and complexity of Frank's neurotic illness, it would be extremely difficult for a dramatist to solve the man's character problems in an entirely satisfactory fashion in the last scene. Here, if not elsewhere in the play, the "linear drive of story" tends to some extent to clash with "psychological drive." Yet Odets has included certain details in the last scene that might serve to lessen the weight of critical censure. Frank Elgin is a man who functions chiefly on the affective, rather than the intellectual, level. Acting is a form of sublimation for Frank. Early in the final scene Bernie, listening to the performance off-stage, remarks: "[Frank's] erratic, in and out—the bursts aren't coming! We'll see . . ." (p. 112). Frank succeeds in the play because he fully identifies with the role. When Frank slaps Nancy-Ellen during the performance he is of course symbolically asserting himself against Georgie—hence the importance of the audition scene in the opening act, where Frank, Bernie and Georgie are identified with the characters in Unger's play—and thus establishing his marriage on a more normal, if perhaps only temporary, basis. The actor informs Bernie: "I'm sorry, kid, firgive me—it just came out that way! That's what he should do there, the Judge—no one wants him, not even his grandchild! And suddenly I got the image—they're caging a lion—like you shove him in the face! Like they do in the circus, with chairs and brooms! And I couldn't hold it back. . . ." (p. 117)

Notice too that Odets is not inclined to stress Georgie's "hope" for the future in a strident fashion. *The Country Girl* is a long way from *Awake and Sing!*. Under the circumstances of a successful first night performance, one might, like Georgie, feel a mingling of "hope" and "uncertainty."

It is not difficult to locate the faults in *The Country Girl*. One might point out, as suggested earlier, the problem of focal unity in the logical structure of the play. In *Group Psychology,* Freud maintains that individual and social psychology are the same. One might argue that in *The Country Girl* Odets shows three characters in a determined effort to make marriage, which is a *social* institution, a "home." In addition, the playwright takes the audience backstage and reveals the economic instability of the acting profession. Nevertheless, one cannot help but feel that *The Country Girl* lacks the social extension of, say, *Golden Boy* or *The Big Knife*. . . . For all its limitations, *The Country Girl* can unashamedly assume its place among the better plays of the American drama. And it can do this mainly on the strength of its character portrayal. . . . Indeed, it is entirely possible that *The Country Girl* will still be playing in revivals long after more "profound" and "socially conscious" plays of the present moment have been consigned to oblivion. As Odets said on this point: "It may be that limitation is the beginning of wisdom." Which recalls Nietzsche's remark: "One must be narrow to penetrate."

Note

1. Ed. note: *The Country Girl* (New York: Viking, 1951), p. 35. Page numbers for quotes are from this edition of *The Country Girl* and are hereinafter cited in the text.

[*The Flowering Peach*]

GABRIEL MILLER

T*he Flowering Peach* opens on a note of negation: Noah's first word is "No!" In the midst of a dream, he is responding to the revelation that God will destroy the world. His first speech is composed of a series of nos, repeated until his wife manages to rouse him. The earth is suffering from a heat wave; the drought motif recalls at once *Rocket to the Moon* and *Clash by Night,* but the world of this play is on the verge of actual destruction, and the rain that is to come will eradicate rather than revive it. Clearly this theme of destruction was intended as an allusion to the dropping of the atomic bomb, the Flood being an entirely appropriate image for what had happened in Odets's world a few years earlier.

Revealing to Esther that God told him that "the earth is corrupt and filled with evil and greed,"[1] Noah remarks that his "soul is sick," a phrase he will repeat throughout the play. Noah, one of Odets's idealists, is sick with despair, appalled by man's transgressions and God's judgment. He even cautions God with comic earnestness later in scene 1: "You're talking a total destruction of the whole world an' this is something terrible" (p. 11). Unsure of his ability to carry out God's commandment—"I'm too old, everybody should laugh in my face! I ain't got the gizzard for it" (p. 11)—he is convinced by an offstage roll of thunder. Odets thus humanizes Noah, making him a rather cranky and often drunken character.

The motifs of negation and destruction in the opening scene are balanced, as usual in Odets's work, with images of beauty and the ideal. After Noah's cries of no and his hesitant speech with Esther about the ark, he hears music, the offstage signal for God's presence, and he moves away from his wife to talk to God. This association of music with the deity makes it a somewhat more complex symbol than it is elsewhere in Odets's work. His God supplies for Noah the Odetsian ideal, the measure of all things, wherein Noah reposes complete faith. But as the philosophic argument of the play will demonstrate, a God who is willing to destroy the world is clearly an ideal to be questioned. By the end of the play, Noah must revise both his opinion of man and his relationship to his God.

Originally published as "The Final Testament" in *Clifford Odets* (New York: Continuum, 1989). © 1989 by Gabriel Miller. Reprinted by permission of the Continuum Publishing Co.

Two other concepts are introduced in scene 2 as images of the ideal. One is *Shabbos,* the Jewish Sabbath, the day of the week sanctified by God, designated as a day of rest and prayer. Noah's family gathers together for the Sabbath meal as Noah tells them of his vision. When this revelation provokes argument among the sons, Noah quiets them by reminding them that it is the Sabbath. The very notion of this ritual day is at odds with the sins of man, which have provoked the Flood: man is to be destroyed because he has strayed from the ideals that the Sabbath represents. Shortly after Noah exclaims, "Shabbos is comin'. . . . quiet in the house" (p. 19), the stage directions read, "The sky is aflame and colors the room." God manifests himself in these colors, as he will at the end of the play in the rainbow, sanctifying the day. Then suddenly appears the Gitka (an animal invented by Odets), which the rest of the family thinks is a mouse, but which Noah recognizes as an emissary from God. It begins to sing "a worldless, sad, and delicate song," and with the song all the animals appear outside Noah's house, standing peacefully in readiness to board the ark. Now everyone understands that Noah has, indeed, been touched by God, and the scene concludes with Noah intoning "the traditional words over the candles." In this fusion of images the first two scenes of *The Flowering Peach* provide one of Odets's most beautiful compositions, a moving evocation of the connection between music and holiness as a counterpoint to the more violent action to follow. At the second scene's end, only Japheth, who will rebel against God's dictum, stands outside of the family group.

These scenes are also effective in contrasting the divine ideal with earthly reality. Odets juxtaposes Noah with his wife Esther, who, like earlier Odets heroines, acts as a foil to her husband's otherworldly preoccupations. Esther deals in the here and now, the practical matters of caring for a house and children. When Noah is involved in his visitation from God, Esther can only interpret his strange manner as a drunken stupor and recommend that he eat breakfast. When Noah then tells her about the Flood, Esther simply warns him to stop talking nonsense and do something useful, like killing the mice in the house. Shortly afterward, she asks Noah, "Answer me a question, a *realism*—why should we be saved?" and Noah responds, "This is not a 'realism'! God's ready to destroy the whole world, so she wants a 'realism'!" (p. 8). Esther's characteristic insistence on realism thus establishes the contrary mode needed to offset and intensify Noah's final words, "I'll tell you a mystery." In part, the play's dramatic tension hinges on the seemingly antithetical nature of these two perspectives.

Noah's chief antagonist in the play is not his wife, however, but his youngest son, Japheth. Noah and Japheth are, in fact, much alike, as Odets emphasizes in a stage direction, describing them as "two outcasts in the more competent and fluent world" (p. 13). Rachel, whom Japheth will eventually marry, says to him, "You're just like your father," while Shem, the oldest son, rightly calls both his father and his brother "fanatics," for both are wholly devoted to their beliefs.

However alike in temperament, these familial antagonists support opposing spiritual concepts, and their essential differences must be clearly recognized if the play's resolution is to achieve the resonance that Odets intended. Japheth believes in man, not God. His faith, unlike his father's, lies not in an idealized future, but in one in which man might reach beyond himself to build a better world, though still not a perfect one. His man-centered philosophy is most vividly expressed in his response to Rachel's question, "What do you believe in?": "Those roads down there! The patterns they make! They're not cobwebs, those roads, the work of a foolish spider, to be brushed away by a peevish boy! Those roads were made by men, men crazy not to be alone or apart! Men, crazy to reach other! Well, they won't now" (pp. 49–50). Japheth can be described as reality's extremist, while his father is a champion of the ideal. Allying himself with God and the associated motifs of music and Shabbos, Noah demands that his world conform to a standard of piety that is far beyond the potentially real. Just as he refuses to accommodate man's imperfect nature in his vision of a virginal future, so Japheth seems unable to accept any idea larger than man himself. Both have much to learn, and both, Odets makes clear, need to change.

Japheth's protest against his father's righteous God, then, creates a serious rift between them. In scene 2 when Noah tells his family of God's plan, Japheth exclaims, "Someone, it seems to me, would have to protest such an avenging, destructive God!" (p. 19), and this is not far removed from Noah's own initial reaction, "You're talking destruction of the whole world an' this is something terrible—!" Noah, of course, has reluctantly acquiesced, but Japheth will not accept such a God and so must oppose his father. For Noah, Japheth's refusal to obey God means that he is a bad son: at one point he shouts, "Disrespect to a father is disrespect to God!" This equation thus draws the larger implication of their dispute, placing it in the context of archetypal father-son conflict.

Declaring that he cannot live with God's edict, Japheth resolves to die with the rest of mankind. The crisis resulting from this decision changes Japheth, who is at first portrayed as a diffident, stuttering boy, intimidated by his two older brothers and in awe of his father. But his determination to defy God's catastrophic judgment affects him deeply, and in scene 3 Japheth seems physically transformed, displaying a new poise: Odets's stage directions read, "This son is no longer a boy. There is a responsible and mature air about him" (p. 25).

The disagreement between these familiar antagonists begins on a comic note in this scene as father and son argue about the correct pronunciation of "tiger," Noah insisting on "teeger." However, debate soon turns more serious as Japheth asserts the need for a rudder for the ark, whereas Noah contends that this is unnecessary, that God will guide the ark. This dispute will persist throughout much of the play. Noah also expresses anger at Japheth's unmarried state, because the new world will require population, but Japheth remains unimpressed with this reasoning: "And what about the bushels of babies who will die in the flood? Since you bring it up . . . is this vengeful God the very God I was taught to love?" (p. 29). Disgusted, he leaves at the end of the scene but returns in scene 4 to help finish building the ark "for the family, not for God" (p. 33). In fact, it is Japheth who does most of the work on the ark, for the rest of the family lacks the necessary skills. The debate over Japheth's decision continues, but he remains unmoved. This father-son struggle comes to an abrupt and rather anticlimactic end in scene 5, which concludes the first half of the play. As the rain starts to fall and the family must board the ark, Japheth still insists on staying behind, when a suddenly rejuvenated Noah strikes Japheth, knocking him unconscious. He is carried aboard.

Noah's transformation has occurred at the end of scene 4. Again he is asleep, and God's visitation is announced by the singing of a bird. When Noah awakens, he has become a younger man: "His eyes are eagle-bright, his reddish hair shows only one streak of gray, and his beard is smaller but glowingly alive!" (p. 42). The father's reinvigoration neatly complements his son's equally dramatic maturation in the earlier scene, for Noah must be physically ready to contest with Japheth in the second half of the play, during which God will remain absent until the final moments. The play's focal conflict is thus refined to the point of father-son debate for the remainder of the action.

The two continuing conflicts that provide the terms of this doctrinal debate are the argument over the rudder and the problem of Japheth's marriage. The question of building a rudder was introduced in scene 3, Noah insisting that, "The good Lord steers the ark, not us" (p. 26), while Japheth claimed that man must guide his own destiny. This argument is resolved in scene 7 when, after hitting a floating house, the ark begins to sink. The family begs Japheth to repair the ark, but he replies with retaliatory irony that all is in God's hands. Noah, finally, yields, remarking that Japheth will use his own judgment, to which Japheth replies, "To use my own judgment, Poppa, I'd have to trust myself." Noah's poignant response, "*Why* don't you trust yourself?" (p. 73) then decides the issue, conceding that man's own efforts may be required to ensure his survival when no divine rescue is at hand.

The opposition of father and son is quickly reanimated, however, over the problem of Japheth's marriage choice. Noah hopes that Japheth will marry Goldie, a woman who saved the young man earlier in the play and who has been invited to join the family on the ark. But Japheth loves Rachel, the estranged wife of his brother Ham, while Ham has fallen in love with Goldie. All the young people want to make the exchange. Noah, however, refuses to sanction this trading of partners, as an offense against God, and he claims ancient authority: "It stands in the books for a thousand years." Esther, ever the practical foil to her husband's fanatical orthodoxy, pleads with him to allow it "for the sake of happiness in the world." Noah's reply is typical: "That's foolish, Tuchter! First place, he won't permit such marriages, the God I know. And secondly, He won't let nothing happen to you, the God I know" (p. 79). Esther's subsequent death at last teaches this zealot that perhaps he doesn't know God anymore, and so he relents: "Jaaphieee! I have trouble. Sonny, help me. I'm in trouble. Children, the whole night is ahead to give thanks to Heaven. Go better now every husband should kiss each wife, as Mother wanted. And I'll go kiss mine and close her eyes" (p. 81).

The specific points of argument between Noah and Japheth thus exemplify a standard generational conflict as well as the theological-philosophical controversy engendered by their predicament. However, the dramatic tension of their situation derives from the strong emotional bond between them. Like his father, Japheth cries out in his sleep to God. When Noah is in trouble, at the outset of the play, it is Japheth he asks for. Later, this "favorite son" begins to question his authority, Noah becomes distressed, and Japheth defends his position by appealing to his father's love: "Because I insist upon a rudder? I can't help it—a rudder is vital to the health of the Ark. Would you want me to lie?" (p. 29). When Esther dies, Noah weeps in Japheth's arms. Rachel points out qualities that she finds in both Noah and Japheth, "love, wrath, gentleness," all positive characteristics. Both father and son are dreamers and idealists, and their spiritual kinship is further underscored by the following exchange:

NOAH: God never said we should steer the ark! Tomorrow first thing you'll take it off!
JAPHETH: And God didn't tell you to invent the hoe and the rake and yet you did!
NOAH: I was a youngster then—what did I know? (p. 68)

Odets indicates that Japheth is right, both about the rudder and about marrying Rachel, but Japheth's position is not allowed to become the decisive one in the ongoing family drama. Clearly both men must temper their views, and the motif of necessary attitudinal change dominates the final two scenes of the play. Odets's implication is that idealism such as Noah's sincere faith may rigidify into a callous piety unless it can be adapted to changing times and novel situations, while rebellious skepticism such as Japheth's may degenerate into a bleak cynicism without some steadying influence of philosophic perspective. At the end of the play Noah elects to live out the rest of his days not with Japheth but with Shem, his capitalist son, because, considered with comic practicality, "It's more comfortable." But Japheth has Noah's blessing—"I pray a beautiful soul shall enter your baby" (p. 84)—for the best hopes for the new generation reside in Japheth and his unborn child.

If the emotional tie between this father and son provides an important human dimension for this modern version of the biblical tale, an equally affective element is supplied in the marital relations each man enjoys with a woman whose personality complements his own. Despite the frequent arguments between Noah and his wife, there is a real tenderness in their dealings with one another. Odets characterizes Esther's gibes at Noah as "harmless," gentle taunts that he has "heard for so many years that he no longer has ears for them" (p. 6). This habit of mockery connects Noah's family to Odets's earlier contemporary Jewish families who also quarrel constantly but take no offense from the exchange of sarcastic remarks. The relationship of Noah and Esther most nearly recalls that of the Gordons in *Paradise Lost,* for both wives display impatience at their husbands' idealism, as well as genuine affection and respect for their principles. After sixty years of marriage, Noah clearly loves his wife, and he even recognizes the rightness of much that she says. His reaction to her death at the end of the play is one of the most poignant moments in all of Odets's work.

Japheth's evolving relationships with Rachel links him further to his father, for this, too, is an authentic love story. As Japheth's confidence in himself grows, so does his capacity for love and his ability to express it. By scene 6 he is able to declare his love for Rachel:

JAPHETH: Rachel, I love you and want to marry you.
RACHEL: I would marry you . . . but your father won't permit it.
JAPHETH: Ham was right—you're changing. Well, I'm changing, too—And my
          father—innocent and stubborn as he is—HE'LL have to change! (p. 59)

Like Japheth, Rachel is at first a youngster lacking in self-confidence. Troubled by her unsuccessful marriage to Ham, she feels unloved by the rest of the family as well. With some encouragement from Esther, however, she eventually responds to Japheth's ardor and asserts her own feelings in agreeing to marry him. Her love will benefit him as well, for Rachel resembles Esther in her admiration for Japheth's idealistic intensity, but she is also practical and realistic. After his declaration of faith in mankind in scene 5, she replies with expedient logic: "If you think people should reach each other . . . the ark is the only place they'll do it now. . . . Japheth, I beg you to think! There is idealism now in just survival!" (p. 50). The echo of Esther's characteristic pragmatism in such exchanges indicates that Rachel's influence will provide the same necessary humanizing balance in Japheth's marriage as can be seen in his parents' relationship. Noah's eventual blessing on their unborn child thus confirms Odets's implication here that man is indeed the measure of things and that the human heart is a surer guide than the law.

This emphasis on human diversity and vitality is elaborated further in Odets's portrayal of Noah's family. Shem and Ham, the other two sons, are types rather than fully delineated characters like Japheth. Ham, as in Obey's play, is presented as a cynic. He is also a drunkard, like his father, but he is not a good husband, and it is not surprising that he can't forge a relationship with the more serious, sensitive, Rachel; instead, Ham is immediately attracted to Goldie, a loose woman. Shem, on the other hand, is the archetypal capitalist. Unlike Morty in *Awake and Sing!* however, Shem is presented as a respectful and obedient son, despite his entrepreneurial zeal. In charge of overseeing his father's business property, he cannot resist moneymaking schemes even in the face of divine judgment. Before the Flood he sells off thirty thousand shekels' worth of land and then hides the money; when Noah learns about it from a tax collector, he is shocked, exclaiming, "Money is unholy dirt on the ark," and Shem can only reply, *"But what am I without my money?!"* (p. 37). Japheth must eventually knock Shem unconscious to get the key to the house where the money is hidden, an act that anticipates Noah's stunning blow to Japheth to get him on the ark.

While on the ark Shem endangers everyone by making and storing manure briquettes to be used and sold as fuel after the Flood. When the manure unbalances the ark, Noah demands that he throw it overboard— "With manure you want to begin a new world?" (p. 64)—while Esther, suggesting that Shem's hoard will benefit the family, defends him. The surface conflict here between individual enterprise and the ideal of community serves the wider purposes of the play's philosophical argument by elaborating Noah's despair over the imperfection of "human beings." The paradoxical duality of physical and spiritual elements is here given its most overt treatment. Man's society, Odets acknowledges, is built in part on a foundation of manure, but his ultimate emphasis falls upon the interdependence of body and spirit, lust and love, the holy and the unholy, for in this manure can grow the flowering peach, the redemptive image that gives the play its title. The discordant variety of life itself, vividly represented in Noah's family, will give rise at last to the new growth that will ensure the future. This acceptance of imperfection within the context of human community, paired with the cautionary emphasis on the grounding of idealism in reality, constitutes Odets's secular gloss on the biblical myth of divine judgment.

The significance of the fruit tree is carefully prepared for during the course of the play. In scene 5, before the family boards the ark, Esther puts on a hat "decorated with fruits, berries, and flowers" (p. 45). As always, fruit is an important symbol in Odets's work, combining allusions to life, growth, sexuality, and nourishment, and Esther's wearing the hat accentuates her importance as a character. Odets obviously sympathizes with her realistic point of view and her desire that love prevail in the relationship between Japheth and Rachel. At the scene's end, as the family hurriedly boards the ark, Esther realizes that she has forgotten her hat and then Noah realizes that he has forgotten the gitka; both are quickly retrieved. The hat and the gitka are thus linked as significant and complementary symbols of the redemptive mission of the ark's passengers.

In scene 8 Odets crystallizes several symbols he has used throughout his career in realizing his most transcendent vision. Noah has sent out the doves in search of dry land. He and Esther have quarreled, and they have not spoken to each other for some time. Esther has been ill, confined to her room, and has not been seen in the play during scene 7 and part of scene 8. When finally she reappears, she asks for the hat; Ham's reaction is that his mother looks "like a queen." Esther requests of Noah, "Marry the children . . . for the sake of happiness in the world," adding that their happiness "is my last promised land" (p. 79). She then complains that the gitka has not sung for a long time. Her final words signal the approach of death: "I'll take the hat to shade my eyes . . Noah, I'll tell you a mystery" (p. 80). Soon afterwards the dove returns with an olive branch in her mouth, the gitka begins to sing a "mourning song," and Esther dies, her hat falling off. In her final scene Esther thus becomes an emblematic figure much like Noah: she has moved from asking a "realism" to telling a "mystery," and in her death the two points of view merge. Further elaborated by the gitka's song and a significant reference to the moon—that Odetsian image of idealized reality—this scene recalls the symbolic richness of *Golden Boy*, *Rocket to the Moon*, and *Clash by Night*. In this significant fusion of music, fruit, and the moon, Esther passes on her vital wisdom to Noah and the family.

The final scene, then, highlights a young peach tree "in profuse and handsome bloom," which is the play's legacy and also Odets's final image. (This symbolic appearance of the flowering tree recalls Strindberg's use of a flowering castle at the end of *A Dream Play*, another work of reconciliation.) Noah can finally bless Japheth's marriage, understanding Esther's vision and recognizing the shortcomings of his own. His final words to God are a request that the world not be destroyed again, indicating that he has learned to trust himself, and the play ends on a note of prophecy, echoing Esther's final words as husband, wife, and Japheth merge: "But what I learned on the trip, dear God, you can't take it away from me. To walk in humility, I learned. And listen, even to *myself* . . . and to speak softly, with the voices of consolation. Yes, I hear You, God—now it's in man's hands to make or destroy the world—I'll tell you a mystery" (p. 85).

It is oddly fitting that *The Flowering Peach* turned out to be Odets's last play, for it takes him full circle from his first full-length work, *Awake and Sing!* Both plays focus on a Jewish nuclear family, both balance the comic and the serious, both deal with the conflict of idealized visions with the demands of the real world, and both project images of utopia. In the earlier play, however, the Berger family never achieved harmony or togetherness, and the worlds of Bessie and Jacob remained far apart, not realizable even in the next generation. Odets the young playwright was too angry and idealistic himself to reconcile viewpoints that he saw as irreconcilable. The later Odets is more chastened, more willing to comprehend and appreciate the paradoxes he was unable to face as a younger man. In an interview before the opening of *The Flowering Peach* he said:

I'm not a kid any more, I'm 47. And at this age I began to ask myself, what happened? Do you want to begin all over again? Who are you and where are you? I went through an examination of personal resources while doing this play. From all this came something, I think, that is very affirmative.

When you start out, you have to champion something. Every artist begins as if he were the first one painting, every composer as if there were no Beethoven. But if you still feel that way after ten or fifteen years, you're nuts. No young writer is broad. I couldn't have written "The Flowering Peach" twenty years ago. As you grow older, you mature. The danger is that in broadening, as you mature, you may dilute your art. A growing writer always walks that tightrope.[2]

In *The Flowering Peach,* accordingly, the basic unsympathetic Bessie has become the more understanding and motherly Esther. Jacob, the idealist who felt that he must kill himself to effect his vision, has become Noah, who is able to survive a cataclysm and learn from it. The Berger children, who ran away from their problems, have become Noah's children, who are able to overcome adversity and grow. Jacob's vision of "O Paradiso" could only remain in his head; ultimately it was only a song on a record that Bessie would break. The Berger house remained one "without an orange." In Odets's final play, however, the visions of paradise have become a possibility, because man has learned to understand his nature and trust himself. In such a world Moe Axelrod's dream, "Ever see oranges grow? . . . one summer I laid under a tree and let them fall right in my mouth,"[3] can become a reality. The peach tree can grow; indeed, it flowers.

Notes

1. Clifford Odets, *The Flowering Peach* (New York: Dramatists Play Service, 1954), p. 7. All references to the play are to this edition and are cited in the text.
2. Herbert Mitgang, "Odets Goes to Genesis," *New York Times,* 26 December 1954, II, p. 1.
3. Clifford Odets, *Awake and Sing!* in *Six Plays of Clifford Odets* (New York: Grove Press, 1974), p. 50.

Clifford's Children:
or It's a Wise Playwright
Who Knows His Own Father

GERALD WEALES

The charting of influences is, at best, a chancy endeavor.

When *Awake and Sing!* opened in New York on 19 February 1935, at least three reviewers—John Mason Brown in the *Evening Post,* Gilbert W. Gabriel in the *American,* and Robert Garland in the *World-Telegram*—compared Clifford Odets's play to *Spring Song,* the Bella and Sam Spewack play that ran briefly a few months earlier. Although the Spewacks' Mrs. Solomon tries to get another character to eat some fruit—as Clara Gordon would in *Paradise Lost* late in 1935—there is very little similarity between the work of Odets and that of the Spewacks. *Spring Song,* like *Awake,* is about a Jewish family and there is an unmarried, pregnant daughter, but the two plays are different in tone, in texture, and in ideational and aesthetic intention. The evocation of the Spewacks' play is an old reviewer's trick. Under the pressure of a deadline, it is convenient to reach for a handle, a work that has a real or imagined likeness to the play under discussion. Such a practice helps a reviewer who has nothing to say, but it also helps one with specific points to make. *Spring Song,* having just passed this way, might provide a familiar starting point for a critical trip across unfamiliar ground. Take the Robert Garland review, for instance. As the second head indicates, he has decided that *Awake and Sing!* is a tragicomedy, and he finds it convenient to say so by comparing it not only to "much that was moving" in *Spring Song* but to "much that was mirthful" in Rose Franken's *Another Language,* a highly successful family play from a few seasons earlier. Reviewers on the weeklies and the monthlies, with more time on their hands, can be more judicious or more imaginative in their comparisons. Thus, Edith J. R. Isaacs in *Theatre Arts* finds *Awake* very like Louis Bromfield's *Times Have Changed,* and Joseph Wood Krutch in *The Nation* guesses that Odets had "learned something of his manner from Hemingway and the other members of the hard-boiled school."

Delivered 21 November 1985 at the University of Wisconsin-Madison, part of "The Odets Symposium," a three-day celebration of the 50th anniversary of *Awake and Sing!* This talk was also published in *Studies in American Drama 1945–Present* 1987, no. 2. Reprinted by permission of Gerald Weales.

The coupling of Odets with Chekhov and Sean O'Casey is a rather more complicated operation. John Mason Brown, who had written *The Modern Theatre in Revolt* back in 1929, might have been expected to find his own way to Chekov (one of the subheads in his review was "Chekhov in the Bronx"), and even John Anderson in the *Evening Journal* could have come to the Chekhov comparison on his own. Still, the Group Theatre had laid the groundwork for seeing Odets in terms of the earlier playwrights. In a pre-opening interview with Morris Carnovsky, the Brooklyn *Eagle* indicated that some members of the Group welcomed *Awake and Sing!* as "the nearest thing to Tchekov" and that others called Odets the "Sean O'Casey of America." Harold Clurman was still making the O'Casey comparison in a piece in the *Herald Tribune* about a month after *Awake* opened, but it was the Chekhov connection that persisted. In fact, it became a bone of contention as a result of a tactical error on the Group's part. Shortly before the opening of *Paradise Lost* on 9 December 1935, a letter from Odets explaining the play was sent to the New York reviewers. As a group, they may have been in need of instruction, but they were not about to accept it from a young playwright—"the theatre's newest wonder boy," as Robert Cole called him in the *Daily Mirror*. The reviews were not as bad as Harold Clurman's account in *The Fervent Years* suggests, but they were bad enough, and most of the reviewers, whether they liked the play or not, could not refrain from picking up and picking on Odets's use of Chekhov as a fellow rejector of theatrical conventions. "Excuse us for not showing the gun in the first act, because it will later be used in the second." The day after the reviews appeared, Harold Clurman turned up in the "So This Is Broadway" column in the *World-Telegram*, trying to mend fences by explaining that the Group did not mean that Odets was as good as Chekhov, only that he might usefully be compared to the Russian playwright, and Odets was found back-pedaling in the same paper a few days later. In a letter to Robert Garland, Odets explained that he was citing Chekhov as an historical example, not as an influence on him. "You have my word for it that I intend to read 'The Cherry Orchard' tonight for the first time in my life." At this distance there is something touching about Odets's attempt to counter the bumptiousness of his first letter with a plea of ignorance.

The Chekhov fiasco apparently continued to rankle Clurman, for in *The Fervent Years,* in a passage that has nothing to do with Odets, he mentions unidentified Chekhovian "parallels and analogies that are academic, empty, and useless." I know the feeling. Years ago, when I was briefly a novelist, I created a character whom I thought was a perfect model of a modern academic achiever; he had written an article called "An Image in Hegel and Bret Harte: An Intuitive Borrowing." Yet, as recently as 1 November 1985, I conjured Oliver Goldsmith to make a point in my *Commonweal* review of the new Lily Tomlin / Jane Wagner play. Clurman is no purer on this matter. Read through *Lies Like Truth* and *The Naked Image* and you will find that

Clurman, who has so many sensible things to say about so many plays, is a relentless analogizer. A single example: To get into his review of *Death of a Salesman,* he cites plays by Arthur Richman, J. P. McEvoy, Elmer Rice, George Kelly, and two by Clifford Odets.

I did not begin this speech with an account of reviewers' strained comparisons and an abortive publicity device (Clurman says it was Helen Deutsch, the Group's publicity representative, who asked Odets to write the infamous letter) to discommend the practice of searching out literary and theatrical influences. I did it to emphasize the pitfalls. Parallels can be dangerous, particularly when theatrical giants are used to smother infant playwrights in their cradles. Yet, they can also be useful as the Chekhov analogy has been on occasion. In his review of *Three Plays,* months before the *Paradise Lost* imbroglio, Stark Young, who tended to find Odets vulgar, could see a likeness to his beloved Chekhov in Odets's use of "the seemingly irrelevant. Speech and emotion follow one on another without any surface connection." Of course, Odets may have picked up that method not from Chekhov but from conversations around the kitchen table in the Bronx apartment in which he grew up. A more verifiable influence on Odets, one not mentioned in the early reviews of his plays, is John Howard Lawson's *Success Story.* Odets, not yet a playwright, understudied Luther Adler in the lead when the Group produced the play in 1932. Almost thirty years later, he recalled that the play had been "a very decisive influence on me, by showing me the poetry that was inherent in the chaff of the street."

This paper has begun to sound like "Clifford's Parents" rather than "Clifford's Children." Let me turn now to my proposed subject with the warning that influences from Odets are even more tenuous than influences on him. "In the thirties," John Gassner once wrote, "scores of playwrights endeavored to write like Clifford Odets." Joe Rasmussen, a character in John O'Hara's *The Champagne Pool,* says, "When I was at Harvard I wrote a play that was such a steal from *Awake and Sing!* that I got embarrassed and called it a parody," and then adds, "But it wasn't Odets, it was pure Rasmussen, which is crap. Crap, crap, crap." Those of us who had to read all those pseudo-Beckett, pseudo-Pinter, pseudo-Albee plays a few years ago (what is it today, pseudo-Shepard?) understand what was pushing Rasmussen. Since we are not O'Hara characters, driven by Rasmussen's breast-beating preachiness, we can even admit that imitations to the point of parody do not have to be crap. Yet, whether Odets imitations are good or bad, whether they come from student dramatists borrowing someone else's shoes to take their first steps on stage, activist writers who see *Waiting for Lefty* as a model, not an inspiration, or commercial hopefuls who confuse the lowercase-*g* group with the capital-*g* Group, they are not what I think of when I ponder the possible influence of Odets on American theatre.

In the speech that I quoted earlier, John Gassner said, "In the final sense, creativity is a public act, and creation in a vacuum is a sheer impossibility." He was emphasizing that works in any period share the same artistic context and that even the strongest writers cannot escape "a style, a technique, an attitude, and a subject matter" prevalent in their time. Gassner's is a sensible if obvious point, and I would like to make an equally platitudinous one by converting his horizontal view of the creative context to a vertical one. "Coletti to Driscoll to Berger," Ralph says at the end of *Awake and Sing!*, "—that's how we work." Ibsen to Chekhov to Odets—that's how we work. And beyond Odets? Several playwrights come to mind, men and women who have strong artistic personalities of their own but who seem to have inherited something from Odets. Or to have dipped at some of the same places into the stream of theatrical history.

Influences, then, or parallels. Before I trot them out, however, let me indicate what I find most characteristic in Odets. His settings, first of all. The families in his early plays, and—after the disintegration promised in *Paradise Lost*—the specialized milieux in which his typically homeless characters find some sense of place, however tentative, however dangerous: the boxing world of *Golden Boy,* Hollywood in *The Big Knife,* the theatre of *The Country Girl.* The special quality of these settings is not that they are realistic, but that they are tangible worlds, rich in detail—shifting solid ground on which Odets's characters can act out the minimal plots he gives them. The plays are relentlessly urban. Even the ark in *The Flowering Peach* seems not to be floating on a Biblical deluge but to have been launched into the East River, perhaps at Hunts Point, which Bessie Berger invoked in her description of Polly Moran's nose. The characters are city folks, familiar types, for Odets recognized, as most good playwrights do, that personality begins in stereotype and, if the dramatist is skilled enough or lucky enough, escapes into complexity.

Second, the language. These city folk have recognizable voices. Much has been made of the verisimilitude in Odets's dialogue, and *verisimilitude* is the exact word. The lines his characters use are not a re-creation of everyday speech; they have the appearance of actuality. There are theatrical antecedents, not only in plays like *Success Story* but in the wisecrack, the indigenous language of American farce. Still, the happy surprise with which the first audiences greeted Odets came from their sense that Joe and Edna, Sid and Florrie sounded like people down the block. The rhythm is urban—New York, Bronx, Jewish—and the locutions and some of the expressions are domesticated imports from the *shtetl.* The vocabulary is ordinary, but it is enriched with pop-culture allusions and grandiose variations on the kind of metaphor that comes easily to the mouths of everyone: she's a dog; he drinks like a fish. Odets transformed the speech he heard around him, went for "the poetry" in it as his comment on his debt to Lawson indicates. He may have avoided the conventional literary language of the American stage, but his lines are as studied, as artificial as those of Maxwell Anderson. When admirers of Odets recall lines now they think of them not as accurate reports from the street; they repeat them for their flamboyance. When I was working on my Odets book up at Yaddo, Alfred Kazin, who had paid his homage to the playwright in *Starting Out In the Thirties,* would sometimes lift a glass of water, smile at me in complicity and, quoting from *Rocket to the Moon,* say "Municipal champagne . . . ah-cha-cha!"

Third, the ideology. I do not mean the specific politics of the early plays, the Communism of *Waiting for Lefty* and *Till the Day I Die,* the implied revolution of *Awake and Sing!* and *Paradise Lost.* I am thinking of the mandatory optimism of 1930s leftism in general, of the Group Theatre in particular. The sense of human and social possibility that prevailed in the Group was so strong that it persuaded Paul Green to alter the tragic ending of *The House of Connelly* and led the usually pessimistic Maxwell Anderson to the upbeat ending of *Night over Taos.* It infected Clifford Odets, and he carried the virus for the rest of his life. His plays are full of corruption, loss, decay (think of *Paradise Lost*), but the man who could alter the title and the substance of his first play from *I Got the Blues* to *Awake and Sing!* was not about to succumb to negation. On stage, at least. The redemptive final moments of his plays sometimes seem gratuitous, ideational overlay on works in which the plots and images seem to be going in another direction. Even in plays like *Golden Boys* and *The Big Knife* in which the protagonists must die, the death is to be seen as "a final act of faith." So Hank says of Charlie's suicide at the end of *The Big Knife.* Our personal lives are at the mercy of the social and economic forces around us, Odets keeps saying in his plays, but alter the circumstances and you tame the forces. "I want the whole city to hear it—fresh blood, arms. We got 'em. We're glad we're living."

This brief description of Odets's work hardly exhausts the elements that are characteristic of his plays, but they will serve as an introduction to the later dramatists that I want to consider. Tennessee Williams and Arthur Miller, for starters. Although Odets is only a few years older than Williams and Miller, they belong to the next generation of American playwright. The most important thing they inherited from the Group Theatre was Elia Kazan. The brisk hero of Odets's *Night Music* turned director before the Group dissolved and went on to stage *A Streetcar Named Desire, Camino Real, Cat on a Hot Tin Roof, Sweet Bird of Youth, All My Sons, Death of a Salesman* and—after the fall had been forgiven—*After the Fall.* What Miller and Williams—particularly Williams—might have got from Odets is a great deal less certain.

There is an odd paragraph in John Mason Brown's review of *A Streetcar Named Desire* in which he seems to be called upon to discuss Williams in terms of Odets although he finds little similarity between the two playwrights except that both "have read Chekhov with profit and affection." Brown's juxtaposition of Odets and Williams has less to tell us about *Streetcar* than it does about the way the play was received in 1947—as a drama about the destruction of the old South. Kazan's Director's Notes suggest that this reading of the play was a central element in his production. For any

Williams-Odets parallels, it is probably more sensible to go to the pre-*Streetcar* Williams. After all, Williams had Group Theatre connections of his own. In 1939, four one-act plays of his earned him a Group award, an event that brought him to New York, to John Gassner's drama class, to Audrey Wood, eventually to Broadway. No one seems very sure about which Williams one-acters were in that prize-winning package, but there is certainly a 1930s sound, if not necessarily an Odetsian sound, to plays like *The Long Goodbye* and *Moony's Kid Don't Cry.* Moony, like Hennie and Ralph, is caught in a domestic trap, made worse by his poverty, and he dreams of escape to the "North woods." It is a paradisal dream like those in *Awake and Sing!,* as amorphous as the Boston plane when it first calls to Ralph, but Moony has no last act in which he can learn how to say, "We're glad we're living." Those first plays were grouped under the title *American Blues* and there was small likelihood of any awake-and-singing name change.

Although the early Williams one-acters are still produced, particularly on campuses, they are so fragile that they cannot bear much scrutiny. For an Odets comparison, it is better to turn to Williams' only urban family play, *The Glass Menagerie.* I am going to ignore Tom as narrator, which is unfair to Williams' play since it has a present action (remembering) as well as a past one. For my purposes, it is the past action that is important—the story of the Wingfields trapped in their St. Louis apartment. It is the 1930s and middle-class Americans were, as Tom so grandiloquently puts it, "Having their fingers pressed forcibly down on the fiery Braille alphabet of a dissolving economy." Or, as Jacob says in *Awake and Sing!,* "Economics comes down like a ton of coal on the head." The narrative fanciness of Tom, the poet in the making, is not characteristic of Williams's stage language. The real eloquence in *The Glass Menagerie* lies in Amanda's speeches, and although their rhythm is very different from those of Odets's characters, they reflect a similar artistic strategy, an imaginative transformation of Southern speech like Odets's reworking of the Bronx idiom. Tom, like Ralph, is in a dead-end job, dreaming of escape. When Amanda says, "Most young men find adventure in their careers," Tom answers, "Then most young men are not employed in a warehouse." Just behind their exchange, I can hear Ralph's "I don't know. . . . Every other day to sit around with the blues and mud in your mouth." At the end of the play, although "the world is lit by lightning," there is no redemptive "thunderbolt" for Tom as there is for Ralph. Tom takes Hennie's way out, cuts and runs, but unlike Hennie, who dumps husband, wife, and the Bronx, he carries his past with him. His is an incomplete escape.

Tom inherits his susceptibility to the past. His mother spends much of her time remembering or inventing her jonquil-filled youth along the Delta. On the surface, Amanda with her chatter about gentlemen callers seems very far removed from Bessie Berger, but the two women have much in common. Both have been infected by the American dream. "Ralph should only be a success like you, Morty," says Bessie. "I should only live to see the day when he rides up to the door in a big car with a chauffeur and a radio." "Try and you will SUCCEED!" Amanda insists. "Why, you—you're just *full* of natural endowments!" Yet, neither of them quite believes her own words. Survival, not success, is the primary goal of the Berger and Wingfield households; both women know that—in Bessie's phrase—"Talk from now to next year— this is life in America." Amanda may know it better than Bessie does since she hustles for pennies in the marketplace—peddling magazine subscriptions, demonstrating some unnamed product in a department store—while Bessie stays at home, a general coordinating the Berger battle against poverty. The ineffectual Myron, who does at least work three days a week, is not much more useful in the struggle than the missing Mr. Wingfield, the "telephone man who fell in love with long distance." Both women have a strong sense of what it has cost them to hold their families together. "Ralphie, I worked too hard all my years to be treated like dirt," Bessie complains, and Amanda says with tears in her voice, "My devotion has made me a witch." Both women know how to use guilt as a weapon. Consider the opening supper scene in *Awake and Sing!*, in which Bessie shuts Ralph up by threatening to leave the table ("I can't take a bite in my mouth no more"), and the confrontation scene in *The Glass Menagerie* in which Amanda chides her daughter over her failure in typing class, wearing, as Laura says, "that awful suffering look on your face, like the picture of Jesus' mother in the museum!" Bessie Berger, Amanda Wingfield—two tough women, so full of vitality that they walk off with their respective plays, almost making us forget that they are chock full of false values. Tennessee Williams may have found his Amanda at home, in his mother, but I find her in *Awake and Sing!*

The connection between Odets and Arthur Miller is more obvious. Miller is overtly political, as Odets is. The works of both men suggest that deception and betrayal are inevitable products of business. Sam Katz cheats his own partner in *Paradise Lost* and proposes that they save themselves by burning the factory for the insurance money. Joe Keller ships cracked engine-heads in *All My Sons* and manages to let his partner take the blame. Yet, not confusing sin with sinner, the playwrights manage to make their tainted small businessmen sympathetic." Should we / Burst into tears when we see the bedbugs move out?" asks Bertolt Brecht in "Letter to the Playwright Odets," the poem that was his response to *Paradise Lost*. The play answers yes. Sam Katz may never be more than pathetic—the failed businessman as impotent husband—but Leo Gordon is attractive in his bumbling way, and he is the character who gets the visionary curtain speech. Miller may sentence Joe Keller to death in *All My Sons,* but by the end of the play the audience, like Joe's son Chris, is moved by a man self-destroyed by his attachment to his society's skewered sense of values. Both dramatists question the American success ethic—Odets in *Golden Boy*, Miller in *Death of a Salesman*—and suggest that the plays' protagonists are the willing victims of their society. Joe Bonaparte becomes a boxer on the assumption that success in America grows out of violence and power. Willy Loman becomes a salesman because he believes "that a man can end with diamonds here on the basis of being liked!" Both characters sacrifice their deeper sense of self to a borrowed image. "Hey, Joe, you sounda like crazy!" says Mr. Bonaparte. "You no gotta nature for fight. You're musician." Biff, at Willy's grave, says, "there's more of him in that front stoop than in all the sales he ever made," and Charley agrees, "He was a happy man with a batch of cement."

Odets and Miller may share a diagnosis of their society's ills, but they differ when it comes to marrying theme to dramatic structure. The tragic— or, at least, fatal—endings of the early Miller plays leave little room for the positive upturn that Odets's ritual optimism dictates. Still, Elizabeth's "He have his goodness now. God forbid I take it from him!" at the end of *The Crucible* suggests Hank's benediction over Charlie in *The Big Knife* and Mr. Bonaparte's "we bring-a him home" at the end of *Golden Boy*. It is interesting that the two playwrights meet when external pressures force Miller into an uncharacteristic romantic affirmation, Odets into a temporary withdrawal from his visionary coda. Miller does not find his way to redemptive conclusions for his plays until works like *After the Fall* and *Incident at Vichy,* and he only gets there by letting his characters succumb to the idea that we are all murderers, a concept that does not mix with the belief in the perfectability of society which permeates the Odets plays even after he has turned his back on specific political solutions.

If Odets and Miller pull away from one another when it comes to ways of packaging their doubts about American society, they do their pulling in very similar settings. In most of their plays they use domestic situations— parent-child conflicts, sibling rivalry, sexual triangles—and Miller's families, like those of Odets, are urban and Jewish, implicitly at least. George Ross called his essay on the Yiddish translation of Miller's play, "*Death of a Salesman* in the Original." John Gassner once credited the two playwrights with "discovering a source of colloquial poetry in New York." The "poetry" that Miller found is that of fitting speeches to characters and to the dramatic moment: it is not the kind of plummy rhetoric Odets uses. There are Miller lines that suggest a watered-down Odets: "He's a man way out there in the blue, riding on a smile and a shoeshine. And when they start not smiling back—that's an earthquake." Or, on the schmaltzy side: "He's only a little boat looking for a harbor." Linda could hardly be expected to see what is ludicrous in her little-boat cliché, but not even Charley, the kidder, manages to give his speeches the double edge that Moe in *Awake and Sing!* brings to a line like "The only thing'll change is my underwear." The wisecrack as social statement. Miller's characters do not play with their words as Odets's do—at least not until Gregory Solomon comes along in *The Price.* Joe Keller and Willy Loman make jokes like the essentially earnest men they are. Miller's language, then, both is and is not like Odets's. Gassner's remark about "colloquial poetry" appears in an essay that gave him no opportunity to ask whether Miller made his "discovery" through Odets as Odets did through Lawson.

Miller and Williams are the obvious playwrights of their theatrical generation to compare with Odets, but I would like to pause for a sentence or two to consider a very unlikely candidate, Carson McCullers. After all, Harold Clurman, who was Odets's first and perhaps most perceptive director, staged *The Member of the Wedding* when it came to Broadway in the 1950s. Clurman was not a one-tune director—he did Anouilh's *Mademoiselle Colombe,* which is hardly Odetsian—but I find family connections between *The Member of the Wedding* and *Awake and Sing!*. The marvelous texture of McCullers's play grows out of conversations that Frankie, John Henry, and Berenice Sadie Brown have around the kitchen table. Apparently aimless talk, it might be described by Stark Young's phrase for what Odets shared with Chekhov—"the seemingly irrelevant." Chekhov does make a token appearance in Clurman's essay in *Lies Like Truth* on the staging of *The Member of the Wedding.* Except at the end of the play, when one violent offstage event piles on top of another, not much seems to be going on in *Member,* but, as Clurman says, "Without action, it would not *play.*" He goes on to spell out what he "sensed" and presumably conveyed to the performers: "The action springs from the twelve-year-old Frankie Addams' desire to get out of herself, to *become connected* or identified with a world larger than that which confines her to the 'ugly old kitchen' which is her world." Frankie Addams? Why that's Ralphie Berger. Of course "the irony of fate" that introduces Frankie to her new friend Mary "in front of the lipstick and cosmetics counter at Woolworth's" is not exactly the "thunderbolt" that awakens Ralph. Still maturation plays come in all sizes—take *Henry IV, Part II,* for example—and *Awake and Sing!* is not only about new political awareness. Like *The Member of the Wedding,* it is about growing up. Frankie Addams is Ralph Berger, but she is also Tom Wingfield, and McCullers did write a first draft of her play in Tennessee Williams's house on Nantucket while he sat on the other side of the dining room table working at *Summer and Smoke.* This influence tracking is a slippery business.

Although Miller, Williams, and McCullers are identified with postwar theatre, they are almost contemporaries of Odets. Let me move now to the end of the 1950s, to a playwright who really belongs to another generation. The first meetings of the Group Theatre took place in the year Lorraine Hansberry was born, and Clifford Odets's last play, *The Flowering Peach,* was produced four years before her first one—*A Raisin in the Sun*—reached Broadway. By introducing Hansberry into this theatrical olio I have been serving up, I am forced to consider the phenomenon of black drama which was relatively unknown—to white audiences at least—when *Raisin* was produced in 1959; now it is an important element in American mainstream theatre. There are obvious similarities between the political climate of the 1930s and the Civil Rights movement of the 1950s and 1960s. The former may have been somewhat more amorphous than the latter, but the two historical moments share the great sense of possibility, the assumption that societal (racial) wrongs can be righted through direct action. Odets, the representative playwright of the 1930s, might be expected to have found new relevance as black theatre followed black politics onto the main stage. "Clifford rather identified with the Negro movement today as he did with the proletarian movement in the '30's," William Gibson said in a *New York Times* interview just before the musical version of *Golden Boy* opened on Broadway. Odets died before the musical went into production, and his book was rewritten by Gibson. Sammy Davis, who played Joe, told Gibson to "Write colored," but he either could not or did not, and the resulting show, in Gibson's book and in the Charles Strouse-Lee Adams songs, is neither black nor Odets.

If there are Odetsian elements in the black theatre movement, we will have to look elsewhere. The last line of the Langston Hughes poem about "a dream deferred" that gave Hansberry her title is *"Or does it explode?"* It did in the 1960s, and part of the fallout can be seen in plays like those by LeRoi Jones, Ed Bullins, Ben Caldwell, and Ron Milner that formed *A Black Quartet*. There is a mix of realistic and nonrealistic elements in black revolutionary drama, as there is in *Waiting for Lefty,* but the black plays are very different, only recalling Odets's work so far as all agitprops have a generic resemblance. A more interesting parallel may be found in a character like Ed Bullins's *The Fabulous Miss Marie*. Although that queen of party-givers is no Bessie Berger, they share an energy and a vividness which reflect their authors' fondness for them even while the plays they inhabit reject the values by which they try to live. There may be Odetsian echoes in the recurrent black family plays—by Milner, by Leslie Lee, by Charles Fuller—but all the black playwrights, whether they embrace her or disown her, have been influenced by Lorraine Hansberry; so let's get back to her.

So far as I know, Hansberry has never acknowledged the influence of Odets as she has that of Sean O'Casey. "The play was *Juno,* the writer Sean O'Casey—but the melody was one that I had known for a very long while." When Robert Nemiroff organized *To Be Young, Gifted and Black,* he put Hansberry's remarks about the Irish playwright alongside Walter Lee's African-warrior scene from Act Two of *Raisin*. Odets is the American O'Casey, as the Brooklyn *Eagle* told us in 1935, and *A Raisin in the Sun,* whatever its Irish echoes, is insistently American. It was Odets, not O'Casey, who made his way into my review of Hansberry's play in 1959, and looking at *Raisin* again recently, I was struck by the hovering presence of Odets. There is a touch of Arthur Miller, too, since Walter Lee Younger, like Willy Loman, has bought the American success dream, although, more Ralph Berger than Willy, Walter Lee is not destroyed by it. There is no black equivalent of Odets's language in *A Raisin in the Sun*. Hansberry's characters do not go in for flamboyant metaphor, for ethnic idiom writ large; there is no signifying monkey here. The eloquence of the Youngers is a product of function; their lines gain strength from dramatic context. It is in the family setting and in the central action of the play that *A Raisin in the Sun* most resembles *Awake and Sing!* The quarrelling affection of the Youngers establishes them as a family as full of love and tension as the Berger household, although in Hansberry's play it is not just the children who want to escape, but the whole family who needs to get out of the twin traps of their crowded apartment and Chicago's Southside. They almost fail to make it because Walter Lee is tempted by the polite bribe the white homeowners offer to keep them from moving into their new house. In the end, tearfully and painfully, he struggles to a realization and a statement of the Younger family pride. It is not an exultant speech like Ralph's in *Awake and Sing!*, but we know that when Mama says, "He finally come into his manhood today," she is also saying, as Moe did, "I wouldn't trade you for two pitchers and an outfielder." There is a similar movement in Hansberry's *The Sign in Sidney Brustein's Window*, which carries the protagonist from a sense of despair, personal and political, through cleansing tears to the tentative promise of "tomorrow, we shall make something strong of this sorrow."

With a little discreet critical sleight-of-hand I should be able to indicate the Odets elements in the works of Edward Albee and the off-Broadway playwrights of his generation, in the political plays of the 1960s, certainly in what the trend-spotters a few years ago began to call a *return to realism.* I have neither the time nor the inclination to take an Odetsian walk through all of American drama since World War II. I want instead to look at the contemporary theatrical scene and to focus on the uses of language. Twenty or so years ago Robert Brustein would occasionally invoke Odets in his reviews when he wanted to commend a playwright's dialogue. He reported that Saul Bellow's *The Last Analysis* contained "some of the most magnificent rhetoric to be heard on the American stage since Clifford Odets," and that Jack Gelber's *The Connection* "offers promise that the language of 'cool' might soon become a pulsing stage rhetoric similar to Odets' language of the blues." Bellow went back to the novel, and Gelber became increasingly interested in theatrical experiments that had little to do with words. Eloquence did not disappear with them. In 1964, the year that *The Last Analysis* was produced on Broadway, Sam Shepard's first plays were performed in New York, and the next year Ronald Ribman turned up at the American Place Theatre. Shepard and Ribman are two of the most inventive writers, verbally as well as dramatically, that the American theatre has seen. I am an enthusiastic admirer of Shepard's way with an extended monologue and with the surprising images Ribman puts in the mouths of his characters—particularly Parmigian in *Cold Storage*—but for the sake of this meditation on Odets, I prefer to look at one of their younger colleagues—David Mamet.

Mamet has a more sophisticated sense of language then Odets had. There are times when an Odets speech—even one that gives pleasure—seems to belong to the playwright rather than the character. Checking the "Municipal champagne" line that I quoted earlier, I skimmed Frenchy's speeches, thinking it sounded like him, only to find it in Phil Cooper's mouth. When Odets is at his best, the words he puts into his characters' mouths help to define them. Hennie does not speak like Ralph, nor Moe like Jacob, although on a stage which they share with Maxwell Anderson's Mio and Miriamne and S. N. Behrman's Leonie Frothingham, they all sound alike. Despite Odets's sense of the connection between the speaker and the spoken, I can think of only one instance—Marcus Hoff in *The Big Knife*—in which a character is conceived primarily as a pattern of words. Mamet, on the other hand, builds his characters verbally. Think of Teach in *American Buffalo* or Shelly Levene in *Glengarry Glen Ross* and try to imagine them outside their speeches. One can see Teach in terms of his paranoia or as a product of his environment or as an image of the American businessman *in extremis,* but the validity of any of these Teaches is essentially verbal. This is because Mamet does not simply define characters in terms of their language; he assumes that the way people speak affects the way that they act. Thus the young man in *Sexual Perversity in Chicago* is incapable of loving a woman fully because he can only see her in the crudest terms, his idea of sex having been fixed by the way he and his older friend talk about "broads" as a "nice pair of legs," a "Very acceptable old ass," and "beautiful pair of tits."

I seem to be talking about the way Mamet's language is not like Odets's, but listen to Teach:

TEACH: I come into the Riverside to get a cup of *coffee,* right? I sit down at the table Grace and Ruthie.
DON: Yeah.
TEACH: I'm gonna order just a cup of coffee.
DON: Right.
TEACH: So Grace and Ruthie's having breakfast, and they're done. *Plates . . . crusts* of stuff all over . . . So we'll shoot the shit.
DON: Yeah.
TEACH: Talk about the *game . . .*
DON: . . . yeah.
TEACH: . . . so on. Down I sit. "Hi, hi." I take a piece of toast off Grace's plate . . .
DON: . . . uh-huh . . .
TEACH: . . . and she goes "Help yourself." Help myself.
I should help myself to half a piece of toast it's four slices for a quarter. I should have a nickel every time we're over at the game, I pop for coffee . . . cigarettes . . . a *sweet roll,* never say a word.
"Bobby, see who wants what." Huh? A fucking *roast-beef* sandwich. (*To* BOB) Am I right? (*To* DON) Ahh, shit. We're sitting down, how many times do I pick up the check? But (No!) because I never go and made a big *thing* out of it—it's no big thing—and flaunt like "This one's on me"

like some bust-out asshole, but I naturally assume that I'm with friends, and don't forget who's who when someone gets *behind* a half a yard or needs some help with (huh?) some fucking rent, or drops enormous piles of money at the track, or someone's *sick* or something . . .

And then Donny says, "This is what I'm talking about," although it is not at all what he has been talking about, and the marvelously confused Gus Michaels of *Paradise Lost* comes wandering into my mind. Mamet likes to explain that *American Buffalo* and *Glengarry Glen Ross* are social plays, attacks on the American business ethic, and although one can agree, as one can recognize the social significance of all the Odets's work, one comes away from Mamet, as from Odets, with the sound of words ringing in the ears. Odets is in *American Buffalo* whether Mamet knows it or not. Not in the casual obscenity which was impossible in Odets's day. A little in the locutions which swallow prepositions and connectives. Most of all in the triumphantly infectious stage language.

That sounds like the proper end of a speech. But not quite. I feel a little like the hot-fur salesman in *Night Music,* pushing the "silver fox" of Odets's influence on American theatre. "Bargain of a lifetime. Don't ask no questions." Those of you who know *Night Music*—and not enough people do—will remember that Steve and Fay did not want the fur. Some of you may feel the same way, but I am better off than poor Gus. I have something else to peddle if the "silver fox" does not go. Clifford's children? Well, maybe. I started out to show how Odets had influenced the playwrights who followed him, but I may have ended with a demonstration of the continuity of American drama. Certain themes, dramatic structures, uses of idiom keep coming back.

"Coletti to Driscoll to Berger—that's how we work."

Index

◆

275